D1379925

# A Year in Your Garden

## Ann Bonar

Marshall Cavendish

**Editor:** David Joyce
**Designer:** Elizabeth Rose
**Illustrators:** David Bryant *(Kitchen Garden)*; Barbara Howes
   *(Flower Garden)*; Mike Bryan *(Shrub & Tree Garden)*

Published by Marshall Cavendish Books Limited
58 Old Compton Street
London W1V 5PA

©Marshall Cavendish Limited 1980, 1983
First printing 1980
Second printing 1983
Printed by Dai Nippon, Hong Kong

ISBN 0 85685 806 4

# Contents

# Introduction

Every gardener's ideal, surely, is to look out on a garden of year-round colour and greenery – beautiful blooms ranged beside sturdy, fruit-bearing shrubs, and a kitchen garden producing a rich harvest of succulent vegetables. But, to be practical, successful gardening is gardening according to the seasons. *A Year in Your Garden* aims to help you achieve ideal results by a careful appreciation of climate and weather, and not merely by applying a rigid monthly schedule.

Weather and climate, which effectively govern the seasons, are not the only vital factors. The condition of the soil is also important. Very few gardens have a humus-rich loam with a perfectly balanced mixture of plant foods, but you can work towards the ideal by adding compost and fertilizers. Regular watering is also a fundamental requirement. Going short of water means going short of food too, so all the right nutrients will not help if there is not enough moisture.

Choose the correct position for your plants as the seasonal planting times come round. Taking account of particular needs for sun, shade and degree of shelter will give the plants the chance they need to show their best. Starting with good stock is also important: strong plants are much more resistant to pests and diseases, and this reduces the need for chemical control.

In the kitchen garden section of this book you will find advice on how to get bumper crops – and nourishing produce on the kitchen table. It includes staples, such as potatoes, as well as the exotics – artichokes and asparagus for example. The flower garden chapters help you create a perennial show of colour, and also cover special features such as rock gardens and ponds, which give a garden its own special character. The third section, on shrubs and trees, ranges from the many beautiful varieties of rose, through ornamental bushes and hedging plants, to the delicious harvests that can be obtained from fruit trees.

Each season begins with a summary of jobs to be done, followed by more detailed instructions on planting times and cropping, pruning, pest control and soil balance – all accompanied by easy-to-follow seasonal charts. *A Year in Your Garden* is not about the mysteries of horticulture. Its theme is that the gardener's real wisdom lies in common sense and an appreciation of climate and weather – the infinitely variable factors which combine to create the seasons of nature.

# Early Spring

This season is the most important one of the gardening calendar. It is the beginning of new growth and a fresh cycle of flowering and fruiting. You will be starting plants off again – admittedly only a few in this early part of the growing season – but you can take advantage of the fact that you will be dealing with only half a dozen or so. Use the rest of your gardening time to get ahead wherever possible before the real spring rush starts in a few weeks' time.

Any gardener who wants to be successful must have the weather at the back of his or her mind the whole time, whether he or she lives in the country or the town. When early spring starts, it is especially important to keep an eye on the weather, as is can change radically in a few hours. This season can be treacherous, blowing hot and cold, with a deceiving, warm, sunny period somewhere in it, during which novice gardeners dash out and sow and plant with great abandon, only to have the seedlings frozen as they germinate, and newly shooting plants blasted by fresh onslaughts of wind and snow.

The message is that the winter has by no means finished, except perhaps in gardens and areas known to be mild and sheltered. However, your main pre-occupation now will certainly be to get things off to a start, by preparing the ground in various ways, and by sowing or planting towards the end of early spring.

Other important jobs that will be necessary for the general run of plants are cleaning up and putting right the damage caused by winter storms, and weeding. This last is well worth doing thoroughly before the weeds start to grow again in earnest. You will save a great deal of time later by grubbing out now, docks, thistles, chickweed, grass and other weeds which established themselves late last autumn, and then sat it out through the winter.

# At~a~glance diary

**Prepare the soil for:** sowing outdoors in seed-beds and planting

**Sow seeds outdoors of:** broad bean, leek, onion, parsnip, summer spinach, spinach beet, Swiss chard (seakale beet)

**Sow seeds under glass of:** Brussels sprout, summer cabbage, summer cauliflower, lettuce, peas, radish

**Sow seeds under glass (in heat) of:** aubergine, celeriac, celery, cucumber, pepper, tomato

**Put to sprout:** main crop potato if not already done

**Plant outdoors:** garlic, onion sets (if conditions are mild) early potato, rhubarb, shallot

**Transplant and prick out indoors:** aubergine, cucumber, pepper, tomato

**Weed and clear:** ground prepared earlier, established asparagus beds, globe artichoke, strawberry

**Prune:** gooseberry if buds pecked out by birds; tips of raspberry canes

**Spray:** soft fruit

**Mulch and feed:** mulch asparagus; feed all fruit if not done previously

**Protect:** brassicas, currant and gooseberry from birds.

**Ventilate:** strawberry under cloches, greenhouse plants

# Jobs to do

**Preparing the soil for an outdoor seed bed**
In order that the seeds you sow get the best start possible, the surface of the soil in which they are sown should be crumbly like breadcrumbs, moist, warm and level; it should contain plant food. You will have done the initial preparation of digging, and manuring where necessary, last autumn or early winter but now, if the weather is becoming less cold and less wet, you can finish off the soil preparation by making a seedbed for the seeds listed in the At-a-Glance Diary.

Choose a day when it seems likely that the weather is changing to mild and showery (probably towards the end of early spring in most gardens) and when the soil is moist but not soaking wet. Rake off sticks, leaves and large stones; break up large lumps of soil with the back of the rake, and weed if necessary by hand or hoe. If the soil surface has been packed down by heavy rain, you may have to lightly fork it first. When clear of rubbish, rake again, lengthwise and crossways until the soil is crumb-like, to a depth of about 2cm (1in). If you cannot sow at once, cover with polythene sheet overnight, so that unexpected rain does not destroy your work.

**Preparing the soil for planting**
At this time, the soil can be got ready for deep-rooting and heavy-feeding crops to be planted in mid- or late spring. This means vegetables like globe artichokes, asparagus, runner (pole) beans, celery, cucumbers, marrows, melons, peas, squashes, perpetual-fruiting strawberries and sweetcorn. For all except asparagus and runner (pole) beans, dig a trench one spade deep and wide, put in well-rotted manure, garden compost or a similar form of bulky organic matter in a layer 7.5cm (3in) thick, and mix it with the soil at the bottom of the trench, using a fork. Then return the topsoil, but mixed with more organic matter if it is inclined to be sandy and to become dry quickly. For asparagus and runner (pole) beans, dig the trench two spades deep, mix humus-providing material as before into the bottom, and also with the soil dug out at the depth of the second spade (see also

*The range of vegetables shown here can easily be grown by the home gardener. Careful choice of variety will make it possible to harvest vegetables fresh all the year round, thus ensuring maximum flavour and food value.*

double digging, Late Autumn). Never try to cultivate the soil when it is wet or cold. Trampling on it, as you will have to if you do any digging, forking, raking or weeding will only damage the structure and result in a bad harvest for one season at least.

The soil which you dug earlier, in winter or autumn, for potatoes, will now need loosening with the fork or rake, the rubbish taken off and V-shaped trenches made, 7–15cm (3–6in) deep and 50cm (20in) apart, to whatever length is required. The heavier and more clayey your soil, the shallower can be the trench: the lighter it is, the deeper. Line the trench with fresh grass mowings, if available, to reduce the possible infestation of superficial scab.

If you are going to try your hand at outdoor grape growing, early in mid-spring is not too late for planting, so you can still get the soil into condition any time in early spring, if it has not been done previously. The sooner, the better, however; for the details, see Late Autumn.

Another luscious and exotic fruit is the melon, which can perfectly well be grown in frames out doors, as well as in an unheated greenhouse. For melons in frames, you should allow one or two plants to each frame. Dig a hole about one spade deep and 45cm (48in) square for each planting site, and mix one or two bucketfuls of rotted organic matter with the forked up soil at the bottom. Use the greater quantity if your soil is shallow or sandy. Return the remaining soil to the hole, but mound it up towards the centre, so that the plants will be growing on a little hump. This prevents water collecting round the base of the stem and rotting it.

If you are trying the mini-melons called Ogen, smaller planting holes only 30cm (12in) square will be needed, and you can fit at least two plants into a Dutch light frame or three into a standard English frame.

For melons to be grown in the greenhouse border, get the soil ready in the same way, allowing 60cm (24in) between each plant.

As the season after this is one of the busiest in the gardening calendar, it is a good idea to get ahead wherever possible, so you could complete the soil preparation for greenhouse tomatoes now. Fork the soil over lightly, and at the same time mix in a slow-acting compound fertilizer such as the J. I. Base. If you intend planting in the middle of mid-spring, do this preparation at the end of early spring, i.e., two weeks before you intend planting. At the same time, put up the support system you intend to use (see Mid-Spring for details of this).

*The crumb-like structure of seed-bed soil is achieved by raking and then cross-raking.*

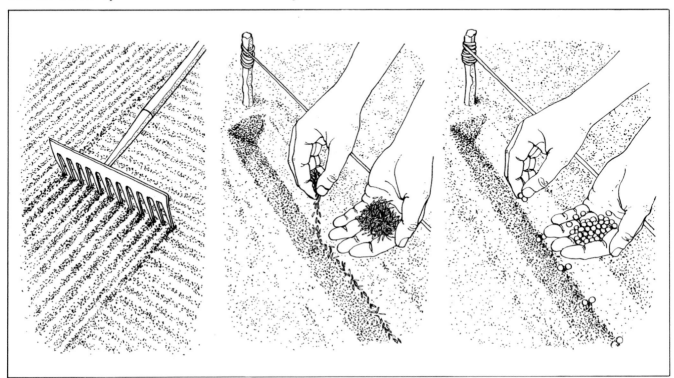

# Sowing and Planting

| Vegetable | Depth to sow | Method | Distance to sow/thin | Distance between rows | Germination time (days) | Remarks |
|---|---|---|---|---|---|---|
| Broad bean | 3.5cm (1½in) | Singly | 15cm (6in) | 60cm (24in) | 8–12 | Sow also in two staggered rows in shallow trench 5cm (2in) deep, 15cm (6in) wide, with one row at each side |
| Leek | 0.6cm (¼in) | Continuously and thinly | 2.5cm (1in) | 15cm (6in) | 21–24 | Thin carefully when 5cm (2in) tall and transplant |
| Onion | 0.6cm (¼in) | Continuously and thinly | 15cm (6in) | 23cm (9in) | 21–25 | Thin in two or three stages *in situ* |
| Parsnip | 2.5cm (1in) | Continuously or station sow | 20cm (8in) | 45cm (18in) | 21–28 | Thin *in situ* |
| Summer spinach | 2.5cm (1in) | Station sow | 20cm (8in) | 30cm (12in) | 10–15 | Thin at stations |
| Spinach beet | 2.5cm (1in) | Station sow | 23cm (9in) | 45cm (18in) | 18–24 | Thin at stations |
| Swiss chard (seakale beet) | 2.5cm (1in) | Station sow | 23cm (9in) | 45cm (18in) | 18–24 | Thin at stations |

Once you have got the soil ready, you can start the first crops off, either from seed or by using parts of mature plants.

## Sowing seed outdoors

When you have prepared your seedbed, and are ready to do the sowing, there are several ways in which you can do it. The standard method is to make a shallow, narrow furrow, or 'drill' in the soil, and then sow a trail of seeds in a single line along it. It makes sense to do this as thinly as you can, with the seeds regularly spaced, as it saves money and, when you come to thinning or transplanting, time. If you do this, one of the easiest methods of sowing is to shake some of the seed into the palm of one hand, take a pinch of it between the thumb and forefinger of the other hand, and trickle it gradually into the drill.

As well as continuous sowing, there is the 'station' sowing method, by which seeds are sown in groups or stations with spacing between them appropriate to the crop. The seeds then germinate in clusters, and when the strongest seedling in each group can be seen, the remainder are carefully taken away. Sometimes only the leaves and stems are removed, so as not to disturb the root of the retained seedling; the decapitated root will die in due course.

You can also sow broadcast, that is, scatter the seed completely and thinly all over a given area, without any attempt at marking rows or producing any sort of order, but this is not very often done. Turnips for turnip tops can be sown like this; early carrots are another possibility. It is a useful method where space is a bit tight, as you can better make use of odd patches than you would if growing in conventional rows. Handweeding and thinning will be made easier if you make sure the patches are not more than two arms' length wide.

Big seeds like broad beans, marrows, runner (pole) beans sow singly, in holes rather than continuous furrows. Peas can be sown in a much wider drill than usual, in fact wide enough to take two or three staggered rows. Pea germination is so erratic it pays to do this; in fact, with any of the larger seeds, it does no harm to sow a few extra in peat pots as reserves for filling in spaces.

You will be sowing seed of the hardiest vegetables only at this time (do not be misled by that warm spell into sowing most of your seeds now): for instance, broad bean, leek, parsnip, summer spinach, spinach beet and Swiss chard. You can also sow onion, but only if the soil is workable and becoming less wet; it is generally better to wait until early in mid-spring.

In addition, if you have a sheltered, warm garden, you can try some, or all, of the seeds listed for sowing outdoors in mid-spring.

After sowing, crumble the soil back over the seeds with your hands, or draw it back with the corner of the hoe, and firm it down. Mark the ends of the rows and label them, and if there is no rain, water gently but thoroughly every evening with a fine spray, and again during the day if the weather is hot and sunny. If the seeds become dry while germinating, they are quite likely to die. Be prepared to cover with cloches or polythene tunnels if the weather turns very cold and/or wet. Both types of spinach will in any case need some form of bird protection, preferably netting.

**Sowing seed under glass**
Many more seeds can be sown under the protection of glass of polythene than can be in the open ground, but in this case they are usually in seed trays or other containers. The method of preparing these is described in Late Winter.

Seeds which can be sown like this in the greenhouse or in a frame with brick or wooden sides, without artificial heat, consist of: alpine strawberries, Brussels sprouts, summer cabbage, summer cauliflower, and peas. Sow them thinly and evenly on the compost surface, and then cover with compost sifted through a 3mm ($\frac{1}{8}$in) sieve, to a 0.6cm ($\frac{1}{4}$in) depth and firm with a 'patter'. Note that the peas are spaced 4cm ($1\frac{1}{2}$in) apart and are covered with 1.2cm ($1\frac{1}{2}$in) compost, and if you sow them in boxes in a frame, make sure the mice cannot get at them. Germination times for these seeds are:

| | |
|---|---|
| Brussels sprouts | 7–12 days |
| summer cabbage | 7–12 days |
| summer cauliflower | 7–12 days |
| peas | 6–12 days |
| alpine strawberries | 14–21 days |

*Potatoes are planted in early or mid-spring. One method of planting is to dig out a trench 15-30cm (6-12in) deep, depending on whether the soil is heavy or light, and to line the bottom of the trench with fresh grass cuttings. This helps to cut down infection by superficial scab disease, a fungus which is unsightly but not particularly harmful.*

## Sowing seed under glass (in heat)

Seeds which can also be sown in containers but which need a little heat supplied are: aubergine, celeriac, celery, cucumber, melon, pepper and tomato; celeriac and celery will germinate in 14–25 days, melon in 7–14 if all are sown in a temperature of 16–18°C (60–65°F) (see the sowing section in Late Winter for temperatures and germination times of the remainder).

Keep a close watch on the development of seedlings and young plants in the greenhouse; they can be quickly burnt or the compost become dry in the heat of the spring sun, as it shines through the greenhouse glazing. Space the plants out as they grow, otherwise they will get leggy.

## Put to sprout

If it has not already been done, maincrop potatoes should be put to sprout as soon as possible.

## Planting outdoors

Besides sowing seed, you can now begin to plant as well. Crops include garlic, onion sets, potatoes, shallots and rhubarb. The soil for these will already have been thoroughly dug in autumn or winter, and limed if necessary. All that you need do to it before actually planting is to fork off any weeds, and break down large lumps. Mark the rows for the garlic, onion sets and shallots, and then work from a planting board alongside the row you are working on, so that the soil is not consolidated by your feet. The board will distribute the pressure of your weight – you will need two boards, by the way.

If the soil and weather are still cold, do not plant the onion sets yet; they will not do well, and it is much better to wait until a suitable time in mid-spring. You will find the method of planting them described there in detail; for garlic planting, see Mid-Autumn.

Early and second early potatoes can be planted now, at the beginning of the season in sheltered gardens and towards the end of early spring in the remainder. Sprouts at planting time should be about 3cm (1½in) long. Rub off all but two or three of the shoots from each set, ensuring that the shoots remaining are at the 'rose' end, that is, the opposite end of the set from where it joined the root of the parent plant, and put them in with the sprouted end uppermost, 30cm (12in) apart.

A tip for a better yield still is to make the trenches slightly deeper than advised, put a forkful of really humusy, rotted manure or garden compost where each set is to be planted, and then put soil on top to ensure that planting will be at the right depth.

*Melons like these – the cantaloupe Dutch Net and Ogen types and the sweet or musk varieties – can be grown by the gardener, with the help of cloches or frames for the hardier kinds, and a greenhouse for the tender varieties.*

After planting, fill in the trenches carefully so as not to damage the shoots, firm down and rake level. You can, at this stage, ridge the sets up so as to protect the growing shoots for as long as possible against frost. The chances are that by the time they emerge, frost will no longer be a possible source of damage.

Shallots should have been planted in late winter, but they will still crop, though a little late, if planted now; watch for bolting during the summer.

When you plant rhubarb, space each crown 75–150cm (30–60in) apart in each direction, depending on variety;

six crowns should be enough for a family of four. You can divide already-established rhubarb by lifting it, and chopping it into several sections, each with one or two buds already showing. The sections which will do best will be those taken from the outer, not the central, part of the parent crown.

Be sure to make the planting hole large enough, spread the roots out comfortably, and return the soil so that the buds are showing above it. Firm down with the feet, and spread a layer of rotted organic matter on the soil that surrounds each of the rhubarb plants.

## Transplanting and pricking out indoors

You should also plant the seedlings which germinated in late winter and which were sown in containers in a gently heated propagator. The process of moving and putting seedlings into a new position is sometimes called 'pricking out', and is a form of transplanting in fact. The seedlings can be of any of the following: aubergine, cucumber, melon, pepper and tomato; the method of pricking out is described in Mid-Spring.

However, if you sowed them in individual small 5cm (2in) peat, plastic or clay pots, rather than seed-trays, they will not need this treatment, though if more than one seed was sown in each pot, they will need reducing to the strongest in each pot. Peppers are very slow to grow when young – do not expect them to develop as quickly as the other crops.

When you are pricking out the tomatoes, which should be when the second true leaf is barely showing, watch for the 'rogues', and do not use them: they will not crop. You can spot them by the unevenly-sized seed leaves.

If the melons were sown towards the end of late winter, they should be ready at some time in early spring for planting into larger pots. All the plants in the marrow family grow very fast when young, and it is not unknown for a seedling sown in a 7.5cm (3in) pot to need more root space four or five days after it has germinated. A 10cm (4in) size, containing John Innes potting compost No. 1, will be needed, and as soon as the young plant has started to grow again in its new pot the temperature can be gradually reduced to below 55°F during the day and, 55–59°F at night, so as to slow down its growth. Otherwise it will come on too fast, and be very expensive in terms of supplied heat.

## Weeding and cleaning up

Clear off the crops which are coming to an end (see the harvesting list), put the remains on the compost heap if free from pests and diseases, and burn the rest.

Clean up all the soft fruit that needs this attention. By the end of the winter, there is likely to be a thin cover of weeds, and also rubbish blown on to the soil by the winter gales, such as sticks and twigs, unrotted leathery leaves and so on.

Weed all sites for which the general cultivation and preparation was done earlier, and also weed established asparagus beds and globe artichokes.

By weeding now, when the weeds are still small, you will prevent perennial weeds from getting a stranglehold, especially in the centre of fruit bushes from which it is virtually impossible to remove them, once established. There are several methods of weeding: forking or hoeing, hand-weeding, or using chemical weedkillers.

If you decide to use chemicals, paraquat is a useful time-saver for annual and small weeds; it has its effect through the green parts of plants and is inactivated when it reaches the soil. There is a new translocated weedkiller available containing the chemical glyphosphate. This is sprayed on to leaves and stems, through which it is absorbed, although the effect will not be as good as application later in the spring. It is also inactivated in the soil.

If you cultivate the weeds out, you will also be aerating the soil surface and so, although it may take a little longer, you will have in fact done two jobs.

Where soft fruit is being grown in beds, you can keep the edges of the beds free of weeds for a year, by watering the soil in a strip approximately 15cm (6in) wide all round the bed with simazine mixed with water. The soil must be clear of weeds to start with, and preferably level, crumbly-textured and moist; then the solution (suspension) can form a cover over and in the upper layers of the soil, through which weeds cannot penetrate. As they germinate so they will be killed. However, perennial weeds, which are tougher, are likely to be able to grow through, though not as strongly as usual.

## Pruning

If the gooseberries have been damaged by birds, such as bullfinches picking out the buds during the winter, cut the bare shoots back hard to leave stubs a few centimetres (an inch or two) long. The bushes will respond by producing new shoots from the centre, though you will not of course have any crop in the summer.

Top the raspberry canes as soon as possible, if this was not done in late winter, tie them in if loosened during

Opposite: *Rhubarb is a trouble-free crop which will continue to provide stems for pulling for many years, provided that it has a good dressing of organic matter annually.*

winter, and also re-tie any of the other cane fruits that need it.

## Spraying
Currants and gooseberries may need treatment against aphids, especially greenfly, and possibly some early hatches of capsid as well, towards the end of early spring. Bioresmethrin, pirimiphos-methyl or malathion can be used; choose a calm day and make sure the solution is exactly the right strength. Young growth can be badly burnt by a strong solution, or by spraying when windy.

## Manuring, mulching and feeding
Spread a layer of rotted organic matter over established asparagus beds if this was not done in autumn. Feed all the fruit with a general compound fertilizer if this was not done in late winter, or late summer last year.

Some gardeners who have to deal with soil which dries quickly find that mulching the surface with straw, where they are growing bush and cane fruits, helps to keep it damp in all but the hottest, droughtiest conditions. The fresh covering that was put on last autumn will mostly have rotted by now, and a new supply of straw should be laid over the ground after any weeds have been removed.

If you do this, put on first the mulch of manure or compost referred to in Mid-Spring and Late Spring, and then cover with straw.

## Protection
Look over the protective netting against birds on the brassica (cabbage) family and make sure it is bird-proof. Pigeons in particular seem to be voracious at this time of the year. Also have a look at that over the gooseberries, and put netting on over the currants, as birds sometimes have a go at the newly developing buds now. This will save you time later, too.

## Ventilating
Cloched strawberries should be expanding their leaves well by now; on sunny days open the cloches a little otherwise the temperature inside shoots up surprisingly high, too high for the strawberry, which is fundamentally a temperate-climate plant. It is not too late to put cloches on now; if done at the beginning of spring the berries should still be ripe before the unprotected ones.

Begin to open the ventilators in the greenhouse more during the day as the sun becomes warmer and more frequent in appearance. Be very careful to close down every night still, all but a crack.

*When planting rhubarb, make sure that buds are just above the soil surface, and that the roots are spread out to their entire length, in a sufficiently deep hole. Doubled-up, cramped roots will result in a poor plant. Finish the planting by mulching, or put the mulch on later, in late spring.*

## Crops to be harvested
sprouting broccoli, heading broccoli (winter cauliflower), spring cabbage, chicory, kale, leek, lettuce (cloched), Savoy cabbage, winter spinach, spinach beet, swede, turnip tops, perennial herbs

## Available from store
beetroot, carrot, celeriac, onion, parsnip, potato, shallot, turnip

# Mid-Spring

The key words in mid-spring are speed and watchfulness. This is the time of the year when the days really begin to lengthen and the sap starts to rise with a vengeance, with the result that dormant seeds sprout and apparently dead plants leap to life with alarming speed, as do plant pests and fungus diseases. The quantity and quality of your harvest will be determined by the amount of seed you are able to sow now and the alacrity with which you spot and stop plant enemies.

The weather will be particularly fickle, perhaps warm during the day and frosty at night or cold and wet for a week at a time. It may blow a gale or it may snow. It is astonishing that Nature has arranged things so that seedlings have to survive such unsuitable growing conditions, but you can help them with protective cloches or tunnels and special soils or composts. Watching the weather in mid-spring is more important than in any other season – you need to be conscious of what is happening to it all the time and to make a mental record for future reference, when you have a bumper harvest or a famine.

Pests such as greenfly and caterpillars will be hatching; birds and mice will be hungry after the winter and the just as damaging but barely visible fungi will be infecting new leaves and stems with disastrous effects. For every one greenfly that is obvious there will be ten more hidden. Get into the habit of using finger and thumb early in the season and look underneath leaves for signs of infestation, not just on top.

Seed sowing outdoors is the major job in mid-spring; the majority of the vegetables can be sown, many of the herbs, and melons and alpine strawberries. You will be doing some more planting too: vegetables grown from crowns such as globe artichokes and asparagus; tomatoes and cucumbers under glass; transplanting the larger seedlings and pricking out the smaller ones.

Frost protection is vital; all sorts of young crops will be needing it, especially potatoes and seedlings which have just germinated. Five degrees below freezing is not very encouraging to a two-day-old seedling. A maximum and minimum thermometer is an exceedingly useful reminder that the night temperature, either outdoors or indoors, may have dropped too far for plant comfort.

# At~a~glance diary

| | |
|---|---|
| **Prepare the soil for:** | outdoor and indoor sowing; outdoor planting |
| **Sow seeds outdoors of:** | beetroot, borage, broad bean, broccoli (sprouting) Brussels sprout, cabbage, carrot, chives, dill, fennel, kohlrabi, leek, lettuce, marjoram, onion, parsley, parsnip, pea, radish, savory (summer) sorrel, summer spinach, spinach beet, strawberry (alpine), Swiss chard (seakale beet), turnip |
| **Sow seeds under glass (in heat) of:** | Aubergine, basil, celery, cucumber, marrow, melon, squash, pepper, pea, sweetcorn, tomato |
| **Plant outdoors:** | globe artichoke, asparagus, sweet bay, cauliflower (summer, hardened off), chives, garlic, mint, onion (sets) pea (hardened off), potato (second early and maincrop) rhubarb, sorrel, tarragon, strawberry, vine |
| **Plant under glass:** | tomato |
| **Prick out or pot on:** | aubergine, Brussels sprout, summer cabbage, summer cauliflower, celeriac, celery, cucumber, melon, pepper, strawberry (alpine), tomato |
| **Thin:** | beetroot, Brussels sprout, summer cabbage, carrot, summer cauliflower, leek, lettuce, onion, parsnip, radish summer spinach, spinach beet, Swiss chard (seakale beet) |
| **Weed and clear:** | weed seedlings from all crops; clear off finishing crops |
| **Pests and diseases:** | caterpillars, greenfly, slugs and snails on any or all crops; mice; big-bud mite (currant); spur blight (raspberry) carrotfly; grey mould, mildew (strawberry) |
| **Mulch:** | all fruit |
| **Feed:** | asparagus, cucumber, melon, strawberry (alpine) |
| **Protect against:** | birds, frost |
| **Train and tie in:** | vine |
| **Ventilate:** | greenhouse plants, cloched strawberries |
| **Choose:** | site for cropping |
| **Harvest:** | asparagus |

# Jobs to do

## Preparing the soil

As you will be sowing a great many vegetable seeds in mid-spring, seed-bed preparation will be one of the most important jobs and you will find the method for this detailed in Early Spring. The soil for sowing seed in containers and for planting outdoors may also be prepared, as detailed in Late Winter and Early Spring.

## Sowing seed outdoors

Seeds to be sown outdoors include those listed in the sowing and planting chart; methods of sowing are listed in early spring. The seeds which were sown outdoors in early spring can still be sown now and they include broad bean, leek, onion, parsnip, summer spinach, spinach beet and Swiss chard (seakale beet). Their sowing requirements will be found in the Early Spring sowing and planting chart.

## Sowing seed under glass (in heat)

You can also sow under glass in a gently heated propagator: aubergine, basil, celery, cucumber, marrow, melon, squash, pepper, pea, sweetcorn and tomato. Basil, marrow, pea and squash will germinate best in a temperature of about 16-18°C (60-65°F), basil in 14-21 days, pea in about 3 days, the other two in about 7-14 (see Late Winter and Early Spring for temperatures and germination times of the remainder). In warm, sheltered areas all these can be sown in containers in brick or wooden-sided frames outdoors. When the seeds have germinated, protect the seedlings from strong sunlight.

## Planting outdoors

Crops which can be planted out this month include globe artichokes, asparagus, summer cauliflower (hardened off), garlic, peas (hardened off), onions from sets, second early and maincrop potatoes, rhubarb, strawberries and vines (see Late Autumn for planting details). Chives and mint, bought-in, can also be planted now, or your own plants can be divided, and the best pieces planted. Sweet bay is

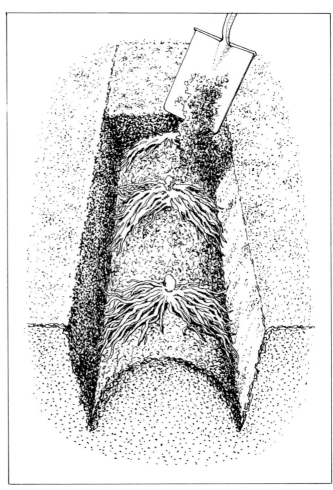

*When planting asparagus, make a rounded ridge down the centre of the trench, and put the crowns on top of it, with the roots spread down its sides.*

another herb which can be planted now, as can sorrel and tarragon from bought-in plants, or by dividing your own.

About ten days before planting the globe artichokes, fork some compound fertilizer into the prepared site, at the rate of 90g per sq m (3oz per sq yd), and clear off any weeds. Plant the crowns so that the buds are just above soil level, with the roots well spread out, and water them in if rain is unlikely. Space them 90-120cm (36-48in) apart each way.

It is usually safe to plant onion sets this month; they do not do well if put into cold soil but, by mid-spring, conditions should be suitable. Sets are onions which have had their growth arrested the previous autumn by heat treatment during which the flower embryo is killed. This means that not only do they mature more quickly, but also that they cannot bolt to flower.

The sets are planted 15cm (6in) apart in the row, with 30cm (12in) between rows, and should be put in so that half the bulb is above ground. Cut off any papery brown leaves at the tips before planting. After a week or so, have a look at the sets; they have a habit of heaving themselves out of the ground, or the birds may have tweaked them right out, mistaking the tips for useful nesting material.

That delectable crop, asparagus, can also be planted now. If your soil is on the acid side, dress it early in the season with sufficient lime to produce a neutral reaction on the pH scale, and fork the lime well in. A week or two later, dig out trenches 30cm (12in) deep and 38cm (15in) wide and then form a rounded ridge about 20cm (8in) high down the centre of each trench with some of the dug-out soil. Put the asparagus crowns 30-45cm (12-18in) apart, on the ridges, so that the roots are spread evenly down the sides, and cover them and the crowns with crumbled soil until the trench is filled in and the crowns are about 10cm (4in) below the soil surface. Firm the soil and water in if no rain is expected.

Make sure there are no weeds whatsoever at this stage, because this is your last chance for getting adequate control over them. After this, any perennial weeds which remain cannot be eradicated completely; chemical weedkillers are likely to damage the asparagus, and hand weeding can never get the roots from under the crowns.

Summer cauliflower is planted out, either from the pricked-out crop if sown very early in the month, or from that sown in frames last month, into soil prepared early in the winter. For success with cauliflowers in summer, they should be planted as early in mid-spring as possible, putting cloches over them if the weather is really bad. Hardening off before planting will be required (see Late Spring for details on hardening off).

## Planting under glass
The remaining planting job to do is that of tomatoes in the greenhouse. This will probably not be necessary until the last week of mid-spring; it is no good planting tomatoes in cold soil, as the roots simply stand still; moreover, they are much more likely to become infected with fungus diseases from the soil.

The greenhouse border soil should by now be in good condition after your winter preparation and all that remains to be done is to make sure there are no weeds, large lumps of soil or stones, and water the surface thoroughly if it has become dry. For supporting the tomatoes, stretch a wire along the row 7.5cm (3in) above the soil, fasten securely at each end to the greenhouse wood or metal framework and run another above it, about 15cm (6in) below the glass of the roof.

The tomatoes are planted so that they are spaced along the bottom wire at 38-45cm (15-18in) intervals, with about 45cm (18in) between rows. Water the root-ball thoroughly, put it into a hole which will take it comfortably and fill in firmly with crumbled soil. Do not water in; then roots will be encouraged to grow and extend in a search for water, but make sure the surrounding soil does not become dry. As the plants grow they can be strung for support (see Late Spring for method).

## Thinning
The seeds which were sown outdoors or in frames in early spring will probably need thinning some time during mid-spring; they include beetroot, carrot, leek, lettuce, onion, parsnip, radish, summer spinach, spinach beet and Swiss chard (seakale beet). Any Brussels sprouts, summer cabbage and summer cauliflower which were also sown in early spring, either in containers or in the ground, can also be thinned. Thinning is a delicate job, and it is important to do it carefully and at the right stage. When the seedlings have one or two true leaves and it is possible to see which are the strongest, thin the rows to leave 2cm (1in) or so between the seedlings and then do it again when the leaves of the young plants are touching so that they are thinned to their recommended final spacing. Try not to disturb the retained seedlings when you are pulling out the unwanted ones and try to leave only those with sturdy upright stems, undamaged by pests.

## Pricking out
This is done with seedlings started in seed boxes, rather than grown singly in small pots. Crops to be treated like this can include any of those sown last month: aubergine,

Opposite: *Although bay comes from the Mediterranean region, it will grow well outdoors in sheltered gardens. It can also be grown satisfactorily in a container. Keep clipped as necessary.*

# Sowing and Planting

| Vegetable or herb | Depth to sow | Method | Distance to sow/thin | Distance between rows | Germination time (days) | Remarks |
|---|---|---|---|---|---|---|
| Beetroot | 2.5cm (1in) | Station sow | 10–15cm (4–6in) | 30cm (12in) | 18–24 | Round and globe types best for general use; thin *in situ* |
| Borage | 1.3cm (½in) | Continuously and thinly | 30cm (12in) | 30–60cm (12–24in) | 4–12 | Thin *in situ* |
| Broccoli, sprouting | 1.3cm (½in) | Continuously and thinly | 7.5cm (3in) | 15cm (6in) | 7–12 | Transplant when four or five leaves present |
| Brussels sprout | 1.3cm (½in) | Continuously and thinly | 10cm (4in) | 15–23cm (6–9in) | 7–12 | Transplant when four or five leaves present |
| Cabbage | 1.3cm (½in) | Continuously and thinly | 10cm (4in) | 15cm (6in) | 7–12 | Transplant when four or five leaves present |
| Carrot | 0.6cm (¼in) | Continuously and thinly or station sow | 5–15cm (2–6in) | 15–30cm (6–12in) | 14–18 | Thin *in situ* |
| Chive | 1.3cm (½in) | Continuously and thinly | 10–13cm (4–5in) | 20cm (8in) | 21 | Thin *in situ* |
| Dill | 0.6cm (¼in) | Continuously and thinly | 20cm (8in) | 50cm (20in) | 7–14 | Thin *in situ* |
| Fennel | 1.3cm (½in) | Continuously and thinly | 45cm (18in) | 45cm (18in) | 14–21 | Thin *in situ* |
| Kohlrabi | 1.3cm (½in) | Continuously and thinly | 25cm (10cm) | 38cm (15cm) | 7–12 | Thin *in situ* |
| Lettuce | 1.3cm (½in) | Continuously and thinly | 15–23cm (6–9in) | 23–30cm (6–12in) | 10–15 | Thin *in situ* |
| Marjoram | 0.6cm (¼in) | Continuously and thinly | 15–23cm (6–9in) | 20cm (8in) | 14–20 | Thin *in situ* |
| Parsley | 1.3cm (½in) | Continuously and thinly | 13cm (5in) | 23cm (9in) | 7–35 | Germinates quickly in warm soil; thin *in situ* |
| Pea | 2.5cm (1in) | Singly | 7.5cm (3in) | 45cm (18in) | 10–22 | Also sow two staggered rows 7.5cm (3in) apart in 15–23cm (6–9in) wide drill |
| Radish | 0.6cm (¼in) | Singly | 2.5cm (1in) | 15cm (6in) | 4–7 | Thin *in situ* |
| Savory, summer | 0.6cm (¼in) | Continuously and thinly | 30cm (12in) | 60cm (24in) | 8–12 | Thin *in situ* |
| Sorrel | 0.6cm (¼in) | Continuously and thinly | 30cm (12in) | 38cm (15in) | 7–18 | Thin *in situ* |
| Strawberry, alpine | 0.6cm (¼in) | Continuously and thinly | 20cm (8in) | 23cm (9in) | 21–25 | Sow in light shade; thin *in situ* |
| Turnip | 1.3cm (½in) | Continuously thinly | 15–30cm (6–12in) | 30–40cm (12–16in) | 7–12 | Lightly shaded site for summer crops; thin *in situ* |

Brussels sprouts, summer cabbage, summer cauliflower (the last three where sown in containers, after thinning), celeriac, celery, pepper, alpine strawberries and tomatoes.

Pricking out should be done when the seedlings have one or both seed leaves, depending on the species, and the first fully true leaf formed. They can be put singly into 5cm (2in) pots or into seed trays 7.5cm (3in) deep, spaced 5cm (2in) apart each way. Fill the container with a good standard potting compost, firm it down and level the surface, so that a 2cm (¾in) space is left at the top. Use only well-coloured and well-formed seedlings and lift them with the roots as intact as possible, using a metal widger. Make a suitably sized hole in the compost, lower the roots and firm the compost over them. The stem of the seedling should be buried almost up to the seed leaves. When the tray is full, water the seedlings with a fine-rosed spray and put them in a sheltered, shaded place for a day or two, while they establish.

The remaining seeds sown in containers last month include cucumber and pea. The cucumbers can be potted on again, if not already done; see Planting Outdoors for peas. Space out all the plants in containers, keep them well watered.

## Weeding and cleaning up
By this time you will have got rid of the over-wintering weeds from established crops and will have cleared sites which are to be sown or planted. Unfortunately, new weed seeds will be germinating all the time, so that you need to go round with the hoe every week, and hoe them off while still in the seedling stage. If time is very short, you can let them grow to form a leafy cover, and then spray with the contact weedkiller, paraquat, mentioned in Early Spring. Provided you restrict the solution to the leaves of the weeds, no harm will be done to any adjacent crops, as the chemical only has effect on the green parts of plants and not on the roots.

Many of the winter crops will be coming to an end and can be dug up and put on the compost heap if not diseased or pest ridden. You can start a new heap (or heaps) at this time of the year, as there will be plenty of fresh vegetative material from all parts of the garden, not just the kitchen garden. The old heap finished in autumn last year can be used for mulching, as it should by now be crumbly and dark brown. For the method of making compost see Late Spring.

## Treating pests and diseases
The soft fruit will be the crops which require most attention to pest and disease control at this season. Greenfly can be infesting any of the bush or cane fruit, or strawberries; it is particularly important to deal with them on the currants as their leaf feeding can severely stunt new growth and so decrease next year's crop. Caterpillars of various kinds may

*Tomatoes grown in the greenhouse need considerable support: one way of supplying it is to use horizontal wires, and attach vertical lengths of fillis to the wires at each planting station. The fillis should be twined round the main stem and not vice versa; side-shoots are cut or broken off when tiny, without leaving any snag.*

hatch and start eating holes in leaves; the first brood of gooseberry sawfly eggs will hatch towards the end of mid-spring and the larvae can feed on the leaves so severely that the bush is completely defoliated.

Big–bud mite in blackcurrants starts to move in mid-spring from the swollen round buds, where it has spent the winter, to newly forming, uninfested buds. The infected buds will not come into leaf – they have been destroyed by the mites feeding – and so you will have a much smaller crop. Another unpleasant fact about this mite is that it carries a virus disease of currants called reversion, which makes the plants revert to the wild type, and eventually virtually cease to crop and grow.

Spur blight sometimes infects raspberries; it is a fungus disease which kills the buds on the new canes. You will find silvery-grey, elongated patches on the canes extending up and down from infected buds, if it is present. Cut all such canes down to ground level and burn; also remove any small, weak canes and thin the remainder if crowded. Diseases spread much more rapidly amongst plants which are growing closely together and where the air is still and moist. Grey mould and mildew will affect strawberries for the same reasons, hence the need to plant at what appears to be rather wide spacings.

Towards the end of the month, the adults of the carrot fly will begin to lay eggs in the soil around young developing carrots. The maggots hatching from the eggs will bore into the carrot roots and feed, wrecking the crop in severe cases. One more brood may appear in late summer, the worst damage being done to the main crops in early summer and late spring. As the adults are attracted by the smell of the carrot leaves, destroy or bury all the thinnings; it is said that parsley sown with carrots camouflages the carrot odour, so that the fly is not attracted. If you sow very early in mid-spring, or wait until late in early summer, you can escape possible attack altogether.

Slugs or snails can devour a crop of lettuce seedlings or parsley overnight; neither are they averse to spinach and seakale beet. Trap them by putting small heaps of leaves and stems near the rows at night and collect them in the mornings, or sink shallow dishes of watered milk and sugar, to which they will be attracted, in the soil. Bands of really gritty material 15cm (6in) wide placed along the rows will provide a physical barrier. Soil which is always damp tends to be badly slug ridden, so improving the draining capability of the soil will help in the long run.

Mice are very partial to peas when newly sown and just germinating. If you have sown in boxes or individual pots, by the time they are planted out they are no longer attractive to mice, but if you have to sow in the open ground, sprinkling the peas with paraffin and then dusting with red lead is a good deterrent. Remember that red lead is poisonous. Traps or proprietary baits also can be used, with the appropriate precautions regarding pets. For detailed treatment of all these troubles see Kitchen Garden Controls and Treatments.

## Mulching
Strawberries, bush fruit and cane fruit can all be mulched with rotten garden compost, manure, spent hops or any similar materials, when the soil is moist and clear of weeds. Vines can also be mulched, but thinly; in fact, if they are fairly vigorous already, there is no need to do this. A moderately thick mulch will be 5cm (2in) deep; a thin one only 1.2cm ($\frac{1}{2}$in). For a heavy dressing, use 7.5cm (3in), but remember that many factors determine the amount of mulch applied and you can vary these quantities as you become more experienced in handling crops and soil.

## Feeding
Little feeding is required this early in the growing season, but you can put a dressing of agricultural salt on to the asparagus some time in mid-spring; 60g per sq m (2oz per sq yd) is the rate. Wild asparagus grows near the sea, so it does no harm to supply the cultivated crop with a little of the common sea mineral, sodium chloride.

Established alpine strawberries can be given a general compound fertilizer, slightly high in potassium. You will find, later in the season, that this will have done much good and increased the crop enormously. Cucumbers and melons in pots, which are waiting for planting out, may need a little help in the form of liquid feeding, again using a mixture which has more potash than nitrogen or phosphorus.

## Protection
Frost is an enemy to be watched for, especially on potatoes, the young leaves and stems of which are very vulnerable. Cover them on those evenings when a night frost is forecast and during the day when snow is a possibility. Some strawberries in sheltered, really warm gardens may be coming into flower at the end of mid-spring, so protect these on cold nights, otherwise you will see the fatal black centre to the flowers which means they have been killed.

All crops, especially brassicas, will need protection from birds; over-wintered crops, and newly sown ones, are vulnerable; pea, lettuce and spinach will need netting – of a close mesh, to keep out the smaller birds – or some other form of deterrent.

## Training and tying-in

One of the commonest methods of training outdoor vines is by the double Guyot system. Each established vine will have one side-shoot or bearer rod trained horizontally on each side of the main stem, and from this will be produced five or six side-shoots. These should be trained straight up and tied to the supporting wires as they reach them. The central shoot which was cut back in the early winter to leave three dormant leaf buds will produce new shoots from these three buds, one to each, and the three new shoots should also be trained vertically up the centre and tied in as they grow. Newly planted vines, put in last winter or this spring, will not have any bearer rods, only the three central shoots, which should be treated as on the established plants.

## Ventilation

The outdoor temperature will, one hopes, be starting to rise appreciably, on sunny days especially, so during the day ventilate the greenhouse for longer periods, and at night begin to leave one or more ventilators open 5cm (2in).

*A splendid crop of Siegerrebe grapes, a good choice for wine and dessert. Strong supports and secure tying are vital, when crops are as heavy as this.*

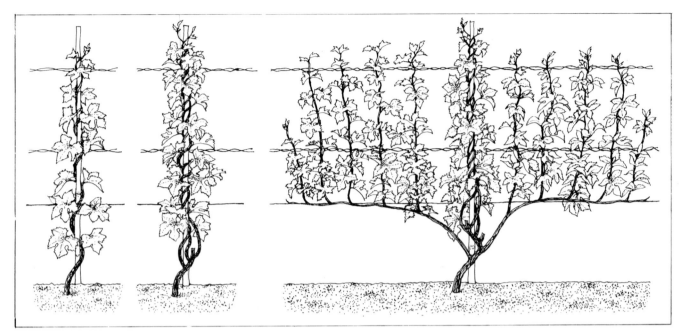

*Double Guyot training of outdoor grapes. In the first summer train leading shoot up its support. Cut back in early winter to leave three buds. In the second summer, train these up their support. In the second winter, pull outside shoots down to side wires, cut off tips and cut central shoot.*

Remember to open those facing away from the prevailing wind, otherwise your plants will be enduring cold draughty gusts instead of warm fresh air gently supplied in moderation. Keep the cloched strawberries well aired.

### Choosing a site for fruit or vegetable growing
You will get the best fruit and vegetables and heaviest crops from bushes, canes and plants if you can grow them in a sunny place, sheltered from wind, and in soil which is slightly acid (alter to slightly alkaline for a few crops), drains well and the topsoil is at least 30cm (12in) deep. Coastal and hilltop sites should be planted with the hardier varieties, and so should northern regions and gardens in frost pockets. By choosing the site now, there is time to clear and cultivate the ground thoroughly before starting with the first crops in mid- to late summer.

### Cutting asparagus
You can begin to harvest asparagus at the end of mid-spring, cutting only a few spears from each plant. Cut about 10cm (4in) deep below the soil surface; there are special asparagus knives with serrated and curved blades available for this. Scrape the soil away carefully before cutting.

## Crops to be harvested

asparagus, broccoli (heading-winter cauliflower), broccoli (sprouting), cabbage (spring), kale, leeks, lettuce (over-wintered), radish (summer), rhubarb, spinach, spinach beet, Swiss chard (seakale beet), turnip tops. All established herbs

## Available from store

beetroot, carrot, celeriac, garlic, onion, parsnip, potato, radish (winter), shallot, swede, turnip

# Late Spring

Warmer soil and rising air temperatures, combined with spring rain, should mean good, fast growth of all crops, but the night temperature may still be dropping surprisingly low, and even occasionally dipping down to freezing. If this is the case, it will account for what may seem to be puzzlingly slow growth of some crops and it will pay handsomely to put cloches at night over such crops as lettuce, peas, onions, radishes, carrots and beetroots.

You will be doing a good deal of planting during late spring; it should be possible to plant outdoors the slightly tender crops such as melons, cucumbers, tomatoes and sweetcorn in normal weather conditions, as well as more peas and early-started runner beans. There are still some seeds which can be sown though they will crop a little late; there are others which it is best not to sow until now in any case.

Pests and diseases will now be a major problem and the succulent growth of plants will make them irresistible to insects, birds and slugs in particular. Finger and thumb work may be all that is needed if done early enough; otherwise there are pesticides which are harmless to all but the pest concerned (see Controls and Treatments).

The new compost heap which was started last month will be piling up fast, which is all to the good. The quicker it is built, especially if there is a lot of fresh green vegetation, the more likely it is to heat up to the high temperature needed for full rotting. Weeds will form a large part of this and, if you are very skilful and careful, you can let the weeds grow to form a good cover without much harm to the crops and then take them off just before they flower, thus getting the maximum of vegetation for the compost heap.

Weeds are said to absorb moisture and food which the crops might otherwise have; they take away the light and provide an alternative home for diseases and insects. On the other hand, bare soil certainly seems to get dry more quickly, weeds can absorb some mineral nutrients which vegetable and fruit crops might not be able to reach and they do eventually provide humus, so they are not altogether bad. It is when they get out of hand that you run into trouble and the perennial weeds have developed methods of increase which are almost invincible.

# At~a~glance diary

**Prepare the soil for:** sowing outdoors in a seed-bed

**Sow seeds outdoors of:** basil, French (kidney) bean, runner (pole) bean, beetroot, broccoli (heading), Brussels sprout, cabbage (for autumn and winter cropping), calabrese, carrot, chicory, cucumber (ridge), dill, endive (curled), fennel, kale, kohlrabi, leek, lettuce, marjoram, melon, parsley, pea, rad ish, savory (summer), squash, spinach (summer and New Zealand) swede, tomato, turnip

**Sow seeds under glass of:** aubergine

**Plant outdoors:** aubergine, basil, bay, Brussels sprout, cabbage (summer) celeriac, celery, chives, cucumber (ridge), marjoram, melon, marrow, mint, pea, pepper, potato, rosemary, sage, squash strawberry (alpine), sweet corn, tarragon, thyme, tomato

**Plant under glass:** aubergine, cucumber, melon, pepper, tomato

**Thin:** beetroot, broccoli (sprouting), Brussels sprout, cabbage (autumn and winter), carrot, chives, kohlrabi, leek, lettuce, marjoram, onion, parsley, parsnip, radish, summer spin ach, strawberry (alpine), Swiss chard (seakale beet), turnip

**Earth up:** potato

**Compost heap:** continue to make

**Mulch:** all outdoor vegetables to be thinned plus globe artichoke French (kidney) bean, runner (pole) bean, cucumber, marrow, tomato, and such fruits as blackberry, blackcurrant loganberry, gooseberry, red currant, strawberry and vine; all herbs

**Feed:** asparagus, lettuce, pea, spinach and spinach beet, Swiss chard (seakale beet), strawberry; tomatoes and peppers in greenhouse

**Stake, train and tie in:** angelica, Jerusalem artichoke, aubergine, runner (pole) bean, indoor cucumber, lovage, indoor melon, pea, indoor tomato, vine

**Weed and clear:** all crops

**Water:** young plants if weather dry; greenhouse crops

**Protect:** gooseberry, strawberry

**Pests and diseases:** birds, capsid bug, carrot fly, celery leaf miner, flea-beetle greenfly, mice, onion fly, slugs and snails

**Deblossom:** perpetual-fruiting strawberries

**Ventilate:** cloched strawberries, greenhouse plants

# Jobs to do

### Preparing the soil

A little bit of seed-bed preparation will be required and there will be some digging outdoors for planting out crops started in the greenhouse, or indoors for planting in the soil inside the greenhouse. It will be much easier now to obtain the right consistency for the soil of the seedbed and digging will be less difficult, with drier soil conditions than in winter or early spring (see these sections for details of soil preparation).

### Sowing seed outdoors

You can still sow outdoors most of the crops listed in mid-spring and some of those listed for sowing under glass in early spring as well as additional crops. They include: basil, beans (French and runner), beetroot, broccoli (heading), Brussels sprouts, cabbage (for autumn and winter cropping), calabrese (a form of sprouting broccoli), carrot, chicory, cucumber (ridge), dill, endive (curled), fennel, kale, kohlrabi, leek, lettuce, marjoram, marrow, melon, pea, radish, savory (summer), squashes, spinach, (New Zealand and summer), swede, tomato and turnip.

For some of these, it would be a good idea to put cloches over the soil where they are to be sown and leave the cloches over the rows until germination has taken place. Then take them off except at night until the seedlings are growing well and the weather consistently warm. Suitable crops are: basil, fennel, French (kidney) bean, runner (pole) bean, cucumber, marrow, melon, squash and tomato.

If the weather is still chilly, you can start these tender crops off in the greenhouse, sowing them singly in individual peat or plastic pots and planting out after germination, under cloches.

Calabrese is an interesting form of sprouting broccoli which is very popular in Italy, where it originated in its wild form near Calabria. It matures as a plant less tall then the winter-sprouting kind and will be ready for picking in late summer, on into mid-autumn. On the top of the stem will be a green head, rather like a small cauliflower, and this should be cut first. The side florets lower down the stem

*Calabrese is a interesting member of the sprouting broccoli family, which can be harvested from mid-summer to early autumn. It has a delicate flavour.*

are then cut as they are produced, when the stem of each is about 10cm (4in) long. Unlike its relative, you should sow it where it is to mature, not in a seed-bed, and thin it in the row.

Chicory and endive are grown to provide salading in autumn and winter, so there is no need to sow them earlier than late spring. Chicory is the crop which forms white-to-pale-green growths shaped rather like a tightly packed cos lettuce about 10-15cm (4-6in) long. These are produced by digging up the roots in autumn, cutting off any remaining summer growth, boxing them and later giving them warmth so that they are forced into renewed growth much earlier than would otherwise be the case with a biennial plant.

Endive is much more lettuce-like; there are two sorts, curled or mossy, which has intricately cut and fringed leaves, and the Batavian endive, the leaves of which are broad and entire. Curly endive is not hardy and should be harvested in autumn, about three months after the sowing date, but Batavian endive can be left in the ground until late autumn or lifted, like chicory, and taken into the greenhouse for blanching. This kind is usually not sown until mid-summer. Chicory and endive are also sown where they are to mature and thinned in the rows.

New Zealand spinach is quite different to ordinary spinach; it grows long shoots which trail along the ground and needs 90cm (36in) of space each way. The leaves are relatively thick. It does not bolt in hot, dry weather and the tips of the shoots and the young leaves can be harvested from mid-summer until the frosts. Keep it well watered in dry conditions.

Swede is grown for use in winter and should not be sown before late spring, otherwise it either bolts (runs to flower) or matures long before you want it, when there are a great number of summer vegetables ready for harvesting. Sow it and thin it where sown; like turnip, it is a brassica, although a root crop, and should be counted as part of that group when working out a cropping rotation.

### Sowing under glass
The only seeds which are still worth sowing in the greenhouse are those of aubergine, and then only if you have a garden which will be warm in autumn.

### Planting outdoors
Although mid-spring is the traditional time for planting maincrop potatoes, it is still not too late to do it now, preferably as early in the season as possible. In any case, with warmer conditions generally, late-planted maincrops often catch up with the earlier planted tubers. You can also plant outdoors the crops which were pricked out or potted on in mid-spring: Brussels sprout, summer cabbage, celeriac, celery, cucumber, melon, pepper, alpine strawberry and tomato.

If the temperature outside the frames or greenhouse is markedly lower than that inside them, you should harden off all these before planting out, especially celeriac, celery, cucumber, melon, pepper and tomato.

These last-mentioned crops are best not put out until the end of late spring, with cloche protection at night, if frosts are still being forecast.

All these crops will be more developed through being given heat at the start, so they will be ready for planting earlier and will be more in need of cloche or frame protection than those not sown until mid-spring. Young plants which have been growing in a nice cosy atmosphere will simply stop growing, at the very least, if suddenly put out into soil and air which are considerably colder, so give them all fresh air during the day, starting about a week before you intend planting. Take them back into shelter later and later in the evening until you are eventually leaving them out all night, preferably one of the warmer nights, and then they will grow straightaway when planted in their cropping positions.

Control of hardening off is easier when dealing with frames, because you can manipulate the frame cover much more exactly, according to the vagaries of the temperature. You will find, as you do more and more gardening, that a frame is a very useful piece of equipment and can have plants in it, at various stages of growth, all through the year. Even in winter you can put pot strawberries in a frame for bringing into the greenhouse to force.

When you plant melons, make a hole with a trowel large enough to take the soil-ball comfortably and then make a shallow mound in the centre of it. Water well, put the soil-ball on the mound so that the surface is slightly above that of the surrounding soil and fill in firmly with crumbly soil. This will ensure that no water collects around the base of the stem, leading to rot. Water the plants in and mulch lightly.

In mid-spring, you may also have sown some crops in gentle heat, such as aubergine, basil, celery, cucumber, marrow, melon, squash, pepper, pea, sweetcorn and tomato; these can be pricked out or potted on and then planted in the open.

The timing of these different stages depends on the date you sowed the seed, the state of the weather and the rate of growth of the various crops. You will have to be guided by the root development in particular, which can to some extent be judged by the amount and rate of the top growth. You should never do a specific job because it is the third week in mid-spring, or the second week of late spring. The plants themselves will show when they need more room or when they are mature enough to go into their permanent positions. In one year you may be able to plant out melons in frames in the middle of late spring, another year early summer may be sufficiently soon. If some of these plants are growing fast and the weather is unsuitable for planting out, you can keep them growing with liquid feeding for two weeks or so.

You can also plant out a variety of herbs: basil, bay, marjoram, rosemary, sage, tarragon, and thyme, whether

# Sowing and Planting

| Vegetable or herb | Depth to sow | Method | Distance to sow/thin | Distance between rows | Germination time (days) | Remarks |
|---|---|---|---|---|---|---|
| Basil | 0.6cm (¼in) | Continuously and thinly | 20cm (8in) | 90cm (36in) | 14–21 | Sow when frost mostly past, or protect |
| Bean, French (kidney) | 2.5cm (1in) | Singly | 20cm (8in) | 45cm (18in) | 10–14 | |
| Bean, runner (pole) | 5cm (2in) | Singly | 20–30cm (8–12in) | 38cm (15in) | 10–14 | Sow a double row staggered and allow 150cm (5ft) between each double row. Choose a site sheltered from wind |
| Broccoli, heading (winter cauliflower) | 1.3cm (½in) | Continuously and thinly | 10cm (4in) | 15cm (6in) | 7–12 | |
| Calabrese | 1.3cm (½in) | Continuously and thinly | 38cm (15in) | 60cm (24in) | 7–12 | Sow and thin where maturing |
| Chicory | 1.3cm (½in) | Continuously and thinly | 23–25cm (9–10in) | 30–45cm (12–18in) | 14–21 | |
| Cucumber, ridge | 2.5cm (1in) | Singly | 90cm (36in) | 120cm (48in) | 5–15 | |
| Endive | 1.3cm (½in) | Singly | 23cm (9in) | 38cm (15in) | 14–21 | |
| Kale | 1.3cm (½in) | Continuously and thinly | 10cm (4in) | 15cm (6in) | 7–12 | |
| Marrow, bush | 2.5cm (1in) | Singly | 90cm (36in) | 75cm (30in) | 5–8 | |
| Marrow, trailing | 2.5cm (1in) | Singly | 150cm (60in) | 90cm (36in) | 5–8 | |
| Spinach, New Zealand | 2.5cm (1in) | Singly | 90cm (36in) | 90cm (36in) | 12–21 | |
| Squash | 2.5cm (1in) | Singly | 150cm (60in) | 90cm (36in) | 5–8 | |
| Swede | 1.3cm (½in) | Continuously and thinly | 20cm (8in) | 38cm (15in) | 6–12 | |
| Tomato, outdoor cordon | 0.6cm (¼in) | Singly | 45cm (18in) | 45cm (18in) | 7–21 | |
| Tomato, outdoor bush | 0.6cm (¼in) | Singly | 60cm (24in) | 60cm (24in) | 7–21 | |

grown from seed, division of established plants, or bought in as young plants. It is also not too late to plant chives and mint, if not done in mid-spring. One plant each of bay, rosemary, sage, tarragon and thyme should be sufficient.

There are three types of celery available nowadays, one of which is self-blanching or summer celery; this does not need to be earthed up and comes into crop early in midsummer. The ordinary kind, which is not ready until mid-autumn, must be blanched.

The self-blanching kind is planted in a square block, fairly closely, with sacking or black plastic sheeting round

*Potatoes are earthed up two or three times during the summer, to protect the haulm, produce a bigger crop and prevent the tubers from turning green. Draw the soil towards the stems, to leave a V-shaped trench between the rows.*

the outside, to keep the light from the outermost plants. Ordinary celery is planted in trenches and the stems wound round with brown paper, corrugated cardboard or plastic sheet, and surrounded with soil as they grow, to produce the long, completely white stems of winter celery. The third kind has stems coloured green or pinkish; like self-blanching celery this is a summer and early autumn type, which will not stand winter cold but nevertheless has the authentic celery flavour.

Sweetcorn also gives better results if planted in blocks. The pollinating tassels at the top of the plant shed their pollen on the female flowers much lower down on the plant; if planted in single rows, the pollen is likely to be blown away and wasted, but planted in blocks, there is a better chance of overall pollination. Sweetcorn is a member of the grass family, which is commonly wind pollinated.

### Planting under glass
In the greenhouse, you can plant aubergine, cucumbers, melons, peppers and tomatoes in their permanent positions or containers.

Melons planted in the border in the greenhouse should have a short cane placed at the back to support the stem until it reaches the lowest wire. Break off the growing tip just above the top leaf, when there are four or five leaves present, to encourage side-shoot development.

### Thinning
Late spring is the time to do most of the thinning that is necessary. Crops which are to be transplanted, as well as those which are to mature where sown, should all be given the extra space that results from this exercise. Crops to be thinned are those sown outdoors in mid-spring: beetroot, borage, broccoli (sprouting), Brussels sprout, cabbage, carrot, chives, dill, fennel, kohlrabi, leek, lettuce, marjoram, onion, parsley, parsnip, radish, savory (summer), sorrel, summer spinach, spinach beet, alpine strawberry, Swiss chard (seakale beet) and turnip. There may also be some thinning still left to do on crops (i.e., leek, onion, parsnip and the spinaches) sown in early spring, if they were sown late and germinated late due to chilly weather.

### Earthing up
If you have not already piled up ridges over your potatoes at planting time, you will need to start earthing up at the beginning of this season or whenever the potato shoots (haulm) are about 15cm (6in) tall. This is done to prevent the tubers being exposed to the light and turning green, to encourage the production of more tubers from the buried part of the haulm, to protect the tubers in case of infection by potato blight and to keep the haulm upright.

To earth up, soil should be drawn up from both sides of the row to form a V-shaped ridge from the top of which about 2.5cm (1in) of the potato stems emerge. It is easier to do this when the soil is crumbly and dryish. If you know the soil is rather infertile, you can scatter compound fertilizer on the soil before ridging, as an insurance against a bad crop. Two to four weeks later, repeat the process.

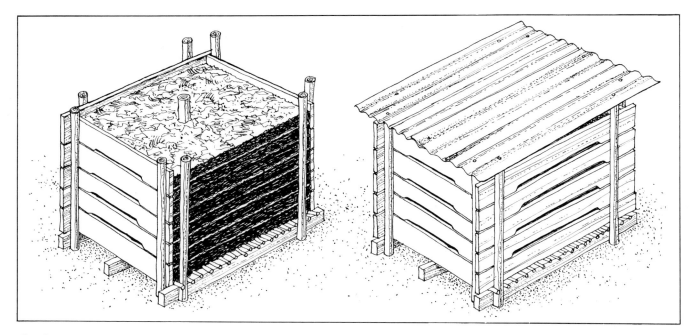

*Garden compost added regularly to the soil will keep it in excellent condition. Compost bins can be wooden-sided, with ventilation beneath them.*

## Compost-heap making

To make good compost, the heap should be made of as much fresh green vegetation as possible and it should be made quickly. It should be made so that air, water, warmth and nitrogen are available to the bacteria which feed on and break down the vegetation into the dark brown crumbly mass which is the source of humus.

Humus is a substance which ensures that the soil structure remains in good condition for plant growth and that it contains nutrients which are available to plant roots. It is most important that soil contains humus and, as the humus is in a constant state of change and breakdown, it has to be replaced; garden compost is one of the most convenient ways of ensuring its presence in your soil. Other bulky organic substances such as farm manure, spent mushroom compost, leafmould, spent hops and seaweed will supply humus, but need to be obtained; they are not on the spot, except in rare circumstances.

The heap can be contained in a wooden box, or by bricks straw bales, breeze blocks, corrugated iron or black plastic sheet. The bottom of the heap should be lifted off the ground so that air can get underneath and there should be a hole or holes up through the heap, so that a chimney-like effect is obtained; air can then go up and help to create what is almost literally combustion. This is all to the good,

as the considerable heat thus produced will result in quicker rotting and destruction of weed seeds, most pests and fungus diseases. Building the heap round two or three poles stuck into the ground will ensure aeration, as they can be withdrawn when the heap is finished.

The heap is built in layers, like a sandwich, first a 10-12.5cm (4-5in) thickness of vegetation, then a sprinkling of an activator or sulphate of ammonia, another layer of vegetation and a sprinkling of lime, and so on until the heap is about 1.2m (4ft) high. Width can be about the same and length as long as convenient. When finished, a sloping roof to keep the rain off is advisable, but the heap should never be completely dry, otherwise it will not rot. You may have to sprinkle it with water as you make it if the weather is dry. Good heaps should be ready six weeks after starting, but usually they take about three months and a heap started in late summer will not be ready until the following spring.

Try not to put hard, woody material into it; this rots very slowly and you will find digging out the compost which is rotted very irritating as your spade constantly strikes sticks and twigs. Also, try not to regard the compost heap as a rubbish dump for plastic, milk-bottle tops, odd pieces of papers, labels, string, stones and particularly glass. The dustbin is the right place for these.

## Mulching

A good deal of mulching is done in this season. It helps to stop the weeds from growing, and putting it on while the soil is still moist, before the summer droughts, will cut down on the time needed later for watering. It also, keeps the soil structure in good condition, encourages worms and supplies some plant food.

You can mulch all those vegetables which have been thinned for the final time, also globe artichokes, French (kidney) and runner (pole) beans, peas and the cucurbits and tomatoes if planted out. If you are not keeping a straw cover on the soft fruit, then the currants, blackberries, loganberries, gooseberries and vines can all be mulched; the raspberries will already have been done as their new shoots start to appear so early.

Strawberries can be mulched with organic matter, if not already done in early spring, and the mulch covered with straw towards the end of late spring. The time to do this is when the berries are still green and swelling rapidly, on a dry day, but when the topsoil is moist. If you straw on to dry soil you will run into trouble later on with hard, small berries because of lack of moisture. An alternative to straw is black plastic sheet, though the slugs tend to congregate under it and come up at night to feed on the berries.

A very light mulch on the herbs will give them that finishing touch which results in first class plants and flavours.

## Feeding

There is still little feeding to do outdoors; another dressing of agricultural salt can go on to the asparagus bed, four weeks or so after the last one, at 60g per sq m (2oz) per sq yd. The quickly growing early crops such as lettuces, peas, the spinaches and Swiss chard (seakale beet) can be liquid fed once a week, also the strawberries for really bumper crops, but most of any feeding necessary comes during summer. In the greenhouse, regular liquid feeding will be necessary for tomatoes and peppers.

## Staking, training and tying

The tall-growing crops will all need supports and should be trained up them or tied to them: Jerusalem artichoke, broad bean, runner (pole) bean, indoor cucumber, melon, pea, indoor tomato and vines. Aubergines and broad beans will need the tops pinched out.

Jerusalem artichokes can grow to 2.1 or 2.4m (7 or 8ft) tall and are fairly strong. They will only need to be attached to stakes or canes if in windy positions. Broad beans need only have a stake or two put at each end of the row and wire run along the outside of the row from one end to the other, so that they are enclosed.

Runner beans must have tall supports, at least 2.1m (7ft) high, very firmly anchored. You can use bamboo canes,

*Runner (pole) beans need picking over every three or four days, so that they continue to flower and produce a crop right through to autumn.*

but wooden stakes are better because they have a rough surface; there are several methods of support.

Indoor cucumbers and tomatoes can be trained and supported on the same system, as single stem cordons. Both will have a great tendency to produce side-shoots from the join between a leaf stalk and the main stem, and in order to channel the plant's energy into fruit production, these should be removed as soon as they appear. A length of fillis (soft string) is attached at each planting station to the lower and upper horizontal wires and then twined round the main stem as it grows. When the stem reaches the top wire, the growing tip is pinched off just above the second leaf above a flower cluster in the case of tomatoes, and at the first leaf above a flower or fruit for cucumbers. Cucumbers will need the tendrils removing.

Indoor melons are trained to develop two side-shoots, pinching out the growing point just above the fourth leaf. The side-shoots from these are also stopped when about 75cm (30in) long and as soon as one fruit has set on each, any sub-side-shoots and tendrils should be removed as they appear. Each plant should be able to carry at least four fruit. A trellis arrangement of wires or string will be necessary to support the melon shoot growth, spaced about 30cm (12in) from the greenhouse glass.

Continue to tie in the three new shoots on established vines, as described in Mid-Spring, and when they reach the top wire, train them along it as convenient. Also continue trying the sub-side-shoots and, on young vines, the three centre shoots. Some herbs may need supporting also; angelica grows 1.5 or 1.8m (5 or 6ft) tall, lovage even taller. Some of the lower growing kinds tend to sprawl about on the ground and get eaten by slugs.

Broad beans should have the tops nipped out when they have grown to their full height and the top cluster of flower buds is visible. This discourages an infestation of blackfly. Aubergine should also have their growing points removed, just above a leaf, so that the length of main stem left is about 15cm (6in); more side-shoots will result and hence more fruit. A stake about 90cm (36in) long will be necessary for supporting the plants. and should be put in position before planting.

### Weeding

Continue to hoe out or otherwise treat seedlings and young weeds; especially keep an eye open for perennial weeds. Leeks and onions are very vulnerable to swamping by broad-leaved weeds, and grass weeds can easily be mistaken when young for seedlings of these crops. Root out seedlings of trees such as hawthorn, ash, sycamore or chestnut while still small. All germinate readily and grow unseen, sending down long tap-roots which make them difficult to remove quickly once they reach about 15cm (6in) in height.

### Watering

There should not be a great deal of this to do outdoors yet, but do make sure none of the young plants runs short. A check at this stage can mean no hearting or curding later or bolting in a few weeks' time. However, in the greenhouse watering will become a major job, especially for plants in containers.

### Protecting

Gooseberry and strawberry fruits will be setting and swelling fast, for maturing in early summer, so they will need netting or other protection from birds. Strawberry flowers may also need protection from frost; newspapers, plastic sheet or straw should be sufficient to ward off the degree of frost that may occur at this time.

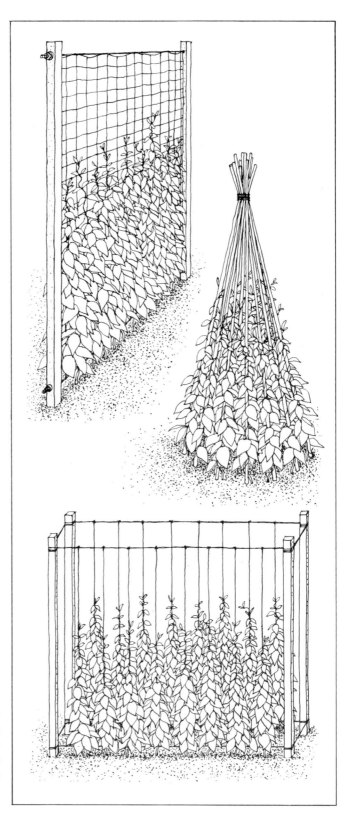

*Various ways of supporting runner (pole) beans (besides the usual one of poles crossing at the top) : the illustration shows them trained up netting; the canes formed into a wigwam; the plants trained up single strings or wires. The first and last method will need guy-ropes at the ends of the rows to prevent collapse while the plants are in full crop.*

## Treating pests and diseases

As with mid-spring, caterpillars, greenfly, slugs and snails, mice, birds and carrot fly will all have to be watched for (see Kitchen Garden Controls and Treatments.) In addition, there are likely to be various specific troubles, some of which may already have appeared. Onion fly can be a great trouble on young onions, when the maggots feed in the developing bulb. The adult looks like a small grey housefly and there may be two broods a year, though the first causes the most trouble, attacking the main crop while young and feeding for about three weeks. Wilting and yellowing leaves are the first signs above ground of attack.

The tiny maggots of the leaf miner fly can start infesting celery and celeriac in spring; leaves become covered in pale brown blisters and stop growing, eventually withering completely. Young plants may be killed or severely stunted. The one or two later broods which may occur are less

## Crops to be harvested

asparagus, broad bean (a few), broccoli (heading-winter cauliflower), broccoli (sprouting), spring cabbage (last), kale, leek (last), lettuce (over-wintered), spring onion, radish, rhubarb, spinach, spinach beet, strawberry (cloched), turnip tops (last). All established herbs

damaging, as the plants are much larger. Picking off affected leaves, if done soon enough, may be all that is necessary.

Capsid bugs can reduce currant, gooseberry and raspberry leaves to tatters by their feeding. They are like very large greenfly but move quickly, running for shelter when disturbed. Attacked leaves will have pinprick holes in them, especially the youngest ones, and sometimes the growing point will be so damaged that it dies and the shoot ceases to extend, thereby diminishing the future crop. Hatching is usually towards the end of late spring; this is one pest for which a preventative spray is a good idea, put on during the last two weeks of late spring.

The cabbage family can be decimated by flea beetles during spring, feeding on the seedling leaves to produce large quantities of small round holes. The beetles are tiny and iridescent greenish black or black and yellow in colour; they hop when disturbed. For controls of all these troubles, see Kitchen Garden Controls and Treatment.

### Deblossoming

If you are growing perpetual-fruiting strawberries, any flowers that may be developing should be removed now in order that a good and continuous crop is produced from mid-summer onwards.

### Ventilating

Cloched strawberries will need airing on sunny days; open the cloches at the tops and ends and move them slightly apart. This allows pollinating insects to get inside. The berries should begin to colour shortly. You can also begin to give the greenhouse a great deal more ventilation.

*A heavy crop of strawberries, protected from mud by straw. A black plastic sheet will do the same job, keep down weeds and discourage pests.*

# Early Summer

By this time your crops will be well into their stride, growing rapidly, flowering and setting fruit. From now on, most of the work consists of routine care, protecting the plants from pest and disease, and at the same time minimising the effects of unsuitable weather. You can still start off some crops, mainly those which are to be stored through the winter, or those which are deliberately being sown late to avoid pest attack, but you may in any case be short of space unless a crop has failed or bolted.

The experienced gardener makes use of all the space available and makes sure that it has some crop or other in it for as much of the year as possible. As soon as one crop is finished, in summer, the ground should be cleared, dug and fertilized and another batch of seed sown or plants put in. This is where the quick-maturing crops are so useful: beetroot, radish, lettuce, carrot, French (kidney) bean, spinach and pea.

Watering will begin to be of considerable importance; the soft fruit season lasts mainly from early to late summer, but at the same time as the plants are fruiting, they are also producing new shoots on which next year's crop will be carried. This puts a great strain on them and if ample supplies of water are not available to the roots, the new growth will be poor or non-existent; if the water shortage continues, the crop will also be miserable.

Vegetables, too, are vulnerable when potential droughts loom; biennial kinds which are cropped in their first season telescope their growth during drought and run to seed (bolt) then, instead of in the second summer. Root crops split or stop growing, only to crack when moisture is supplied eventually; the fruiting vegetables drop their fruits while still embryos or their flowers fall without setting. Do not let a dry spell go on for too long without watering; a week of hot dry weather, even if the soil is moist at the beginning, is quite long enough, and you should then water heavily at intervals of a few days, until the drought is over. Pests and diseases will still be with you, so will the weeds.

# At~a~glance diary

**Prepare the soil for:** sowing outdoors

**Sow seeds outdoors of:** French (kidney) bean, runner (pole) bean, beetroot, borage carrot, chicory (Sugar Loaf), dill, endive (curled), kale, kohlrabi, lettuce, parsley, pea, radish, swede, turnip

**Plant:** bay, broccoli (heading and sprouting), Brussels sprout, cabbage, celery, cucumber, kale, leek, marjoram, marrow, melon, rosemary, sage, sweetcorn, tarragon, thyme, tomato

**Thin:** basil, beetroot, broccoli (heading), Brussels sprout, cabbage, calabrese, carrot, chicory, dill, endive, fennel, kale, kohlrabi, lettuce, marjoram, parsley, radish, savory (summer), summer spinach, swede, tomato, turnip

**Earth up:** potato

**Compost heap:** continue to make

**Feed:** globe artichoke, asparagus, aubergine, cucumber (indoor) garlic, lettuce, pepper, pea, strawberry, tomato

**Stake, train and tie in:** Jerusalem artichoke, aubergine, runner (pole) bean, blackberry, cucumber (indoor), loganberry, marrow, melon, pea, raspberry, squash, tomato, vine

**Prune:** red currant

**Water:** all

**Weed and clear:** all crops

**Protect:** all newly planted out brassica, currant, gooseberry raspberry, and strawberry from birds

**Pests and diseases:** caterpillars and maggots of various kinds, greenfly, capsid bug, slugs and snails, birds, mice, flea beetle, brassica clubroot, red spider mite, whitefly

**Deblossom:** perpetual-fruiting strawberry, pepper, aubergine, male cucumber flowers under glass

**Pollinate:** melon

**Increase:** mint, rosemary, sage, strawberry, tarragon, thyme

**Shade:** greenhouse, cloches and frames

**Ventilate:** greenhouse, cloches and frames

**Order:** strawberry plants

**Harvest:** asparagus, potato, rhubarb

# Jobs to do

## Preparing the soil
There is little to do beyond getting the soil into condition for sowing seeds, mostly in rows where the plants are to mature, rather than in seed beds or containers for transplanting.

## Sowing seed outdoors
Most of the sowing has been done by now, but there is still time to get a crop of some quick-growing vegetables and there are others which will grow steadily until the autumn and need the long growing period. Seeds to sow are: French (kidney) bean, runner (pole) bean, beetroot, borage, carrot, chicory (Sugarloaf), dill, endive (curled), kale, kohlrabi, lettuce, parsley, pea, radish, swede and turnip.

Beetroot, carrot and swede should be sown and grown for winter storage, so will need thinning to the widest spacings given in Mid- and Late Spring. Sown in a position where they are not exposed to sun all day, they will be less likely to bolt. Peas to sow at this time should be the first-early dwarf varieties, which take only 11-12 weeks to mature and will fit under cloches in autumn.

*Well-filled pea pods can be obtained by digging in plenty of manure or compost, and ensuring a good supply of water.*

## Thinning

There will be a variety of late-spring-sown crops to thin, if not already done, including: basil, beetroot, Brussels sprout, broccoli (heading), cabbage, calabrese, carrot, chicory, dill, endive, fennel, kale, kohlrabi, lettuce, marjoram, parsley, radish, savory, summer spinach, swede, tomato and turnip. Thinning is easier when the soil is on the dry side, but if it is, water the remaining plants to make sure their roots are firmly in contact with the soil.

## Planting

This will be one of the main jobs to do in early summer as the winter brassicas, celery, leeks, sweetcorn, tomatoes and the cucurbits will all be ready to go out. The soil for all these will already have been prepared and will only need

transplanting and should have a ball of soil round the roots when lifted. Water the plants well as they grow.

Self-blanching celery is generally grown in a square block, planted on the flat, without digging trenches first. Lift the young plants with their roots as intact as possible, and plant so that the roots are covered, but not the stems, otherwise they will tend to sucker. Water in and erect a sacking or black plastic sheet barrier round the block to keep the outside plants blanched; the inside ones will be shaded by one another.

Winter celery is planted in trenches; dig out the prepared site to 15-25cm (6-10in) deep and 38-45cm (15-18in) wide. Put the young plants, 23cm (9in) apart, in a row along the centre. Lift them from their containers with as little disturbance to the roots as possible, set firmly in the soil and

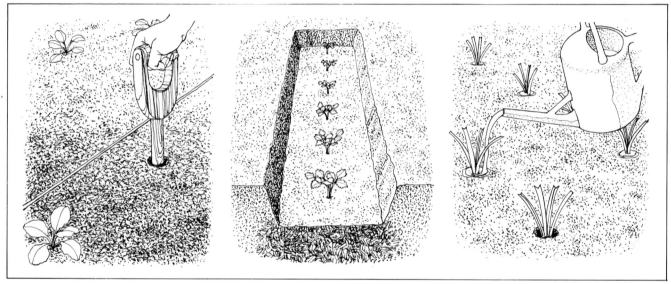

*Correct planting is important. Brassicas should be planted up to the lowest leaf, in a hole made with a dibber. Celery is planted in a trench, and leeks are dropped into a hole.*

loosening on the surface and clearing of possible annual weeds. (For preparation see Early Spring.)

The brassicas – sprouting and heading broccoli (winter cauliflower), cabbages including Savoys, Brussels sprouts, kale and kohlrabi – can all be transplanted to their permanent positions as soon as they have developed four or five leaves. Do not choose plants which have gone 'blind' – that is, lost their growing point, or those with leaves which have a bluish tinge, as it means their roots may be damaged in some way. Make a planting hole with a wooden dibber, or trowel, water it, put in the plant up to the first leaf and firm the soil round the roots. Plants should be watered before

water in. Celery needs plenty of water, so it is wise to water the site beforehand if at all dry. You can also plant in a double staggered row, using the wider trench spacing, and leave 30cm (12in) between plants, to make later work easier. The dug-out soil at the sides of the trenches can be used for quick-growing, catch crops before earthing up is needed in late summer.

Leeks can be grown on the flat and blanched as they grow, but it is easier to make holes with a dibber, drop one leek plant into each hole and then fill the hole up with water to settle the soil round the roots. Trim the roots back a little, and cut the tips off the leaves before planting so that they do not trail on the ground and rot. Leeks should be transplanted when about 15–20cm (6–8in) high.

Sweetcorn is another crop which is planted in a block; put in the plant complete with peat pot, firm well in and water thoroughly. Sweetcorn should be 10-15cm (4-6in) tall when transplanted; if the nights are still chilly, below 13°C (55°F), cover with cloches, but remove during the day.

Tomatoes will do best if they can be planted close to a south-facing wall with shelter from cold winds. Plants should be about 15-20cm (6-8in) tall at planting time, with the first flower truss just showing. Move them with a good ball of soil round the roots, put in a supporting stake (for cordon tomatoes) about 120cm (48in) high at the same time and water in after firming the soil round them.

The cucurbits are planted in the same way as melons (see Late Spring).

The Mediterranean type of herbs can still be planted out: bay, marjoram, rosemary, sage, tarragon and thyme. Although they are plants from hot, dry habitats, water them in and water occasionally thereafter, otherwise they will not take when transplanted.

## Earthing up
Maincrop and second early potatoes will need earthing up once or twice more during early summer, but stop once the tops have grown sufficiently to touch those of the rows on each side (see Late Spring for details).

## Compost heap
Your heap will be growing fast and should be turned once or twice, sides to middles, or sides can go on top. Keep it within manageable proportions, and start another as soon as it is about 150cm (60in) high.

## Feeding
Feeding begins to become more important from now on; the last dressing of agricultural salt can be given to asparagus, at 60g per sq m (2oz per sq yd). Globe artichokes can be given a general liquid feed at ten-day intervals from now until autumn, and aubergine, lettuce, peppers, peas and tomatoes can also be liquid fed: give all but lettuce a potash-high liquid fertilizer. Lettuce will do better with one which has a high nitrogen content. Garlic can have a single dressing of compound, potash-high fertilizer, well watered in, to bring the bulbs up to a really good size. It should by now be about 45-60cm (18-24in) tall; remove the flower if one appears. Liquid feeding of strawberries can continue and all greenhouse plants need regular liquid feeding.

## Staking, training and tying in
Raspberries, blackberries and loganberries will be producing new shoots which will lengthen very quickly, so these will want tying in, up the centres of the plants. Continue to tie and train such tall-growing crops as Jerusalem artichoke, aubergine, runner (pole) beans, indoor cucumber, indoor melon and tomato. Trailing marrows and squashes need only guiding as to the way they should grow, and the tips pinching out if they are out-growing their space.

Runner beans should be supplied with some form of support as soon as possible; there are various methods but whatever you use, make sure that it is really well anchored. A row of fully grown runner beans presents a massive barrier to the wind and, if it gets blown down, it is not really possible to erect it satisfactorily again.

Melons grown in frames or under cloches can be trained so that they produce two or four main shoots per plant. Take out the growing tip just above the fourth or fifth leaf, and side-shoots will be produced in the axils of the leaves, one

*Many herbs enhance the flavour of vegetables: marjoram is one whose leaves have a highly individual flavour. It is a herb that well goes with tomato dishes and salads.*

to each axil. As these grow they will produce flowers, and one on each shoot should be allowed to set a fruit, if there are four side-shoots. If you have only allowed two side-shoots to a plant, each can carry two fruits. The small Ogen melons can be allowed to carry several fruits to each side-shoot.

The fruiting side-shoots will produce sub-side-shoots and sometimes the flowers will be produced on these, rather late, instead of on the main stems. These minor shoots and all subsequent ones should have the growing tip removed above the third leaf, to keep them in the space available. If need be, they can be kept shorter still.

Continue to tie in all the vine growth; when the sub-side-shoots reach the top wire, train them along it, or cut back to the top wire, to prevent undue crowding. As a general principle, the more leaf that is left the better the flavour of the fruit, and especially wine made from it.

The aubergines sown in late spring will need stopping any time now, at about 15cm (6in) tall.

Remove the runners from strawberry plants, unless you want to keep some to establish a new bed next year.

## Pruning

If the red currants are strong, vigorous bushes, they can be summer pruned, starting just as the first fruits are beginning to colour. Cut the side-shoots on the main branches back to just above the fifth leaf on the *new* growth; do not do it all at once, but spread the pruning over about two weeks. Start with the oldest side-shoots, which will be nearest the centre of the bush.

## Watering

Keep all soft fruit well watered, even if a dry spell lasts only a few days. Their demands for moisture are great, from now until late summer, and lack of it can mean two, not one, poor crops. During hot weather, melons under frames or cloches will need heavy watering every two or three days. Similarly, the vegetables should not be allowed to become thirsty; water all well with a fine spray for several hours, and then leave for several days. A dribble every day does more harm than good. Crops in the greenhouse will need a good watering every day in hot weather, preferably using water which is at air temperature.

## Weeding

By now, there should be fewer weed seeds germinating and crops should have developed sufficiently to make it difficult for them to survive in any case. However, in wet seasons, you will be kept busy with the hoe; it is essential to get the weeds out while young, as they will grow very fast and will be very troublesome to deal with, if neglected.

## Protecting

Strawberries will be coming up to full crop this month, so get them netted as soon as possible, if not already done. Make sure any netting which is already in place is well pegged down round the edges, remembering that blackbirds in particular will slip under the tiniest gap. The currants, gooseberries and raspberries will also be swelling fast – you may already be picking gooseberries for cooking – so protecting them is another priority job.

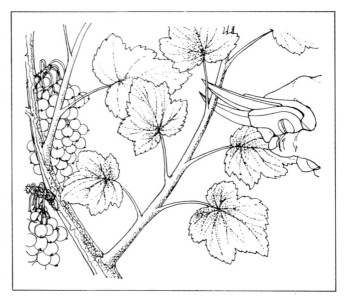

Above: *The new shoots of red currants will grow and ripen better if the bushes are thinned a little as they grow, by cutting the new side-shoots back to just above the fifth leaf. The leading shoots can be left unpruned.* Opposite: *Cabbages with solid large hearts like these will win a prize at any show.*

Cover your newly planted brassicas with bird-proof netting which should be strong enough to remain over them until harvesting next winter and spring.

## Treating pests and diseases

Caterpillars, carrot and onion fly maggots, greenfly, capsids, flea beetles, celery leaf miner, slugs and snails, birds and mice may still be with you, but, unfortunately, there will now be a variety of other plagues. This is a bad time for hatching of various pests, but do not expect your plants to be invaded by all that follow; it is best to be forewarned in case any appear. Cabbage root fly maggots will bore into and feed on the roots of the young brassica plants, and the first signs will be wilting, slow-growing plants.

Caterpillars of the cabbage white butterfly may appear from now on, eating large holes in the leaves of any of the brassicas; gooseberry sawfly may produce their second brood of caterpillars this month. Club-root of brassicas is a serious, soil-borne fungus disease infecting the roots; it results in the roots being swollen and distorted and infected plants die. Starting the seeds in sterilized compost in seed trays helps to avoid infection. Pea moth maggots are also a possible danger, feeding on the peas within developing pods; raspberry beetle maggots can hatch in the flowers and feed on the developing fruitlets.

In the greenhouse, red spider mite may begin to feed on leaves; it can be seen with a hand lens on the leaf undersides. It thrives in dry, hot conditions, so keep the greenhouse well damped down by hosing and you will do much to keep it at bay. Whitefly may also appear; these pests look like minute white moths on the undersides of the leaves and make the whole plant very sticky wherever they feed (see Kitchen Garden Controls and Treatments).

## Deblossoming
Perpetual-fruiting strawberries should have the flowers removed until the end of early summer. The flowers of peppers should be thinned out, otherwise they produce a lot

*Opposite: Strawberries like these can be picked from late spring to early autumn, by choosing the right varieties and by using the right methods of growing. Below left: Tying in new raspberry shoots: space them out so that the fruiting canes are not crowded. Below right: The new canes of loganberries are trained up the centre of the fan of fruiting canes.*

of small fruit. If aubergines are beginning to flower, remove all but four or five once these have set fruit. Remove also the male flowers from cucumbers in the greenhouse; if you do not the fruits will be bitter and mis-shapen.

## Pollination
Melons under glass, and possibly some in frames and cloches, will be the better for assistance with pollination (see Mid-Summer for method).

## Increasing stock
You can take cuttings of the following now: rosemary, sage, tarragon and thyme, using the tips of new shoots, about 2.5-5cm (1-2in) long, and putting them in 7.5cm (3in) pots of cutting compost. Stems of mint which have rooted can be separated off the parent plant and planted to start a new clump.

For a new strawberry bed, you can use the best plantlets your established plants will now be producing. The first or second on each plant will be the strongest and can be pegged

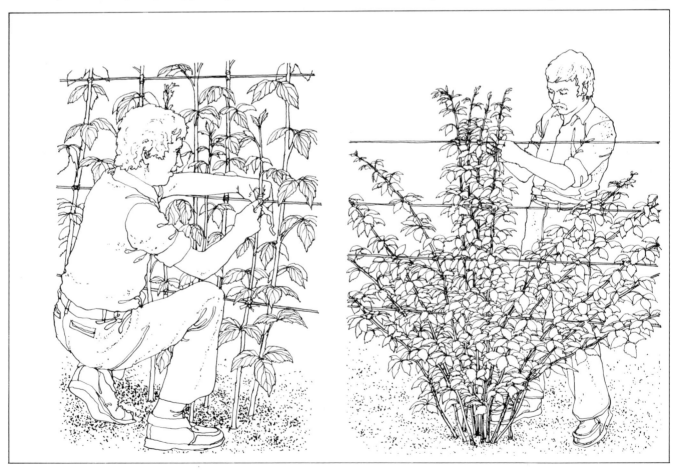

*Crunchy radishes not only add zest to a salad, but colour too: Sparklet and French Breakfast are two examples of the white-tipped red variety of radish.*

down so that it either roots into the soil, or into 7.5cm (3in) pots of potting compost, plunged into the soil. Cut off the runner beyond the chosen plantlet, but do not sever the plantlet from the parent until it is well rooted.

## Shading
The greenhouse will need shading from now until the end of summer, either by painting with a proprietary mixture, or with blinds; frames and cloches for melons and frame cucumbers should also be treated. Without it, fruit and leaves will be burnt brown as the heat of the sun's rays is concentrated by the glazing material.

## Ventilating
All the air possible should be given to greenhouse plants during the hotter weather, when the outside temperature rises above 21°C (70°F), opening the doors as well as the ventilators. Damp down the paths, borders, staging, and the inside of the glazing two or three times a day until late afternoon, but no later. This allows the greenhouse to dry off before night, otherwise the humidity will be so great that fungus disease will be encouraged to grow rapidly. Damping down can be done with a rosed watering-can, or with a hose with a spray nozzle attached; it lowers the temperature, and decreases the rate at which plants give off moisture as water vapour.

Frames and cloches can be opened or removed entirely, though melons like lots of warmth, provided they are shaded, and great humidity.

## Ordering
If you intend starting a new plantation of strawberries later in the summer, this is a good time to order them from the nursery, for delivery in late summer.

## Harvesting
Many more crops will be available in early summer, but you should stop cutting asparagus at the beginning of this season and allow the shoots to grow naturally so that the crowns can replenish themselves. Similarly, rhubarb should not be pulled after the middle of early summer, but completely remove flowering stems. Potatoes should be harvested as for maincrops (see Late Summer) but dig them up only when wanted.

## Crops to be harvested
asparagus, bay, broad bean, French (kidney) bean, black currant, beetroot, borage, carrot, chives, gooseberry, horse radish (established), kohlrabi, lettuce, marjoram, mint, onion (Japanese)

## Available from store
onion (spring), parsley (a little), pea, potato (earlies), radish, red currant, rhubarb, rosemary, sage, shallot, spinach, strawberry, Swiss chard, tarragon, thyme, turnip

# Mid-Summer

With the middle of summer there comes a lull in gardening activities. Most of your crops will be well on with their growth and, apart from routine training, watering and feeding, will not need much help from you. In fact, some of them will reach or finish their harvest stage and you will be more occupied with picking, cutting and lifting than previously. Cleaning or clearing the ground they have occupied should be fitted in when the ground is moist and catch crops or winter crops put in to replace them, according to your rotation plan.

The gardening cycle is continuous and as crops finish you can start off others; even in summer you can be putting in plants for harvesting late next winter and in spring, while you are still lifting this season's harvest.

This is the best time for herb gathering and drying; most herbs will begin to flower and the leaves can be harvested now, or the seeds collected later in mid-summer, depending on which part of the plant is used for cooking. Those which have been harvested can be cut back, and should then produce growth from which you can take a second crop in autumn.

The hottest weather of the year can occur in mid-summer, with the longest periods of drought, so be prepared for considerable watering. A large water storage tank comes into its own now, especially if watering the garden from the mains is temporarily prohibited by the local council; keep it tightly covered so that no light at all can get in and so that mosquito larvae, other insects and small mammals cannot infest it. The mulches you put down earlier in the season should be helping to keep the moisture in the soil; black plastic sheet on top of these will ensure even more retention.

As far as troubles are concerned, they are much like early summer, except that greenfly will be much less in evidence. They will have reached the final winged stage of their life cycle, when they fly off to other plants than crops, or die, after laying eggs. Blight on potatoes and tomatoes should be watched for and mildew may begin to appear on a variety of plants, as it thrives, like red spider mite, in warmth and drought. Wasps and ants are a nuisance in some years.

# At~a~glance diary

**Prepare the soil for:** sowing and planting outdoors

**Sow seeds outdoors of:** French (kidney) bean, beetroot, borage, cabbage (spring), carrot, chicory (Sugar Loaf), endive (Batavian Green), kale (Hungry Gap), kohlrabi, lettuce, parsley, spinach (summer), turnip

**Plant:** Brussels sprout, broccoli (heading), cucumber (ridge), cabbage, kale, kohlrabi, leek, marrow, melon, squash, tomato

**Thin:** beetroot, borage, carrot, chicory (Sugar Loaf) dill, endive, kale, kohlrabi, lettuce, parsley, radish, swede, turnip

**Earth up:** winter celery

**Compost heap:** continue to make

**Feed:** globe artichoke, aubergine, French (kidney) bean, broccoli (heading and sprouting), Brussels sprout, cabbage, chicory, cucumber (indoor), endive, garlic, kale, kohlrabi, leek, lettuce, pepper, rhubarb, spinach, strawberry, tomato

**Stake, train and tie in:** Jerusalem artichoke, aubergine, blackberry, broccoli (sprouting), Brussels sprout, cucumber, loganberry, marrow, melon, pea, raspberry, squash, strawberry (runners), tomato, vine

**Prune:** gooseberry

**Pollinate:** melon

**Deblossom:** aubergine, pepper, cucumber under glass

**Water:** all, but particularly runner (pole) bean, black currant, celeriac, celery, all cucurbits, gooseberry, loganberry, potato, raspberry, red currant, strawberry

**Weed and clear:** continue on all crops

**Protect:** all brassicas, soft fruit, tomato, against birds

**Ventilate and damp down:** greenhouse, frames and cloches

**Pests, nutrient deficiencies and diseases:** birds, caterpillars, celery leaf miner, leaf hoppers, maggots mice, mildew, potato blight, red spider mite, slugs and snails, tomato blight, tomato leaf mould, tomato magnesium deficiency, whitefly

**Layer:** blackberries

**Order:** soft fruit

**Harvest:** globe artichoke, runner (pole) bean, black currant, cabbage, cauliflower, celery, cucumber, garlic, herbs grown for leaves, kohlrabi, onion, shallot, strawberry

# Jobs to do

## Preparing the soil for outdoor sowing

As with early summer, there are still some crops which can be sown, either for quick maturing or for storing through the winter; one or two of the latter can be left in the ground in winter and pulled or picked as required. They will all be sown where they are to grow, so no separate seed bed will be needed (see Early Spring for method).

## Preparing the soil for planting

Late summer is the time to start planting strawberries, so the ground for these, if vacant, can be prepared now. They will do best in a sunny place, on a slightly sloping site and, if you have the time, they will develop the best root system in soil which has been double dug. A mildly acid soil, pH 6.5, is preferable, though neutral will do. Alkaline soil can lead to nutrient deficiencies and should be avoided if possible. While digging, mix in rotted garden compost, or similar bulky organic material at the rate of about half a garden barrow load per square metre (sq yd). Clear off all weeds thoroughly – couch grass, bindweed, ground-elder and other perennials – roll the dug soil lightly and rake.

## Sowing the seed outdoors

You can sow seeds of the following: French (kidney) bean, beetroot, borage, cabbage (spring), carrot, chicory (Sugar-loaf), endive (Batavian Green), kale (Hungry Gap), kohlrabi, lettuce, parsley, radish, spinach (summer), turnip.

The beetroot sown now will be for salads; it will not have time to grow sufficiently for storage and round varieties should be chosen. Cabbage for spring cutting can be sown where it is to grow, though if you have no space for the time being it can go into a seed-bed and be transplanted in autumn. Carrots can be grown both for salads and immediate eating and for storing. The lettuce-leafed endive is hardier than the curled endive, which will not survive past mid-autumn. Kale will provide 'greens' next spring and early summer. Kohlrabi should be sown early in mid-summer to ensure its maturity by autumn.

*Beetroot is one of the vegetables which can be grown for ornament as well as use – a useful attribute where there is shortage of space.*

Lettuce sown now will be just matured by autumn; any sown later will need cloche or tunnel protection. Parsley will provide fresh leaves through the winter from this sowing. This will also be the last date for sowing summer spinach; after this change to the prickly-seeded, winter variety. Turnips sown now will provide roots for storage.

*Before blanching celery, remove the side-shoots, make sure the plants are dry and free of slugs, then start to earth up.*

## Planting outdoors

The brassicas sown in late spring will be ready for planting now (see Early Summer for method). Moist soil and watering in are more important then ever. Leeks will also be ready to go in – in some ways this later planting is better than the conventional one of early summer, since you will have more of the crop ready at a time – spring – when there is a dearth of fresh vegetables. If not already done, you should plant as soon as possible outdoors, ridge cucumbers, marrows, squashes, melons and tomatoes. It is just worth planting them still, although a lot will depend on whether the summer is a good one.

## Thinning

Continue to thin crops, mainly those sown in early summer: beetroot, borage, carrot, chicory (Sugarloaf), dill, endive, kale, kohlrabi, lettuce, parsley, radish, swede and turnip. Thinning is done more easily in dry soil, but water the rows afterwards to settle the soil down round the plants that you have left in place and ensure that they are all very firmly anchored.

## Earthing up

The winter celery planted outdoors in late spring will need its first earthing up towards the end of mid-summer. Any suckers at the base of the plants should be removed; look for slugs on the plants nearby and in the soil. Then wrap brown paper round the stems; this practice is mainly an insurance to prevent soil getting into the centre and you can dispense with it if you are careful, or you can twine string round the stems up to the leaves. Pile soil from the top of the ridges loosely round the stems up to about 10cm (4in) high. You will be doing this again twice more in the growing season, about once every four weeks. Pick off any leaves infested with leaf miner as you work.

## Compost heap

If you finished one heap in early summer, or one is just finishing now, make sure that there is some moisture in them; they can get very dry at this time of the year. If the bottom of the first heap is ready you can use it for preparing the strawberry bed.

## Feeding

Routine liquid feeding should continue on more or less the same crops, with some additions, as last month: globe artichoke, aubergine, French (kidney) bean, chicory, endive, leek, lettuce, pepper, and tomato. If the early sown summer spinach is beginning to slow down in its leaf production, a liquid feed every week or so will do it no harm. The brassicas planted last month will be the better for an occasional liquid feed, too, especially if it is one which contains more potash than phosphorus or nitrogen. Do not overdo it, otherwise you will have 'blown' sprouts, loose curds on the cauliflower and leafy 'soft' cabbages.

If your soil is light and stony, give the rhubarb a solid feed, watered in, of a compound balanced fertilizer. Garlic which was spring-planted can also be given a dry feed, watered in, but use a potash-high compound, such as a tomato fertilizer. Continue to liquid feed the greenhouse plants, but stop feeding the strawberry bed when the crop has been picked.

## Staking, training and tying in

A final tie can be given to the Jerusalem artichokes if you are supporting these, and to the aubergines if they need it. Pinching out the tips of the artichoke stems will keep their height down. Runner (pole) beans will have done their own climbing and supported themselves; cucumbers, marrows and squashes will need ends of side-shoots stopped to keep them in the space allowed, and to divert energy into fruit production.

Peas will need the support of brushwood twigs or chicken or plastic netting; tomatoes will need stout stakes, well driven in, and sometime in the next few weeks should have the growing point pinched out at about the second leaf above the fourth flower truss. Fruit from flowers produced later than this will not ripen, although it may set. Brussels sprouts and sprouting broccoli are the better for being tied to strong supports, otherwise summer gales can have them very quickly lying on the ground and pulling them upright always damages them. The new shoots on blackberries, loganberries and raspberries will need tying in.

In the greenhouse, tomatoes, cucumber and melons will need stopping; tomatoes can be allowed to carry six or seven fruit trusses before being stopped. Continue to remove runners from strawberry plants, as they will be produced in even greater quantities as the crop begins to end and the bed will become a tangle if left. Let perpetual flowering strawberries flower normally from now on, to crop from late summer. Tie in vine growth as in early summer.

*Tomatoes are an immensely satisfying crop to grow, whether indoors or out. With only the protection of an unheated greenhouse they can produce large, evenly-sized trusses of fruit.*

## Pruning

You may find it necessary to prune gooseberries in mid-summer, if there is an outbreak of mildew. This will infect the tips and young leaves. Cutting them off well back to healthy growth will do a great deal towards controlling the disease, without harming the shape or growth of the bushes.

## Deblossoming

Continue to remove male flowers from greenhouse cucumbers and from peppers if flowering heavily. When vine flowers have finished setting, remove all the bunches except about ten to twelve on each plant, ensuring that those remaining are spaced out evenly, one to each sub-side-shoot.

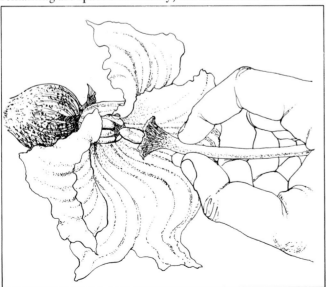

*Like redcurrants, gooseberries can be summer pruned. For fewer but large berries, they are pruned in the same way, or they can be pruned in mid-summer, to cut off the tip growth if there is an outbreak of mildew, back to healthy tissue.*

## Pollinating

Though frame and cloche melons can set with the help of pollinating insects, you can make certain of getting the fruit when and where you want it on the plant, by hand pollination. Ridge cucumbers will set a good crop without your help.

## Watering

Runner (pole) beans are deep-rooting, fast-growing plants, with a great demand for moisture. If you prepared the soil thoroughly and have kept it mulched and watered during dry periods, you should have no trouble with either the pods dropping as soon as set, or withering when half grown. Keep them well watered, though, mid-summer can be particularly drought-prone. Celery, celeriac, the cucurbits, tomatoes, potatoes and the soft fruit have priority on any water available, but all crops should have it when natural water is not forthcoming.

Left: *Although melons are likely to be pollinated by bees and other insects, you can make sure that the fruits come when and where you want them on the plant by hand-pollinating. Remove the petals from a male flower and push the cone into the centre of the female flower, behind which there will be a round swelling, the embryo melon.* Right: *The standard method of supporting runner (pole) beans.*

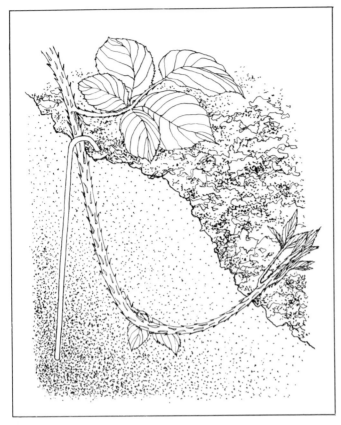

Above: *Tip-layering blackberries is an easy way of increasing your stock of plants. Bury the end of a new shoot, except for the tip, in the soil and hold it down with a wire hook for extra security.* Below: *The cut-leaved blackberry is decorative as well as being a good crop-bearer. It is vigorous and needs plenty of space.*

## Weeding

Less arduous than earlier in the season, this job is still necessary here and there; annual weeds can have several cycles in one growing season and proliferate uncomfortably fast in wet weather. Hoeing, mulching or chemicals are all ways of keeping control.

## Protecting

Blackbirds are attracted to tomatoes, so you may find that both outdoor and indoor kinds need to be guarded; soft fruit and brassica guard netting should be kept in order.

## Ventilating

Continue to keep the greenhouse well aired, open frames and tunnels on the hottest days and separate cloches more, or less, depending on the temperature. Those over the early strawberries can be removed, if not already done, cleaned and stacked on their ends, one inside the other. Damp down the greenhouse as last month.

## Treating pests and diseases

Two fungus diseases which can ruin crops and decimate plants from now on are blight on potatoes and tomatoes, and mildew on a variety of plants. Blight causes more trouble in wet summers, as the spores are spread by rain splashing; infected leaves have dark brown blotches on them, tomato fruits have brown patches, slightly sunken, and potato tubers will be found to have brown patches in the flesh. Regular spraying with a fungicide every ten to fourteen days will keep the top growth protected and clean.

Mildew takes the form of powdery white patches on the upper surfaces of leaves and spreads in mid-and late summer and early autumn, during dry weather, when there are heavy dews. Strawberries, gooseberries, all cucurbits, lettuce, peas, cabbage, onion, spinach and turnip can be afflicted; if you see it early enough, removal of affected parts, and watering the plants well, will often be all that needs to be done.

Apart from these, red spider mite, whitefly, caterpillars and maggots, celery leaf miner, leaf hoppers, slugs, snails, birds and mice are the other competitors for your crops besides you. Tomato moth caterpillars, large green or brown beasts, appear in the greenhouse (see Kitchen Garden Controls and Treatments).

Tomato leaf-mould is a fungus disease which spreads rapidly in greenhouse conditions and can kill plants. The spots appear yellowish green on the upper leaf surface and are velvety grey beneath. Remove affected leaves and spray with a fungicide; some varieties are resistant.

Indoor tomatoes may also begin to show magnesium deficiency signs, in the form of yellow patches on the leaves between the main veins. It usually starts to appear on the leaves about half way up the plant. Spraying with a solution of magnesium sulphate at 28g per 4.5 litre (2 oz per 1 gal) of water, four or five times at ten-day intervals, should restore the leaves to their normal green.

## Layering
Blackberries and loganberries will have produced new shoots sufficiently long by now to be used for propagating. Bury the tip of a new shoot in the soil 15cm (6in) deep and, for additional security, pin it down where it enters the soil with a bent wire or wooden hook. By late autumn it will be well rooted and can be transplanted to a nursery bed for a year. Do not use your own plants for propagation unless you are absolutely certain they are free from virus.

## Ordering
Although late autumn is several months ahead, mid-summer is not too soon to order new plants of cane and bush fruit, if you wish to renew your stock. By sending your order off early, you will get the best choice of plants, and receive them at the time you want them.

*Like kale, ornamental cabbages can be extremely attractive, as this picture shows, and are often to be found in the flower garden or in use in flower arrangements.*

## Harvesting

From now until the end of early autumn, vegetable cropping will be in full swing; the main soft fruit harvest will occur during mid-summer, though you can continue to pick soft fruit also until autumn, if the right varieties are being grown.

Globe artichokes will be ready for cutting, taking the king heads first, that is, the one at the top of each main stem. Cut the bud when the tips of the scales are just beginning to separate and are no longer tightly closed. Blackcurrants will be picked throughout mid-summer; if the variety is one which ripens the whole strig (cluster) at once, you can cut off completely the fruiting branch, down to a good new shoot, or down to ground level, if it has grown rather long. Red currants grow differently, and need a different method of pruning, so the strigs should be picked off individually.

As you cut the cabbages and cauliflowers pull the stump right out, roots and all, chop it up and put it on the compost heap, unless it is infected with pests or diseases, when it is better burnt. Kohlrabi should be lifted when the swollen

*French (kidney) beans are more than welcome at the end of spring for their delicate flavour.*

stem is about the size of a golf-ball, for the best flavour. You can still eat them when tennis-ball size, but they begin to be tough and less tasty at that stage.

At the end of mid-summer you should be able to pick the first runner (pole) beans, lift the first of the self-blanching celery and cut some ridge cucumbers. Autumn-planted garlic will be ready and should be left to dry in the sun for a few hours after lifting and cleaning, as should the Japanese varieties of onions sown in late summer last year and the shallots planted in winter. Summer-fruiting strawberries will come to the end of their season; pick off the bad ones with grey mould infection at the same time as picking the good berries and destroy; greenhouse tomatoes should come into full crop.

Herbs with leaves which are used in cooking can be cut for drying now; they will have the best flavour if the plant they are taken from is just ready to start flowering. Strip them on a dry, sunny morning, after the dew has dried, but before mid-day, and spread them in single layers on trays to dry in a dark, warm, well ventilated place. Then put them in airtight, dark containers, as exposure to the light and air quickly releases their essential oils.

## Crops to be harvested

globe artichoke, black currant, broad bean, French (kidney) bean, runner (pole) bean, beetroot, cabbage, cauliflower, carrot celery (self-blanching), cucumber (greenhouse), cucumber (ridge) fennel, garlic, gooseberry, kohlrabi

## Available from store

lettuce, loganberry, onion (Japanese), potato (early and second earlies), raspberry, radish, red currant, seakale beet, spinach, strawberry, tomato, turnip. All foliage herbs

# Late Summer

Your main concern during the next few weeks will be harvesting the crops in the vegetable garden, though even amongst the soft fruit, there will still be crops to pick and even finish off and one or two others just starting. Provided the weather is reasonably warm and dry, you should be able to cut and lift all through late summer, some for immediate eating, and some for storing in winter. Storage nowadays can of course include deep freezing, but alternatives to this are salting, pickling and bottling; these are all quite adequate methods of preservation.

A lot more of your working time will be taken up with cleaning ground where crops have finished, particularly on the soft fruit front. Late summer is a good time to do this; there will be little in the way of weeds, the ground will be easy to work on and bonfires will burn prunings readily. But continue to put soft vegetation on the compost heap; the straw and other debris from the strawberry bed rots down well, and can be used if not badly infested with pests or diseases.

Watering will still be necessary, if the odd seasonal thunderstorm has not provided the necessary moisture. However, many crops will be coming to or passing their peak, and the already shortening days and weaker sunlight will be decreasing the risk of bolting, so in a normal growing season irrigation will now be less demanding. In fact, water should be withheld from certain plants, so that maturity is not delayed.

More crops for the winter can be started off now than during mid-summer and, while they will probably germinate without any trouble in the warm soil, make sure that they have sufficient moisture. Avoid subjecting them to a droughty few days or weeks once they have sprouted, because it will be difficult to get another batch well established before the winter cold and rain begins. Herbs ripen their seed at this time of the year, so it is a good time to sow them, giving the less hardy ones cloche protection in bad winter weather. There are some which have such a short viability that they will not germinate if kept until next spring, so it pays to sow them now.

# At~a~glance diary

**Prepare the soil for:** sowing and planting outdoors

**Sow seeds outdoors of:** angelica, French (kidney) bean, cabbage (spring), caraway, chervil, coriander, lettuce, lovage, mushroom (spawn), onion (Japanese), radish (summer and winter), spinach (winter), spinach beet, Swiss chard (seakale beet), turnip

**Plant:** strawberry

**Thin:** beetroot, borage, cabbage (spring), carrot, chicory (Sugar Loaf), endive, kale (Hungry Gap), kohlrabi, lettuce, parsley, radish, spinach (summer), turnip,

**Prune:** black currant, gooseberry, raspberry

**Weed and clear:** black currant, gooseberry, loganberry, raspberry, red currant, strawberry, vegetables and herbs where necessary

**Stake, train and tie in:** blackberry, broccoli (sprouting), Brussels sprout, cucumber, loganberry, marrow, melon, raspberry, strawberry, tomato

**Feed:** globe artichoke, aubergine, French (kidney) bean, chicory, cucumber (indoor), endive, leek, lettuce, parsley, pepper, tomato

**Water:** all, especially in dry weather

**Earth up:** celery

**Blanch:** endive (curled)

**Protect:** aubergine, blackberry, blackcurrant, all brassica, raspberry, strawberry, tomato

**Compost heap:** continue to make

**Pests and diseases:** birds, blights, caterpillars, greenfly, greymould (Botrytis cinerea), maggots, mildew, red spider mite, slugs, snails, whitefly

**Harvest:** aubergine, marrow (including courgette) onion, potato, sweetcorn

# Jobs to do

*Angelica is a handsome plant in its own right and adds distinction to any herbaceous border. For culinary use the young stems are gathered in late spring and candied.*

### Preparing the soil for outdoor sowing

Seeds of a few vegetables can still be sown outdoors now, where they are to grow and mature. They should fit in with your rotation plan for next year, as some of them will remain in the ground until next spring or early summer. Space should become increasingly available as the spring sown crops complete their growth and are harvested.

For sowing and growing Japanese onions, the rows or drills should have a slightly different preparation to the normal one. Dig out a wide drill, 30cm (12in) across, and 20cm (8in) deep, put a 7.5cm (3in) layer of rotted organic matter in it and replace the topsoil, but mix it thoroughly with the manure, at the same time adding a slow-acting organic fertilizer such as hoof and horn at about 45g per 1.8m (1½oz per 72in) run. Firm the soil down very well and top up the trench if necessary until a space of about 2.5cm (1in) is left. Do this preparation about 10 to 14 days before sowing.

### Preparing the soil for planting

The soil which was dug and manured in mid-summer for strawberry planting during this season should be further prepared by scattering and lightly forking in a dressing of a compound fertilizer. If the weather is dry, it should be watered in. The time to do this is about ten days before you plan to put in the strawberries, so that their roots do not have to contend with neat fertilizer as soon as planted. If there was no time to dig the ground earlier, it is not too late to do it now, provided it is done early in the season with the object of planting right at the end of it, or even in early autumn.

### Sowing seed outdoors

Late summer is a particularly good time for sowing seeds of herbs, many of which are ripe at this time, as well as some vegetables to provide winter crops. Seeds include: angelica, French (kidney) bean (to cloche later), cabbage (spring), caraway, chervil, coriander, lettuce (to cloche

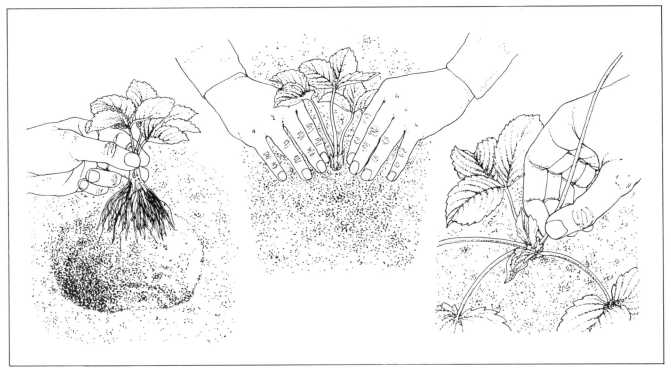

Above: *Planting strawberries: make sure the hole is large enough to take the roots spread out to their fullest extent, and firm the plant in so that the crown is neither buried nor so high that the roots will be easily exposed by rain. Finally, remove any runners which are present when planting or which develop later.* Opposite: *Sweet peppers are a delicious vegetable.*

later), lovage, onion (Japanese), radish, spinach (winter), spinach beet, Swiss chard (seakale beet), turnips (for tops). Sow all these where they are to grow, though the cabbage may also be sown in a seed-bed and then transplanted.

French (kidney) beans are most likely to produce a picking or two if sown at the beginning of late summer, kept well supplied with moisture, and cloched in early autumn at night. Cabbage sown now will produce small, unhearted spring 'greens', or can be left to heart for cutting in late spring and early summer, a time often rather short of fresh vegetables. Lettuce sown now will, like the beans, need protection in autumn if they are to heart satisfactorily by mid-to late autumn and, if you already have endive coming along, this is more likely to produce a worthwhile and better tasting crop. Lettuce outdoors now are rather chancy and much depends on the weather.

The recently introduced varieties of Japanese onions are useful in that they will mature in early and mid-summer, so filling the gap in supplies of onions between the old and new season's crops. However, very careful timing of sowing the seed is essential; the last two weeks are best for the milder gardens, the first two for the chillier ones, with the middle of late summer being the optimum date in many cases. Sow the seed very thinly; mixing it with sand helps ensure even distribution, and cover it with sieved soil 2.5cm (1in) deep. Protect at once from birds and make sure there are no weeds at any time from now until the onions are well established after transplanting.

Most radish sown at this time should be the winter varieties, which produce large roots, weighing up to 0.45kg (1lb) each. Skins can be red or black, roots long or round, and they can be left in the ground during the winter, to be lifted when wanted, or stored in the same way as other roots. Summer radish can still be sown but are best in a little shade, otherwise they bolt.

Spinach to sow now is the winter variety, with prickly, triangular seeds; this and spinach beet and Swiss chard (seakale beet) will all provide leaves during autumn and early winter and again from early spring. Protecting with cloches when the weather turns cold will prolong the picking period. Turnips should be sown in rows 7.5cm (3in) apart and not thinned, as sowing at this time is done to provide tops for 'greens' in spring.

Late summer is a good time to attempt growing mushrooms outdoors and a simple way of doing this is to lift and

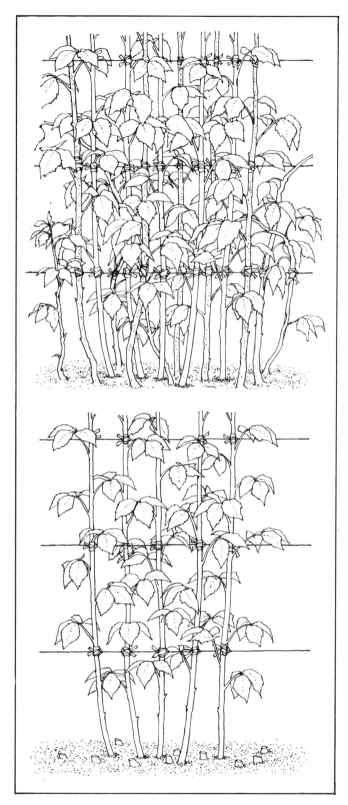

roll back pieces of turf in lawn or meadow, lightly fork the soil beneath, and scatter mushroom spawn over the surface, replacing the turf when this has been done. Moist soil and a warm, humid atmosphere should result in mushrooms in autumn though, the crop being a rather perverse one, you may find mushrooms appearing in totally different places from where you originally sowed the spawn!

## Planting

The recommended time for planting strawberries used to be early to mid-autumn, but experiment has found that by planting in late summer, the plants in general produce a heavier crop in their first season. There is, however, the danger that the soil is dry and rather short of moisture reserves at planting time and that rain is light and spasmodic until autumn, so that you will probably need to keep watering for some weeks after planting.

Put in the plants at spacings of 45cm (18in) between plants and 60cm (24in) between rows. There are two schools of thought about methods of planting: the usual advice is to plant on a slight mound in a shallow hole, so that the roots are spread out and hang down in order to ensure that the crown is not buried, as can easily happen. The alternative and less general recommendation is to plant in a shallow hole sufficiently wide to take the roots spread out naturally, but without a mound in it, the theory being that rain will not then wash the soil away from the upper roots, and that the plant is unlikely to be forced out of the ground by frost, both of which might happen with mound planting. Whichever method you adopt, make sure that the central buds and growing points of the crowns are not covered, and that the plants are well firmed in.

## Thinning

Last month's sowings will need thinning: beetroot, borage, cabbage (spring), carrot, chicory (Sugarloaf), endive, kale (Hungry Gap), kohlrabi, lettuce, parsley, radish, spinach (summer) and turnip. The second brood of carrot fly maggots may hatch some time during the next few weeks, so bury the carrot thinnings in the compost heap to avoid attracting the adults. Thinning provides a good opportunity to weed at the same time.

*The best time to prune summer-fruiting raspberries is as soon as the crop has been picked, which is usually some time in late summer. Raspberry pruning is very simple: all that needs to be done is to cut the fruited canes right away, down to soil level. The number of new canes is reduced to about five of the strongest, and these are spaced along the wires and tied in.*

## Pruning

Gooseberries should have the pruning detailed in mid-summer completed by the middle of late summer at the latest. All the raspberry canes which have carried this summer's crops should be cut completely away, down to ground level; weak, short canes and those that are broken, mis-shaped or diseased should also be removed. The remaining shoots should be reduced to about five or six strong ones to each plant, retaining those nearest to the original row. Raspberries are prolific in their production of suckers, in all directions, and can become a nuisance if not strictly confined to the space assigned to them. Loganberries should also have their fruited shoots pruned off completely and all but four of the strongest new canes removed. As their canes are so long, it is easier to cut them in sections rather than attempt to drag away one complete—and possibly very prickly—length of stem.

If you have not already done it while picking, the fruited branches of blackcurrants can be cut off, either to just above a strong new shoot, or down to ground level, if it is one of the oldest branches. Removal of some of the weakest of the new shoots at the same time will let in light and air to the remaining growth, so that it can ripen well.

## Weeding and cleaning up

The soft fruit will take most of your attention on this front; as the plants, bushes and canes finish cropping, they should be restored to respectability after the neglect occurring during harvesting.

You can be quite ruthless with the strawberry bed, either removing all the foliage with a grass hook and then raking off all the debris, straw and weeds, or you can burn it over, if the weather is dry. The straw will catch well and produce enough heat to burn the remaining rubbish and burning does away with disease spores, weed seeds in the surface soil and pests. The plants will sprout new leaves quickly and often produce a second flowering and fruiting, if the autumn is warm and cloches are put over them. After cleaning, fork up the paths and give a dressing of a potash-high fertilizer round the plants, watered in, followed by a mulch of organic matter.

All the currants, raspberries and loganberries should be freed of any weeds and debris and the soil very lightly forked to break up the hard surface that will have resulted from picker's feet. Soft fruit is surface rooting, so must never be deeply dug. Then put on a potash-high fertilizer, water in and mulch, or straw several centimetres (inches) deep. Fairly heavy mulches of this kind are necessary to make sure of regular, heavy crops every year.

## Staking, training and tying in

The new raspberry canes that remain after pruning should be tied individually to their supporting horizontal wires, so that they are separated evenly in the space available. The same should be done to the loganberries, taking the new shoots down from the centre, separating them, and training them in the fan method shown. Blackberries will be coming into full flower, and with these it is still only a case of tying in selected new shoots. Pruning will not be necessary until mid autumn.

Strawberries will still need de-runnering, a job which gets neglected in the press of picking; those which have been potted or rooted direct should be detached, ready for planting in a few weeks' time.

Melons will slow down their growth this month and concentrate their energies on swelling their fruit, so it will only be a case of keeping them tidy and nipping back the occasional new growth. Any embryo fruits which form now should be taken off, to prevent competition with selected fruit. Cucumbers and marrows also will only need occasional attention; they are prolific croppers and this is their peak cropping period: their vegetative growth will have more or less finished.

If outdoor tomatoes have not already been stopped above the fourth flower truss, do this as soon as possible. Indoor tomatoes will have been stopped for some time, but you can remove one or two of the lowest leaves completely, cutting

*Loganberries can be pruned and trained in late summer. Cut the old canes completely away, and spread the three or four best canes out in a fan shape to right and left, then tie in.*

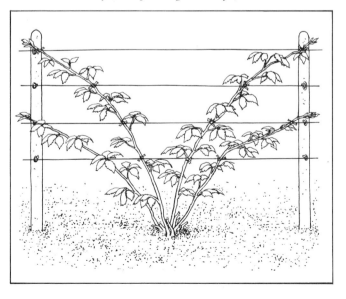

them off cleanly and flush with the main stem. This increases air circulation and prevents spread of fungus diseases such as leaf-mould.

Sprouting broccoli and Brussels sprouts will probably need another tie by now; secure supports at this time can make all the difference between good and bad crops next winter, especially with the early varieties of Brussels sprouts which crop from mid-autumn. Tie in vine growth, if necessary, as in early summer.

## Feeding

Routine liquid feeding of the crops listed in mid-summer can continue, i.e., globe artichoke, aubergine, French (kidney) bean, chicory, cucumber (indoor), endive, leek, lettuce, pepper and tomato. If parsley sown in mid-summer is a little slow to grow, a nitrogen-high liquid feed until autumn will give it the boost it needs. Similarly, indoor tomatoes will need more nitrogen now and less potash, to keep their vegetative growth going; leaves are the food factories of a plant and without them it cannot form good flowers and fruits. They may also need extra magnesium.

## Watering

As the melon fruits cease to swell and begin to ripen, the amount of water given to them should be decreased until none is given. The leaves will begin to pale and turn yellow as a result, but the plants will be nearly at the ends of their lives and will no longer need water. Keep the runner beans,

## Tomato Fruit Troubles

| Trouble | Cause | Remedy |
|---|---|---|
| Green area round stalk– greenback | Too much sun, lack of potash, susceptible variety | Supply shade; do not de-leaf too much; give extra potash; grow resistant varieties |
| Black sunken patch on base of fruit opposite stalk end – blossom-end rot | Shortage of water when fruit was swelling | Always keep well watered |
| Orange and pale yellow patches – blotchy ripening | Lack of potash | Use potash-high liquid feed |
| Halo spots on fruit – ghost or water spots | Due to infection with *Botrytis cinerea* spore which has since dried up | None needed, but is a sign that there were damp, chilly conditions at some previous stage |
| Cracking and spitting | A large water supply following a dry period | Always give sufficient water to ensure regular, even growth |
| Pale-brown sunken blotches on fruit, not very noticeable | Tomato blight (fungus disease) | Remove infected fruit and leaves; spray with fungicide |
| Pinhead-sized fruits which do not grow | Imperfect fertilization, too dry an atmosphere at pollination time | Spray plants daily overhead at flowering time |
| Grey fur round calyx | *Botrytis cinerea* (grey mould, fungus disease) | Remove infected parts; raise temperature and spray with fungicide |
| Black spot-like sticky substance on fruit | Sooty mould growing on honeydew produced while whitefly feed on leaves | Remove worst infected parts; introduce parasitic wasp; spray with insecticide |
| Holes in fruit | Tomato moth caterpillars, blackbirds, slugs and snails | Handpick green or brown caterpillars; protect with netting; put down slug pellets |

For chemicals, see Controls and Treatment section

*When onions have finished growing and are ready to be harvested, they need to be dried in the sun for a few hours. Hanging them in lines allows the wind to help this process.*

celeriac, celery, cucumbers, marrows and soft fruit all well watered still and do not forget the remainder of the vegetables, especially newly germinated seedlings, recently planted brassicas and the root crops.

### Earthing up

Celery can be given its first earthing up, if planted late, or its second, about four weeks after the first (see Mid-Summer for details).

### Blanching

Curled endive can be blanched during late summer if sown in late spring; you should wait until it is fully grown before blanching, usually about twelve weeks after sowing (see Early Autumn for method).

### Protecting

Any brassica crops should be well guarded against birds, whether newly planted, just sown or well established. Autumn-cropping raspberries and blackcurrants, perpetual-fruiting strawberries and blackberries, and swelling grapes, can be subject to bird damage; tomatoes are also attractive and birds will even have an exploratory peck at aubergines.

### Compost heap

The first heap of the season may already have been partially used on the soft fruit; any that is not sufficiently well rotted can be added to the new heap, in a layer taking the place of any activator you may be using. The remains of plants, after harvesting has been completed, will make excellent compost material, provided it is not infected with diseases or infested with pests. If you suspect virus disease infection burn or otherwise destroy such plants. As there is no cure for viruses and they are easily spread, addition to the compost heap will only serve as a centre for further infection.

### Treating pests and diseases

Red spider mite and whitefly can still be causing great trouble in the greenhouse, unless you have been keeping it well damped down and well ventilated. If there are some plants badly infected, it is best to pull them out and burn them; you will not lose much of the crop as it is near the end of the growing season and you may lose what crop there is on the other plants if you leave the unhealthy ones to grow. Whitefly can also be a plague outdoors, on cabbages and other brassicas; if you suspect the presence of one or two adults, treat the plants at once before the pests become an epidemic.

Greenfly should still be watched for on peppers; mildew can affect many crops and blight on potatoes and outdoor tomatoes can spread rapidly in late summer if wet and cool. As in mid-summer, caterpillars and maggots, grey mould (*Botrytis cinerea*) slugs, snails and birds are all likely to be around. Underground slugs can do a lot of damage to maincrop potatoes at this time and it may be more satisfactory to grow only second earlies.

### Harvesting

Aubergine will probably be ready for cutting towards the end of the month; the purple-skinned kinds will be purple right from the time they first set and will be ready for picking when they have stopped increasing in size, are glossy and remain indented when pressed. Marrows are tastiest if cut when about 25cm (10in) long; they can be used as courgettes (zucchini) when they are much shorter.

The normal summer-fruiting kinds of blackcurrants and raspberries will finish cropping at the beginning of late summer, if they have not already done so, but towards the end of this season in good warm weather, the autumn-fruiting kinds will start to ripen.

Onions will be ready for lifting some time this month; do this on a dry day if possible, clean the soil off them and leave them to dry in single layers on wire netting trays or hanging on a frame as illustrated. The second early, and the first of the maincrop potatoes can come up also; spread them out in the sun for an hour or two and then store (see Early Autumn for methods of storing onions and potatoes).

Sweetcorn is another possible crop for harvesting in late summer. The cobs will be ready when the 'silks' are brown and moist, but not dry and shrivelled, about three weeks after they have appeared. The ripe kernels will produce a creamy white liquid when pierced, but a watery liquid or virtually none at all shows under- and over-ripeness.

## Crops to be harvested

globe, artichoke, aubergine, blackberry black currant, broad bean (last), French (kidney) bean, runner (pole) bean; beetroot cabbage, calabrese, carrot, cauliflower, celery (self-blanching), cucumber, endive, kohlrabi, lettuce

Herbs: the seeds of caraway, coriander dill, fennel, lovage; the leaves of basil bay, borage, chives, dill, fennel

## Crops to be harvested

lemon balm, lovage, marjoram, mint parsley, rosemary, sage, summer savory winter savory, sorrel, tarragon, thyme.

## Available from store

loganberry, marrow and courgette, melon, onion, pea, peppers, potato radish, raspberry, spinach, spinach beet, squash, strawberry, sweetcorn, Swiss chard (seakale beet)

# Early Autumn

Traditionally the season for harvest festivals, early autumn is a satisfying time when you can reap the results of the year's labours and not bother too much about routine jobs. You should have a glut of vegetables to cut, lift or pick, either for immediate use or for storing in one way or another. Several of the root crops are stored in containers in garden sheds or put into clamps; other vegetables – and also fruit – can be deep frozen, bottled, or preserved by salting or drying. Seeds and leaves of herbs are usually dried but leaves can also be deep-frozen, in ice cubes.

The weather is likely to be warm and humid, with occasional rain, mostly calm and often sunny, a very pleasant time during which the gardener can generally relax his or her vigilance and leave the crops largely to their own devices. However, towards the end of the period, the night temperature can drop steeply and quickly towards freezing, so you should be ready with cloches, tunnels, newspapers and so on for safeguarding some of the newly germinated crops and those which are coming up to maturity. The latter are generally those being grown out of their normal season, since you are trying to prolong the crop, so they may need a little fussing over.

However, in some years this can be a very wet period, with constant rain. If this is the case, the weeds will grow very fast and it is essential, whenever there is a day without rain, that you get them thoroughly cleared, otherwise next spring will be a nightmare, and your over-wintering crops will be poor and stunted.

The general work such as watering, feeding, training, thinning, spraying and so on will diminish considerably, but as many vegetables come to an end, the remaining stems, roots and leaves should be dug up and composted, the ground raked and either prepared for a new over-wintering crop or left to follow for a few weeks, keeping an eye on the weeds.

# At~a~glance diary

**Prepare the soil for:** sowing and planting outdoors

**Sow seeds outdoors of:** borage, cabbage (spring), endive (Batavian), lettuce, lovage, onion, radish, savory (winter), turnips (for tops)

**Plant:** strawberry

**Thin:** angelica, cabbage (spring), caraway, chervil, coriander, lettuce, lovage, radish, spinach, spinach beet, Swiss chard (seakale beet), turnip

**Cloche:** French (kidney) bean, beetroot, carrot, endive, kohlrabi, lettuce, parsley, pea, radish (summer), strawberry

**Blanch:** endive

**Earth up:** winter celery

**Mulch:** rhubarb

**Feed:** cucumber, pepper, tomato

**Water:** especially all seedlings and young plants, if weather is dry; cucumber, pepper, strawberry, tomato

**Weed and clear:** all ground where crops have finished; seedling weeds elsewhere

**Compost heap:** continue to make

**Protect:** blackberry, blackcurrant, brassicas, grape, raspberry, strawberry, tomato from birds

**Pests and diseases:** cabbage caterpillars, greenfly, grey mould, (Botrytis cinerea), mildew, red spider mite, slugs, snails, whitefly

**Store:** beetroot, carrot, garlic, onion, potato, shallot, turnip

**Harvest:** grape

# Jobs to do

**Preparing the soil for sowing and planting outdoors**
There are only half a dozen or so vegetables which are worth sowing at this time, and only one fruit – strawberry – which can be planted, so little soil preparation is necessary, but follow instructions for seed-bed preparation (in Early Spring) and for soil preparation for strawberries (in Late Summer).

**Sowing**
Vegetable and herb seeds which can still be grown are: borage, cabbage (spring), endive (Batavian), lettuce, lovage, onion, radish, savory (winter), turnip (for spring greens). If you want lettuce as early as possible next spring, now is the time to sow it and over-winter under cloches; select a hardier variety, such as the cos (Romanie) kinds.

Borage germinates very easily and will even flower during mild periods in winter, so you can often go on using fresh leaves until the end of early winter. This is the latest period

*The curled form of endive should be ready for blanching at this time of the year, and is a good alternative to lettuce.*

for sowing summer radish, endive and turnips for tops. The last named is likely to be rather a hit-and-miss crop, a matter of filling up a space that would otherwise be empty, or of augmenting a rather sparse programme of fresh spring vegetables.

Onions sown in early autumn should provide mature bulbs in mid and late summer next year and spring onions in late spring. However, they are not an easy crop to grow successfully unless you have a sheltered garden; if you can sow the Japanese varieties in late summer, you are likely to have more success with them. The ordinary autumn varieties sown at this time should be sown a little more thickly, as germination may not be as good and the seedlings are likely to be more vulnerable. For successful over-wintering, the young plants should be about 15cm (6in) tall by the middle to end of mid autumn. Keeping them thoroughly weeded is especially important.

**Planting**
The only planting that can be done at this time is that of strawberries, as early in early autumn as possible, choosing a time when the soil is moist and rain forecast (see Late Summer for instructions on planting).

**Thinning**
The seeds sown in late summer will need their first or second thinning now and they include: angelica, cabbage (spring), caraway, chervil, coriander, lettuce, lovage, radish, spinach, spinach beet, Swiss chard (seakale beet) and turnip.

Seeds will be less quick to germinate at this time of the year and less quick to grow; you may find that some, particularly Japanese onions, are not ready for thinning until the beginning of mid-autumn.

If the cabbage have been sown where they are to grow, they can be thinned progressively to a spacing of 30cm (12in), but if in a seedbed, thin to about 13-15cm (5-6in) and expect to transplant later this season. Lettuce which are to be cut later in autumn should be thinned to a 23-30cm (9-12in) spacing.

## Cloching

During early autumn, you should be ready to put cloches over various crops, to maintain warmth round them and ensure that they mature. Such crops include lettuce, French (kidney) bean, pea, summer radish, carrot, beetroot; also kohlrabi, parsley and endive may need cloching if they are being a little slow, perhaps because of unseasonable chills or late sowing in mid-summer. Strawberries which were de-leafed in late summer can be covered at night to start with and then during day as well, once the blossom has set and there begins to be a nip in the air. The perpetual-fruiting kinds will be the better for protection as well, but the alpine varieties, being so hardy, can be left without cover and will still ripen in mid-autumn. There are many different kinds of cloches available, from your local nursery or garden centre. Glass and various kinds of plastic materials are used for glazing; height and width vary and you will find something suitable for most crops.

*Lettuces grow well in autumn if protected by cloches, such as these Chase barn cloches above. A modern substitute for glass cloches is the plastic tunnel, cheaper but not so long-lasting.*

## Blanching

Endive is a good, tasty, salad vegetable, provided it has been properly blanched, otherwise it has a bitter flavour. Exposure to light produces this unpleasant taste so plants must be covered completely. The curled varieties should be dealt with first, as they will not stand cold weather; they are simply covered with a plate or saucer, depending on their size, to blanch all but the outside leaves. Do this when the plants are completely dry, make sure there are no slugs lurking in the centre and then cover the plants with cloches. Blanching will take about two to three weeks. Alternatively, to blanch the whole plant, cover with a clay pot and stop the drainage hole with putty or similar material so that it is light-proof.

Batavian (lettuce-leaved) endive takes longer, about four to six weeks to blanch. All the leaves are gathered together so that the outside leaves surround the inner ones and are tied together at the top or secured with a rubber band. Then the cloche protecting them is itself covered completely with black plastic sheet.

## Earthing up

Winter celery can be given its final earthing up soon after the beginning of early autumn. Tie the stems together at the top and then add soil so that only the tops of the leaves show. The soil should be smoothed and evenly sloped so that rain runs off it; the plants can then be left until wanted for lifting, from the time of the first frosts onwards. Earthing up should be done gently, so as not to constrict the plant. Do not put fertilizer on the soil used: it could damage the stalks.

## Mulching

There is only one crop that need be treated with a top-dressing, in early or mid-autumn, and that is rhubarb. A prolific producer of leaves and stems, it needs equally prolific quantities of humus and nutrient and will make best use of the humus if applied during the next few weeks.

## Feeding

This job has almost come to an end; only the greenhouse crops will have sufficient growing time left for it to be worth feeding them. Cucumber, pepper and tomato can have

## Weeding and cleaning up

Many crops will finish this season – some will already have been pulled out – including aubergine, broad bean, French (kidney) bean, summer cauliflower, summer cabbage, self-blanching celery, pea, spinach and spinach beet, Swiss chard (seakale beet), and sweetcorn. Tomatoes should finally be picked by the end of early autumn and, if green, put to ripen in warmth; the haulms can be consigned to the compost heap, as can those of the maincrop potatoes when the crop has been lifted. If the fruits of melons and squashes have all ripened, their stems and leaves will also make good

*Blanching endive : use a plate for curly endive, a clay pot with the hole blocked, or a cloche covered with black plastic.*

liquid feeds until they finish, or until the end of the month, whichever comes first. Both melons and aubergines will be or have been harvested.

## Watering

This also will apply mainly to the greenhouse plants, though sometimes in the first two weeks or so of early autumn, the weather can be quite dry and the seedlings and young plants will need help with moisture. A fine spray is best for the seedlings. The soil for the strawberries and the runners if dry should be soaked the night before planting.

compost, but marrows often go on cropping well into mid-autumn and it is worth leaving the plants in the ground.

With quite a lot of space becoming free at once, it will be a matter of roughly levelling the soil after the crops have been dug up, eliminating any weeds and leaving well alone, unless you have planned for some overwintering crops to be sown or transplanted into these cleared patches. But nature abhors a vacuum and they will fill up with weeds while your back is turned; get the seedling weeds out while they still look as though they are not worth bothering about. Otherwise wet weather will be on you and, unless you like working in the rain, there will be few chances to deal with them before next spring, when you will be more concerned with the start of your new season's crops.

## Compost heap

Early autumn is another period, like spring and early summer, when the heap grows very quickly and, because of the quantities of green material put on to it now, and the relative warmth of the weather, will rot well, until the end of early autumn. After this, as every living organism slows down and prepares for the winter, the heap will itself become dormant until about the middle of late winter.

## Protecting

As in late summer, the soft fruits – blackberry, black-currants, grapes, raspberry and strawberry – should be defended against our feathered friends (feathered fiends, according to some gardeners). Brassicas and tomatoes, too, should be fortified against aerial attacks.

Above: *Varieties of blackcurrants will fruit in late summer and early autumn.* Below: *Raspberries can also be added to the autumn bounty of fruits.*

## Treating pests and diseases

Cabbage white butterflies will still be very much in evidence, laying quantities of eggs, and their caterpillars can still shred the leaves of brassicas into delicate lace. Grey mould in the greenhouse, on peppers, cucumbers and tomatoes and mildew outdoors, on many plants, may still be present, but it is not really worth spraying them at this stage; hand picking is usually sufficient to keep these diseases under control.

There may still be some red spider mite, whitefly and greenfly around indoors, but slugs and snails are likely to become real pests again, on lettuce, endive, celery and some of the root crops, such as potatoes, carrots, turnips and celeriac. On these they follow after a primary injury or infection.

## Storing

There are various ways of storing crops, as well as a surprisingly varied assortment that can be preserved by traditional storing, rather than the modern method of deep freezing, which is not, in fact, suitable for all vegetables and fruit and, in any case, involves a large outlay.

*Autumn is the time to store many of the vegetables sown and planted in spring. Root crops such as carrots or beetroot can be stored in sand or peat in lidded wooden boxes which are proof against mice and frost. Potatoes are often put into outdoor clamps, protected by layers of straw and soil. Onions need only to be thoroughly cleaned, dried and hung in ropes in a cool, dark place.*

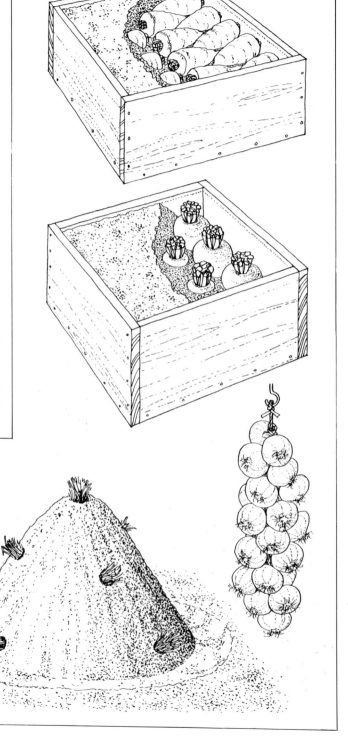

Potatoes, carrots, beetroot and turnip can all be lifted now for storing indoors in cool but frost-free sheds, rooms or cellars. All should be cleaned of soil and any top growth remaining, and allowed to dry in the sun for an hour or so. Beetroot should have the leaves and stems screwed or cut off to leave a length of about 5cm (2in); carrot and turnip growth can be cut off much closer to the crown.

Dry peat or sand can be used as the storage material and the roots put in layers, alternating with the peat or sand, heads to tails. Finish with a layer of packing material and then a lid which fits tightly so that no light (or mice) can get in. Use roots that are firm, uninjured and free from disease.

Potatoes are treated in the same way, but can go straight into the container without peat or sand; they must be kept completely dark, otherwise they turn green, and/or produce sprouts.

If you have very large crops, or no suitable storage building, you can clamp all these. Clamps consist of a conical or rectangular heap of vegetables built up on a thick layer of straw with a shallow trench dug out round the base of the clamp. The vegetables are covered with a layer of straw and then with soil which has been smoothed down with a spade so that rain runs down and off it, rather than into it. At intervals a plug of straw is left sticking through the soil to allow for ventilation. Crops will keep perfectly well in these clamps, even in frosty weather; of course the thicker the layer of soil, the more frostproof are they. When frost threatens, remove the straw plug and replace with soil.

Onions are easily stored. Clean off soil and cut off roots and tops, leave to dry in the sun and then string together. Lastly, either put them in single layers in trays or hang in dry, cool and dark conditions, until needed. Treat shallots and garlic in the same way.

### Harvesting

A new crop which can be harvested during early and mid-autumn is that from your vines; depending on the variety, grapes can be picked during the next six weeks or so. If you had cloches over them, however, you may have picked a few already. If they are for wine-making, they should be left on the vine longer than those for dessert, so that as high a sugar content as possible is obtained.

*Chives grow best in a warm border with some shade. They make a good edging for a vegetable plot.*

## Crops to be harvested

aubergine, globe artichoke, French (kidney) bean, runner (pole) bean, blackberry, blackcurrant, cabbage, carrot, cauliflower, celery (self-blanching), cucumber, endive, grape, kohlrabi, lettuce, marrow and courgette
Herbs: the leaves of basil, bay, borage, chives, dill, fennel, lemon balm, lovage, marjoram, mint, parsley, rosemary, sage, summer and winter savory, sorrel, tarragon, thyme

## Available from store

melon, mushroom, onion, pea, pepper potato, radish, raspberry, spinach, spinach beet, squash, strawberry, sweetcorn, Swiss chard, tomato, turnip

# Mid-Autumn

From now until next spring, there will be no really warm weather; the temperature will go down gradually but steadily and only crops which are really hardy will survive outdoors. Even some of these will need protection in the worst weather, but you will be relying mainly on the brassicas and roots for your vegetables in winter. The spinaches, unprotected, will provide pickings until late autumn and from early spring, but with cloches you can get more in early and late winter, by prolonging the first growth period, and bringing on the second one early.

It is not a good time to sow seed for new crops; there are some that could be tried, such as lettuce, spinach, peas and broad beans. However, autumn is so far advanced by this time that it will be difficult to get these germinated, let alone well enough established by winter to survive cold weather, even with the help of cloches. Broad beans are generally sown in late autumn if they are to over-winter, and sowing towards the end of mid-autumn does not produce much gain. In many years, the crop from the late autumn sowing is itself very little earlier than that sown in early spring.

Most of your work will consist of lifting the remaining root vegetables for store, clearing ground, and generally tidying up after the confusion and rush of harvesting. Cutting down, pruning, dividing and weeding, and giving the greenhouse a thorough clean out, are some of the mid-autumn jobs; those that occupied most of the summer work, such as feeding, watering, training and staking, spraying and compost heap making, will be virtually unnecessary.

Some soil preparation can be done for planting soft fruit including vines, in late autumn, and also some basic digging, in certain circumstances, though the large part of this can be done in late autumn and early winter.

It is possible to pick fresh leaves from some of the herbs for much of the winter, either with the help of cloche protection outdoors, or by lifting some, potting them and putting them in the greenhouse. It is a good time to divide some of the hardy herbs as well, if they are past their best.

# At~a~glance diary

**Prepare the soil for:** planting blackberries outdoors

**Put in supports for:** currant (red and black), gooseberry, loganberry, raspberry, vine

**Plant:** garlic

**Transplant:** cabbage (spring), lettuce, onion (Japanese)

**Thin:** borage, cabbage (winter), endive, lettuce, lovage, onion (all), radish (all), savory (winter), turnip

**Cloche:** beetroot, carrot, chives, endive, kohlrabi, lettuce, parsley, radish (summer)

**Prune and train:** blackberry

**Blanch:** endive

**Lift:** chicory

**Compost heap:** finish and cover

**Weed and clear:** Jerusalem artichoke, asparagus, French (kidney) bean, runner (pole) bean, brassicas (summer varieties), marrow, pea, pepper, spinach (summer), squash, all ground where roots are growing; vine after harvesting

**Mulch:** asparagus, rhubarb, vine, soft fruit

**Pot:** basil, marjoram, mint

**Greenhouse:** clear out, wash and sterilize/fumigate

**Increase:** by division, globe artichoke, lemon balm, chives, horseradish, lovage, pot marjoram, mint, savory (all); by cuttings, currant (red and black), gooseberry

**Pests and diseases:** cabbage caterpillar, mildew, slugs, snails, whitefly

**Store:** Jerusalem artichoke, carrot, celeriac, marrow, parsnip, squash, swede, turnip

# Jobs to do

*Red currants are fruits seldom seen in the greengrocer's shop now-a-days, so it pays to plant one or two bushes of your own, if you like redcurrant jelly or preserve. Preparation for planting is best done in mid-autumn if possible.*

**Preparing the soil for outdoor planting**

As the next season, late autumn, is the best time to plant vines outdoors, preparation of the soil towards the end of mid-autumn is advisable to give it time to absorb any organic matter and fertilizers you may think it necessary to add. For the best crops of grapes, whether they are for dessert or wine, choose a sheltered position facing south, gently slop-ing, and with a well-drained, slightly alkaline soil. Although vines need good drainage at the roots, and warmth in autumn, they are much hardier than is generally realized and will survive frost without difficulty. Choosing varieties which mature early and quickly is also important.

Since the vines are going to be cropping for twenty years and more, the soil should be dug two spits deep, a little manure or compost mixed into the bottom of the second spit, and the soil returned. It does not need to be particularly fertile, but if it is extremely gravelly, shingly or sandy, some rotted compost or farm manure should also be mixed into the top spit. Total rate of application can be about 4.5kg per sq m (10lb per sq yd). If this is not available, bonemeal, a slow acting organic fertilizer, can be mixed in instead, at 90g per sq m (3oz per sq yd). When preparing the soil, dig out each planting site so that it is about 60cm (24in) square.

In all gardens but those where winter is severe, planting in mid-autumn will ensure a good long growing period and produce the biggest cloves. You will get best growth if the position is not in a frost hollow and gets a reasonable amount of sun and if the soil is medium to light in texture. At the beginning of mid-autumn, single dig the site and mix in a moderate amount of rotted organic matter.

You can also prepare the soil now for planting the bush and cane fruits in late autumn, the traditional time for such planting. Since all make heavy demands on the soil's food and moisture content throughout their lives, it is important to ensure that the soil is in good heart to start with, other-wise none will do really well, however much you add manure, food and water later. Currants will crop for at least twenty years, the cane fruit for about fifteen, so preparation should not be skimped.

Currants do well on the heavier, moister soils with a slightly acid pH; a position sheltered from wind is important, otherwise they will suffer from 'run-off'—at flowering time pollinating insects will not work the blossom because of wind, and the clusters of flowers will wither without setting. If a windy place is unavoidable, supply some kind of protection in spring, even if only temporary.

Single dig the entire area; bushes will need a spacing at least 1.5m (60in) each way, and the root system, though shallow, will spread underground at least the width of the top growth above ground. Each bush should produce 4.5-5.5kg (10-12lb) of fruit in a single cropping season though in the first few, the crop will only be in the region of 1.5-3kg (3-6lb) per bush.

Mix in a good dressing of rotted garden compost or manure; the rate should be about one garden barrowload per 1.7sq m (2sq yd); it can be less on heavy soil and should be a little more on sandy ones. This may sound rather a lot, but the bushes will be cropping for many years and need a really good start.

While the site is being dug, make sure you get up all the weeds, including their roots; trying to eradicate bindweed, ground elder, couch grass and horsetail from a black or redcurrant planting, once the bushes are eastablished, is not possible. Pieces of root always remain in the soil, twined in the roots of the bushes, and if you try to spray the top growth with a translocated hormone weedkiller, harming the bushes as well is unavoidable. If the site is badly weed infested, it is worth waiting until the following early autumn, and clearing it at intervals until it is thoroughly weed-free, otherwise you will have endless trouble.

For cane fruit – raspberry, loganberry and blackberry – the soil should be prepared in much the same way. Raspberries are a little more particular about the type of soil, and if you have a really heavy soil or a very sandy, shallow one, they will not do well. Alkaline soil should also be avoided; a slightly acid one is best. Loganberries and blackberries are not so fussy and will accommodate themselves to most conditions. As with currants, sun and shelter from wind will give the best and most regular crops for all three. The fruiting laterals of raspberries in particular are liable to be 'blown out', i.e., damaged by wind so badly that they break off.

If you have the space, avoid planting any of these in soil which has recently been down to cane fruits, as there is the possibility that there may be soil-living eelworms present, which carry virus diseases common to cane fruits. Once plants are infected there is no cure; crops will become light and poor and plants will be stunted and weak and should be lifted and destroyed.

Single dig the soil, and break up the bottom of the trench or hole with a fork, adding organic matter at the same time. If the soil is very heavy, with a clay subsoil, it is advisable to dig deeper, to two spades' depth, and then fork up the lowest layer. Turn the soil, mixing it with more rotted garden compost, manure or leafmould and ensure that the quantity added is in the region of 12 litres (2½gal) per plant.

The cane fruits are planted in rows; raspberries will produce between 0.24 and 0.45kg (½ and 1lb) of fruit per 30cm (12in) of row and blackberries about 2.5-5kg (5-10lb) per plant. Loganberries crop slightly more heavily. About a week before planting, mix some bonemeal with the soil, about 21g per 90cm (¾oz per 36in) run of row.

## Supporting

Vines are planted at spacings of 120-150cm (48-60in) between plants, and 150cm (60in) between rows. They will need a support system of wires and posts, and this can be put in after the soil has been prepared. Wooden posts of chestnut or oak, 2.1m (84in) long, treated with preservative on the lowest 60cm (24in), should be driven into the soil at each planting site so that there is about 1.5-1.8m (60-72in) left above ground. Wires of 2.5mm (1/12in) gauge are run horizontally from post to post, the lowest 38cm (15in) above the ground, the next 75cm (30in) above the ground, and third 120cm (48in) above it. A single strand should be strung along the tops of the posts, for netting support later. Make sure that the wires are really firmly and rigidly attached to the posts, as the shoots and fruit will be a considerable weight, and will have to present a large surface area to possibly gale force winds.

For raspberries, perhaps the simplest method is to use a system of strong posts at each end of the row and spaced along it at about 2.4m (96in) intervals. Attached to these are three single horizontal wires, spaced 45cm (18in) apart, the first being 45cm (18in) above the ground. Posts should be similar to and erected in the same way as those for the vines, though only 45cm (18in) need be driven into the ground. There should then be 1.8m (72in) projecting above it. Raspberries are spaced 45cm (18in) apart with 1.5m (60in) between rows, so you can either prepare separate sites or dig out a trench about 60cm (24in) wide.

Blackberries and loganberries can develop strong, fast growing shoots 2.4m (96in) and more long, so need very sturdy supports and plenty of space. Concrete posts are frequently used by commercial growers; these have the advantage of being permanent and needing no attention, whereas wooden ones need preservative treatment and, even so, may decay. Cast iron 2.5cm (1in) piping can sometimes be obtained and is effective, though rather grim looking. Wires will have to be wound round them and tied to them.

Spacing between plants will need to be about 1.2-3.6m (48-144in), depending on the vigour of the variety and the amount of room it needs. If you plant in rows, allow 1.8m (72in) between them. The training system of wires and posts is similar to that for raspberries but attach the wires so that they are 30cm (12in) apart, the first one 60cm (24in) above the soil, and use four rather than three.

*Loganberries are a crop not grown as much as they should be: they have a delicious and distinctive flavour and crop well every year.*

## Planting

The only crop you need put in at this time is garlic. If you have a garden which is, in most winters, only moderately cold, you can get a good start with garlic by planting it now, especially in mild, sunny autumns. The cloves will root and produce shoots in a few weeks, but will then stand still until spring, surviving all but the severest weather. A well drained soil ensures the best survival rate. About a week before planting, mix some bonemeal with the soil, about 21g per 90cm ($\frac{3}{4}$oz per 36in) run of row.

You can use the grocer's bulbs; choose the ones with the biggest individual cloves. Separate the cloves, taking the outside ones only, and plant them so that there is a 2.5cm (1in) depth of soil over them. They may already have started to sprout – the green tip should be pointing upwards when planted. Allow 15cm (6in) between each clove and 30cm

(12in) between rows. Sometimes cloves are very large, about 2.5cm (1in) in diameter, and such specimens will need to be planted deeper, with 5cm (2in) of soil above them.

## Transplanting

There may be a little transplanting to do now, depending on your method of growing some crops; Japanese onions and spring cabbage can be moved into their permanent sites from seed-beds. If you have been short of space, you will have had to use a seed-bed and wait until the chosen sites become free. These two vegetables should be moved as early in mid-autumn as possible, with the usual precautions about moist soil and planting the best specimens.

The Japanese onions should be spaced about 13cm (5in) apart. Remember that the miniature bulb which will already have formed should be sat on the surface of the soil and the roots put into a hole so that they go straight down.

Some gardeners transplant lettuce at this time of the year as well, from a seed-bed. This does no harm when the winter months follow, but transplanting lettuce in spring frequently leads to bolting; the check produced by lifting, together with the rising temperature and increasing day length all encourage the plants to run to seed.

## Thinning

If you sowed a few crops in early autumn, they are likely to be at the stage of needing the first thinning by now, perhaps the second, if sown early in warm, moist weather. They include: borage, cabbage, endive, lettuce, lovage, onion (Japanese and ordinary), radish (summer and winter), savory and turnip. Turnips grown for tops only are thinned in two stages, first to 5cm (2in) apart, and then to 15cm (6in).

## Cloching

Crops to be newly cloched or which should have cloche-cover maintained over them are: beetroot, carrot, chives, endive, kohlrabi, lettuce, parsley and radish (summer). Chives, lettuce and parsley will need to be cloched continuously until spring but the remainder should be eaten or lifted for storing or blanching by early winter.

## Pruning and training

As the blackberry crop finishes towards the end of mid-autumn, the fruited canes can be cut off completely and the new shoots produced this year tied to the supporting wires to take their place. Most varieties are very prickly and tough gloves are a must for handling the stems. The best method of attack is to cut the old growth at ground level, cut the stems into sections and then unfasten them from the wires.

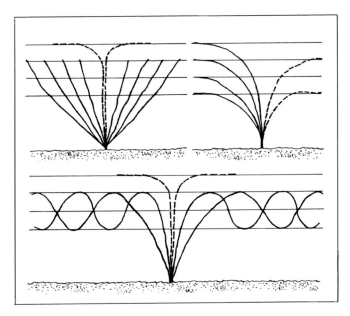

*Three methods of training blackberries:* top left: *the new canes are trained up the centre;* right: *they are taken to one side;* below: *the fruiting canes are interlinked, not fan trained.*

Unfasten the new growth also, lay the canes out separately on the ground and prune off all but eight to ten of the strongest and healthiest. Then tie them to the wires in one of the patterns illustrated.

## Blanching
Towards the end of mid-autumn, you can begin to blanch the first few Batavian varieties of endive, remembering that they take about four to six weeks. Either cloche them, if this has not already been done, and cover the cloche completely with black plastic sheet, or tie the outside leaves up round the inner leaves. However, with the possibility of much colder weather suddenly occurring, the latter method is not so suitable. If the temperature does drop, you can lift the plants with a good ball of soil round the roots and put them into boxes of soil in the greenhouse or a shed; then cover them with black plastic, and blanch them there.

## Lifting
Now is the time to lift chicory so that it can be stored under cover and forced as required through the winter. At the end of mid-autumn, or thereabouts, dig up the chicory, keep the plants which have a crown of 2.5-5cm (1-2in) diameter and strong healthy roots, and discard the remainder. Trim off any remaining leaves and cut the roots back to leave a length of about 20cm (8in). Then pack them horizontally in layers

in a box of moist sand or peat, in a dark place and a cool temperature; 2-7°C (35-45°F) is best, otherwise they may start into growth before you want them.

## Compost heap
The last of the weeds, stems and leaves of crops and similar material will go on the heap during the next few weeks; some of it will probably rot, but the outermost layers will remain the same until next winter or early spring. The heap should now have some protection put above it to ward off heavy rain and snow.

## Weeding and clearing
Mid-autumn will see the end of the marrows, squashes, peppers, runner (pole) and French (kidney) beans, the summer brassicas, peas and summer spinaches. The remainder of the root crops will be lifted execpt for one or two which can safely be left to over-winter in the ground. All these empty spaces will need raking and lightly forking to get rid of weeds and, in some cases, you can start the winter digging (see Late Autumn). After the grape harvest, the soil round the vines will certainly need attention to weed removal.

The asparagus bed will need clearing up before the winter; the shoots left to grow in summer should be cut down to ground level and composted and any weeds thoroughly cleared out. The stems of Jerusalem artichoke, too, can be cut right down, but leave an appreciable stump, otherwise it can be difficult to know exactly where to dig in winter when you want a few tubers for cooking.

## Mulching
If the rhubarb was not mulched in early autumn, do it as soon as possible now. The asparagus can also be given a good mulch over the entire bed; because of its coastal origin, compost containing seaweed will be particularly beneficial. Vines can be mulched if this was not done in late winter or early spring, after the grapes have been picked. If you are one of the gardeners who needs to straw the soft fruit, this form of mulch can go on now, if it was not put on in late summer; put it on to weed-free soil if possible, though a thick covering will choke the majority of weeds.

## Potting
Much of the work that needs to be done in mid-autumn is best got through in the first two weeks, which are often fine, mild and sunny, the last of the good weather. Potting herbs for winter use is one of the jobs to do at this time; marjoram, mint and basil can all be lifted, put into a proprietary potting compost in suitably sized pots and

boxes, and taken into the greenhouse, cold frame, or the home to go on a sunny windowsill. The top growth of all should be cut down to leave stems about a quarter of their original length. In a moist compost and moderate temperature they should produce new growth slowly and steadily.

## Cleaning the greenhouse

Giving the greenhouse a spring-clean, or rather an autumn-clean, is essential if the ongoing intensive cultivation in it is to be satisfying and successful. Although it provides protection for plants and the growing conditions can be manipulated as you wish, it also provides an ideal environment for a variety of pests and diseases, which have ample food supplied to them continuously, warmth and shelter from predators. Their rate of increase can be astronomic if you do not keep a very watchful eye on them all the year round.

Some will over-winter as pupae or eggs, or go into aestivation as adults until the spring in cracks in woodwork, under staging and in any odd corner. It pays to scrub down the inside of the greenhouse thoroughly, including the framework, staging, roof and floor, if it is paved or concreted, and to wash the glazing. Cleaning the latter is particularly important at this time, as crops being grown through the winter in a greenhouse will need all the light possible. Often you need only use clear water, in copious quantities, to wash away or drown insects and fungal spores. However, if you had much trouble with one or other, or both, you could use a sterilizing solution of formalin – a 2% solution – remembering to wear gloves while using it and that the fumes can be irritating to eyes, nose and throat. All plants should be removed from the greenhouse, until the smell of the solution has completely disappeared. Pots, tools, seed trays and so on can be plunged into the solution for forty-eight hours, and not used again until free of odour.

An alternative to formalin is the use of sulphur candles which, when alight, give off fumes of sulphur dioxide. These effectively penetrate cracks and crevices difficult to reach when scrubbing. Fumigation is preferably done at night, and the greenhouse should be air-tight and empty of plants. The fumes from burning sulphur are also poisonous, so take suitable precautions for yourself, family and pets.

A dry sunny day will make the job easier; you can stand any plants that are to over-winter outdoors while you do it, and dry out the inside more thoroughly and quickly than in dull or wet weather. Any old tomato haulms, cucumber leaves, and melon, together with all roots, should be pulled up and dispatched to the compost heap; pots, tools, thermometers, watering cans, hoses and so on put outside, and water tanks emptied, before starting the cleaning.

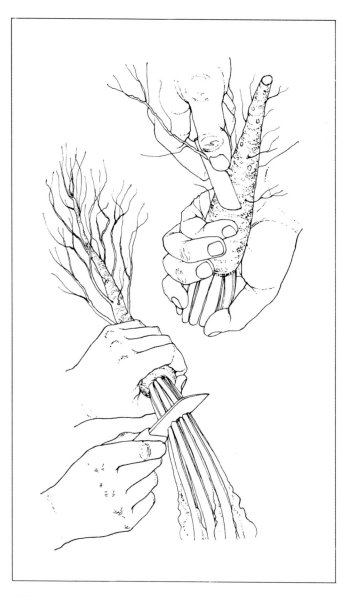

*When chicory is lifted to be stored for blanching later on in winter, keep those with a 2.5-5cm (1-2in) diameter crown, cut off the remains of the leaves, and trim off the fibrous roots. Cut the main root to about 20cm (8in) and pack in moist peat.*

## Increasing perennial crops

As the cost of plants is rising, like everything else, propagating from your own plants, provided they are not virus-infected, will not only provide you with new free plants but will probably also result in better plants in the long run, as you can give them much more attention and care than the nurseryman, who is dealing with thousands at a time rather than half a dozen.

Division is a very simple method of increase, applicable in mid-autumn to globe artichokes, lemon balm, chives, horseradish, lovage, pot marjoram, mint and both the savories. When dividing, plants are dug up with as much root intact as possible and the crowns chopped through vertically with a trowel or spade, so that there are several pieces, with dormant buds and/or some top growth on each piece. Pieces from the edges of the crown will be the strongest – the central part will be the oldest and should be regarded as compost heap material.

This method applies to all the above, except the globe artichokes, which are not lifted. Instead, the suckers which they will have produced during the growing season at the base of the plant can be detached and planted; those which are about 25cm (10in) tall will establish best. Cut off the sucker from the parent with a little of the crown attached and some roots, and plant it as soon as possible by the method described in Mid-Spring. For spacing of herbs, see Mid-Spring also.

Another method of propagation is by cuttings, in the case of the bush fruit: gooseberry and currants. Use hardwood cuttings of new shoots produced this season; the bark should have turned light brown almost to the tip. Blackcurrant cuttings should be about 23-30cm (9-12in) long, those of red and white currants about 38cm (15in) long, because they are grown with a 'leg', that is, with a short length of main stem or trunk. Blackcurrant bushes, on the other hand, consist of several shoots coming directly out of the ground which crop along their entire length. The cuttings are prepared and planted as shown in the illustrations, and in approximately a year's time will be ready for planting in their permanent positions. Remember that they should not be allowed to crop until the second summer after planting.

Gooseberry cuttings will be about 25cm (10in) long and are less easy to root, so take more than you need in case of failure. Also, the earlier in mid-autumn they are taken the better, while the soil and atmosphere are still warm.

## Treating pests and diseases

By now you can virtually cease to be on the lookout for plant troubles, though slugs and birds will still be with you. There may be the odd spot of mildew here and there, patches of whitefly on the outdoor brassicas and, in a mild autumn, caterpillars can still be causing considerable trouble on cabbages. Since the brassicas will be in the ground is frozen. Marrows and squashes also can be stored, in a cool, dark shed or room for several weeks after cutting, preferably in a net hanging from the wall or ceiling.

## Storing

You can start to lift the remainder of the root crops and put them into store: carrot, celeriac, parsnip, swedes and turnips, also Jerusalem artichokes, although the latter taste better if left in the ground and dug as required. The other root crops will also survive in the soil until late winter, but the difficulty with all these is getting at them when the ground is frozen. Marrows and squashes also can be stored, in a cool, dark shed or room for several weeks after cutting, preferably in a net hanging from the wall or ceiling.

## Harvesting

Winter celery should be just about ready by the end of mid-autumn, although the flavour is said to be better when it has been frosted. Grapes grown for wine making should be picked in about the middle of this period, but a good deal depends on the season, the amount of sunshine there has been, and the type of wine that is to be made. Red cabbage, except for the variety Rugby Ball, should be lifted before the frosts really begin to bite.

## Crops to be harvested

Jerusalem artichoke, beetroot, blackberry, cabbage, carrot, celeriac, celery, cucumber, endive, grape, lettuce, marrow
Herbs: the leaves of bay, borage, chives, fennel, lemon balm, lovage, mint, parsley, rosemary, sage, winter savory, sorrel, tarragon, thyme

## Available from store

mushroom, parsnip, pea, pepper, radish, spinach, spinach beet, squash, swede, Swiss chard, turnip

# Late Autumn

The season for plants to grow is more or less over now; the annual crops will have finished and the biennial and perennial ones will become dormant in late autumn if they have not already done so. There is still a little life left though; there is one vegetable crop which will germinate if seed is sown, some of the soft fruit will still produce roots from cuttings taken early in the season, and all one- or two-year-old plants of soft fruit will continue to put out roots.

However, the cooling temperature and the regular decrease in the hours of daylight ensures a halt in the cycle of growth and a chance for the gardener to do what jobs can be done rather more slowly. Since most gardeners now only have weekends in which to deal with their plants, it is just as well that there is less to do. One of the major winter jobs which will be in full swing from now until the end of early winter is the annual digging, whenever the soil is fit to work, as well as preparing it for planting.

Another major job to be done and completed, if possible, in late autumn, is soft fruit planting (except strawberry). In fact, much of this season's work is concerned with the fruit crops, since another job is the completion of the pruning, which is more easily done once the leaves are off the plants. Some pruning could have been finished in the summer, but the lack of time and difficulty of seeing the shoots clearly when in leaf makes it less convenient at that season.

The greenhouse will be in use for a few crops which are being blanched or forced; you may perhaps be trying lettuce there as an overwintering crop instead of outdoors under cloche and there may be some herbs in pots. All will appreciate some fresh air during the day, but, apart from ventilation, occasional watering, and removal of leaves from the roof glazing, the greenhouse will not need attention.

# At~a~glance diary

**Prepare the soil for:** sowing and planting indoors

**Dig:** for general cropping

**Sow seed of:** broad bean

**Plant:** blackberry, currant (red and black), gooseberry, loganberry, raspberry, rhubarb, vine; plant blackberries and loganberries which were layered last autumn, and also hardwood cuttings of gooseberry and currants (red and black) which were taken and rooted in the previous autumn

**Prune:** blackberry, currant (red and black), gooseberry, loganberry, raspberry, vine (after planting only)

**Lift:** rhubarb

**Force:** chicory, rhubarb

**Blanch:** endive

**Protect:** bush fruit such as gooseberries and the currants from attacks by the birds

**Ventilate:** greenhouse

**Increase:** by hardwood cuttings, the bush fruit such as currants (red and black) and gooseberries; by suckers, raspberries

# Jobs to do

**Preparing the soil for outdoor sowing**
In mild areas, it is worth sowing the longpod varieties of broad beans, to stand through the winter, but you will not need to prepare the soil for sowing other seeds. Since broad beans have large seeds, there is no need to try and reduce the soil to the fine tilth required by the tiny seeds. The autumn rains would make this difficult, so digging the soil as advised in early spring, raking it to remove the larger lumps and stones and to level it, will be sufficient.

*In mild, sheltered gardens, broad beans can be sown in late autumn to provide an early crop in late spring of the next year.*

### Preparing the soil for planting outdoors

It is still possible to plant soft fruit, except vines and rhubarb, at the beginning of early winter, so you can prepare the soil for this during the next few weeks (see Mid-Autumn for method).

### Digging

Cultivating the soil by digging is a major routine job in the vegetable garden. It is most conveniently done in late autumn or early winter, partly because most of the ground is clear of plants and partly because leaving it until later in winter runs the risk of the ground being frozen, covered in snow or waterlogged.

There is a school of thought which advises 'no digging', the idea being that in Nature the ground is not cultivated; the necessary improvement or maintainance of the soil structure is carried out by worms, small mammals, insects and other soil fauna, provided an annual mulch of organic matter is put on. The arguments for and against both points of view are considerable and you may like to experiment with both techniques in your garden.

As far as digging is concerned, the type called single digging is the most useful and the easiest. It only involves digging the top soil out to a depth of the spade, putting it on one side and then forking up the bottom of the hole or trench, and lastly, returning the top soil mixed with organic matter.

It is standard practice to mark out a strip, dig a trench across the width of the strip, barrow the soil to the other end of the area to be dug and fork up the bottom of the trench. Then make a second trench next to it and throw the soil from this forward into the first trench, mixed with manure, garden compost, etc (see Early Winter for details on bulky organics). You can spread the manure over the soil before digging, or have it ready in a barrow and add it to the bottom or top of the trench, mixing it thoroughly with the returned soil.

Double digging repeats the process, but to a depth of the length of two spades' blades; two trenches need to be dug, and two lots of soil removed for use at the finish. Half trenching, or bastard trenching, comes between the two; in that method the soil is dug to one spades' depth, and the bottom is then forked or dug to the length of the tines or spade blade, but not removed. With both half trenching and double digging, manure should be mixed with all the soil which is loosened.

*Three types of digging are illustrated here: single digging, half-trenching and double digging.*

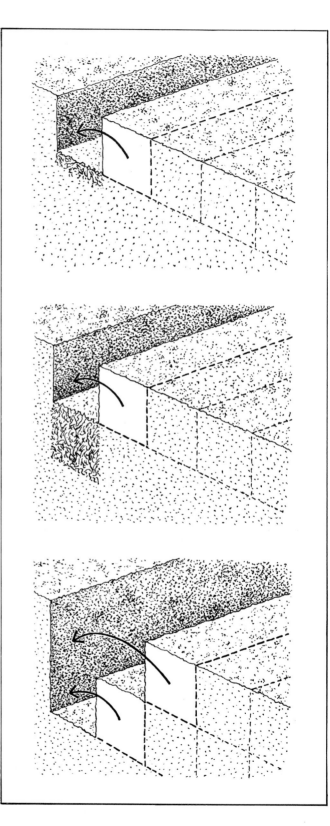

Half trenching can be used if you suspect a compacted layer is building up just below your usual depth of digging. Double digging can be used for heavy soils, for permanent crops, or for those soils which are shallow and need food and humus added to increase the depth of useful growing medium.

### Sowing outdoors

The longpod varieties of broad beans can be sown outside, the sooner the better, at the same spacings and depths advised in Early Spring. You may have to cloche them in

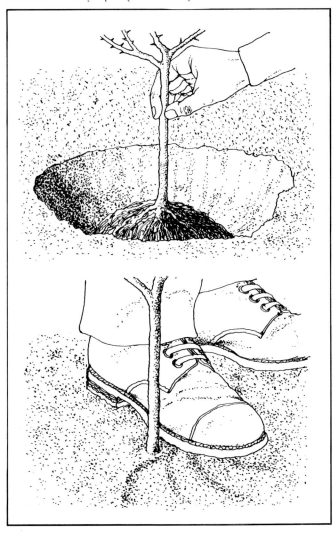

*When planting a gooseberry bush, make sure that it is in the centre of the hole and that the roots are well spread out. Plant so as to leave a good length of main stem or 'leg' clear of the soil.*

really cold weather, but take the cloches off if the temperature rises or the sun comes out, otherwise the plants will come on too fast, get soft and be severely frosted. Winter is not an easy time to get broad beans going; the most successful plants will be in the sheltered and milder gardens.

### Planting outdoors

The main plantings will be of blackberry, currant, gooseberry, loganberry, raspberry and vine. Prepare the plants by cutting any broken roots back to just behind the injury, and shorten a little any very long ones. The planting method for all these is more or less the same. A hole should be dug out at each planting site of sufficient width and depth to enable the roots to be spread out to their fullest extent, as naturally as possible. When planting has finished the soil mark on the stem should, in general, be at the same level as the surface of the soil in which the plant now is.

When you have put the plant roots in the hole, hold the stem with one hand and crumble the soil back over them with the other, shaking the plant occasionally so that the soil settles naturally round the roots and firming the soil as it is filled in. Finally, tread it down round the plant, add more soil so that there is not a hollow round it, firm this also, and then rake the surface lightly. Water in if the weather or soil is dry.

Although the main method is the same for all these, there are some slight variations for each fruit. For instance, you will probably find it easier to deal with raspberries by digging out a complete trench along the row and then setting the plants in it at the appropriate spacings, instead of making a separate hole for each plant.

Blackcurrants should be set in the soil so that the soil mark on their stems is 5cm (2in) below that of the soil level. This is to encourage more shoots to come from below ground to make certain that they form a plant with several main branches. Red currants and gooseberries are always grown with a short, single trunk, or 'leg', and the difference between the two is due to the habit of growth and fruiting characteristics (see under Pruning). Because of these characteristics red currants and gooseberries should have any suckers or buds rubbed off the roots; and buds on the 'leg' should also be removed.

You can plant rhubarb as well now, or in early spring; you will find the method of planting detailed there.

If you took cuttings of fruit last autumn, or layered blackberries and loganberries, you can lift these now and plant them in their permanent positions. Raspberry suckers can also be chopped off from the parent plants, dug up and lined out in trenches.

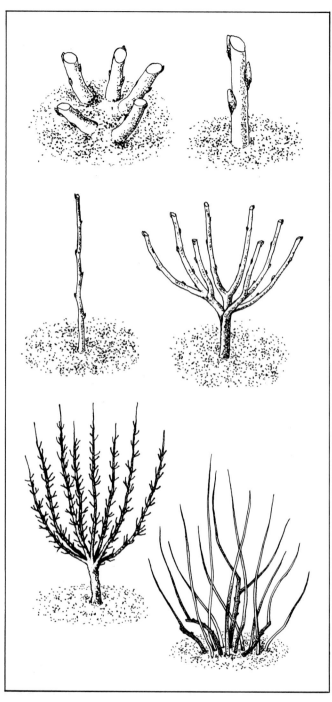

*Pruning: cut blackcurrants down after planting to leave two or three buds, and vines to leave three dormant buds. A raspberry cane should be pruned after planting to about 23cm (9in); red currant shoots are cut by half. Mature red currants can be spur-pruned, blackcurrants have most of the old growth removed.*

## Pruning

There is no doubt that fruit bushes and cane fruit, if left unpruned, produce small crops, often damaged and diseased, and they may even not crop at all in some years. To get heavy crops of fruit every year, whatever the weather, is a skilled job, which takes some years of experience. The production of such crops is helped by good pruning. This channels the energies of the plant into producing fruit, balanced by the production of leaf and shoot, and removes surplus growth which chokes the bushes, and may be a source of fungus disease and a home for vagrant pests. When pruning, cuts should always be made just above a bud, and should be smooth and clean, without any snags left, otherwise disease gets into the snags.

There are two lots of pruning to do in late autumn, if you have planted a new collection of soft fruit and you still have some of the old. Newly planted cane and bush fruits should all be cut back hard, as soon as planted. All will arrive from the nursery or garden centre with varying lengths of new shoots but, although these would produce a crop the following summer, this would weaken the plant, and it is better to prevent the plants from fruiting. The same applies to stock you have rooted yourself.

Blackcurrants should be cut back so that the three or four shoots are reduced to short stumps, each with only two or three buds. Red currants and gooseberries are pruned so that the main shoots are reduced to half their length; short, weak or straggling shoots should be cut off competely, flush with their point of origin. Raspberry canes should have no more than 23cm (9in) left after pruning; loganberries and blackberries should be treated in the same way. Vines are also pruned hard, but the degree varies, depending on which method of training you are using. With the double Guyot method, the cane should be cut down, if not already done in the nursery, to leave three strong buds, any weak ones being removed.

The routine pruning of established fruit bushes is mostly done at this time, as soon as the leaves are off, finishing off the summer pruning of some and doing all the pruning on others. You may have started on the blackcurrants in late summer and you can now finish the job by thinning out the new shoots, so that the remainder consist of the strongest, spaced well apart, with room in the centre to let in air and light. You can either cut shoots right down to ground level, if several years old, or cut younger ones back to a strong, new side-shoot halfway down them. Work on the principle of cutting back shoots by slightly more than half, rather than less, otherwise the bushes get very tall — up to 1.8m (6ft): aim for a neat, vase-shaped structure.

Red currants are trained to form a goblet-shaped bush, with about eight to twelve main branches, evenly spaced. The tips of each of these main branches are cut off to a length of about 10cm (4in) of the new season's growth. The new growth on the side-shoots is cut to leave only 2.5 or 5cm (1 or 2in) of it, so that short side-shoots, fruiting spurs, are built up along the length of the stem.

It will take two or three years after planting to form the number of main branches required, but you can allow the bushes to fruit in the second summer after planting. In order to obtain the main branches, cut the new growth on the leading shoots back by half in the second and third winter after planting and at the same time cut back any side-shoots to produce spurs, as already described. The aim is an open-centred bush with well-spaced branches.

The formative pruning of the bushes is done in the same way as red currants but, as many gooseberry varieties have a drooping habit of growth, it is important to cut to a bud on the *upper* side of the branch or shoot.

You can also prune and tie in blackberries and loganberries, if there was no time to do it in mid-autumn, or the blackberry crop had not finished.

Autumn-fruiting raspberries and blackcurrants can be pruned now: deal with them as with summer fruiting kinds.

## Lifting

If you are thinking of forcing rhubarb, late autumn is the time to start lifting it. Use three-year-old crowns, dig them up and leave on the surface of the soil until they have been exposed to wind and frost for a few days.

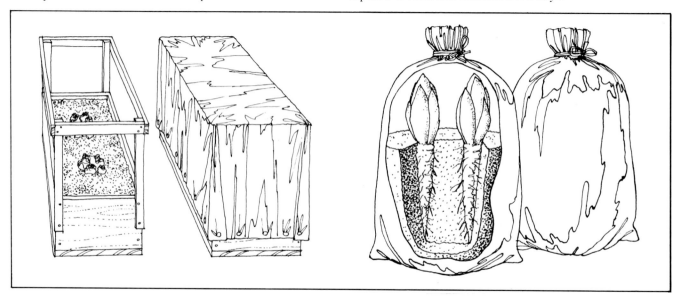

*Rhubarb can be forced by packing it into boxes of moist soil or peat, draping these with black plastic and supplying warmth. Similarly, chicory will produce chicons if the roots are given moisture and warmth and kept dark.*

Gooseberries can be spur pruned in the same way, if you want very large berries, for dessert, but you can also get crops of more but smaller berries with much less hard pruning. This latter method consists of cutting the new season's growth on the ends of the main branches back by a quarter, removing weak, straggling, crossing and very old shoots completely, and cutting some of the new season's side-shoots back to about 7.5cm (3in) in length. Space these cut-back side-shoots evenly all over the bush, so that there is room to pick reasonably easily.

## Forcing

Towards the end of late autumn you can force the first batch of rhubarb, and thereafter do it in succession every week or fortnight, or whenever it is wanted, remembering that it takes about four to six weeks from the time the crowns are taken into warmth to pulling the stalks. Pack the crowns into large boxes full of moist soil or peat, cover them with black plastic sheet draped over a framework, and supply a temperature of 4-10°C (40-50°F). When growth is well started, raise it to 16-18°C (60-65°F) but not more, otherwise rotting can occur. Crowns will not be fit for use again afterwards and should be thrown away.

You can also start to force chicory, and carry on through the winter as it is wanted; about a month is needed to produce acceptably sized chicons. Each root will produce one head, 13.5-20cm (5-8in) long. Plant the roots vertically, 7.5cm (3in) apart in moist soil, peat or sand, using boxes or pots of a sufficient depth to take the roots comfortably. Either cover the crowns 2.5cm (1in) deep, or mound up the growing medium to about 17.5cm (7in). The latter method produces much more tightly packed chicons. If the soil is not to be mounded up, cover the container with black plastic sheet on a framework. Temperature should be 10-16°C (50-60°F). If any light at all reaches the chicons, they will taste bitter.

## Blanching
Continue to blanch endive; the moss-curled type will finish about now, but the Batavian variety may remain outdoors for blanching if the autumn is mild, until the end of the month. However, you should lift it if frost is forecast (see Mid-Autumn for blanching methods).

*One of the ways of making sure of a good crop of gooseberries like these is to protect the bushes from late autumn through the winter against birds pecking the dormant fruit buds.*

## Protecting
Bullfinches can start pecking out the buds of gooseberries as early in the dormant season as late autumn, so it is well worthwhile putting netting over them as soon as possible.

## Ventilating
The greenhouse will need some ventilating, unless the weather turns exceptionally cold; you may have a few plants in it or a lettuce crop overwintering and all will be the better for a little fresh air. Condensation on the glazing may be a problem, even with ventilation, and should be wiped off, otherwise it considerably cuts down the transmission of light. Even if you are forcing plants, it pays to supply a little air, but at least the daylight hours are usually warmer than the night, so that extra heat should not be needed.

## Increasing
You can still take cuttings of bush fruit, but as early in late autumn as possible, since dormancy is imminent and the production of roots from the base of the cuttings is rapidly becoming unlikely.

## Crops to be harvested
globe artichoke, Brussels sprout, cabbage, cauliflower (winter-heading broccoli), celeriac, celery, chicory, endive, leek, lettuce, parsnip, parsley, radish (winter), rhubarb, spinach (winter), spinach beet, swede, Swiss chard, herbs in pots

## Available from store
beetroot, carrot, garlic, marrow, onion, potato, shallot, turnip

# Early Winter

The shortest day occurs near the end of early winter, when there may only be six or seven hours of daylight, and not very bright daylight at that. All through this period the days get shorter and shorter, and the temperature may drop steadily until it is at or below freezing at night and not much higher during the day. There will be little time for garden work; even if the ground is not frozen, or even snow-covered, it may be very wet and there may be incessant rain.

Even more than in late autumn it is important to finish jobs whenever an hour or two can be snatched. After this season winter will set in with a vengeance and you may not be able to get out into the garden again until early spring. The routine digging and improving the soil will be the main preoccupations; your planting should be finished as soon as possible, so any further preparation of the soil outdoors for planting will not be necessary. It is frequently said that planting can be done at any time in the winter, in mild and dryish periods. However, with the prospect of prolonged waterlogging, or prolonged frost and snow, losses of fruit bushes and canes are quite possible, if there has not been time for their roots to get a firm grip on the soil in autumn or early winter.

The pruning of soft fruit should also be finished off, and then a winter spray can be applied while the plants are completely dormant, to control various troubles.

Amongst the vegetables, the brassicas should be well covered against birds and well staked against winter gales. Leaf crops under cloches may need tidying and weeding once the last cutting for the winter has been made. Continue to keep an eye open for weeds on the unprotected vegetables, too.

# At~a~glance diary

**Dig:**      all ground

**Improve the soil:**      for all crops

**Prepare the soil for:**      indoor planting of tomatoes

**Force:**      chicory, rhubarb

**Prune:**      cane and bush fruit such as blackberries, currants (black and red), gooseberries, loganberries and similar berries, raspberries, and also vine

**Spray:**      cane and bush fruit, as detailed under pruning.

**Clean:**      crops under cloches, brassicas

**Stored crops:**      look over for damage from rotting

**Harvest:**      remaining root crops, some brassicas, e.g. heading broccoli (winter cauliflower) Brussels sprouts, cabbage, celeriac, Jerusalem artichoke, kohlrabi, parsnip, winter radish, swede, turnip

**Protect:**      the following brassicas by attack from birds, particularly pigeons: Brussels sprouts, sprouting broccoli, cabbage, kale, heading broccoli (winter cauliflower)

# Jobs to do

## Digging

If this job has not already been started in late autumn, you will do yourself a good turn by starting as soon as possible. Turning out to dig later on in winter can be very unpleasant and if it gets missed altogether, there is a chance of failure with various crops in the following season. If you are a regular 'no-digger', that is a different matter, but if you have decided that your system of cultivation involves digging, it will need to be done regularly for consistently good results. For the method, see Late Autumn.

## Improving the soil

It is while digging that you can take the opportunity to alter the condition of the soil and improve it if necessary. You may own a garden the soil of which contains a good deal of sand, shale, or stones; all these help to ensure that water drains through it quickly and that it is short of plant food. Since the mineral nutrients that plants require can only be absorbed by them if they are dissolved in moisture, in such soils there will be a shortage of plant foods, hence you need to treat such soil so that it retains water.

However, you may have to deal with the other extreme, which is the heavy soil that sticks to the spade in lumps when it is wet, and cracks into 2.5cm (1in) wide crevices if allowed to be dry for any length of time. It easily becomes water-logged and unfit for plant growth and if it becomes compacted from weight of machinery or your own feet, it may take a whole growing season before the structure is restored to anything like normal. So the time of cultivating it has to be chosen carefully, unlike the sandy soil, which can be worked at more or less any time. Against this disadvantage, however, must be weighed the fact that these heavy clay soils are highly nutritious to plants and the quantity of moisture they contain ensures that they remain moist many weeks longer than free-draining soils, especially as the subsoil is often almost pure clay.

*Green manuring: digging growing plants into the soil to increase the humus content. A cheap, clean and easy method.*

You may have a chalky soil only a few centimetres (in) deep, on top of a subsoil of pure chalk or you may have to deal with a soil largely consisting of peat, if you live near moorland. The former will be excessively alkaline and prone to become dry, the latter will have a very acid reaction and retain so much moisture that you can squeeze a handful out like a sponge. Of course, you may be lucky enough to have a good soil which does not possess any of the extreme characteristics described or which only needs a little titivating to keep it in good order.

All these different types of soil can be considerably improved over the years by mixing with them that now rather rare substance, rotted organic matter. This is so often quoted as being the answer to the gardener's prayer that one tends to lose sight of what it is and why it is so important.

Rotted organic matter consists of the decaying or decayed remains of animals or plants and it provides humus, a substance the physical properties of which ensure that the drainage of water and the supply of air (and hence oxygen) are adequate for health of roots and that mineral nutrients are present in a form that roots can absorb. Organic matter in the soil ensures that there is a variety of small and even microscopic animals present, such as worms, nematodes, bacteria and insects, all of whose various activities on and in the organic matter result in its gradual change and decomposition into humus.

Woodland soils into which leaves have rotted over years and years are some of the best there are. When trees are

*All sorts of materials can be used as mulches ; one is spent hops, which supply a lot of organic matter but not much plant food.*

cleared and the site used for cropping, its initial fertility is considerable but, unless it is maintained by the return to the soil of most of what is taken out of it, the fertility gradually decreases and the end product is desert.

It is not necessary to add vast quantities of organic matter, except when first dealing with very poorly structured soils; a little goes a long way and will keep all the processes necessary to maintain a good structure ticking over steadily. Standard types of organic matter are: garden compost, leafmould, farm manure of various kinds, poultry deep litter, spent mushroom compost, spent hops, straw, peat and seaweed. Some other less conventional ones are: bark, shoddy (wool or cotton waste), wood shavings and sawdust, hair, feathers, sewage sludge, fishmeal, leather, coffee waste and green manure.

Farm manure, sewage sludge, fishmeal and poultry deep litter are often available as products with proprietary names; these have been heated and dried to remove possibly harmful bacteria, and in some cases deodorized, so that the end product is inoffensive and easy to handle. Garden compost is available from your own garden in the form of plant waste materials which have been, in effect, re-cycled. The garden soil should become richer in nutrients over the years if you are also adding compound fertilizers. You may also be able to make leafmould; it is less nutritious than compost, but a very useful humus supplier.

Spent mushroom compost is excellent; the original compost is very rich and the mushroom crops do not take much fertility from it, so that although it is called 'spent', it is by no means finished as far as green plants are concerned. It may be very alkaline, however; your supplier will be able to tell you. If it is, use it sparingly or mix it with other manures. Spent hops consist of the haulm of the hop plant and the hops themselves after use in brewing; their value is mainly in the humus they contribute, as there is little nutrient present. Peat contains even less plant food, but is an excellent sponge and supplier of humus; straw is similarly low in nutrients and not such a good sponge. Shoddy, wood shavings, sawdust, hair, feathers, leather waste, coffee waste and bark are all very slow to rot. They will supply humus, but only very gradually during a period of several years and only a little plant food.

The time to add any of these types of organic matter, if they are to be dug in, is autumn and winter, the earlier the better, so that as large a part as possible has been integrated into the soil by bacteria and worms by the time of planting or sowing in spring. A standard rate of application for the average crop, to an average soil, of rotted farm manure (pig, cow or horse) or garden compost is about 4.5kg per sq m (10lb per sq yd). For soils which are already in good heart, 2.2kg per sq m (5lb per sq yd) is sufficient, especially if you intend mulching in spring or summer. For those which are poorly structured and/or lacking in plant food, 6.7kg per sq m (15lb per sq yd) is not too much. The variations on these rates can be considerable, but if you use them as a basis, you can alter them in the light of your own experience, as you come to know your soil, the needs of the varying crops and local weather conditions.

### Preparing the soil for planting indoors

You can start to prepare the soil now in the greenhouse for planting tomatoes in the spring. Growing tomatoes regularly every year in the same place runs a considerable risk of fungus disease building up in the soil, or root-infesting

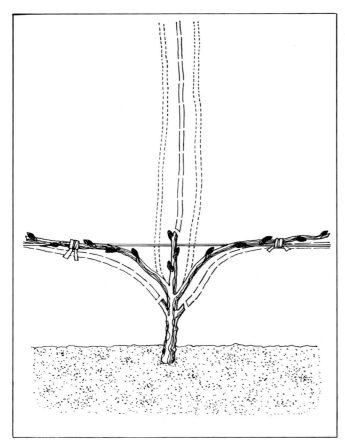

*Pruning outdoor grape-vines: cut off the fruited rods, gently tie down the new shoots to right and left, and cut the central rod down to leave three dormant buds – or four for insurance.*

eelworms, and these troubles will mean that infected plants will be slow to grow, with wilting and yellowing leaves and stunted shoots.

Provided you have not previously had trouble, you can dig the soil roughly to produce a broken up surface and then flood it, preferably with a sprinkler attachment to the hose. Both these practices ensure that the soil is moistened evenly, which would not be the case if a stream of water were spouted out onto a smooth, compacted soil surface. The soil needs to be really wet to a depth of 50cm (20in) and you can water it in two or three stages.

If the soil is markedly acid, you should put on a dressing of lime to make the pH value 6.0-7.0, though tomatoes will grow well in a fairly wide range of pH values, up to about 7.5. This lime dressing can go on before the last watering, applied evenly in powder form. You can flood and lime at any time in early winter, or early in mid-winter; the remaining preparation will be done in late winter.

If some of your plants grew badly last year and you have been growing them in the same soil for some years, it will need replacing or sterilizing. Sterilizing should be done as soon as the old plants have been pulled out, using form-aldehyde; then you can follow with flooding and liming and the rest of the preparation.

### Forcing
Continue to force chicory and rhubarb in succession as it is wanted (see Late Autumn for method).

*Chicons can easily be produced by planting the roots in a pot, and covering this with another pot to keep out the light.*

### Pruning
Finish the pruning of cane and bush fruits as soon as possible, and if you did not get the vines pruned in late autumn you can still do it during the next few weeks. As the sap of the vine becomes active much earlier than with other fruits, it is necessary to finish the pruning before mid-winter, otherwise the cut surfaces 'bleed'.

If you are following the double Guyot method of pruning, the tow main rods which carried the fruiting sideshoots should be cut right back to stubs. Two of the three new shoots which have been trained vertically are now tied down horizontally, one on each side of the main stem, and cut back to leave five or six buds. The remaining shoot which is to produce the replacement fruiting shoots next year is cut down to leave three good buds, or four if you want one as an insurance.

## Spraying

Early winter is a good time to do any winter spraying that may be necessary. As far as soft fruit is concerned it is not usually a big job; the pests and diseases that can occur in gardens on these fruits are nothing like as troublesome or varied as on the tree fruits. Often all that is needed is one thorough spraying with tar oil winter wash to destroy the overwintering eggs of aphids, leaf suckers and leaf hoppers. It will also burn off any moss or lichen on the shoots and so help to cut down fungus disease by destroying protection for the overwintering spores.

Since the eggs and spores are tiny, the spray should be applied until it drips off the ends of the shoots. It will burn grass and kill herbaceous plant and vegetables, so be careful if any of these are growing close to or in between the rows. It will not be necessary to spray vines.

## Protecting

Brassicas should be safely guarded against birds, and securely staked against winter storms. The outer leaves of the winter cauliflower should be half broken and bent over the florets to protect them against frost.

*Winter cauliflowers provide a welcome variation; the curd can be protected from frost by bending the outer leaves over it.*

## Crops to be harvested

Jerusalem artichoke, Brussels sprout, cabbage (including Savoy), cauliflower (winter-heading broccoli). celery, chicory, endive, parsnip, radish (winter), rhubarb (forced), spinach (winter), spinach beet, swede, Swiss chard

## Available from store

beetroot, carrot, garlic, marrow, onion, potato, shallot, turnip

## Cleaning

Winter spinaches, lettuce, endive and brassicas may need the occasional tidying and hoeing round. Yellowing leaves should be taken off the brassicas and the endive ground cleared when the crop is finished.

## Stored crops

Some time in early winter, it would be advisable to have a good look at the roots, potatoes and other crops in store. However careful one is to keep only sound, healthy specimens, there are always one or two which start to rot, and the quicker they are removed the better, before they contaminate the remainder. You may also find, in spite of taking precautions, that mice and rats have found a way into the containers or clamps and have had a hearty feed.

## Harvesting

Since the worst winter weather will probably start in mid-winter, early winter is a good time to get up some, if not all, of the roots remaining in the ground, in case it becomes frozen hard or covered in snow, and put them into store. This will include Jerusalem artichoke, parsnip, radish and swede. If the weather becomes very bad, it is possible to dig up cauliflower, and also cabbage with roots attached, and store them for two or three weeks in a dark cool shed, hanging upside down. If the roots are enclosed in polythene bags containing a little moisture, they will last even longer.

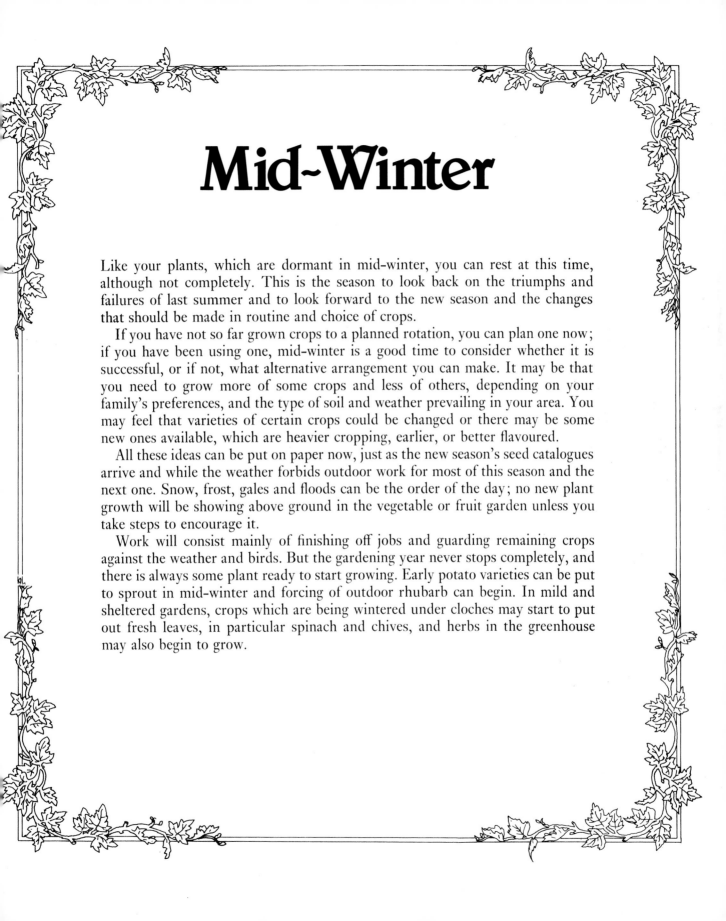

# Mid~Winter

Like your plants, which are dormant in mid-winter, you can rest at this time, although not completely. This is the season to look back on the triumphs and failures of last summer and to look forward to the new season and the changes that should be made in routine and choice of crops.

If you have not so far grown crops to a planned rotation, you can plan one now; if you have been using one, mid-winter is a good time to consider whether it is successful, or if not, what alternative arrangement you can make. It may be that you need to grow more of some crops and less of others, depending on your family's preferences, and the type of soil and weather prevailing in your area. You may feel that varieties of certain crops could be changed or there may be some new ones available, which are heavier cropping, earlier, or better flavoured.

All these ideas can be put on paper now, just as the new season's seed catalogues arrive and while the weather forbids outdoor work for most of this season and the next one. Snow, frost, gales and floods can be the order of the day; no new plant growth will be showing above ground in the vegetable or fruit garden unless you take steps to encourage it.

Work will consist mainly of finishing off jobs and guarding remaining crops against the weather and birds. But the gardening year never stops completely, and there is always some plant ready to start growing. Early potato varieties can be put to sprout in mid-winter and forcing of outdoor rhubarb can begin. In mild and sheltered gardens, crops which are being wintered under cloches may start to put out fresh leaves, in particular spinach and chives, and herbs in the greenhouse may also begin to grow.

# At~a~glance diary

**Dig:**      all ground as necessary

**Improve the soil:**      by liming as necessary, according to the results obtained from testing with a proprietary soil-test kit

**Put to sprout:**      potato (early varieties)

**Force:**      chicory, rhubarb

**Spray:**      all soft fruit, e.g. blackberries, currants (red and black), gooseberries, loganberries and similar berries, raspberries

**Choose:**      new varieties of vegetables and soft fruit from the new season's catalogues

**Prune:**      vine

**Ventilate:**      all glass

**Stored crops:**      look over for damage or rotting, particularly in beetroot, carrot, onion, parsnip, potato & swede

**Plan:**      arrangement and type of fruit to be grown; rotation of vegetables so as to avoid pest and disease build up and to make the best use of plant foods in the soil

# Jobs to do

**Digging**
Finish the digging and manuring as soon as possible, when the weather and soil conditions permit.

**Improving the soil**
Another method of improving the soil, besides manuring, is liming. It is important to do this carefully and not to lime indiscriminately; it is easy to overlime but almost impossible to reduce the alkalinity to a desirable level. Although liming the vegetable garden was formerly regarded as a routine annual job, it is by no means essential and it can easily do more harm than good. A very alkaline soil can result in deficiencies of several mineral nutrients in certain plants,

because the alkalinity reacts upon these nutrients so that their nature is changed, and the roots of such plants cannot absorb them.

So it is important to find out what the pH value of your soil is – that is, the degree of acidity or alkalinity – before liming it. The pH value is a scale of values in which neutrality (the point exactly between acidity and alkalinity) is 7.0; anything lower than this is acid, and above it, alkaline.

*Testing soil to discover its pH : by using a soil-testing kit the acidity/alkalinity value can be determined. A soil sample is placed in a glass tube, indicator solution added to it and the mixture thoroughly shaken. The colour change gives the pH.*

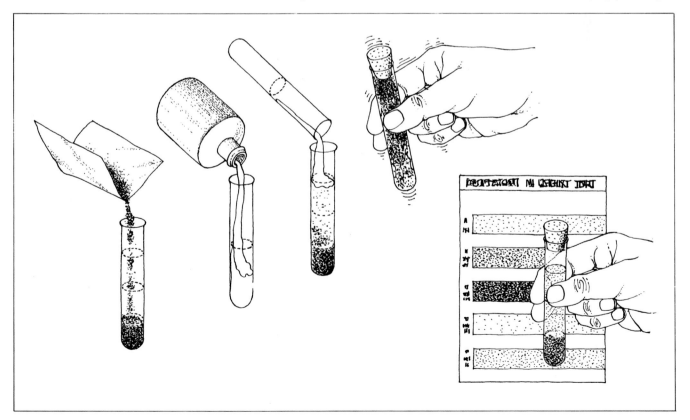

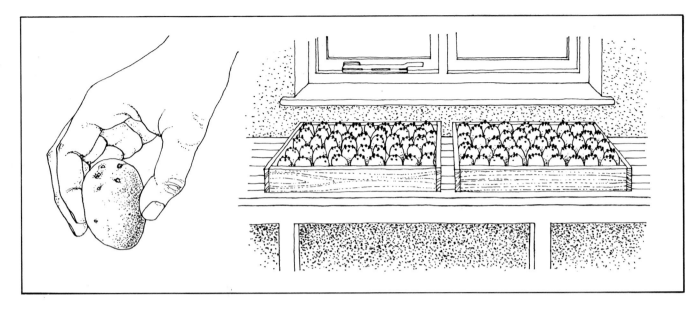

*If potato tubers are encouraged to sprout before being planted, they will crop earlier and more heavily. They are put in a cool, light place, with the 'eyes' upwards, for about eight weeks.*

You can test your soil with a proprietary soil-testing kit available from garden shops—directions for using it will be given with the kit.

Lime has an additional structural benefit on heavy clay soils; due to a chemical and physical reaction with the clay particles, it helps to improve the drainage and aeration. Some soil-borne fungus diseases, such as clubroot of brassicas, are encouraged in acid soils and a little lime will help to keep them at bay.

There are two sorts of lime chiefly used in crop gardening: hydrated (slaked) lime (calcium hydroxide), and ground limestone (calcium carbonate). Hydrated lime is quick acting and caustic; it will burn plant leaves and stems; ground lime is slow acting and safer to use. Its effect is gradual and long-lasting (chalk is similar to ground limestone but less slow in its effect).

Lime can be put on about six weeks after adding organic matter, not at the same time, otherwise it reacts with it so that nitrogen is given off and lost as ammonia. Better still, put it on in the year you are not manuring a particular piece of soil, for instance where root crops are to be grown. If you add it in the same season as organic matter, even with a gap of several weeks between the two applications, there will still be some loss of nitrogen. Lime should be sprinkled evenly all over the area to be treated, at the rate recommended on the soil-testing chart, and then forked lightly in. If you do not have access to such a chart, average rates of ground limestone to apply to a soil of pH 5.0 are: 210g per sq m (7oz per sq yd) for sandy soil, 300g per sq m (10oz per sq yd) for loam, and 420g per sq m (14oz per sq yd) for clay soil. Soft fruit has no particular preference for acid or alkaline soils, but grows marginally better in those which are slightly acid, about pH 6.5.

## Sprouting

Mid-winter is the time to get early varieties of potatoes going, so that they are ready for planting in early spring. Small tubers are used, about the size of a hen's egg, and they are put in single layers in containers in a light cool place, to encourage the dormant buds or 'eyes' to start growing; where the 'eyes' crowd together is the top of the tuber.

## Forcing

Chicory and rhubarb can still be forced in succession. Outdoor rhubarb can also be forced by covering the crowns with boxes, buckets or barrels, and then piling leafmould, straw or garden compost round and over the containers, so that the plants are in the dark and protected from cold. Depending on the weather, stems should be ready for pulling about six weeks later.

Opposite: *Crop rotation of vegetables to avoid the occurrence of pests and diseases in the soil, and to make use of all the nutrients. In the first year in the first section plant the brassicas; in the second section grow potatoes and some of the potash-loving crops, and in the third put the beans, some roots and the marrow family. Move them all on one plot in the second year.*

## Spraying

If the winter wash was not applied in early winter, it can still be done in mid-winter, or even in late winter, although by that time there will be many other jobs to do.

## Choosing crops

The new season's vegetable seed catalogues are published during early and mid-winter and it is a good time to order your new stock. There will be new varieties to try, old ones which were successful to re-order, others to discard and completely new vegetables to experiment with. Your family's likes and dislikes need to be remembered; the expensive vegetables are well worth growing and those that are not available in most shops are particularly desirable to grow: Jerusalem artichokes, chicory, endive, calabrese, celeriac, winter radish and kohlrabi are prime examples.

As with vegetables, you can choose the most suitable fruit varieties at this time, but it is much more a 'one-off' job; once done, you will not need to choose again for many years, except for stawberries. But make sure that you get plants certified free from virus disease; certified schemes will be mentioned in the nursery catalogues. Varieties of fruits and vegetables are listed and described separately.

## Pruning

If the vine pruning has not been done, this should be completed with all possible speed.

## Ventilating

On the occasional fine, mild day, give the greenhouse, cloches and frames, a good airing, otherwise keep the ventilators only just open. Clean off any condensation from the inside and any snow from the roof outside. In bitterly cold weather, shut down the ventilators completely, until the weather changes for the better again.

## Stored crops

Check the roots, potatoes, onions and so on occasionally for rotting and mice attacks; also check the temperature in case of frost if they are in an outdoor store.

## Planning

Growing plants to provide food will be much more sucessful if you take time, before planting or sowing, to think about various aspects of their cultivation. The soft fruits, for instance, are permanent crops which are likely to be in the ground for at least twelve years. It is worth taking care over choosing the site, aspect, soil and its initial treatment. When planning the layout of the plants, remember that room

# Sowing and Planting

| Group A manure in autumn–winter | Group B manure in autumn–winter, potash-high fertilizer before or planting | Group C general fertilizer before sowing/ planting |
|---|---|---|
| broccoli, heading (winter cauliflower) | Jerusalem artichoke | beetroot |
| broccoli, sprouting | aubergine | carrot |
| Brussels sprout | garlic | parsnip |
| cabbage | onion | radish |
| cauliflower | pepper | **manure in spring** |
| kale | potato | bean, French |
| kohlrabi | shallot | (Kidney) or |
| swede | tomato | runner (pole) |
| turnip | | celeriac |
| | | celery |
| | | cucumber |
| | | marrow |
| | | pea |
| | | squash |
| | | sweetcorn |

Movables: broad beans, chicory, endive, leek, lettuce, spinach, spinach beet, Swiss chard (seakale beet)

Permanents: globe artichoke, asparagus, rhubarb

should be allowed, not only for growth, but for comfortable picking, pruning, spraying and cultivating.

Choose sunny and warm sites where there is shelter from wind. Blackberries and loganberries will tolerate a little shade. A position with easy access to water is advisable, as soft fruit often needs some irrigation in most summers. Unless you are very cramped for space, keep the fruit separate from the vegetables, except during the first year or two, while the bushes and canes are growing. The space available between the plants in the early stages can be used for the smaller vegetable crops.

Vegetables are nearly all annual crops; one or two are permanent and some are biennial. In order to make use of all the nutrients available at different levels of soil and prevent the build-up of soil-borne disease and pests, the various vegetables should be grown on different pieces of ground each year.

There are many vegetables grown, but the business of what to grow where can be simplified, since they can be put into three groups: the brassicas and leaf crops, the root

*Kohlrabi may look like a sputnik but it tastes delicious, eaten at the right stage. It should be lifted when it is about the size of a golf-ball to be at its tastiest and tenderest.*

## Crops to be harvested

Brussels sprout, cabbage, cauliflower (winter-heading broccoli), celery, chicory, leek, rhubarb (forced)

## Available from store

beetroot, carrot, garlic, onion, parsnip, potato, radish (winter), shallot, swede, turnip

*Swiss chard is one of the few dual-purpose vegetables: the leaves can be cooked and eaten like spinach, and the stems like asparagus – which they resemble in flavour.*

crops and the legumes. The remainder which do not fit exactly into these groups can be put with one or another of them, according to their cultivation requirements. To practice crop rotation, you divide your vegetable plot into three, and grow each group on them in turn. A suitable plan is shown in the diagrams, which also take into account the manurial and fertilizing needs of each vegetable.

At the end of the first growing season, each group moves on one, so that A goes to B's place, B goes to C's place, and C goes to A's place. At the end of the second growing season, all move on a place again and by the time the fourth growing season starts, each group is back in its original site.

The most important point about rotation is that brassicas do not occupy the same ground more than one year in three. The crops that need potash particularly, as well as some manure but not as much as group A, are all in group B, and can follow the brassicas. The crops that should not be grown in ground manured the previous winter are the roots, but they do appreciate a little fertilizer. With them, you can group those crops for which manure is dug in during early spring, as they will not be planted out until late spring or even early summer.

The manure for the brassicas should be put on in autumn

if possible; some gardeners advocate planting them in ground immediately after lifting early potatoes so that they are grown on ground manured for a previous crop, but this can mean that the soil is rather loose and soft, and may lead to 'blowing'.

The group of movables can be fitted in where suitable, remembering that they are mostly leafy crops and need to grow fast, so that group A or B would probably be best. However, leek remains in the ground most of the year, so would perhaps fit best with group A; lettuce and radish are particularly quick-growing, so make good catch crops, and endive might fit in after a crop of early beetroot or carrot. Permanent crops which are not included in the rotation are globe artichoke, asparagus and rhubarb. Lastly, tradition has it that onions are best in the same bed every year, if they do well in it, but they are subject to various diseases, so it would seem advisable to include them in a rotation, which also takes into account the manure and fertilizer needs of each vegetable.

# Late Winter

The main change in the climatic conditions during this season is the appreciable lengthening of the days. The temperature may still be low; there may be snow and frost throughout late winter or there may be constant rain and flooding. Even so, the increase in the quality of light and in its strength will be affecting temperate climate plants so that they become ready to grow later, if not during the next few weeks. When they do grow, it will be very quickly.

In spite of chilly conditions, some crops will grow if planted outdoors; others will germinate from seed if sown indoors in warmth. Soil and compost can be prepared for these and, in fact, much of your work this season will consist of preparations, though there will still only be a little to do. The state of the soil outdoors will prevent much cultivation, but indoors you can finish the preparation of the greenhouse border soil for tomatoes, and you can prepare the composts for sowing seed and for those composts that will be needed later for mature plants.

When the weather permits, fertilizers can be given to a variety of fruit and vegetables. An occasional stroll round the plants will show you what damage has been caused by the winter weather and where tying-in is needed, whether of trained fruit or protective netting. It will show the need to get out a patch of weeds missed in the autumn and a general tidying up and clearing off of rotting leaves, twigs, and crops which are finishing.

The management of the greenhouse will need extra care now that you are starting off some crops in it. The light transmission should be as good as possible and the heat provided by the propagator should be steady. Fresh air, not draughts, should come in through the ventilators, and newly germinated seedlings should not be allowed to run short of water.

# At~a~glance diary

**Prepare the soil for:** sowing and planting outdoors, sowing and planting indoors

**Sow seeds outdoors of:** broad bean

**Sow seeds under glass (in heat) of:** aubergine, pepper, tomato

**Plant outdoors:** Jerusalem artichoke, shallot

maincrop potato; earlies if not already done

**Prune:** raspberry

**Lime:** as necessary, if not already done

**Fertilize:** Jerusalem artichoke, asparagus, soft fruit such as blackberries, currants (black and red), gooseberries, loganberries and associated berries, raspberries; soil to be sown or planted later this season or early in the next

**Cloche:** strawberries

**Protect:** against birds: brassicas, currants, shallots, gooseberries; against cold: stored root crops, plants under cloches and young plants in greenhouse

**Stored crops:** look over for damage or rotting, especially such crops as beetroot, carrot, onion, parsnip, potato and swede

# Jobs to do

### Preparing the soil for outdoor sowing

There is only one crop which can really stand being sown outdoors in late winter: broad beans. As with sowing them in late autumn, there is no need to produce the fine, crumb-like soil advised in early spring. The soil is unlikely to be in a fit state for such cultivation but, provided it is reasonably level, and free from lumps, stones and rubbish, it should provide a satisfactory seed-bed for broad beans (see Late Autumn for details).

### Preparing the soil for outdoor planting

This should be done as early in late winter as possible, to give the soil time to settle and absorb any fertilizer applied,

*There are various containers in which seeds can be sown; the standard one is a wooden seed-tray, although modern trays are plastic. Seeds can be sown singly in individual but continuous plastic pots, or in peat cubes, which can be planted.*

so that the crops to be planted, Jerusalem artichokes and shallots, can be put in well on time. You will have done the initial digging and clearing during the autumn or early winter; all that remains to be done now is to fork over the top few centimetres (inches), remove any weeds and apply fertilizers if required (see Fertilizing, below).

### Preparing the soil for sowing indoors

When sowing seeds in artificial warmth under glass, it is usual to sow them in containers, and for good results it is best to use a special soil mixture, or compost. One of the most commonly used standard composts is called the John Innes seed compost, and it consists of : 2 parts medium loam, 1 part granulated peat and 1 part coarse silver sand (parts by volume). With 36l (1 bushel) of this is mixed 44g (1½oz) superphosphate and 21g (¾oz) ground limestone. All these ingredients should be put through a 0.6cm (¼in) mesh sieve. For best results, the loam should be sterilized before mixing.

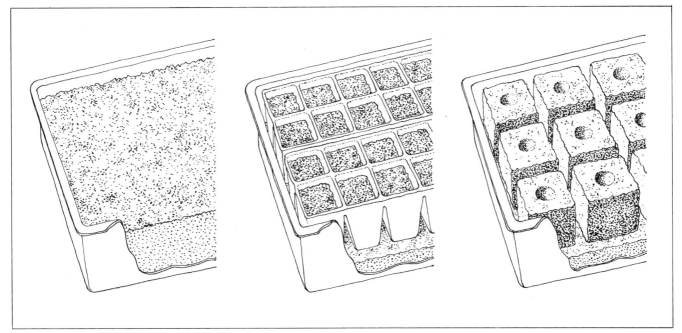

This mixture will be free from pests, fungus diseases and weed seeds; it will be of a consistency which provides the best drainage and aeration for most seedlings and will provide the right kind of plant foods, There are other proprietary seed composts available, usually consisting of a mixture of mainly peat and coarse sand, and instructions for their use are provided with the container.

The containers, which can be plastic or wooden seed-trays, pots or pans, should be filled evenly with compost, firmed down so that 1.2cm (½in) of space is left at the top for watering after germination of the seeds, and the compost then watered from the bottom.

### Preparing the soil for planting indoors

Towards the end of late winter is not too early to get the soil in the greenhouse borders ready for planting the slightly tender crops that you wish to harvest earlier than is possible outdoors. The preparation of the soil for

*At this time of the year it is a good idea to assemble and inspect all containers to ensure that they are ready for the new season.*

tomato growing will have been started in early or mid-winter and you can complete this now by digging to a depth of one or two spits, at the same time mixing in rotted manure, garden compost or similar material. You can also add a slow-acting organic fertilizer now, or wait until early spring. A suitable fertilizer is the John Innes Base, which consists of: 2 parts superphosphate, 2 parts hoof and horn and 1 part sulphate of potash (parts by weight). After thorough mixing, 120g (4oz) is added to each square metre (sq yd).

If you live in a mild and sheltered area you should be able to plant the other tender crops out in the greenhouse at the end of early spring, so you can prepare the soil for these also – aubergine, melon and pepper. For the details see Early Spring. All are heavy feeders and need a rich soil.

### Sowing seed outdoors

The real rush with sowing vegetable seeds does not come until mid-spring and in late winter the only one that can be attempted is broad bean and that only in warm gardens. For details of sowing, see Early Spring.

### Sowing seed under glass (in heat)

You can start off some of the tender vegetables towards the end of the late winter, provided you can give them some warmth. To avoid warming the entire greenhouse, a propagator is very useful and is a kind of miniature heated greenhouse in itself, usually heated by electricity. In various sizes, can be heated to a variety of maximum temperatures, and may or may not have thermostats fitted.

When you are deciding which vegetables to grow in this way, and how many, remember that they will quickly get too big for the propagator and will need to be moved out into a much lower temperature, unless you are proposing to heat the greenhouse temporarily for a few weeks with a paraffin heater. If you are not going to heat the greenhouse, you can get over the problem to some extent by hardening them off gradually and thus slowing down their growth, or you can buy a much larger propagator than is needed for the seedlings and spread the young plants out in it, until either the temperature outside rises sufficiently, or they have been suitably hardened.

Late winter is a tricky time to start off seeds, even if you can supply the temperature they need. The light is not as good as it would be at their normal germination times and problems come once they have developed into young plants. However, with care and a good deal of attention, it is possible to get them going successfully. Seeds to sow are: aubergine, pepper and tomato; temperature should be maintained both day and night at 16-18°C (60-65°F). Germination times will be: aubergine, 14-21 days; pepper, 7-14 days, and tomato, 8-14 days.

All can be sown in prepared seed-trays, spacing the seed evenly on the surface of the compost and then covering with about 3mm ($\frac{1}{8}$in) of finely sieved, moist compost.

*Strawberry plants, put into a heated greenhouse in late winter, may bear ripe fruit by mid-spring.*

*Tomato seedlings grown in individual pots will be stronger than if they are sown broadcast.* Right: *Shallots are planted at half the bulb's depth, after the withered leaves have been cut off.*

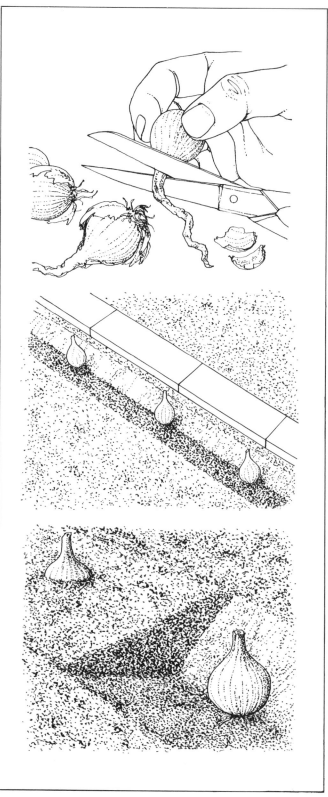

You can also sow them in individual, 5cm (2in) pots of clay, plastic or peat, sowing two or three in each, and later removing the weakest, to leave one seedling in each pot.

Firm the compost and give a light sprinkle with water if it is at all on the dry side, then cover with brown or white paper and top with glass or plastic sheet. The glass or plastic keeps in the moisture, and the paper traps any condensation and prevents drops falling on to the compost and possibly disturbing the seeds.

### Planting outdoors
Late winter is supposed to be the traditional time for planting shallots, though often the soil is too wet or cold. Mild conditions will get best results and you may find that you have to wait until early spring for the soil to dry or the temperature to rise. Shallots are grown from sets;

plant each 15-20cm (6-8in) apart, in rows about 38cm (15in) apart. Before planting, cut off the withered brown remains of the leaves, otherwise the birds tweak them out of the ground. Sit the sets just below the surface of the soil. Do not press them into the ground, but make a shallow depression to put them in, and pull a little soil round them to half way up the bulb.

Jerusalem artichokes can be planted any time in late winter or early spring. Choose tubers about the size of a hen's egg, and plant in holes 15cm (6in) deep and 45-60cm (18-24in) apart; rows should be about 90cm (36in) apart. You can expect to start seeing shoots in two to four weeks' time, depending on the weather.

### Sprouting
Maincrop varieties of potatoes can be put to sprout in late winter, in the same way as the earlies were (see Mid-Winter). It is still possible to start the earlies off and get the crop at a reasonable time, provided you do it as early this month as possible.

### Pruning
Raspberries should have the tips of the canes cut off now. They may have died back or been broken during the winter; moreover, shortening the very long canes of the modern varieties makes picking more manageable and encourages the plants to produce more fruiting laterals.

### Liming
This should be dealt with quickly, as the time for applying fertilizers is approaching; as with manures, lime can react with certain fertilizers so that plant foods are lost, particularly those such as sulphate of ammonia, superphosphate and basic slag. To be on the safe side, never apply lime directly before or after putting on a fertilizer.

### Fertilizing
As many plants will soon be starting to grow in earnest and as you will be sowing and planting new crops during the next two seasons, late winter is a good time to put on any mineral plant foods that you may think necessary. There will then be time for them to be dissolved in the soil moisture and become part of the soil complex; they will undergo various changes under the influence of the soil constituents, both living and inert, which will ensure that plant roots can absorb them, along with the soil water. Plants can only 'drink' the mineral nutrients from the soil; the particles must be dissolved in water before the plant can make use of them via the roots.

*A well-grown shallot plant should have about eight or ten new bulbs of moderate size, and five or six if the bulbs are large ones.*

Of course, plants feed in other ways; as a result of the process known as photosynthesis, the green parts of the plant, especially the leaves, make (or synthesize), in the presence of light (*photo* = light), sugar and oxygen from the water and carbon dioxide of the air; sugar is then turned into starch and stored in this form. This is a very simplified version of the way plants feed and live but it is worth remembering that they need other foods than mineral nutrients and they obtain some of these from the air and rain.

Fertilizers and the soil are the main sources of supply of mineral nutrients; plants must have, in particular, nitrogen (N), phosphorus (P) and potassium (K), and in general

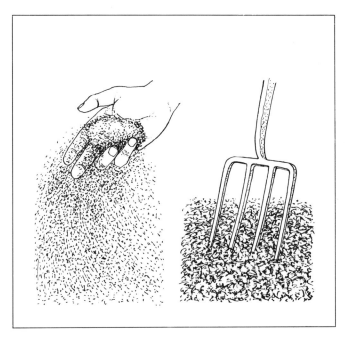

*When applying a powder or granular fertilizer to any plant, always sprinkle it evenly over the area round the plant, and then rake or water in.*

these three must be provided in larger quantities than other minerals. Calcium, magnesium and sulphur are needed in moderate amounts, comparatively speaking, and there are a good number of nutrients or elements such as iron, manganese and boron which need only be provided in tiny quantities. These are called 'trace' elements.

Modern fertilizers may contain mostly one element in a usable form – these are sometimes called 'straights' – for instance, sulphate of ammonia, or they may contain several (the compound fertilizers), when N, P and K (and other nutrients) will be contained in them in varying proportions. Whatever type of fertilizer it is, there will be an analysis on the container which shows the percentage of the nutrient or nutrients in the fertilizer. Sulphate of ammonia is usually standardized at 20-21 per cent N; a compound fertilizer will show an analysis of, for example, 6 per cent N, 9 per cent $P_2O_5$, and 12 per cent $K_2O$. In the case of phosphorus and potassium, for technical reasons, their content is expressed in terms of the phosphoric acid and potash content, rather than the pure element. None of them in fact is present in element form – nitrogen is there as a compound chemical substance, not as nitrogen gas – but the percentage given is a guarantee of the quantity of the nutrient content and the amount of fertilizer to be applied can be based on these figures.

The three major plant nutrients, N, P and K, have varying functions. Nitrogen affects the growth of leaves and stems, and ensures a good green colour and strong, vigorous development. Lack of it results in yellow or pale green leaves and stunted, slow-growing plants. Phosphorus affects root growth and is especially important for the roots of seedlings and young plants. Potassium is associated with the maturity of the plant: flowering, fruiting, development of seeds and colouring. Lack of phosphorus is not easily detected, though short, rather 'hard' plants, with purplish tints to the leaves, are some of the more obvious symptoms. Lack of potash will be obvious in poor fruiting, reddish or brown leaf edges, small and few flowers and little formation of seed.

These major plant foods also affect other processes in the plant and react with one another according to how much of each is absorbed. Trace and minor elements have various jobs to do as well, so the business of plant feeding is a complicated one. Adding fertilizers to the soil needs to be done warily, never in larger quantities than advised by the manufacturers and, if possible, according to the results of a soil analysis, which can be done with a soil-testing kit, or by a professional adviser.

However, if neither of these is available, provided you have used organic matter earlier and you are careful with quantities, you should not do any damage. The organic matter will act as a buffer if too much fertilizer is given and as you build up the soil fertility with it, you will be able to do with less and less fertilizer. Eventually, there may not be a need to add any at all.

When you do apply fertilizers, sprinkle them evenly over the soil surface in exactly the quantities advised, about ten to fourteen days in advance of sowing or planting and mix them into the top few centimetres (inches) with a fork. The soft fruits can be fed towards the end of late winter, if not treated the previous late summer; use a compound fertilizer with more potash in it than nitrogen or phosphorus, since they are fruiting plants. Asparagus and Jerusalem artichoke can be given potash, preferably as wood ash, at the rate of 120g per sq m (4oz per sq yd) to established asparagus and rather more to the artichokes.

Bulking the fertilizers with coarse sand is one way of getting them spread evenly, or you can mix them with sieved soil. It is usually simplest to give a compound fertilizer, though if a crop has a particularly heavy demand for one nutrient, a straight can be used instead. In general the leafy vegetables will need more nitrogen; the roots, tubers and bulbs, as well as the fruiting vegetables need

*There are many different sorts of cloches available: it is a case of choosing the size and type most suited to your crops.*

potash and all when young need phosphorus. Note that marrows, including courgettes, need nitrogen, rather than potash, although they are a fruiting vegetable.

## Cloching
If you want to bring on strawberries early, covering them with cloches now will give fruit late in spring, earlier in warm gardens. Clear the plants of weeds and debris first, fertilize if necessary, and then cover. Straw will not be necessary as the berries will keep clean when protected. Other crops may begin to grow again; clean up these also and clear the cloche itself of mud and debris.

## Protecting
Safeguards against birds and cold will still be very necessary, in particular for brassicas, shallots, gooseberries and currants (birds) and stored root crops, vegetables under cloches and young plants in the greenhouse (cold).

## Stored crops
Continue routine inspections of these and increase the frequency of inspection, as all crops will be ageing and will rot more quickly and have less resistance to infection.

## Crops to be harvested
broccoli (purple sprouting), Brussels sprout, cabbage, cauliflower (winter-heading broccoli), chicory (forced), leek, rhubarb (forced), Swiss chard (protected)

## Available from store
jerusalem artichoke, beetroot, celeriac, garlic, onion, parsnip, potato, radish (winter), shallot, swede, turnip

# Controls & Treatments

With good cultivation and careful management of the soil, you should be able to ensure that crops are strong and healthy. Plants which always have the food and water they need are seldom badly infected with disease or attacked by pests and are often not infested at all. Plants which have become weak are the main targets and an epidemic is generally a sign that you have not supplied or ensured the right growing conditions.

What is known as 'garden hygiene' is important. It means keeping the garden clear of piles of various objects: bricks, stones, corrugated iron and wire netting, pots and boxes, twigs and branches, polythene sheet and so on, all of which provide homes and shelter for small and large pests, such as mice, rabbits and insects, and for sources of infectious diseases.

Many weeds are alternative hosts for these troubles; the remains of crops left in the ground can also be the starting point for infestations, so can plant supports and protection. If you have concrete paths, keep them free of soil; keep grass paths mown and gravel paths clear of weeds.

When you are buying new stock, order from nurseries or garden centres which supply plants certified free of disease (where there are certification schemes in force for a particular species), and which have a good national reputation. Tempting though it is, don't accept offers of plants from friends unless you know the plants to be clear of diseases; they are so often infected, in particular with virus, which may not be apparent.

Various 'biological' methods of control are beginning to be available to gardeners, for the control of red spider mite and whitefly so that chemicals do not have to be used. There are also many predatory insects naturally present in the garden; ladybirds are a well-known example. By not using chemicals or by using those specific to the pest, these beneficial insects will survive and help to keep down the marauders of your crops.

If you do have to resort to chemicals, there are some modern kinds which are particularly safe and effective. Bioresmethrin is one of these, similar to pyrethrum, but even better and safer. Another safe but older one is derris; it needs to be used fairly frequently for best effects. Remember that it is a fish poison, and keep well away from ornamental ponds. Malathion is still the safest and least persistent of the phosphorus insecticides, but bioresmethrin seems likely to take its place. Benomyl is a systemic fungicide which will control grey mould (*Botrytis cinerea*) and mildew; however, it is a worm killer, and it seems that these diseases are becoming resistant to it, so we may have to return to sulphur and copper. Diazinon is a useful soil insecticide which breaks down very quickly. Methiocarb is the best of the snail and slug killers if you are desperate, but there are other, safer ways of dealing with these pests if you must kill them.

There are various other chemicals which may need to be occasionally but in general, you should be able to sidestep their use by cultural methods of control, hand picking of pests and the use of natural predators. In any case, there is usually too much crop and the occasional nibble or scar on some of it is nothing to lose sleep about.

If, early in your gardening career, you need to sterilize soil, before you have got it into good condition, there is a widely available liquid sterilizer called formalin which will kill pests, fungal and bacterial diseases and weed-seeds. It is diluted with water in a 1:49 ratio and is then given off as a gas when mixed with soil. Treated soil should not be used for planting until all smell has left it; this will take between two and six weeks. The solution is unpleasant to use, as it is irritating to the eyes, nose and throat. Full instructions for use are provided on the container.

Sometimes the greenhouse may need a thorough cleaning out by fumigation, using sulphur candles. These, when lit, give off sulphur dioxide gas, which will kill fungal diseases and red spider mite. The greenhouse should be tightly sealed, and is best treated overnight. Both this and formalin are poisonous to warm-blooded animals and must be used with great care. *Always* keep all pesticides out of the way of children and household animals and wash out all containers and sprayers thoroughly after use.

There are various kinds of plant troubles: insect pests and fungus diseases (which are likely to cause the most trouble), bacteria, viruses, nutrient deficiencies, weather damage and attacks by small mammals (mice, voles, squirrels, rabbits, coypu) and birds.

The main insect pests, fungus diseases, and harmful mammals and birds are detailed in the list which follows. Of the remainder, the symptoms of bacterial infection are usually a liquid, unpleasant-smelling rot and black or brown discoloration. Root crops in store, and occasionally celery, are most likely to be troubled and are best destroyed. Viruses infect the nucleus of the plant cell and any chemical which would destroy them would also destroy the plant. Infected plants must be completely lifted and destroyed as soon as seen, so that healthy plants remain healthy. Viruses are mostly spread by the feeding of sucking insect pests, especially greenfly. Symptoms of virus diseases may be yellow discoloration of the leaves, stunted and slow growth, malformation of leaves and flowers and little or no crop.

Nutrient deficiencies rarely occur in the average garden; lack of nitrogen is one of the few that may be apparent in plants growing in quick-draining soils. Lack of iron and lack of magnesium may show in alkaline soils; symptoms are yellow-to-white discoloration of the young leaves, for iron, or yellowing between the veins and later of the whole leaf, in the older leaves, for magnesium. These are the most likely nutrient deficiencies but, provided you manage the soil as advised, you should not run into this kind of trouble.

The weather is always with us and some damage to plants will occur which is unavoidable. Hail pitting of leaves and fruits, tearing and breaking, blackening and browning of leaves by wind is typical. Cracking and splitting of fruits, roots and tubers due to irregular supplies of water is another type of damage, when heavy rain or watering follows a dry period. Scorch of seedlings and scalding (browning) of tomato leaves and grape fruits by too hot sun can be prevented by shading. Blackening of strawberry flower centres by frost can be warded off with coverings on cold nights.

Eating of bark, nibbling of stored crops, attacks on peas and beans, removal of strawberries by mice and squirrels, and damage from birds, especially pigeons, sparrows, bullfinches and blackbirds, on brassicas, the onion family, bush fruit buds, fruit generally and tomatoes, can all be warded off with netting draped securely above and round the plants.

*Potato virus diseases can ruin the crop, if the haulm is infected; they are transmitted by aphids, but seed potatoes are certified clean. This is typical leaf-roll virus.*

# Pests & Diseases

*Aphids (greenfly, blackfly, currant-leaf-blister aphid, root aphids)*

Tiny insects 2mm ($\frac{1}{8}$in) long, green, black, pink, grey, blue-grey, cream. Found in great numbers on undersides of youngest leaves and tips of shoots, which become curled and discoloured as the result of feeding; new growth is severely stunted. Root aphids mostly found on roots of lettuce. Feed by sucking sap from plant with pointed, stylet-like mouthparts. Hatch from over-wintering eggs in early spring, cast skins several times as they grow, and one or two produce a winged adult form, the last generation of which lays eggs to over-winter. The wingless forms are all female and produce young aphids asexually. Spray in winter with tar oil winter wash, or with bioresmethrin, derris or malathion in spring and summer.

*Big-bud mite (blackcurrants)*

Migrates in mid-spring to healthy buds; difficult to control, but some effect obtained by spraying with lime-sulphur when flower clusters look like miniature bunches of grapes. Remove and destroy swollen buds.

*Blackfly*, see *Aphids*

*Blight (potato and tomato)*

A fungus disease which produces dark brown, later black, blotches and spots on leaves and stems, and brown patches in the flesh of tubers; sunken areas in the skin indicate them. Most severe infections during wet summers, especially in warm weather. Apply protective sprays containing copper or zineb early in mid-summer and then every two to three weeks until autumn. Destroy infected haulm and tubers when crop harvested.

*Cabbage root fly (all brassicas)*

Tiny white maggots feed on roots of seedlings and young plants, causing swelling and malformation. First brood

*Big-bud mite in blackcurrants is a serious trouble; the mite infests the new buds as they develop in spring and, as a result, they do not leaf and fruit. The mite carries the virus disease reversion, which results in very small crops.*

appears late in mid-spring, second one late in early summer, sometimes a third in the middle of late summer. Eggs are laid by adult flies in soil near plant roots; maggots pupate in soil over-winter. Surround young plants with 15cm (6in) diameter black plastic sheet or plastic foam discs placed on soil, to prevent egg laying or treat soil with bromophos at planting time.

*Cabbage white butterfly and cabbage moth (all leafy brassicas)*
Yellowish-green and black, or brown or green caterpillars, up to 2.5cm (1in) long when fully grown, feed on outer leaves and hearts. Hatch from eggs laid on leaves in spring and become chrysalids after four weeks. Second, third and fourth generations may occur, feeding until late autumn. Handpick caterpillars; crush eggs on leaves or dust leaves with derris.

*Capsid*
Green, fast-moving creatures, like greenfly, but much larger. Feed in a similar way, but cause much worse damage. Leaves with pinprick holes, later tattered; growth severely stunted, flowers one-sided. Spray plant and soil with dimethoate.

*Carrot-fly (carrots, celery, parsley, parsnip)*
Tiny white maggots tunnel into roots. Eggs laid in soil by adults in mid-spring; second brood of maggots appears in late summer and sometimes a third in autumn. Sow maincrop carrots at end of late spring, very thinly. Apply diazinon to soil.

*Caterpillars*
Various colours and sizes; feed on leaves. Handpick; treat with derris or fenitrothion.

*Celery leaf fly (celeriac, celery, parsley, parsnip)*
Eggs laid in leaves by adults, spring to early summer. Maggots hatch to feed on internal leaf tissues, causing pale brown blisters; leaves die. Second brood in late summer, third brood in mild seasons in autumn. Handpick leaves, spray with malathion in a severe attack.

*Clubroot (all brassicas)*
A fungus disease carried in the soil, which infects the roots, producing swollen, contorted and rotten tissue. Seedlings and young plants can be destroyed. Leaves wilt and turn grey-green. Dip roots of transplants in a mixture of pure calomel at 60g per 0.6 litre (2oz per pint) of water or 14g ($\frac{1}{2}$oz) thiophanate-methyl before planting in sterilized compost. Destroy infected plants, including the roots; improve soil drainage and maintain pH at 7.0. Do not plant in infected ground, if possible, for at least seven years.

*Flea beetle (turnip, swede, beetroot, cabbage, kale, radish)*
Tiny blue-black, or black and yellow beetles, which hop when disturbed. Feed in spring on seedling and young leaves, making small circular holes. Adults live through winter and lay eggs in early summer. Dust leaves with derris at once if any signs of damage seen.

*Gooseberry sawfly*
Caterpillars feed on leaves, leaving only skeleton of veins. Eggs laid on leaves in mid-spring; green and black caterpillars hatch from these, and a second brood can appear in early summer, with a third in late summer. Central leaves are attacked first. Handpick and spray with fenitrothion or derris if necessary.

*Greenfly*, see *Aphids*

*Grey mould (Botrytis cinerea)*
Fungus disease which produces grey furry mould on leaves, stems, flowers and fruits. Plant tissue rots and discolours. Worst in cool, damp conditions. Spreads rapidly in stuffy greenhouses. Handpick and destroy diseased parts; improve ventilation and raise temperature; spray with benomyl.

*Leaf-hopper*
Tiny insect pest which feeds by sucking sap from leaves, producing patches of cream-coloured mottling. Occurs on the underside of leaves and hops when disturbed. Wings develop as insect matures. See *Aphids* for control.

*The most serious disease of brassicas is a fungus called clubroot, which is soil-borne and infects the roots. These swell and decay, and the plants cease to grow and eventually die.*

*Mildew, powdery*

Fungus disease, symptoms of which are powdery white substance on leaves, stem, flowers and fruit. Infects tips of new shoots and youngest leaves first. Remove infected parts and spray with benomyl or dinocap. Mildew on lettuce is a different type called downy mildew, which needs treating with zineb.

*Onion fly*

Adults lay eggs in soil near young plants in late spring, and maggots hatch from eggs and enter bulbing portion of stem on which they feed. When fully grown they return to the soil, where they pupate until the following spring. Leaves of attacked plants turn yellow and wilt; bulb rots. Destroy attacked plants. Treat soil with diazinon before sowing seed or planting sets.

*Potato blight*, see *Blight*

*Raspberry beetle*

Ripening and ripe fruit that contain white maggots may rot. Adult beetles lay eggs in blossom in early summer (in blackberry in mid- to late summer). Spray with derris when the fruit begins to colour.

*Red spider mite*

Minute sucking pests, only visible with a hand lens. Pale red or yellow, feed on undersurface of leaf. In bad infestations webbing is produced, and there will be many white skins, cast as the mites moult and grow. Life cycle is completed in a month, and in hot dry, conditions, they multiply very rapidly. Leaves become mottled, greyish, bronze or yellow, papery and wither. In greenhouse, they will overwinter as adults, and feed in warm conditions. Destroy badly infected plants or plant parts, and spray with bioresmethrin, malathion or dimethoate. Use biological control, the predatory mite *Phytoseiulus perimilis*. Alter the environment so that it is damper and less warm.

*Slugs and snails*

Eat irregular holes in leaves, stems, flowers and fruit. Feed by night, and hide during the day. Present all year. Use methiocarb pellets on soil surface; surround plants with 15cm (6in) wide bands of gritty material. Sink shallow containers of sugary water, stale beer, or diluted milk in soil near crops. For underground slugs, improve soil drainage; liquid slug-killers are, unfortunately, only partially effective.

*Spur blight (fungus disease)*

Found on raspberry canes, as silvery elongated patches surrounding buds, which are killed, New infections occur in spring. Cut out infected canes and thin remainder. Disease usually appears amongst crowded plantings, and on canes weak from lack of food and/or water, so improve

*One effective way of controlling pests and some diseases in a greenhouse is to use smoke-cones which give off toxic vapours.*

growing conditions. Spray remainder of canes with a copper-containing fungicide or with benomyl.

*Tomato blight*, see *Potato blight*

*Tomato leaf-mould*

Fungus disease which may appear in early summer. and be very bad by mid-summer, when it is usually first noticed. Spots on leaves spread into patches and leaves killed; spreads rapidly in conditions of high humidity and temperature and crowded planting. Remove infected part and spray with benomyl. Some varieties are resistant.

*Whitefly*

Minute, white, moth-like insects, whose larvae feed on the undersurface of leaves by sucking the sap from the tissue. In large numbers they severely weaken the plants and produce a sticky substance on which grows black sooty mould, making the plants extremely messy. Introduce the parasitic wasp *Encarsia formosa*; spray with bioresmethrin. Treat as soon as seen, otherwise very difficult to control. Destroy worst infected plants or parts of plants.

# THE FLOWER GARDEN
## Early Spring

In early spring, there is a good deal that you can begin to do in the flower garden, unlike the kitchen garden, where the real work does not start until mid-spring. This season is one of the best for planting and transplanting herbaceous perennials and you can also deal with some bulbs, rock plants and plants grown from seed sown last year.

Although early spring can be treacherous in its weather, blowing hot and cold alternately, you can take advantage of a few mild days which help to dry the soil, and put in plants which, being hardy, will not be harmed if the weather then turns cold. The state of the soil is more important than the temperature; those with sandy soils can move plants more or less at will, but those who have to deal with sticky clays will do better to pick their time for planting, so that plant roots do not have to contend with rather too generous quantities of water. If you are doubtful about moving plants, remember that those with thick fleshy roots are the ones least likely to establish in wet soils.

Another of your main jobs will be getting the lawn into good condition after the winter rains and cold; the grass will start to grow again during the next few weeks and as soon as it does, you should begin the reviving treatment for both turf and soil.

Seed sowing outdoors can begin and the soil will need preparing for this; hardy annuals will be the main type of plant sown, though herbaceous perennials can also be grown from seed. Though they may take longer to become flowering plants than those perennials bought from garden centres and nurseries, they are considerably cheaper and you will be certain that they are strong and free of pests and diseases.

Half-hardy annuals and bedding-plant seeds can be sown in the greenhouse: in frames you can sow dahlias and sweetpeas in containers. Cuttings of various kinds can also be taken in the greenhouse.

# At-a-glance diary

**Prepare the soil for:** sowing and planting outdoors

**Sow seeds outdoors of:** hardy annuals (see Table of Hardy Annuals in Early Summer)

**Sow seeds under glass of:** dahlia, herbaceous perennials, rock plants

**Sow seeds under glass (in heat) of:** half-hardy annuals and bedding plants (see Table in Mid-Winter)

**Plant:** biennials, herbaceous perennials, gladioli, montbretia, autumn-sown sweetpea

**Divide:** herbaceous perennials, snowdrop clumps

**Lawn care:** rake, brush, top, spike; treat moss with lawn and/or a proprietary moss-killer

**Put to sprout:** achimenes, large-flowered begonia, dahlia, gloxinia (sinningia)

**Prick out:** half-hardy annuals, begonia (fibrous-rooted and large-flowered), dahlia, gloxinia (sinningia), streptocarpus

**Pot, topdress:** greenhouse plants (foliage and summer-flowering kinds): e.g., asparagus, cacti, chlorophytum, ferns, fuchsia, hippeastrum, hoya, Italian bellflower jasmine, passion flower, pelargonium, succulents tradescantia, zebrina

**Stop:** late-flowering chrysanthemums

**Increase:** chrysanthemum, dahlia, fuchsia, pelargonium by cuttings

**Greenhouse:** ventilate; space out and protect young plants from sun

**Weed and clear:** over-wintering weeds, weed seedlings from amongst annual seedlings, beds, borders, rock gardens

**Compost heap:** use as mulch; start new heap

# Jobs to do

## Preparing the soil for outdoor sowing

The soil in beds and borders should be prepared for sowing seed as soon as it becomes workable. Drying winds and sun will hasten this condition and, when you find that it no longer sticks to your shoes, you can begin to fork the top few centimetres (inches) and break up the lumps. The initial deep digging should already have been done in autumn or early winter.

Remove stones and weeds as you fork and dust a dressing of superphosphate onto the soil surface as you work, making sure that it covers the area evenly. An average application rate is 45g per sq m (1½oz per sq yd).

Do this seed-bed preparation about ten days before you intend to sow, and then, on the actual day if possible, use a rake to level the surface and reduce the lumps of soil to an even smaller size, like crumbs. If done the day before, cover with plastic sheet overnight to protect from heavy rain.

## Preparing the soil for outdoor planting

There is little work to be done here, as the bulk of it should have been done a few months ago and it is merely a case of forking the surface, removing weeds and other debris, and mixing in a general fertilizer dressing, preferably a slow-acting mixture, such as hoof and horn and bonemeal, or a 'straight' (e.g. dried blood), each at about 60g per sq m (2oz per sq yd). This is done about a week in advance of planting, to give the soil time to absorb the nutrients and so that plant roots do not come into direct contact with the fertilizer particles.

## Sowing seed outdoors

Seeds to sow outdoors towards the end of early spring will be hardy annuals (see Early Winter for list). Since these are all hardy, there should be no difficulty in growing them, but of course the same rules for successful germination apply to these seeds as to any other – they must have moisture, a fine soil surface and, even if they are hardy, a temperature above freezing. So it will pay you to cover the soil in some way for a few days before sowing, with cloches, plastic sheet or tunnels to warm it up a little.

Scatter your seed evenly and thinly on soil which has been watered with a rosed watering can if the surface is dry and rake or sprinkle a very light covering of soil over the seed, so that it is covered to about twice its own depth. Protect from birds (see sowing grass seed, Mid-Spring).

*A carefully planted rock garden in its full spring glory: iris, grape hyacinths, the Pasque flower, forget-me-nots and honesty combine beautifully.*

*Nothing is more evocative of spring-time than the primrose, whose pale yellow flowers bloom in both sun and shade.*

You can also sow sweetpeas outdoors this month, in the place in which they are to flower. The trenches for them having been prepared in early winter, the seed should be sown 10cm (4in) apart and 5cm (2in) deep; you can sow a double, staggered row, with 25cm (10in) between the rows. However, sweetpea sowing at this time is somewhat of a last resort; results will not be as good as from autumn sowings and flowering will be much later, in mid-summer. For method of support, see staking, Mid-Spring.

### Sowing seed under glass
If you have frames, or can acquire one or two and put them in a sunny sheltered place, you can sow dahlia seed in them, in boxes or pans. They will all be collections of mixed colours, not named cultivars, but they can be bedding dahlias or the normal larger, decorative kind. They need a temperature of about 13-16°C (55-60°F) to germinate, so you should wait until late in early spring before sowing in a frame; alternatively you can sow them in the greenhouse (without heat) or in a gently warmed propagator in the greenhouse.

Other seeds to sow in warmth will be half-hardy annuals and bedding plants. The earlier in the month you sow these seeds, the earlier they will flower, but whenever you sow them, the resultant plants should not be put outdoors until thoroughly accustomed to lower temperatures, and preferably after any likelihood of night frosts. If they have grown very large and have to be put outdoors before the weather is right, cloche protection will help to prevent actual damage, though they are likely to stop growing temporarily.

If you want to try your hand at growing herbaceous perennials and rock plants from seed, early spring is the best time to sow it, if you have glass protection. Artificial heat is not essential, though a little will hasten germination, but they are hardy plants – don't forget that most rock plants come from mountain sites where there can be snow into mid-spring, or even later.

### Planting and dividing
The main plantings will be of herbaceous perennials, either of new plants, or of plants you already have, which need digging up, dividing and then replanting. This kind of plant grows well for three or four years, but then becomes straggly and does not produce as many or as good flowers. The centre of the crown becomes bare and the new growth appears round the edges, so that gaps start to appear, especially with such plants as golden rod (solidago), Michaelmas daisies and rudbeckias.

When you dig up the plants, lift them with as much of the root intact and unbroken as possible, then pull the crown apart into several good sections, each with buds and/or new shoots on it. You will find that the parts with most life in them will tend to detach from the more or less dead central part. If the crown is very tough and thick, with a mass of tangled roots, you can lever it into sections or use a really sharp knife to cut through the crown, but not the roots – disentangle these by hand.

You can take the opportunity to clear the crowns of any weeds that may be infesting the roots, and to clear out debris such as old stalks, leaves, stones, and slugs and snails, which all provide shelter for disease and other pests.

Make the planting holes large enough to take the roots of the plants spread out, without cramping and doubling up; roots put in bent back on themselves suffer a kind of strangulation and although the plant may not actually die at once, it grows slowly and is permanently weakened so that it dies prematurely. Put the plants in to the same depth as they were, filling the hole with crumbled soil, firm it in with the heel, rake the surface and water in if there is unlikely to be rain within the next few hours.

*The double-flowered Asiatic ranunculus, planted in spring, are in vivid bloom in early summer.*

You can also dig up and divide snowdrops in early spring, as soon as they have finished flowering; they re-establish very quickly and suffer no harm from lifting while the leaves are still green. In fact, if left until autumn and then dug up and divided, they take much longer to recover, and may not flower in the winter following.

Sweetpeas which were sown in autumn can be planted in their permanent flowering positions, and staked at the same time (see staking, Mid-Spring). If you were unable to get biennials into their flowering beds last autumn, they should be moved as soon as possible this season.

Montbretias and gladioli are summer-flowering bulbs (technically corms) planted in early spring, preferably towards the end of it. Montbretias will do best if started into growth before planting, as begonias are, by putting them into damp peat in trays in a frame. As soon as they start to produce green tips and the beginnings of roots, plant them with 5cm (2in) of soil above them and about 10cm (4in) apart. They are very undemanding plants and although it is generally advised to divide them every three years, they will flower for at least twenty years without this. Well-drained soil, slightly starved growing conditions and a sunny place will give the best flowering.

Modern gladioli are varied as well as extremely pretty. There are three main groups of hybrids: the large-flowered, which are the best-known sort; the miniatures, or *primulinus* kind, which includes the Butterfly type; and the early-flowering *colvillei* hybrids; the last named are slightly tender and are therefore usually grown in pots, being planted in autumn and kept in a cool greenhouse for

flowering in early to mid-spring. They can be planted outdoors, but only in really warm, sheltered places, and will then flower in early summer.

Gladioli are sun-lovers and lovers of dryish, or free-draining soil or compost; plant them 10cm (4in) deep and 15cm (6in) apart. You will get a succession of flowers if you plant them in batches, once every ten to fourteen days until the end of mid-spring. The large-flowered kinds should be planted in rows 30cm (12in) apart, the miniatures about 20cm (8in) apart.

### Lawn treatment
The lawn at this time of the year always looks rather sorry for itself, thin, limp and messy with leaves and twigs. As the temperature rises and the grass starts to grow, you can help to revive it more quickly and strongly by raking, brushing, topping and spiking, in that order. This work results in aerating the soil and the turf and removing possible pests.

Use a springbok rake, rake first in one direction and then at right angles across this; next brush, using a stiff brush to bring the grass upright and then cut the grass. Set the mower blades high, so that the grass is left about 2.5cm (1in) long; a harder cut can be given at the next mowing. After cutting, with the collecting box on, spike the lawn – you can use an ordinary garden fork for this. To do any real good, the tines should penetrate 10cm (4in) deep, but 7.5cm (3in) is better than nothing. Do this all over the lawn, about 12 or 15cm (5 or 6in) apart.

Rolling a lawn, to keep it level, used to be considered essential but nowadays it is thought to do more harm than good, by compacting the soil, especially since modern mowers have a roller fitted automatically. If there is moss on the lawn, raking should not be done until the moss has been treated, since raking only serves to spread it.

### Treating moss on lawns
Moss thrives in damp conditions; it will spread rapidly in wet weather, but it will also appear where the soil is extremely acid, where it is compacted and lacking in air and where it is lacking plant food. In all these conditions, the lawn grasses become weak and cannot compete with invaders. Moss can be burnt out with lawnsand bought ready-mixed, or made up at home of 3 parts sulphate of ammonia, 1 part calcined (burnt) ferrous sulphate and 20

*Bergenia, or 'elephant's ears', a neglected plant, flowers from mid-winter into early spring and even later. The glossy evergreen leaves are decorative in themselves.*

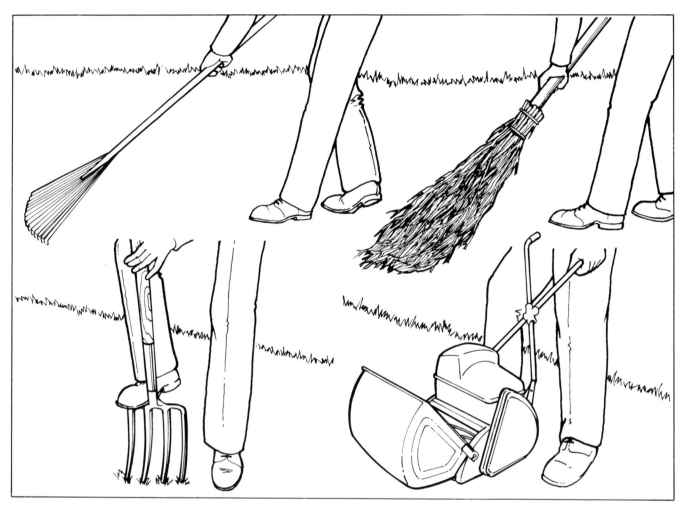

*Rejuvenating the lawn after winter: rake with a springbok rake, brush thoroughly, 'top' the grass and aerate with a garden fork afterwards to a depth of about 10cm (4in). If the lawn has moss on it, do not rake until the moss has been treated: raking will spread it.*

parts sand. This mixture is applied dry at 120g per sq m (4oz per sq yd); it must be put on evenly, otherwise the grass may be permanently damaged, and watered in if there is no rain after 48 hours. The grass is likely to be discoloured, brown or blackish, but this is temporary. When the moss is black and dead, then it can be raked away.

Proprietary moss killers containing mercury can also be used and there are one or two mercurized lawnsands available; the mercury will kill the moss spores as well as the vegetative growth.

However, for the permanent eradication of the moss, conditions for the growth of the grass must be put right and this means that you must ensure good soil aeration, an adequate food supply, frequent cutting to avoid the shock given by occasional very hard cutting, and a sufficient water supply in hot and/or dry weather. It is mostly summer droughts and watering long after it was first necessary that result in the invasion of the turf by coarse and weed grasses, weeds, moss and disease.

### Sprouting

You can put achimenes, large-flowered begonias and gloxinias (sinningias) to sprout in moist peat if this was not done last month, but not in the propagator; the greenhouse will be sufficiently warm, if you are maintaining the minimum temperature. It is quite likely that some of them have already started to produce new shoots. Dahlias can be started as well, to provide shoots for cuttings. Take off any rotting tubers and put the healthy crowns in 15cm (6in) deep boxes, covering the tubers with moist peat or soil.

## Pricking out

By now, the seeds sown last month in the propagator will be seedlings that need pricking out; they will include half-hardy annuals, and such slightly tender bedding and greenhouse plants as begonias (fibrous-rooted and large-flowered), dahlia, gloxinia (sinningia) and streptocarpus. In general, seedlings should be moved when they have two seed leaves and the first true leaf just appearing, in other words when they are large enough to handle. Lever them out, breaking the roots as little as possible, and drop each seedling into a hole in the compost which is large enough to prevent the roots being cramped, and deep enough to ensure that most of the stem is buried; the leaves should be just above the compost surface. Space them 5cm (2in) apart each way.

Quite often each seedling has a long main root or tap root; if you look closely at the tip of this, you will see that it finishes in a kind of rounded point, and it is there that the seedling takes in most of the food it needs. If that gets broken off, it will have to rely on the much less strong side roots to absorb food and may even have to grow a new root. While this is happening, it cannot absorb sufficient water, and this is why so many pricked out seedlings wilt as soon as they are moved. Clumsy lifting can damage a seedling so that the mature plant is never strong. Another important point in pricking out is to do it as soon as the seedling can be handled. The shock of moving is much greater when they are larger and there will be much more root to handle (and to damage); they may even have run short of food.

*Snow-in-summer*, Cerastium tomentosum, *flowers for several weeks and is good ground-cover but needs restricting.*

Once firmed into the compost, the seedlings should be gently watered with a rosed watering can and put in a shady place; a polythene tent over them will keep the atmosphere moist and help to stop any tendency to flag.

## Potting and topdressing

Plants which are grown permanently in the greenhouse will need new compost every one or two years; if they are not particularly strong or fast growers, they can simply be topdressed, instead of completely repotted. Cuttings which were put to root last month may need potting into individual pots by now.

Plants to repot could include all foliage plants, such as tradescantia, zebrina, chlorophytum, asparagus and ferns, summer-flowering plants such as pelargoniums (geraniums), the Italian bellflower (*Campanula isophylla*), jasmine, fuchsia, hoya, cacti and other succulents, cobaea (cup-and-saucer plant) and passion flower (*Passiflora caerulea*).

In general, use a pot one size larger than the one the plant is in, and do not disturb the root-ball unless the roots have become very long, when they can be cut back to the root-ball, and the ball loosened a little. If the maximum size of the plant has been reached, use a pot the same size, but remove all the compost carefully from the roots, put a little new compost in the pot, and centre the plant on this, so that compost can be crumbled in evenly all round the roots.

When you repot, have the new compost ready in the greenhouse so that it is at the same temperature as that in which the plants are growing and use completely clean pots, plastic or clay. If new, clay pots should be put to soak in water for about twenty-four hours, otherwise they will absorb all the water you give to the compost which is intended for the plant and you will constantly be watering but getting poor plant growth. Put drainage material, such as pieces of broken clay pot, in the base of the clay pots, and then repot the plant.

Cacti can be difficult to handle because of their prickles; gloves will help and tongs are even better, the kind that form two halves of a ring, as they do least damage to the spines.

Pelargoniums which have been overwintered in the greenhouse can now be transferred to individual pots about 15 or 17.5cm (6 or 7in) in diameter, whatever size will take the roots without cramping them too much. Use the J.I. potting compost No. 2 with one part extra of coarse sand added, as pelargoniums like well-drained soils.

Topdressing consists simply of removing the top 2.5cm (1in) or so of compost and replacing it with fresh. Plants treated like this will need to have liquid feeding started much earlier than repotted plants. Hippeastrums can be started now if this has not already been done (see Late Winter).

Cuttings, such as early- and late-flowering chrysanthemums, which rooted last month, may also need potting now into their own pots. Pelargonium cuttings which were rooted last autumn can now also be transferred to larger pots.

## Stopping

At some time during early spring, if not before, late-flowering chrysanthemums will have grown to about 15cm (6in) in height and should be stopped, to induce them to produce sideshoots and more flowers in due course. Stopping is a way of halting the upward growth of the main stem completely, and diverting the plant's energy into the production of side growths from the axil of the leaves. Most chrysanthemum cultivars tend to produce these growths in embryo, but they do not develop, unless the plant is stopped. To stop the plant, the growing tip and first pair of leaves are pinched off between finger and thumb.

*Potting a rooted chrysanthemum cutting: use a 9cm (3½in) diameter pot, and put small pieces of crock, curve side upward, over the drainage hole. Fill in some of the potting compost, centre the roots on this and fill in compost round them, firming it at the sides with the fingers.*

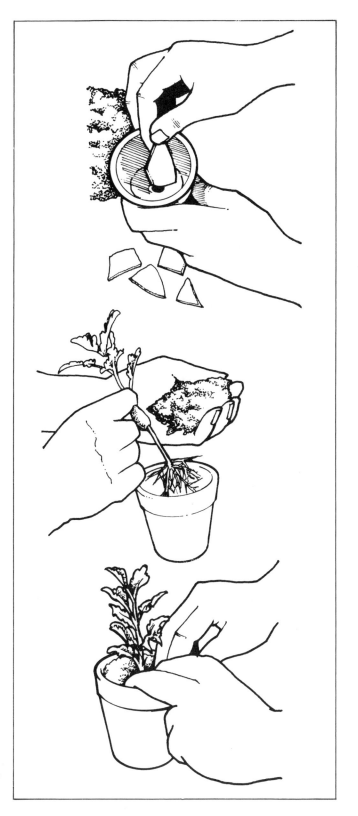

## Increasing from cuttings

Cuttings to take and root in warmth in early spring include the early-flowering and the last of the late-flowering chrysanthemums (see Early Winter for method). Others include dahlias and fuchsias if new growth has started and pelargoniums – if these were not cut back last autumn – for flowering next winter in the greenhouse (see Early Autumn for method).

As with all 'soft-tip' cuttings, the ends of the new shoots should be used, while they are still green and soft and have not become hard and/or brown. Cut off a length of shoot about 7.5cm (3in) long, cutting just below a leaf or pair of leaves. Cut off the lowest leaves and put the cutting in the compost, so that half its length is buried. Make a sufficiently deep hole first with a dibber or pencil, against the side of the pot, and make sure the base of the cutting is resting on the compost at the bottom of the hole. Rooting occurs more quickly with cuttings placed at the side of the pot. Then fill in firmly with compost so that the cutting cannot be shifted with a gentle tug on a leaf. Water in, cover with a blown-up polythene bag and put in a warm shady place until the stem begins to lengthen, when rooting will have occurred. You can then take off the polythene bag.

Three or four cuttings can be put in a 9cm (3½in) diameter pot; hormone rooting powder can be used as an insurance. This method can be used for all soft-tip cuttings, no matter what the plant. Never use a shoot which has a flower or flower-bud on it, as it will not root.

## Greenhouse management

Since the outside temperature is rising and plants are beginning to grow, you can dispense with artificial heat on sunny days, though it will still be necessary at night. Ventilation can be increased during the day and condensation should cease to be a problem. Pricked-out seedlings and potted cuttings will need spacing out as they grow, to avoid their becoming drawn; the need for water will steadily increase and germinating seeds must have an eye kept on them constantly, to avoid sunburn, drought and overcrowding because the pricking out has not been done quickly enough.

## Weeding and tidying

In early spring, most weeding will be a matter of clearing off any weeds that have managed to survive the winter after a late germination last autumn; however, lawn weeds are best left until late in mid-spring. Where seeds are sown outdoors, weed seedlings should be dealt with as soon as they become obvious.

Beds and borders will need tidying to remove leaves, twigs and other debris. Rock gardens especially can be very messy after the winter: some plants need cutting back to remove dead growth, the soil needs forking lightly with a hand fork, and grit or gravel replaced where rain has washed it away. If conditions are dry enough, you can burn off the dead leaves and stems of pampas grass, otherwise cut them off and rake out debris from round the plants.

## Compost heap

Last year's compost heap can be used as a mulch for permanent plantings, if a mulch was not given in the autumn, otherwise it can be kept for later use. A new heap can be started with this year's weeds and grass cuttings (see Mid-Spring for method of making).

## Plants in flower

Anemone, Bergenia, Crocus, Chionodoxa, Doronicum, Eranthis (Winter aconite), Hyacinth, Iris unguicularis (syn. I. stylosa) Kingcup (caltha), Lenten rose (Helleborus orientalis), Polyanthus, Primrose, Primula (in variety), Pulmonaria (lungwort), Saxifraga (in variety), Scilla, Tulip (species)

## Greenhouse

Cineraria, Freesia, Lachenalia, Primula (from early summer sowing), Schizanthus, Hyacinth (gently forced), Narcissi (gently forced), Tulip (gently forced)

# Mid~Spring

This season can be one in which plants really start to grow, so that you can be very busy, both outdoors and in the greenhouse. Sometimes, on the other hand, new growth is slower to appear and extend, because the weather is dry and cold with east winds, although sunny. Flowers appearing at this time will last longer, but growing plants from seed outdoors can be more difficult than in early spring. Although half-hardy annuals can be sown outside towards the end of mid-spring, it is often better not to be in too much of a hurry with them and to wait until late spring.

Planting is safer, but even so, herbaceous perennials may need aftercare in the form of watering, though summer droughts are a long way off. Rock garden plants will not mind chilly conditions if these occur, but their more fragile roots will affect their ability to absorb water, so they will also need watching.

Another major job in mid-spring is making a lawn from seed; this is one of the best times to sow grass seed, especially for colder regions where autumn-sown grass seed is less likely to produce a good lawn. Here again, germination can be dodgy, as it is quite possible to sow grass seed and then not have it germinate for three weeks, because of lack of rain.

You will find that conditions in the greenhouse are getting rather crowded, if you have let your enthusiasm run away with you. Seeds will be germinating, seedlings will need pricking out, pricked-out plants will need potting, so will rooted cuttings, new growth will be providing cutting material, and plants put to sprout will need potting. Provided the temperature is rising outdoors, some of these can go into frames, but if it remains cold, you will have to do some expert juggling and fitting in.

Insect pests of all kinds will be hatching or emerging from winter dormancy and a few diseases will begin to appear, quickly or slowly, depending on the temperature. Be ready to deal with these, if they look like getting out of hand.

# At~a~glance diary

**Prepare the soil for:** sowing seed and planting outdoors

**Prepare compost for:** sowing seed and potting under glass

**Sow seeds outdoors of:** hardy annuals (see Table of Hardy Annuals in Early Summer); also some of the

**Sow seeds under glass of:** half-hardy and bedding plants: dahlia, nasturtium, salpiglossis, ursinia, xeranthemum (everlasting) and zinnia; lawn grasses half-hardy annuals and bedding plants (see Table in Mid-Winter)

**Plant outdoors:** allium, crinum, gladioli, herbaceous perennials, montbretia, rock garden plants, autumn-sown sweetpea if not done in early spring

**Thin:** seedlings from seed sown outdoors in early spring

**Lawn care:** mow new lawns grown from seed; mow and feed established lawns

**Stake, train and tie in:** sweetpea

**Compost heap:** continue to make

**Weed:** annual flower and lawn grass seedlings, herbaceous beds and borders, paths

**Prick out:** half-hardy annuals and bedding plants sown in early spring, seedlings in frames

**Pot:** achimenes, begonia, chrysanthemum, gloxinia pelargonium, pricked out seedlings, streptocarpus, plants permanently in pots and not repotted in early spring

**Stop:** early-flowering chrysanthemum

**Increase:** chrysanthemum, dahlia, delphinium, fuchsia from cuttings

**Greenhouse:** water and ventilate

# Jobs to do

### Preparing the soil for sowing seed outdoors

One of the bigger jobs to do in the spring is producing a lawn from seed. The soil should have been thoroughly dug in autumn or early winter and most of the weeds removed. Now it needs a final cleaning up, about a week before you intend to sow, by forking the top few centimetres (inches) to remove weeds and rubbish, and to break up large lumps of soil. Add a compound fertilizer dressing with an analysis of about 7:7:7 (see Mid-Winter) when you do the forking. A week later, on the day you sow, you can rake to make the soil surface really fine and to do some rough levelling, and then make a finished level, using a line, pegs, boards and a spirit level. Once you are sure there are no bumps and hollows, tread the seed-bed to consolidate it lightly, and give a final raking, standing on boards, to produce the right tilth.

Seed-beds for flowering plants can also be prepared now, as in early spring.

### Preparing compost for sowing seed under glass

If you did not have time to make up compost in late winter or early spring, it should be mixed as soon as possible so that it has a little time, at any rate, to blend together.

### Preparing the soil for planting outdoors

Much of the planting in mid-spring is the same as in early spring, with some additions, so you can follow the instructions given in that season, and make sure that any fertilizer added goes on a few days in advance of planting.

### Preparing compost for potting under glass

As with the seed composts, so potting composts need to be made early in mid-spring and left in the greenhouse to warm up to the same temperature as the one in which the plants are growing.

### Sowing seed outdoors

Grass seed should be sown fairly early in mid-spring; it takes about seven to ten days to germinate and perhaps

*There are water-lilies in many colours besides the usual white, and types to suit all pools, whether shallow or deep.*

another ten to fourteen before the first cut can be made. A windless day is best; marking out the area in square metres (yards) with lines will help you to make sowing more even.

Average rate for sowing seed is about 45-60g per sq m (1½-2oz per sq yd), using the higher rate if birds are likely to be a nuisance or germination conditions a bit problematical. Another way of ensuring evenness of sowing,

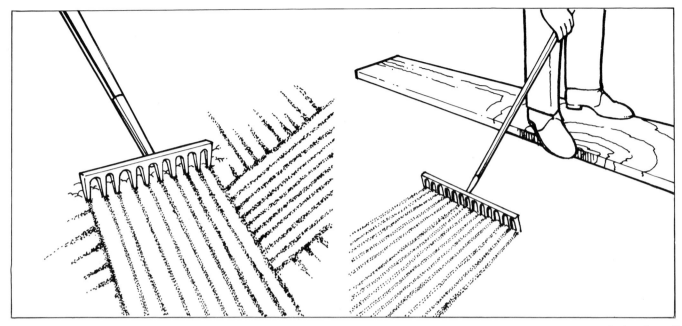

when doing it by hand, is to sow half the seed in one direct-ion and the remainder at right angles to it. This evenness of sowing is important, otherwise you will start with a patchy lawn, and subsequently you will never be able to produce an evenly thick sward. Large areas can be sown with a fer-tilizer distributor, to which a metering roller for sowing seeds is attached. Again, two half sowings are advisable.

After sowing, a very light raking, then cross-raking, can be done to give the best results, though if time is short, this can be dispensed with. Finally, bird inhibitors can be put on or, on small areas, black cotton strung above the soil. Seed treated against birds can be bought, but loses its viability quickly, so should be used in the season for which it was intended and not kept for later use.

Hardy annuals can be sown this month with more chance of a good display later on; germination in early spring can be risky due to treacherous weather conditions. You can add to those suggested for early spring: aster, dahlia, layia (tidy tips), nasturtium, nicotiana, salpiglossis, sweet sultan, ursinia, xeranthemum (everlasting flowers) and zinnia. It is not quite too late for sweetpeas but those sown now will not flower until late summer.

If you have a nursery bed, which is really rather in-dispensable for flower as well as vegetable gardening, you can also sow seed now of bulbs such as crocus, lilies and snowdrops and of herbaceous perennials and rock plants, giving the seeds cloche protection if the temperature is down to freezing at night. Sow as thinly as possible, especially the bulbs.

*Preparing a seed-bed for sowing a new lawn. Rake the soil surface to a fine crumb-like consistency, standing on a board, and then rake crosswise for final levelling and evenness.*

### Sowing seed under glass
In the greenhouse you can sow the same half-hardy annuals and bedding plants as last month but, unless the weather is very cold, you should be able to do without artificial heat during the day. You can also sow cobaea and ipomoea, and freesia for flowering during autumn and early winter. Cobaea and ipomoea have rather large seeds and grow quickly once they have germinated, so sowing them singly in 5cm (2in) pots, preferably peat pots, makes it easier to deal with their first potting.

Ipomoea in particular does not like its roots being dis-turbed; if they are, the first two or three true leaves tend to turn yellow and then white, the plant ceases to grow and eventually dies. This yellowing will also appear if the young plants are kept in bright sunlight or if the temperature drops below 16°C (60°F). They do need to be kept really quite warm, both in the compost and air temperature and if you can supply a temperature of nearer 21°C (70°F), so much the better.

Freesias can easily be grown from seed, and if it is sown now in a temperature of 16°C (60°F), the first flowers will start to appear in mid-autumn. They grow an unusually long taproot, so the deeper the container the better; the depth should be at least 17.5cm (7in). Use a compost con-taining soil, such as J.I. potting No. 3, and sow the seeds spaced 2.5cm (1in) apart and at the same depth. A 23cm (9in) pot will take about nine or ten seeds. The leaves and stems tend to be rather long and straggly, especially the stems, so 37.5cm (15in) long split canes with string threaded across them should be provided for support. Place them round the container edge and in the centre, so that the plants grow up through a supporting network. After germination, the temperature can be lowered a little.

## Planting outdoors

As in early spring, you can plant or lift and divide herbaceous plants, but it is advisable to do this as early in the month as possible, as growth will really be getting under way.

This is the best time to plant rock garden plants as well, preferably when they have just finished flowering, though they can be moved or planted successfully while in flower. You must then do it quickly, with as little damage to the roots as possible, water them in and make quite sure they do not want for water while establishing. Cool, moist weather conditions are best.

Violets can be planted now, either bought plants, or crowns from your own plants. Crowns are pieces separated from a parent plant, each with plenty of roots. Violets thrive if planted where they are protected from summer sun at midday and given a moist, humus-rich soil. They must be watered in after planting, unless rain is imminent. If you see any signs of violet midge trouble, pick off the affected leaves (see Flower Garden Controls and Treatment section).

Gladioli can be planted during mid-spring, at intervals of a week or so to provide a succession of flowers; allium, crinum and montbretia can all be planted at the beginning of the season. Alliums tend to prefer a sunny place and gritty soil and, given these, some species will naturalize so well that they become a nuisance.

*Crinum × powellii* produces beautiful deep pink, lily-like flowers in late summer and autumn; its large bulbs should be planted 15cm (6in) deep and about 23cm (9in) apart. A well-drained soil, to which plenty of rotted organic matter was added in winter, is required, and a sunny place at the foot of a south or west-facing wall. Once planted, it can be left alone for many years, provided it is mulched each spring. Planted with agapanthus, the blue African lily which likes much the same conditions, the resulting combination of flower colour is very pretty.

*In spite of its name, the Skunk Cabbage,* Lysichitum americanum, *does not smell and is a handsome waterside plant.*

## Thinning

The seeds sown outdoors in early spring will need thinning some time during the next few weeks. Thinning means removing some of the seedlings which have germinated, to allow the remainder enough space to grow and mature fully. It should be done when they are just large enough to handle, to leave roughly 5cm (2in) between each remaining seedling; thin a second time when they have produced five or six true leaves, so that there is about 10-20cm (4-8in) between the plants, depending on their final height.

*The wild white daisy has been bred and selected so that strains of seed will now produce double rose-pink flowers.*

## Mowing

A new lawn which has been grown from seed may need its first cut by the end of mid-spring, if conditions for germination and growth have been good. The grass blades will then be about 5cm (2in) long. Before cutting, you can roll it once, with a light roller, to firm the roots of the young plants into the soil. Set the mower blades high, make sure they are razor sharp and then take only the top off the grass, about 1cm ($\frac{1}{2}$in).

Mowing of an established lawn can get into full swing, as the grass will be growing quickly, and you can reduce the height of cut to 0.5-1cm ($\frac{1}{4}$-$\frac{1}{2}$in) by the beginning of late spring. Mow the lawn with the collecting box attached, otherwise the clippings will choke the sward. Hot, dry weather is the only time the mowings can be left; they will then conserve moisture. If you have time, brushing with a stiff broom before you mow will maintain good aeration of the turf and prevent the build-up of a mat of vegetation on the soil surface.

## Feeding

Established lawns can be fed, using a compound lawn fertilizer or, if you want quick but not long-lasting results, sulphate of ammonia, 15g ($\frac{1}{2}$oz) in 4.5L (1 gal) of water, put on with a spray or with a watering-can with a rose. Dry fertilizer must be put on evenly, at the rate recommended by the manufacturers, as a patchy application will only result in burning the grass and quite possibly killing it. Another requirement is moist soil, with the chance of rain within a few hours.

## Staking, training and tying

Sweetpeas planted in early spring after being overwintered will begin to elongate rapidly and should be supplied with 2.5m (8ft) stakes, such as bamboo canes, one to each stem, to which they can be attached with sweetpea rings. Attach twine or wire to the tops of the canes along the row and support each end cane with a strong stake. Tendrils and side-shoots should be taken off as they appear. Tendrils take the place of a leaflet; side-shoots grow from the join between the main stem and a leaf stem. There is more about the training of sweetpeas in Early Summer.

## Compost heap

The new one can be started in earnest, as weeds germinate along with your hardy annuals and new lawn. Give it a base of brushwood or bricks spaced well apart, so that air can get underneath, and surround it with a wooden framework, straw bales, rigid plastic, or black plastic sheet. Build it 120-150cm (48-60in) high, about the same width and any convenient length. Sticking a pole in the centre will ensure that there is a kind of chimney going through the heap, up which air can be drawn when you withdraw the pole at the finish of building.

## Weeding

The main weed problem will be in the annual beds and patches and on the seed-bed provided for your new lawn. If both areas were not properly fallowed, there will be as many, if not more, weed seeds as cultivated seedlings, germinating merrily and growing faster. You can water on a solution of a new lawn weedkiller about a week after the grass germinates, otherwise you will have to remove the worst weeds by hand. However, with large areas this is impracticable, but usually as the grass grows and is cut, the weeds will be overcome, as these annual kinds cannot compete with the grass and withstand frequent cutting at the same time.

Amongst the annuals, handweeding will be necessary and with the smaller areas is quite practicable. Elsewhere in the garden, hoeing or handweeding will keep aliens at bay, if your perennials and groundcovers are not sufficiently closely planted to prevent their obtaining a toe-hold.

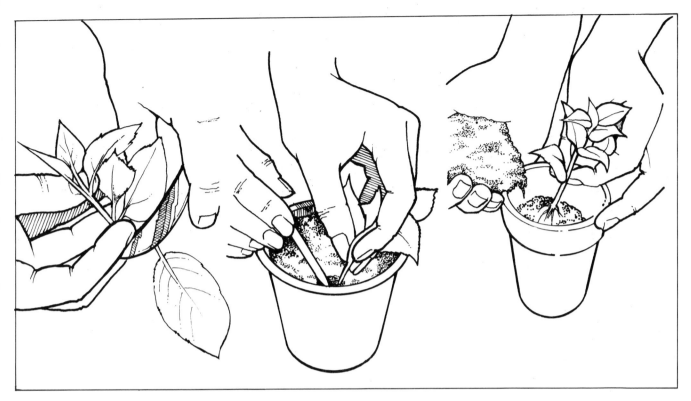

This is a good time of the year to eradicate weeds on paths; you can either water them with a weedkiller which lasts for six months, or you can remove them by hand and then apply one which lasts a year (see Flower Garden Treatments and Controls section).

## Pricking out

The half-hardy annuals and bedding plants sown in artificial heat two or three weeks ago will need to be pricked out into boxes. Seeds sown in frames may have germinated sufficiently well for these seedlings also to need pricking out (see Early Spring for method).

## Potting

The corms and tubers that you started in early spring in moist peat can be transferred to individual pots, 12.5-17.5cm (5-7in) in diameter for all but the achimenes. Do not completely bury the tuber or corm and use a rather peaty compost. Achimenes can be very slow to sprout but when the shoots are about 5cm (2in) tall, transfer the tubercles to 15 or 17.5cm (6 or 7in) pots and plant them about 7.5cm (3in) apart. At the same time, put in 15cm (12in) long split canes for the upright growing kinds.

Rooted cuttings such as those of early- and late-flowering chrysanthemums and pelargoniums can be potted

*Making a soft tip cutting: The tip of a new young shoot is cut off cleanly below a leaf or pair of leaves so that it is about 7.5-10cm (3-4in) long. The lowest leaves are removed, the cutting half-buried in a hole in the compost at the side of the pot and firmed well in. When rooted, the cutting is grown on in its own pot in good potting compost.*

or potted on. Be guided by the state of the roots; if they have filled the soil ball and are just spreading round the outside, the plants are ready for new pots, about 2.5-4cm (1-1½in) in diameter larger than the old ones. Roots coming through the drainage hole or wound round and round the base mean the plant is long overdue for a larger pot.

Late-flowering chrysanthemums, if the cuttings were taken in early or mid-winter, may be ready to go into their final pots, 23cm (9in) in diameter. Use J.I. potting compost No. 3. Such potting is likely to be necessary at the end of mid-spring (see Late Spring for method).

Pricked-out seedlings may also need to be moved into their first pots, using a size which the roots can fit into comfortably without being cramped. If they have one or two long roots, with plenty of shorter, finer ones, it does no harm to shorten the long ones to a convenient length.

Repot or topdress those plants permanently in containers which were not done in early spring.

### Stopping
Early-flowering chrysanthemums can be stopped in the same way and for the same reasons as late-flowering kinds (see Early Spring).

### Increasing
Dahlias, fuchsias and delphiniums can be propagated from cuttings. The dahlias put to sprout in early spring should have long enough shoots by now to provide cuttings; use those about 5-7.5cm (2-3in) long. If you cut them off to leave a stub, this will produce more shoots later on.

Fuchsia cuttings can be made in the same way from the newly produced shoots (see Early Spring for method). Outdoor delphiniums should also have sprouted by now and, if the slugs have left any, the same length cuttings can be made from the shoots and put in sandy compost in the frame. It may still be possible to take cuttings of early-flowering chrysanthemums.

### Watering
Greenhouse plants will be needing more and more water; there are various ways of doing this according to the equipment and time you have available.

### Ventilating
Continue to increase the ventilation in the greenhouse as the weather gets warmer. Turn the heat off when possible, but make sure the seedlings and rooted cuttings do not catch a chill. Frame lights can be raised during the day, or removed altogether in sunny weather.

### Treating pests and diseases
Mid-spring sees the big hatch of insect pests, especially greenfly, the universal pest of plants. Other sucking insect pests such as leaf suckers and leaf-hoppers also appear from tiny overwintering eggs on weeds, bushes and trees, and caterpillars of all kinds will begin to eat leaves, as well as stems and, eventually, flowers. Leatherjackets may make a final onslaught on lawn grasses before they pupate – they account for pale brown patches of dead grass on many lawns in spring. Diseases will not be quite so troublesome for a while yet, apart from grey mould (*Botrytis cinerea*), but peonies will need watching for blight and bud disease at this time (see Flower Garden Controls and Treatment section).

*Cosmos is a freely-flowering annual for sowing outdoors in spring to flower from mid-summer. It comes from Mexico and grows and flowers best in a sunny place and poor soil.*

## Plants in flower
Anemone, Arabis, Aubrieta, Bluebell, Chionodoxa, Crocus, Daffodil, Forget-me-not, Grape hyacinth, Hyacinth, Kingcup (caltha), Lamium maculatum, Lenten rose (Helleborus orientalis), Lithospermum, Narcissus, Polyanthus, Primrose, Primula, Scilla, Tulip, Violet

## Greenhouse
Calceolaria, Hippeastrum, Lachenalia, Primula obconica, Schizanthus

# Late Spring

The season of late spring is probably the busiest one of the year in the flower garden. It is an in-between time; the spring display is finishing and these plants need to be tidied up and allowed to rest. Those which are coming on to take their place will be growing fast and will need constant attention. You will also be able to start off some of next year's spring-flowering plants. The grass will be growing so rapidly that the lawn will need cutting every week.

In late spring there can be a slow but steady rise in temperature. By now, winter is definitely over, though there may be strong cold winds blowing through the whole period, but in sunny sheltered gardens some days can be really hot. The night temperature is the important one now and a constantly low one, even sometimes down to freezing, explains why some plants and seedlings are very slow to grow. This is where cloches and frames are so useful for protecting and bringing plants on so that they are ready for the hot weather.

There will be some soil preparation to do outdoors for sowing and planting; late spring is the best time to plant submerged water plants, including water lilies. The scene in the greenhouse can also be fairly active, with pricking out, sowing and potting all to be done, for summer displays of exotic plants and for flowering next winter and early spring. The greenhouse will need even more care with temperature control, and watering will be increasingly necessary.

Watchfulness will be the key word for pests and diseases. Greenfly and caterpillars will be the most annoying of these in general, though on certain plants there will be specific troubles through the season: capsid bugs on chrysanthemums, earwigs on dahlias, mildew on Michaelmas daisies or rust on antirrhinums. Birds are occasionally a nuisance, but not nearly to the same extent as they are on vegetables and fruit.

# At~a~glance diary

| | |
|---|---|
| **Prepare the soil for:** | sowing seed and planting outdoors |
| **Prepare compost for:** | sowing seed and potting under glass |
| **Sow seeds outdoors of:** | hardy and half-hardy annuals (see Table in Early Summer and Mid-Winter): biennials, Canterbury bells, double daisies, foxglove, hollyhock |
| **Sow seeds under glass of:** | cacti, cineraria, cobaea, ipomoea |
| **Plant outdoors:** | allium; half-hardy annuals and bedding plants; crinum, dahlia, gladioli; herbaceous perennials; pansy, rock plants, water and waterside plants |
| **Prick out:** | half-hardy annuals and bedding plants |
| **Pot:** | chrysanthemum, dahlia, delphinium, fuchsia, pelargonium grown from cuttings; half-hardy annuals and bedding plants if getting large; greenhouse plants permanently in pots that are ready; cobaea, ipomoea |
| **Thin:** | hardy annuals |
| **Harden off:** | freesia, half-hardy annuals and bedding plants |
| **Lift:** | spring-flowering bulbs if site is needed for summer bedding |
| **Rest:** | freesia, lachenalia, any outdoor spring-flowering bulbs which have been brought on early in pots |
| **Stake, train:** | delphinium, erigeron, euphorbia, lupin Michaelmas daisy, peony, poppy and pyrethrum outdoors; achimenes, begonia, freesia and climbing plants indoors |

# Jobs to do

## Preparing the soil for sowing seed outdoors

You will need to fork and rake the soil into a good condition for sowing various seeds, mostly in beds and borders, and it should be much easier to do than it was earlier in the spring. A section of the nursery bed will need to be prepared for seeds as well. In all cases, do try to make sure the seed-bed is level and evenly firm, otherwise you will have patchy germination and weak plants. Hollows and bumps mean that seeds are washed by rain into clumps, and soil which has been firmed too thoroughly will be badly drained.

## Preparing compost for sowing seed under glass

This in fact may have already been done, if you made up a good quantity in mid-spring. If you are short of time, you can use ready-made John Innes Seed Compost. If not, follow the details for seed-compost preparation given in Late Winter.

## Preparing the soil for planting outdoors

As with early and mid-spring, soil preparation consists of forking and removal of weeds, stones and general rubbish. Also, it is a good idea to add compound fertilizer if you are going to grow chrysanthemums and dahlias or if your soil tends to be the quick-draining type. Plant foods are washed through the latter before the plant roots can absorb them.

Since water plants, water lilies in particular, usually are best planted in pools during late spring, the sites or baskets should be prepared now. You will get the best results if you can plant direct into the pool bottom, but this does mean emptying the pool completely. If you do this, spread a layer about 12.5 or 15cm (5 or 6in) deep of good loam all over the pool base and firm it down well.

Alternatively, you can plant the aquatics which grow under water and up through it in baskets, filling them with good loam put through a 1cm ($\frac{1}{2}$in) sieve. Bonemeal mixed with this at the rate of 60g (2oz) per container will supply long-lasting food. Prepare this mixture about a week before you intend to plant.

## Preparing compost for potting under glass

Potting composts may again be necessary, depending on what you are growing; there are all sorts of plants which can go into their final containers in late spring and you may need a good deal (see Late Winter for recipes and quantities).

## Sowing seed outdoors

Seeds to sow in the open are half-hardy annuals, annuals if you are behind (they should produce a display but late in the summer), and biennials for next spring, such as Canterbury bells, double daisies, foxglove, sweet william, *Verbascum bombyciferum* (mullein) and wallflower. Technically speaking, sweet williams are perennial, but are treated as biennials.

The half-hardy annuals will do best if you can put cloches over the seed-sowing site a few days in advance and then keep the cloches on at night until there is no longer any risk of frost.

If you can get the biennials sown now, they will be magnificent in spring next year as they will have had the longest possible growing season. Seed is sown in a seed-bed and the seedlings thinned and then transplanted to another part of the nursery bed to grow on through the summer until final planting in autumn.

This is the general method of cultivation but there are exceptions and, if you are short of time, it is possible to leave the young plants where they are, provided they have been well spaced out by thinning, until planting time in autumn. Verbascum is not transplanted at all, but planted direct from the seed-bed to its permanent position the spring after sowing. Hollyhocks, which are usually treated as biennials, can also be grown as perennials, though they tend to deteriorate rather rapidly.

## Sowing seed under glass

In the greenhouse, seeds to sow now are some of those plants which flower in their pots next winter and spring, such as *Primula malacoides* and cineraria; cobaea and

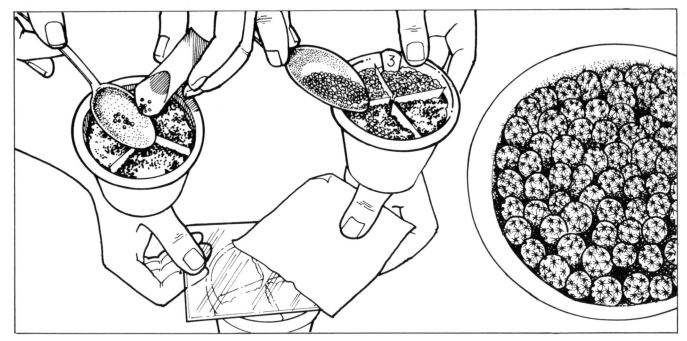

*Sowing cactus seed: Use a pan with plenty of drainage material and very sandy compost; sow thinly and keep warm and covered until germinated. Prick out seedlings a year later.*

ipomoea can also be sown for flowering later on this summer and in autumn, as can cactus seed, but the plants from these will not flower until next year at the earliest.

Cacti sown in late spring should germinate within about 7-14 days, but can be left in their seed containers until next spring as they are very slow to grow. Keep the seedlings in a little shade, otherwise the leaves discolour; when young, cacti do not like bright sunlight. Water occasionally but carefully.

Primula seed is very fine, difficult to sow and difficult to germinate. Mix it with sand for even sowing; use a sandy compost and a pan rather than a pot. Cover the seed with a light, fine covering of compost, then cover the pan with a piece of glass and put in a shaded place, making sure that the compost remains moist but not soggy. Temperature should be about 13-16°C (55-60°F). Germination may take several weeks and will be rather erratic when it does start.

## Planting outdoors

Towards the end of late spring, you will be able to put out the bedding plants and half-hardy annuals, provided they have been well hardened-off in a frame. There is no point in planting earlier than this unless you have a sheltered garden; too often this kind of plant gets put out early in late

spring or even in mid-spring and, although it may not be killed as a result, it will be stunted and slow to grow so that no time is gained.

Choose a warm day, make sure the soil and the root ball are moist before planting and plant in the evening; warm them in lightly and cover with cloches if the temperature is below 10°C (50°F) at night. Spacing depends on the height and spread of the mature plant (see table, Mid-Winter) and can be between 10 and 45cm (4 and 18in).

Hardened-off rooted dahlia cuttings can similarly be planted in spring with cloche protection to start with, as can dormant dahlia tubers which will be just starting to sprout. Spacing can be anything from 23-90cm (9-36in) apart, depending on whether the plants are bedding, the miniature pom-pom type or the giant-flowered decoratives. They will need good, large holes to take the roots or tubers comfortably, and stakes put in now will save a lot of worry later on. Dahlia top growth can be considerable and, although a single stout stake just behind the plant is sometimes sufficient, they often need several additional lighter ones on the outside, round which string can be tied. The stakes should be rammed firmly into the soil and need to extend at least 90cm (36in) above it for the taller varieties.

Submerged water plants – such as water lilies, pickerel and dwarf reedmace – can be planted now. You can also plant those that grow at the water's edge, or in mud or shallow water. The submerged aquatics can go into containers, with the crown just protruding above the compost surface. A layer of clean gravel or shingle on the surface will help to discourage fish from exploring the compost and keep the plant in position.

If you plant directly into loam, do it very firmly with the roots well spread out and anchor the crowns with a few stones as an extra insurance against floating. When you run the water in do so gradually, a few centimetres (inches) at a time, with about a week between additions, until the pool is full. Baskets can be lowered straight into their positions in the pool.

There is still time to plant allium and crinum (see planting, Mid-Spring), and the last of the gladioli (see planting, Early Spring). Pansies sown under glass in early spring will be ready for planting outdoors, after hardening off in a frame; they should begin to flower in late summer. The herbaceous perennials and rock plants grown from seed sown in early spring can also be planted where they are to grow, for flowering, in most cases, for the first time next summer.

## Pricking out
By now, the half-hardy bedding plants and annuals sown in mid-spring will need transferring to trays of potting compost; a standard seed-tray will take about 25-30 seedlings.

## Potting
The cuttings of dahlias and delphiniums may need one transitional potting before planting outdoors, into 7.5 or 10cm (3 or 4in) pots. Chrysanthemum, fuchsia and pelargonium cuttings can also be moved into pots. Fuchsias can go into a final pot size of at least 20cm (8in) diameter for flowering; pelargoniums will be satisfied with a 12.5-15cm (5-6in) diameter. Thereafter they will all remain in pots either in the greenhouse or outdoors in good summer weather.

The final potting for early and late-flowering chrysanthemums needs to be done with more care than usual, as the plants will be in their pots for anything from four to eight months and they will be growing vigorously and flowering profusely. They will need 23cm (9in) pots and J.I. potting compost No. 3; some gardeners make up a No. 4 mixture, for especially good blooms.

Pots, whether clay, plastic or whalehide, should be well crocked for best results and a little compost put on top of the crocks. The plants should be turned out of their present containers; if they are firmly entrenched a pointed stick pushed through the drainage hole should help to loosen them. Drainage material is removed from the base of the rootball and the plant set centrally in its new pot, so that the

*One of the most handsome biennials, the foxglove is a lover of shade and moist soil, but it will grow in most sites.*

surface of the rootball is 2.5-5cm (1-2in) below the pot rim. Compost is then poured in round it and rammed firmly down with a wooden rammer until the container is full. Firm, even potting is very important. Each plant should be given three bamboo canes, about 90-105cm (36-42in) long, spaced evenly round the edge of the pot. Finish by watering and standing the plants in a sheltered place free from the midday sun for a few days, after which they will take any amount of sun.

The half-hardy annuals and bedding plants sown in warmth in early spring and then pricked out may need small pots by now; they can be kept in these pots if the weather is cold and wet, but should be accustomed to lower temperatures ready for planting outdoors late in late spring or at the beginning of early summer.

## Thinning
The hardy annuals sown outdoors last month are the group of plants that will need thinning now. It is important to do it while they are still tiny, otherwise they quickly become straggly, lie about on the soil and never grow into the stout plants that will provide the display expected of annuals.

## Hardening off
As soon as freesia seedlings are showing about 1-2.5cm ($\frac{1}{2}$-1in) of leaf, they can be moved into a cold frame and hardened off for two weeks or so. Then stand them in the open, in a cool, lightly shaded place for the summer; too much warmth will delay flowering.

Half-hardy annuals and bedding plants, whether pricked out or potted, can be put in a frame also, to become gradually accustomed to lower temperatures. Increase ventilation until no protection is supplied, even at night, unless the temperature drops below 10°C (50°F).

## Lifting bulbs
The spring-flowering bulbs such as daffodils, crocus, hyacinth and tulips will have finished flowering or be nearly finished and, if they are growing outdoors, can be treated in one of two ways.

If the ground in which they are growing is not wanted for summer plants, they can be left where they are and the leaves allowed to die naturally. The leaves will manufacture some of the food the bulb needs to develop its flower embryo for next spring. Daffodils have actually produced this embryo by the end of late spring and if the leaves are cut off to tidy up the bulbs or because they were growing in the lawn, flowering is unlikely. Such bulbs will often produce offsets instead.

If you have spring bulbs growing where you have planned a display of summer bedding, you can dig up the bulbs as soon as flowering is over and replant them at once in a spare, slightly shaded corner. The technique is to dig a shallow trench and lay the bulbs in at an angle, so the leaves are lying on the soil surface; fill in the trench with crumbled soil and then water if at all dry. This is known as 'heeling in'. Provided the roots have not been badly damaged in the process of digging up, the bulbs will suffer no harm and will continue to ripen. Once the leaves have withered completely, they can be dug up at any time and eventually replanted. Whatever you do, remove the flower heads when they have died, unless you want the seed.

## Resting bulbs
Bulbs growing in the greenhouse which flowered through early and mid-spring will also be coming up to their resting and ripening time. These could include freesia, hyacinth, lachenalia, narcissi and tulip, in fact any of the outdoor spring bulbs which you may have brought on for early display.

Watering should continue while the leaves remain green but as soon as the tips begin to turn yellow, the quantity and frequency of watering should be gradually decreased. When the leaves have completely withered, no more watering should be done. It does no harm to liquid feed with a potash-high fertilizer during and after flowering, but this is not necessary once the plants start to die down. When growth has finished, the containers can be put under the greenhouse staging, laid on their sides for the summer.

Freesias are, however, an exception. These should be removed from the compost; you will find, when doing this, that the corms have buried themselves much deeper than the seed was originally sown. There will be one large and several smaller corms to each plant and, unless you want to go into the business of freesias as cut flowers, it is best to keep the largest corms only and do away with the remainder. You could grow them on, but it takes two to five years to produce flowering corms, depending on their size, and you will need a great deal of compost and space if you do decide to raise freesias in this way.

Clean the corms you are keeping of compost, roots and dead leaves, lay them in a single layer in a seed tray and store them in the dark, ideally in a temperature between 19 and 30°C (68 and 86°F). Too high a temperature or storage in sun results in 'petrified' corms; too low a temperature produces 'sleepers', which do not flower but which also do not die. They will grow normally if planted the following summer, having missed a year.

## Staking/training

The herbaceous perennials will be growing fast and many of them will need supports. There are just as many that can be grown without staking (see tables, Early and Mid-Autumn), but the older, more popular perennials usually need some support. Amongst these latter are delphinium, erigeron, some euphorbias, lupin, peony, poppy, pyrethrum and Michaelmas daisies if growth is well enough advanced.

Bushy twigs like pea sticks, bamboo canes, stakes such as those which are used for dahlias and extending wire rings are some of the supports available, used in conjunction with fillis (soft string), plastic-covered wire, sweetpea rings or twist-ties. If put on when growth is about 30cm (12in) high and the stems attached so that the plants do not look bundled up and can grow naturally, the supports should be quickly masked by leaves.

Some of the lilies may also need staking; a single cane is sufficient for one plant. Chrysanthemums, dahlias and sweetpeas will already have been staked when planted or sown.

Indoor plants with growth which may be long enough to need support include achimenes, begonias, freesias from seed and climbers. The pendula begonias and some achimenes are natural trailers, very good for growing in hanging baskets. Most pot plants can be staked with split bamboo canes but there are special, extending, wire stakes for the double-flowered begonias; they finish in a kind of cup or half ring on which the flowers rest. Because their length can be manipulated, they can be used for a variety of begonias.

Sweetpeas will need frequent attention every three or four days, to remove tendrils, attach the stems to the supports and remove sideshoots. There is more detail – and a line illustration – covering this aspect of the care of sweetpeas in Early Summer, in Tying/Training.

*Various methods of staking plants.* Left: *This shows one of the best ways of staking dahlias, with a tripod of stout stakes on the outside of the plants.* Right: *Twiggy brushwood is suitable for many border perennials.*

## Cutting back/deadheading

The remains of flowers should be removed from spring-flowering bulbs and herbaceous perennials. Rock plants such as aubrieta can be trimmed with shears and this treatment, far from being brutal, in fact clears out 'dead wood' to such an extent that some flower a second time, especially if encouraged with a little feeding after cutting.

## Feeding

Hippeastrums which have finished flowering and are now ripening their bulbs will be encouraged to flower next year if given a liquid fertilizer with a higher potassium content than nitrogen and phosphorus. Potassium is the nutrient thought to be most related to the maturity of plants and it can, to some extent, make up for a lack of sun.

Other container-grown, spring-flowering bulbs, such as daffodils and hyacinths, can be treated in the same way until they die down; details of the frequency and quantity of fertilizer applications will be given by the manufacturer.

## Mulching
A layer of rotted organic matter about 1-2.5cm ($\frac{1}{2}$-1in) thick on the soil surface round such plants as annuals and herbaceous perennials, especially peonies and hellebores, will do much to prevent water being lost from the soil when the hot weather comes. If the soil is dry, do not put the mulch on, as it will simply do a good job of keeping the soil dry; wait until the rains come, or water heavily with the hose before mulching.

## Lawn care
During normal weather conditions in temperate climates, the grass on lawns will need cutting every seven to ten days and every five days if the grass mixture is a really fine one and the turf of bowling-green texture.

If the grass is cut less often, much greater length of grass blade is removed from each grass plant per mowing. The fine grasses do not respond well to this occasional severe cutting, with the result that the coarse grasses have less to compete with and so flourish. The end product is a lawn consisting mainly of rye grass, annual meadow grass, creeping bent, even couch and an increasing proportion of weeds and moss.

Cutting very frequently, on the other hand, weakens the coarse grasses and encourages the finer ones. Since much of the mixture which provides a fine lawn consists of sheep's fescue, this is not surprising; the fescue originates on hills and downs cropped continuously by sheep, rabbits and other grazing animals, so that over the centuries these grasses have developed constitutions which ensure their survival in the face of such attacks.

A good height at which to keep the grass is 1cm ($\frac{1}{2}$in) if it is really fine, otherwise 2cm ($\frac{3}{4}$in) will be short enough. The best finish will be obtained with a mower which has about 8-10 blades on the cutting cylinder. The current view on removing grass cuttings is that mowing should be done with a collecting box or bag attached to the mower, otherwise the mowings lying on the lawn surface encourage worms, spread weeds and prevent aeration, but in dry weather they can be left to act as a minor mulch.

*Many of the greenhouse fuchsias, like this one, are almost hardy. With only a little heat in the greenhouse, they will flower all through a mild winter.*

Late spring is one of the best times to treat lawn weeds with a selective hormone weedkiller, since the weeds will be growing fast and the chemical will be rapidly absorbed and equally rapidly spread round the plant in the sap. Feeding the lawn in mid-spring will have encouraged growth in any case. Use the weedkiller evenly, whether in solid or liquid form; in general, apply it about two days after the last cut, and leave two or three days at least before the next cut. Hormone weedkillers are extremely potent, and whether you are using a solution or powder form, it is essential to choose a calm, windless day for application (see Flower Garden Controls and Treatment section).

## Shading
Sometime in late spring, the greenhouse should have shading applied to it, especially if it is a three-quarter span or lean-to against a south-facing wall. This is often chosen as an ideal situation for a greenhouse and certainly it protects from north winds and obtains the maximum effect from the sun's heat. But it can get extremely hot and glaringly light, conditions in which only cacti are happy.

Shading is essential; hessian, chain laths, plastic sheet or Venetian blinds all provide temporary shading which can be made automatic, depending on the light conditions, or you can put a wash on the glass. An easily made, inexpensive one consists of a mixture of quicklime or fresh hydrated lime and sufficient water to give it the consistency of milk; adding a little size to the mixture helps it to stick. There are proprietary washes as well; one of these becomes transparent when rained on but remains opaque in sunny weather and also, unfortunately in dull, dry weather.

## Weeding
Weeding amongst small plants is vital if you want a good display of bedding and annual plants, from mid-summer until autumn. The biennials in the nursery bed should be carefully watched, too, and perennial weeds in borders amongst herbaceous perennials should be systematically eradicated while still tiny, otherwise you will never be rid of such unwelcome plants as ground-elder, bindweed and oxalis. The hoe and the handfork are great allies for cultivated ground; paths, drives, paved terraces, patios, garage aprons and steps can be kept clear with chemical weedkillers (see Flower Garden Controls and Treatment section).

## Compost-heap making
The material for this will mainly be lawn-mowings, which are excellent as they heat up quickly, weeds, and cut-back spring-flowering plants. There may also be some excess

plant growth in the pool, which will need clearing out, and there are bound to be leaves, which seem to come down whatever the time of the year. As you make the heap, alternate layers of vegetative material with activator or sulphate of ammonia or, better still, with a thin layer of animal manure.

## Watering

Unless the weather is unseasonably hot, watering will be confined to the greenhouse plants and will be a daily necessity. Water which is at the same temperature as the atmosphere is best, so there should be a tank containing it in the greenhouse. A galvanized iron one, covered so that light is completely excluded, will ensure that the water remains clean and free from algae, dirt, insects, disease and even small mammals. A water-butt outdoors to collect drainpipe overflows should also be covered, but it is difficult to keep the water clean in these. A strainer on the end of the pipe will help but may result in flooding unless cleared out regularly. Butts made of polythene or plastic tend to encourage the growth of algae internally. The same is true of watering-cans; galvanized or painted ones are best.

## Ventilating

Roof ventilators in the greenhouse can be left open permanently; side ventilators can often be opened during the day and on really hot days doors can be left open. The temperature can also be lowered by damping down, that is, sprinkling the floor, staging, walls and plants with water two or three times a day.

Frames must be ventilated, too; this is very important, as they will contain various young plants which will be wanted for planting out at the end of late spring or early summer. On warm, sunny days, the lights can be pushed back completely and as the night temperature rises, they can be propped open at night, gradually being lifted more and more until they are left off altogether, unless the temperature is still dropping below 10°C (50°F) at night.

## Treating pests and diseases

Greenfly and caterpillars will be the main problems but another pest which will become an unseen nuisance from now on is the capsid. This is a green insect which feeds by sucking the sap from young leaves and shoot tips and from flower buds, with the result that the flowers, if they develop at all, are misshapen, lopsided and stunted. Dahlias and chrysanthemums are particularly vulnerable.

Capsids are about ten times larger than greenfly and quick-moving; they drop to the ground when disturbed, so are often missed. Damaged leaves will have pin-prick holes to start with, but rapidly become tattered and new shoot growth stops. This is one case when precautionary spraying is advisable, before damage or pests are seen, at the beginning of late spring and again as the manufacturers advise.

Another unseen pest which can do a lot of damage to narcissus bulbs is the narcissus bulb fly. The adults lay eggs in the soil close to the bulb's neck and the maggots which hatch bore into the bulb and feed in the centre for about two months from early summer onwards. Even if the bulbs do not die at once, the following year they will produce only a few short leaves. Dusting the soil round bulbs with an insecticide in the middle of late spring helps and should be repeated twice more at about two-week intervals.

Slugs and snails will need trapping or otherwise treating and there may be some grey mould in the greenhouse, which can be dealt with satisfactorily by hand removal (see Flower Garden Controls and Treatment section).

## Plants in flower

Achillea, Aethionema, Alyssum, Anemone, Aquilegia, Arabis, Arenaria, Armeria, Convallaria Daisy, Dicentra, Erysimum alpinum, Euphorbia, Forget-me-not, Foxglove, Globe flower (trollius), London Pride (Saxifraga x urbium), Mimulus, Pansy, Primula rosea, Saxifraga (mossy), Tulip, Wallflower

# Early Summer

Early summer can be one of the most attractive times of the year in the garden. Plant growth is at its lushest and freshest, leaves and flowers are clean, bright and not yet battered by summer thunderstorms and many of the herbaceous perennials are in full flower. They will provide the main display of colour but the hardy annuals will be coming along fast and will begin to make themselves obvious by the end of early summer.

Most of the initial work of sowing, planting, pricking out and thinning will have been done, but if you were rushed in spring, the remnants of these jobs will need to be cleared up. A final potting can be given to many greenhouse residents and thereafter this will only need to be done occasionally, unless you are into taking cuttings of everything in sight.

With a chance of really hot weather any time from now through the rest of the summer, watering will become one of the more important jobs, particularly in the greenhouse. A few days without rain on sandy soils and plants will become distressed, particularly the small ones and those just planted out. The temperature in the greenhouse will probably need lowering, rather than the reverse, and cuttings in frames should be allowed some ventilation, too.

There will be quite a lot of tidying-up jobs, such as deadheading, training, stopping and tying but some of these could be called hard work, though they are essential for good displays of flowers, whether first or second flushes. One heavy job which will need doing if you want to sow a lawn in autumn is cultivating the site, as a preliminary to fallowing it for the summer. You could leave it till autumn, but the weed crop is likely to be fairly heavy if you do and will appear at the same time as the new grass seedlings.

# At~a~glance diary

**Prepare the soil for:** sowing seed and planting outdoors

**Prepare compost for:** sowing seed and potting under glass

**Sow seeds outdoors of:** Canterbury bells, double daisies, forget-me-not, foxglove hollyhock, mullein (Verbascum bombyciferum), primulas, polyanthus, primrose, sweet william, wallflower; herbaceous and alpine perennials, aquilegia, aubrieta, alyssum, armeria, delphinium, lupin, oriental poppy

**Sow seeds under glass of:** cineraria, calceolaria, Primula malacoides, P. obconica, P. sinensis, P. stellata

**Plant outdoors:** half-hardy annuals and bedding plants, dahlia

**Prick out:** cineraria, cobaea, ipomoea, Primula malacoides sown in late spring, other primulas sown in early summer if they have grown fast enough

**Pot:** late-flowering chrysanthemums, cineraria, cobaea, coleus, ipomoea, Primula malacoides; plants permanently in pots as required; rooted cuttings of fuchsia and pelargonium

**Thin:** hardy annuals, half-hardy annuals and bedding plants, biennials

**Transplant:** biennials sown in late spring

**Feed:** pot plants repotted in early and mid-spring, hippeastrum, spring-flowering bulbs if still growing, sweetpea, lawns on light soils

**Stake:** border carnations, freesias if not already done

**Train, tie in:** chrysanthemum, dahlia, delphinium, sweetpea, violet

**Divide:** auricula, iris (bearded), polyanthus, primrose

**Weed:** as necessary, including pools

**Routine work:** mow, deadhead, water, make compost heap ventilate and damp down greenhouse

**Pests and diseases:** caterpillars, capsid bug, flea beetle, greenfly, leaf miner, mealy bug, red spider mite, rust, whitefly

# Jobs to do

### Preparing the soil for sowing seed outdoors

With the summer season officially here, the main seed-sowing period is over and you may in fact have more than enough work on your hands without adding to it. However, through lack of time, some seeds that should have been sown in late spring may have been left out and there are plants which should be sown specifically in early summer. Soil can therefore be prepared in the usual way for sowing (see Early Spring) in the nursery bed.

### Preparing compost for sowing seed under glass

Again there is little work to be done here, except to ensure a display next winter and spring and, if you do not have any seed compost left over from late spring, make up a new batch and cover it with black plastic sheet until needed.

### Preparing the soil for planting outdoors

Planting may also be a case of catching up with late spring or of planting which has been delayed due to bad weather, but in any case, clear the site of weeds and rubbish, scatter a little compound fertilizer on the soil and fork it a few centimetres (inches) deep, about a week before planting.

You can also, with advantage, choose a site for a new lawn and start to prepare it now. Cultivate it by digging or with a rotavator to 23cm (9in) deep or to the depth of the topsoil and leave roughly broken up. You may find grey-brown caterpillars and bright-yellow 'worms' in it as you do so, especially if it is old turfland or meadow; these are leather-jackets (daddy-long-legs larvae) and wireworms which should be destroyed, though birds may do this for you as you work.

The ground can then be dressed with rotted organic matter at 2.5kg per sq m (5lb per sq yd), or coarse peat at 3kg per sq m (6lb per sq yd) and left fallow through the summer. This results in weed seeds germinating: these can be hoed off at intervals, each time a fresh infestation appears,

until most of the weed-seed population on the site has been destroyed. You can alternatively use a 'new lawn' weed-killer at the time of grass germination, but the seedling weeds do provide compost-heap material. After hoeing, rake the soil to an even, smooth surface.

If you are dealing with a heavy soil, it is well worth while mixing in coarse sand as you cultivate, at a rate of 6kg per sq m (14lb per sq yd).

### Preparing compost for indoor planting

From now until autumn, you should always have a supply of compost ready for potting, as plants permanently in pots may need re-potting and others grown from seed will need potting on at irregular intervals through the summer (see potting compost, Late Winter).

*Achimenes are a delightful rhizomatous greenhouse plant, flowering for many weeks in summer.*

*Sweet williams are one of the oldest cultivated flowers, dating from medieval times. They will self-sow regularly.*

### Sowing seed outdoors

Seeds to sow outside in early summer can be any of the biennials sown last month, though they will flower some weeks later next spring, and also forget-me-nots, but leave these until late in early summer. Primulas, polyanthus and primroses can be sown outdoors in a shady nursery bed.

There are also some herbaceous perennials which will grow easily from seed sown now, in a nursery bed, to be transplanted in early autumn to their permanent places. They include aquilegia, delphinium, hollyhock, lupin, oriental poppy and such rock plants as aubrieta and armeria. It is worth trying any seed you have available now from perennials and rock plants, as germination of fresh seed, sown as soon as ripe, is nearly always better than if left until the following spring. Plants from early and mid-summer sowings will then be strong enough and large enough to survive the winter weather.

### Sowing seed under glass

*Primula malacoides*, sown in late spring, may also be sown now, to flower late in winter and in early spring next year; *P. sinensis*, *P. stellata* and *P. obconica* can be sown now as well. Cineraria is another beautiful greenhouse plant for winter flowering which needs to be sown now, for flowering with the primulas. There are some glorious colours amongst modern cinerarias and you could fill a greenhouse with these plants alone. The range of colour covers pink, rose, white, purple, light and royal blue, crimson and bi-colours.

Calceolarias are also showy flowering pot-plants for early-summer sowing to bloom in early spring; the range of colour is quite different, covering shades of yellow and orange, bronze, scarlet and cerise, often heavily spotted with red or bronze. They provide a complete contrast in form, too, with petals fused to form a pouch, instead of the single rays of the daisy-like cinerarias. Calceolarias are a little more sensitive to low temperatures than cinerarias and should always be free from frosts, with a temperature in winter preferably between 7° and 10°C (45 and 50°F).

### Planting outdoors

It should be perfectly safe by now to plant dahlias outdoors; if night frosts are still about, then the weather is very unseasonable and you will have to keep the plants in frames a little longer or cover them with cloches, if not too tall. Treat bedding plants the same way, provided they have been hardened off.

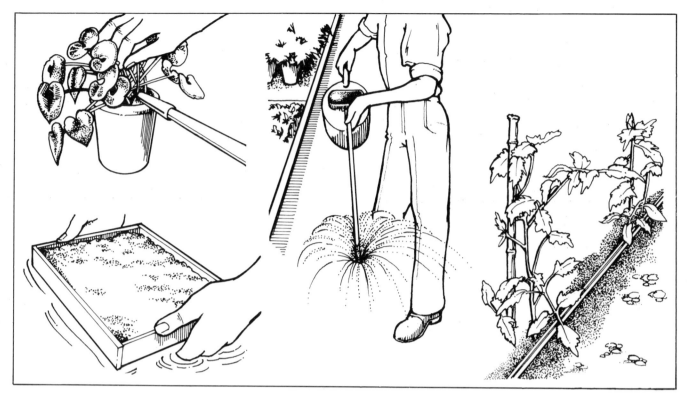

## Pricking out

There will be little pricking out to do in the greenhouse. The cinerarias and *Primula malacoides* sown last month will probably be ready sometime this month to go into trays or, if you only have a few, into pans. Keep them as cool as possible and move them out into a cold frame, shaded from sun, as soon as they have recovered from pricking out. Cobaea and ipomoea should go into 9cm (3½in) pots unless you have sown them singly in 5cm (2in) peat pots, where they can stay until the roots begin to show through the sides or base.

## Potting

Plants to go into their final pots and stand outside are the late-flowering chrysanthemums (see Late Spring). Fast-growing or vigorous plants permanently in pots, such as chlorophytum, cissus, jasmine, passion flower and trade-scantia, will need re-potting. Seeds sown in late spring and pricked out at the end of that season may need individual pots in early summer, 5 or 7.5cm (2 or 3in) in diameter, depending on the size of the rootballs. These will be cinerarias and *Primula malacoides* and they can then go into a shaded cold frame. Cobaea, ipomoea and coleus will also need potting on; the size will depend on the size of the root-ball and this in turn depends on the time of sowing, or, in

*Watering of plants needs to be done according to the type of plant and its needs. Spout watering from a can to the side of the pot prevents rotting of succulent stems—in cyclamen, for example; a seed-box is put into a shallow tray of water; a greenhouse is damped down to lessen the need for water; trickle watering supplies food as well.*

the case of coleus, on the size of the plant when bought in late spring. Cobaea and ipomoea will both need quite large final pots, about 20cm (8in), while coleus do well in 12.5 or 15cm (5 or 6in) sizes. Fuchsia and pelargonium rooted cuttings will need larger pots, probably their final size (see potting, Late Spring).

## Thinning

Any half-hardy annuals and bedding plants, hardy annuals and biennials you sowed in late spring outdoors will all need thinning this month; you will probably have to do two thinnings, one at the beginning and one at the end of early summer, depending on the weather and the time at which you sowed them. All the biennials but mullein will only need thinning once, because they will be transplanted before being put in their permanent positions. Mullein is sown where it is to flower, and will therefore be thinned twice, to a spacing of about 45cm (18in) each way.

# Hardy Annuals

| Name | Time of flowering; flower colour | Height and spread cm/in | Type of flower |
|---|---|---|---|
| Bartonia (Mentzelia) | mid–late summer; yellow | 45–60 x 30cm (18–24 x 12in) | saucer |
| Chrysanthemum, annual* | mid-summer–mid-autumn; all colours but blue | 45–60 x 22.5cm (18–24 x 9in) | daisy |
| Clarkia* | mid–late summer; pink, red, purple, white | 45–60 x 30cm (18–24 x 12in) | carnation |
| Convolvulus, annual | mid–late summer; blue, rose, white, yellow | 15 x 15cm (6 x 6in) | trumpet |
| Cornflower* | early–mid-summer; blue, pink, white | 35–60 x 20–30cm (14–24 x 8–12in) | brush |
| Echium (viper's tongue) | summer; blue, purple, rose | 20–30 x 25cm (8–12 x 10in) | bell |
| Eschscholzia* | summer; yellow, orange, rose, crimson, pink, white | 12.5–30 x 12.5–20cm (5–12 x 5–8in) | poppy |
| Godetia* | mid–late summer; red, white, salmon | 25–60 x 12–30cm (10–24 x 5–12in) | saucer, double |
| Larkspur* | summer; blue, rose, white | 30–90 x 22.5cm (12–36 x 9in) | spike |
| Limnanthes* | spring–summer; yellow and white | 15 x 15cm (6 x 6in) | saucer |
| Linaria (toadflax) | early summer–early autumn; crimson, pink, blue, violet, yellow | 22.5–30 x 15–22.5cm (9–12 x 6–9in) | two-lipped |
| Love-in-a-mist (nigella) | summer; blue, pink, white | 37.5–45 x 25cm (15–18 x 10in) | brush |
| Love-lies-bleeding (amaranthus) | early–late summer; crimson, green | 75 x 37.5cm (30 x 15in) | tassel |
| Marigold* | mid-summer–early autumn; orange, yellow, mahogany | 15–45 x 10–20cm (6–18 x 4–8in) | daisy |
| Mignonette | early–mid-summer; greenish, strongly fragrant | 22.5–30 x 15–22.5cm (9–12 x 6–9in) | insignificant |
| Nasturtium (non-climbing) | mid-summer–autumn; yellow, orange, red, bronze, cream, crimson | 15 x 10cm (6 x 4in) | trumpet |
| Phacelia | mid–late summer; deep blue | 22.5–45 x 15–30cm (9–18 x 6–12in) | bell |
| Poppy, annual | summer–autumn; red, pink, white | 45 x 20cm (18 x 8in) | saucer |
| Night-scented stock | mid–late summer; lilac-mauve | 30 x 20cm (12 x 8in) | spike |
| *Salvia horminum* | mid-summer–early autumn; purple, pink, violet | 60 x 22.5cm (24 x 9in) | coloured leaves |
| Sunflower | early–late summer; yellow | 210–240 x 37.5–45cm) (84–96 x 15–18in) | daisy |
| Sweetpea* | early summer–autumn; all colours | 210–240 x 15cm (84–96 x 6in) | pea |
| Sweet sultan (centaurea) | mid–late summer; purple, pink, yellow, white | 45–60 x 20cm (18–24 x 18in) | brush |
| Viscaria* | summer; mauve, pink, blue, red, white | 25–35 x 15–20cm (10–14 x 6–8in) | star |

*\* = can be sown in autumn to over-winter*

Although it is generally thought that wallflowers do best if transplanted, they become much stronger plants if sown where they are to flower and thinned there twice. If this is done, the rows should be about 23cm (9in) apart and the plants thinned to a final spacing of 15cm (6in). Since they are part of the same family (*Cruciferae*) as the cabbage tribe, they should not be grown in acid soil, nor should they follow plants from that family, such as stocks.

## Transplanting

At the end of early summer, the biennials may be ready for transplanting. If wallflowers are to be moved do it when

*As well as being delicate and beautiful in colour and a graceful shape, freesias have an exquisite fragrance.*

there are three true leaves present, and about the same size is right for the other biennials also. Wallflowers can then be planted 10cm (4in) apart in the rows, with 30cm (12in) between the rows, to make weeding easier. All these little plants need moving and replanting quickly, with as much of the root system intact as possible, from moist soil into moist soil, with a watering-in afterwards. Do the job in the evening, so that they do not have to contend with possibly hot midday summer sun before their roots have absorbed water from the new site.

## Feeding

Pot-plants which were repotted in early and mid-spring will have used a good deal of the nutrient in the compost, and regular liquid feeding can start from now on, unless

they have grown so much that repotting or potting on is necessary. Hippeastrums should be fed, together with any other spring bulbs still growing. For really prizewinning sweetpeas, liquid feeding will do wonders, though with good trench preparation during winter, they may be growing so fast that extra feeding is unnecessary. Lawns growing on light soils will need a powder feed at half the normal rate, applied when the soil is moist and watered in; little and often is the guide to feeding turf on sandy or 'hot' soil. Cacti do not need feeding unless they were not repotted in the spring and then only once every four weeks or so.

*The border peony, with its lovely colouring and full-blown flowers, is the personification of early summer.*

## Staking

Most plants that need staking will already have been secured but border carnations will develop their rather floppy and comparatively long flowering stems during the next few weeks. A little help in standing up will mean a better display but don't tie them rigidly to the supports right up to the buds, otherwise they will lose much of their charm. Stake freesias if not done already (see sowing, Mid-Spring).

## Tying/training

Continue to tie in chrysanthemums, dahlias, delphiniums, lilies and sweetpeas as they grow and keep an eye on other tall-growing plants which may not be as sturdy as they look. Sweetpeas may begin to develop flowering stems towards the end of early summer in warm gardens; watch for the embryo flower buds at tips of the stems, otherwise you will be removing them automatically as sideshoots.

Early- and late-flowering varieties of chrysanthemums will need stopping; violets should be de-runnered, otherwise the parent plants flower less well. Take the runners off with as much stem as possible.

## Dividing

Some plants – such as polyanthus, auriculas and primroses – can be increased by division in early summer. You will find that they have produced plantlets at the side of the parent crown; these can easily be split off with roots attached, replanted in a shady place until autumn and then planted where they are to flower.

Bearded irises can be lifted after flowering and divided every four or five years, otherwise they get crowded and flower badly. This is the time when they grow new roots, so dig them up, keep the new younger root or rhizome and throw away the old central crown. Replant so that the rhizome is only just below the soil surface; a little showing above the surface does no harm. Bonemeal mixed into the soil before planting at about 120g per sq m (4oz per sq yd) will help the roots.

## Weeding

Continue to hoe or use weedkiller to keep weeds at bay. By now duckweed and blanket weed may be starting to grow in pools; duckweed is the tiny, light-green, one-leaved floating weed which collects in large groups on the water surface and blanket weed is the long, hair-like, dark green strands which grow submerged in the water. Chemical control in garden pools is not possible as cultivated plants will also be damaged, so frequent raking all through the growing season is necessary to keep these two water weeds under control. In pools well stocked with goldfish and freshwater winkles, the blanket weed will be eaten.

## Routine work

Continue to mow the lawn, deadhead unless seed is required, water outdoors (do not forget freesias) and in the greenhouse and build the compost heap. Keep the greenhouse well ventilated and damped down.

## Treating pests and diseases

Greenfly and capsid will continue to be a nuisance, various caterpillars will be about, including one rather beautiful velvety green kind which lives mostly on delphiniums, and Sawfly larvae feeding on the leaves of Solomon's Seal

*Bearded irises can be increased by dividing the rhizomes after flowering, keeping the youngest end part for replanting, with leaves attached. Cordon sweetpeas are tied to a stake, and the side-shoots and tendrils removed as they grow.*

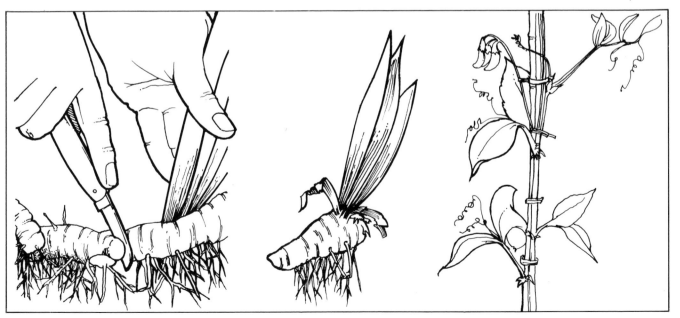

(*Polygonatum multiflorum*). A pernicious new pest is leaf-miner, which can do surprisingly bad damage, considering it is such a minute larva. The maggot hatches from eggs laid in the leaf tissue and feeds in the tissue, making winding, pale-coloured lines (tunnels) or pale-brown blisters as it moves about. Leaves can be so badly infested that they wither completely; chrysanthemums and cinerarias suffer badly. They will also be found on a variety of other plants but if the plants are growing in the ground they will not suffer so badly; it is the potted plants which seem to have little resistance. Remove affected leaves and destroy and spray the remainder with an insecticide.

Sometimes flea beetles attack seedling and young wall-flowers but an insecticidal dust applied as a precaution will solve this trouble; the symptoms of infestation are small round holes in the leaves and tiny, hopping, dark-coloured beetles. Whitefly, small white, moth-like creatures, can become terrible pests on greenhouse fuchsias, usually if the plants are kept too dry and hot. Likewise red spider mite on most greenhouse plants; it feeds on the sap, mainly in the leaves, and makes webs. A hand lens will show the light red, round adults on the undersides of the leaves.

Damping down the greenhouse keeps it more or less free of pests as well as cooling it and making the air humid. Mealybug is another greenhouse dweller, partial to hippeastrums but not averse to other potted plants. Blobs of white fluff on your plants are highly suspect and are likely to contain the bug, feeding on the sap.

Rust fungi can be a problem on such plants as hollyhocks and antirrhinums, pinks and carnations. Although they are not as widespread as the insects mentioned, they are very damaging where they do occur, resulting in early leaf-fall, and poor, stunted plants. Symptoms are raised, bright brownish-red spots on the under surface of leaves, easily missed until it is too late. Grow resistant varieties if available, avoid crowded conditions, and hand-pick diseased leaves, following with a fungicidal spray (see Flower Garden Controls and Treatments).

## Plants in flower

Achillea millefolium, Alyssum, Antirrhinum, Annuals (hardy and half-hardy sown in early spring) Aquilegia, Arabis, Astilbe, Campanula, Carnation, Catmint (nepeta), Cerastium tomentosum (snow-in-summer), Chamomile, Daisy, Day lily (hemerocallis) Delphinium, Dicentra spectabilis, Erigeron, Euphorbia, Forget-me-not, Geranium, Gentiana acaulis, Geum, Gladioli, Globe flower (trollius), Helianthemum, Heuchera, Iris (in variety), Lamium maculatum, Lily (in variety), Lithospermum diffusum, Lobelia London pride (Saxifraga x urbium)

## Plants in flower

Lupin, Pansy, Pelargonium, Peony, Phlox (dwarf), Pickerel (Pontederia cordata), Pink, Poppy, Primula (in variety), Pyrethrum, Red hot poker (kniphofia), Roseroot (Sedum roseum), Wild strawberry (Fragaria vesca), Solomon's Seal (Polygonatum multiflorum), Stonecrop (Sedum acre), Sweet william, Verbascum,

## Greenhouse

Begonia, Cacti, Fuchsia, Ipomoea, Jasmine, Pelargonium, Streptocarpus (old plants)

# Mid-Summer

Like early summer, this is a good season for a colourful display in gardens grown mainly for ornament. The herbaceous perennials will still be in flower and the annuals and bedding plants will really start to come into their own in the next few weeks, filling out their growth and covering the soil with a patchwork of brilliant colour. For a sheer display of dazzle, there is nothing to beat the hardy annuals when they are grown really well.

Your main concern will be to see that the plants have enough water; mid-summer can be the hottest, driest time of the year, only interrupted by thunder-storms, when the rain comes down so fast that the dry ground cannot absorb it and it runs away to the lowest point. Watering by hose, sprinkler or can will be nec-essary throughout the period and the lawn especially should be kept moist. Mulches put on earlier in the year will prove their worth now.

The greenhouse, too, will need much attention in the form of watering the plants and damping down; constant watering does of course wash the nutrients out of the composts before the roots can absorb them so you may have to increase the frequency of liquid feeds and repotting.

There will be a little planting and seed sowing, some thinning and transplanting and a general titivation of the displays in the form of deadheading and trimming. Some training will still be necessary and disbudding of dahlias and chrysanthe-mums to produce large blooms can start, but the work is not anything like the spring rush or the winter labour. Plant growth in general has reached its maximum and, as it will remain at this peak for some weeks, you can relax.

# At~a~glance diary

| | |
|---|---|
| **Prepare the soil for:** | sowing seed and planting outdoors |
| **Prepare compost for:** | potting under glass |
| **Sow seeds outdoors of:** | pansy |
| **Plant outdoors:** | colchicum, autumn-flowering crocus, Nerine bowdenii, seedling alpine and herbaceous perennials sown in early summer |
| **Transplant:** | biennials, pansies if large enough |
| **Prick out:** | cineraria, calceolaria, primulas malacoides, obconica, sinensis, stellata |
| **Thin:** | hardy annuals, half-hardy annuals and bedding plants, biennials |
| **Pot:** | calceolaria, cineraria, Nerine sarniensis, primulas malacoides, sinensis, stellata plants permanently in pots |
| **Start:** | cyclamen (old tubers), freesia (from corms) |
| **Lift:** | spring-flowering bulbs, biennials |
| **Deadhead or trim:** | all plants and flowers that have died down |
| **Disbud:** | early-flowering chrysanthemum, dahlia |
| **Feed:** | greenhouse plants, cacti if not repotted in spring, sweetpeas, lawns in cool weather |
| **Layer:** | sweetpea |
| **Increase:** | border carnations from layers, bearded iris by division |
| **Water:** | all as required |
| **Weed:** | pansy seedlings, lawns in cool weather |
| **Routine work:** | mow, build up compost heap, treat pests and diseases, ventilate and damp down in greenhouse |

# Jobs to do

*Summer-flowering jasmine is hardy in sheltered places and its fragrant flowers will perfume the garden all summer.*

### Preparing the soil for sowing outdoors

This is only a case of preparing for one group of plants, which are to be transplanted, so a small seed-bed can be got ready in the nursery-bed; it will not be long in use (see Early Spring for details of preparation).

### Preparing the soil for planting outdoors

Most of the planting now will be of autumn-flowering bulbs, so look for a place where the soil is naturally medium to well drained and on the sunny side. Mix in plenty of grit if it is not, about 3.5kg per sq m (7lb per sq yd), and a little rotted organic matter, if the soil is poor, at 1.5kg per sq m (3lb per sq yd). These bulbs are used, in their natural habitats, to very good drainage and baking sun in summer; you will find that most bulbs grown in such conditions, if you have them, will seed themselves without any encouragement.

### Preparing compost for potting

Here the work to be done consists of potting on pricked-out plants from seed, so the compost should be the J.I. potting No. 1 type or whatever you are using as its equivalent (see Late Winter).

### Sowing outdoors

This is an excellent time to sow pansies in order to have plants in flower from late spring onwards next year. If you have a heavy soil, the beginning of mid-summer is the most suitable time, and for warm gardens and sandy soil, the end of the period is preferable. The timing is fairly important: too soon and they will grow large enough to be badly damaged by wind and frost before flowering, too late and they will be so small when ready for planting that they will not establish before winter. Sow the seed thinly in rows about 20–25cm (8–10in) apart, making the drill about 2.5cm (1in) deep and just covering the seed firmly. If the soil is dry, water the rows before sowing, and sprinkle gently but thoroughly after the soil has been returned. Pansies need a well-drained soil.

## Planting outdoors

Colchicum, autumn-flowering crocus and *Nerine bowdenii* can be planted in mid-summer; the depth of planting should be about 7.5-12.5cm (3-5in) for colchicum, 7.5cm (3in) for autumn-flowering crocus and sufficiently shallow for nerines for the neck of the bulb to be just above the soil surface. Both the crocus and the colchicum produce their flowers before the leaves at the end of late summer and in early autumn and will grow and flower best in a sunny place, though dappled shade is not unsuitable. *Nerine bowdenii*, from South Africa, will need sun and a wall to back the bed in which it is growing. Plant all these bulbs at a spacing of a few cm (in) from each other, and leave undisturbed for several years.

You can also plant outdoors in their permanent places the perennial seedlings produced last month; spacing will be roughly in proportion to the height of the plants, allowing a space between each plant of a kind, two-thirds of its height: e.g., aquilegias 30cm (12in) high would have 20cm (8in) between plants.

## Transplanting

Any biennials sown in late spring which are to be transplanted should be moved now, in the way advised in that season and there may also be some from early summer, if they were sown early enough and have come on well. Pansies sown at the beginning of mid-summer may need transplanting at the end of it (see Late Summer for method).

## Pricking out

Seed sown in the greenhouse in early summer will need moving into trays and will include cineraria, calceolaria, and *Primula malacoides*, *obconica*, *sinensis* and *stellata*. Done at the beginning of mid-summer, they may well need potting up separately by the end of it, especially the cinerarias and calceolarias. They can all go into the cold frame when pricked out.

Primulas, polyanthus and primroses, sown in early summer, will need pricking out 7.5cm (3in) apart each way, still in shaded places.

## Thinning

There may still be some late-sown hardy annuals and half-hardy annuals and bedding plants that need a final thinning; early-summer-sown biennials will need one or two thinnings in mid-summer.

*An herbaceous border, skilfully planted like this one, will provide brilliant colour from spring to autumn.*

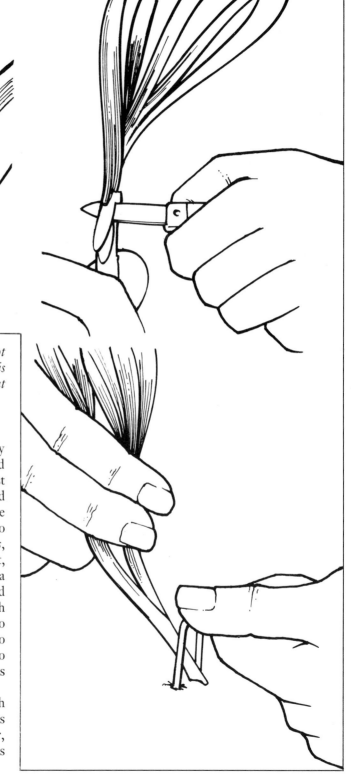

*Layering border carnations: A new shoot which has not flowered has the lower leaves removed, then a slanting cut is made partially through the stem on the underside. The cut stem is pinned down into fine soil to root.*

## Potting

The greenhouse plants grown from seed sown in early summer, *Primula malacoides*, *sinensis* and *stellata*, and calceolarias and cinerarias, may need to go into their first pots towards the end of mid-summer. Cinerarias and calceolarias are likely to fit 7.5cm (3in) pots but primulas are slow to grow and have delicate little roots to start with, so 5cm (2in) diameter pots will suit them. *Primula malacoides*, sown in late spring, may now need a 7.5cm (3in) pot, cobaea and ipomoea will be coming on fast and could use a 15cm (6in) pot or even their final size pot, 20cm (8in), and cinerarias from late spring may need a 7.5cm (3in) pot. With good compost and careful potting, it is often possible to skip a pot size and jump straight from 7.5cm (3in) to 12.5cm (5in), which saves time and compost. You can do this with many plants, the exceptions being the ones such as primulas, which are fastidious about drainage.

Any plants permanently in pots should be given fresh compost and larger pots as required, if you find the roots are well on to the outside of the soilball. By now, however, only the most vigorous and fast-growing will need this treatment.

*Nerine sarniensis*, which is really not frost-hardy, unlike *N. bowdenii*, should be potted during mid-summer for flowering in early autumn; each bulb should have a 12.5cm (5in) pot and should just have its neck above the compost surface. A cactus compost would not come amiss, as they do like good drainage; after planting, give the bulb a good soak, let the superfluous water drain off and then give it a sunny position. The leaves will appear during or after flowering.

## Starting

Freesia corms can be started off, in J.I. potting compost No. 3, planted with their own depth of compost above them. Put ten in a 20cm (8in) pot; they should begin to flower in early winter. Once potted, the freesias should be put outdoors in a cool, lightly shaded place and kept moist.

Cyclamen corms can also be potted to start them into growth for flowering in early winter; they are quite likely to start themselves off and produce new leaves from a completely dry corm sometime in mid-summer. Use J.I. potting compost No. 2, and a 12.5-15cm (5-6in) pot for most corms, though the really large old ones will need 20cm (8in) pots. Make sure the surface of the corm is above the compost.

*The curious flowers of the passion-flower will set to produce egg-shaped fruit, orange in colour and edible.*

## Lifting

The spring-flowering bulbs that have died down completely can be lifted and cleaned if the ground is required for other plants; in any case it is better to lift tulips, otherwise they become weedy or flower badly, or mice eat them. Biennials which have finished flowering can also be dug up and consigned to the compost heap. You will probably have a bonus in the form of self-sown seedlings from some of them, so don't be too hasty to remove all the plant seedlings that appear; they may not be weeds.

## Deadheading/trimming

Continue to remove flowers as they die, taking the stem off completely at the same time, as it is no use to the plant and will die in any case. Plants which will particularly need this attention are delphiniums, heuchera, iris, London pride, lupin, lythrum, monarda, pelargoniums, peony, poppy, pyrethrum and any annuals and bedding plants with flowers which have faded.

Catmint (nepeta) and *Campanula porscharskyana* will flower again in early autumn if the flowering stems are cut off and, in fact, they may already be producing good new growth. Rock plants which flower profusely on creeping growth will respond in the same way to similar treatment.

## Disbudding

You can begin to disbud the early-flowering chrysanthemums now, if you want one large bloom on each sideshoot. It is likely that there is a miniature flower-bud showing at the tip of each shoot and other tiny growths in the axils of the leaves below it. These will also produce flowers if left to grow but should be snapped off without removing the leaves so that the plant's energy is concentrated on the top flower-bud. The smaller these shoots are when removed, the less shock it is to the plant. However, if you want sprays of flowers, do not disbud but leave them to grow. The plants will be at different stages of growth, depending on variety, so it is a question of doing the disbudding all through mid-summer as they become ready, rather than all at once.

Dahlias can also be disbudded in the same way and for the same reasons; the more sideshoots you allow on a plant the smaller the flowers. Dahlias can carry more blooms of a reasonable size than chrysanthemums and less disbudding per stem is needed, usually only the removal of the two side-buds just below the top one. If each plant has many sideshoots the lower ones can be removed to good effect and the plant allowed to carry the remainder.

## Feeding

Continue to liquid feed sweetpeas as in early summer and greenhouse plants where necessary, including hippeastrums; these may start to die down now and when they do, feeding should stop. Cacti not potted in spring may need one liquid feed in mid-summer. Lawns on sandy soils can have another half-strength powder feed, but not if the weather is hot and dry, because the grass is likely to be burnt. In these weather conditions it will not be growing much, so food is rather superfluous. Early autumn is the time when lawns should be given close attention, to put them in good condition for winter (see Lawn care, Early Autumn).

## Layering

Sweetpeas that were planted in early spring can be layered now to prolong their lives, by detaching them all completely from their canes, laying the stems along the ground beside the row of canes and then training the stem up the fourth or fifth cane along from the original support. The last few plants can have the canes from the beginning of the row transferred to them. In this way, they will have another 60cm (24in) of cane to climb up and so produce more flowers.

*Disbudding a chrysanthemum.* Left: *The side buds round the top central bud are removed to leave the latter on its own.* Centre and right: *Saving home-grown seed. Cut the seed-heads, hang up to dry, and roll and sieve to remove chaff.*

## Increasing

Bearded irises can be divided if not already done (see Early Summer for details).

Border carnations can be layered and this is done as follows. Choose a new shoot which has not flowered, take off the leaves up to within about 10cm (4in) of the tip and then make a slanting cut just below a leaf joint, partially through the stem on the side which will be closest to the soil. Bend the stem until it touches the soil, pin it down with a bent wire just before the cut, and then gently pull the end of the stem more or less upright so that the cut is open and in contact with the sandy compost which you now put over and round the cut stem. The upright part of the stem can be attached to a small support. Rooting should occur within a few weeks.

Mid-summer is the time to take regal pelargonium cuttings, as they finish their flowering season now and new shoots suitable for cuttings will begin to lengthen (see Late Summer for method).

## Watering

Give water where needed to all outdoor plants and in particular keep the lawn well supplied with water; using a sprinkler is best. Give sweetpeas a good soaking at intervals in dry weather. Water hippeastrums less and less as the leaves begin to wither but continue to water other greenhouse plants as they need it. Do not neglect your freesias in pots outdoors, nor any plants in frames, such as cinerarias or primulas; they will all need water. Cinerarias are very prone to wilt in hot sun and must have lots of water at these times.

## Weeding

Little will be required, but pansy seedlings are easily swamped by weed seedlings germinating with them, so watch these right up until they need transplanting. Lawns can still be treated for weeds but preferably not in hot, dry weather; however, in such weather they are no more likely to be growing, with one exception, than the grass is. It is in cool damp summers that weeds cause most trouble and it is then that hormone weedkillers are most effective. The one exception is the yellow-flowered sucking clover, which spreads rapidly in hot weather and on sandy soils. As it is an annual, removal before flowering will do a great deal to prevent its appearance the following year. Hand removal is usually sufficient but a selective weedkiller can be used, if need be (see Flower Garden Controls and Treatment).

## Routine work

Continue to mow (without the collecting box in dry conditions), make the compost heap and deal with pests and diseases as in early summer. Keep the greenhouse well damped down and ventilated.

## Plants in flower

Agapanthus, Anemone (Japanese), Allium, Antirrhinum, Annuals (hardy and half-hardy sown in spring), Aquilegia, Campanula, Carnation, Centaurea, Chamomile, Daisy, Day lily (hemerocallis), Delphinium, Forget-me-not, Geranium, Geum, Gladioli, Gypsophila, Iris (English), Lily (in variety), Lobelia, Mimulus, Pansy, Pelargonium, Phlox (dwarf and tall)

Poppy, Red hot poker (kniphofia) Rudbeckia, Scabious, Sweet william, Verbascum, Veronica, Water lily

## Greenhouse

Achimenes, Begonia, Cacti, Campanula isophylla (Italian bellflower), Cobaea, Gloxinia, Hoya, Ipomoea, Jasmine, Passion flower, Pelargonium, Streptocarpus, Thunbergia

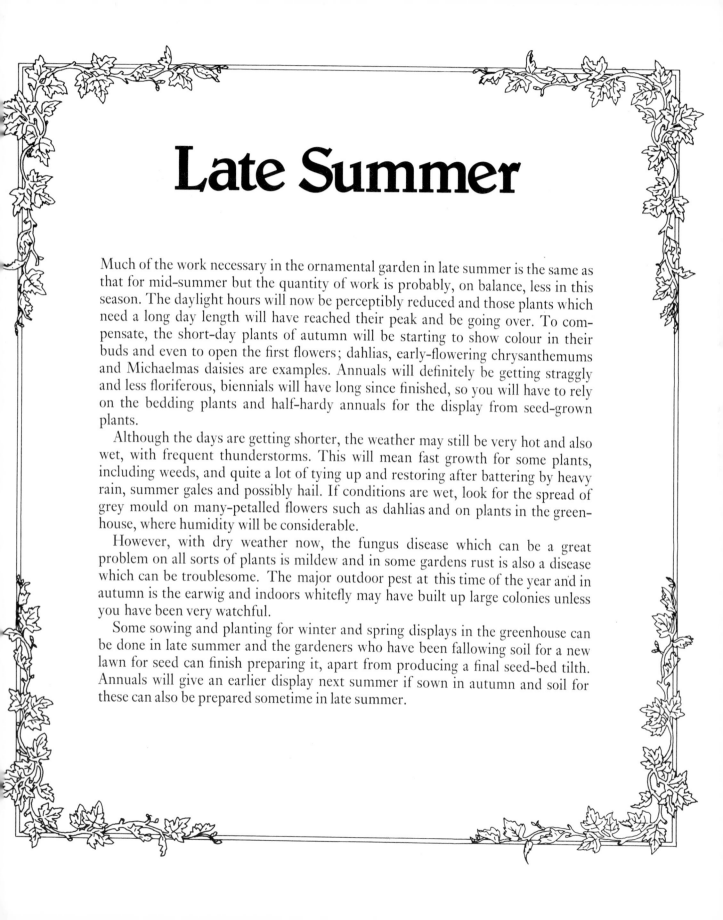

# Late Summer

Much of the work necessary in the ornamental garden in late summer is the same as that for mid-summer but the quantity of work is probably, on balance, less in this season. The daylight hours will now be perceptibly reduced and those plants which need a long day length will have reached their peak and be going over. To compensate, the short-day plants of autumn will be starting to show colour in their buds and even to open the first flowers; dahlias, early-flowering chrysanthemums and Michaelmas daisies are examples. Annuals will definitely be getting straggly and less floriferous, biennials will have long since finished, so you will have to rely on the bedding plants and half-hardy annuals for the display from seed-grown plants.

Although the days are getting shorter, the weather may still be very hot and also wet, with frequent thunderstorms. This will mean fast growth for some plants, including weeds, and quite a lot of tying up and restoring after battering by heavy rain, summer gales and possibly hail. If conditions are wet, look for the spread of grey mould on many-petalled flowers such as dahlias and on plants in the greenhouse, where humidity will be considerable.

However, with dry weather now, the fungus disease which can be a great problem on all sorts of plants is mildew and in some gardens rust is also a disease which can be troublesome. The major outdoor pest at this time of the year and in autumn is the earwig and indoors whitefly may have built up large colonies unless you have been very watchful.

Some sowing and planting for winter and spring displays in the greenhouse can be done in late summer and the gardeners who have been fallowing soil for a new lawn for seed can finish preparing it, apart from producing a final seed-bed tilth. Annuals will give an earlier display next summer if sown in autumn and soil for these can also be prepared sometime in late summer.

# At~a~glance diary

**Prepare the soil for:** sowing seed outdoors in early autumn, planting outdoors

**Prepare compost for:** sowing and potting under glass

**Plant outdoors:** colchicum, autumn-flowering crocus Madonna lily

**Sow seeds under glass of:** cyclamen, schizanthus

**Pot:** calceolaria, border carnation (layered), cineraria, daffodil, freezia, hyacinth, Iris reticulata, lachenalia, narcissus, primulas malacoides, obconica, sinensis, stellata

**Transplant:** pansy

**Disbud:** early-and late-flowering chrysanthemums

**Deadhead:** annuals, half-hardy annuals, pelargoniums

**Feed:** chrysanthemums, greenhouse plants as needed, sweetpeas, lawns on light soils

**Stake:** freesia

**Rest:** hippeastrums

**Increase:** pelargoniums from cuttings

**Routine work:** mow, water, weed, build up compost heap

**Pests and diseases:** capsids, caterpillars, earwigs, greenfly, leaf miner, mealy bug, mildew, red spider mite, rust, whitefly

# Jobs to do

Above: *The Roman hyacinth is a slightly more tender variety of the common hyacinth, which was developed from it.*

### Preparing the soil for sowing outdoors

If you would like to have annual flowers in bloom in late spring and early summer next year, early autumn is the time to sow them and you should therefore prepare the soil during the next few weeks. As they will flower where sown, you should choose a site which is reasonably sheltered from wind and cold, so that they survive the winter. Fork the soil to the depth of the tines and mix in an average-to-light dressing of organic matter, depending on whether the soil is mainly clay or sand, and remove all weeds and large stones as you go.

The site that has been left fallow for sowing a lawn in early autumn can now have lime mixed into it, if the soil is too acid, to bring it up to a pH of about 6.0-6.5. You can take the opportunity at the same time to break the soil up into a reasonably smooth texture, levelling it as you go and cleaning it of weeds and stones.

### Preparing the soil for planting outdoors

There is little to do here; the same plants as were planted late in mid-summer can still be put in, so soil preparation will be as for that season.

### Preparing compost for sowing seed and potting

You will need compost for both these jobs; the potting will include all sizes of plants and bulbs for Christmas flowering, which will do perfectly well in standard composts.

### Planting outdoors

The plants to go in in late summer are the autumn-flowering bulbs but they should be planted as soon as possible, otherwise you will find that they are starting to sprout before being put into the ground. They include colchicum, autumn-flowering crocus, *Nerine bowdenii* and, although a few weeks earlier than other lilies, you can plant the Madonna lily *Lilium candidum*. It should be planted so that the bulb is only just covered with soil, preferably sitting on some silver sand, with a little more sand mixed into the soil round it. As with all lilies, be careful not to damage the fleshy roots. It will do best in slightly alkaline soil and a sunny place, though shade will not come amiss.

### Sowing seed under glass

Seed of schizanthus and cyclamen can be sown in pans or seed trays filled with a standard seed compost. Schizanthus seed sown now, for flowering in spring, should be well

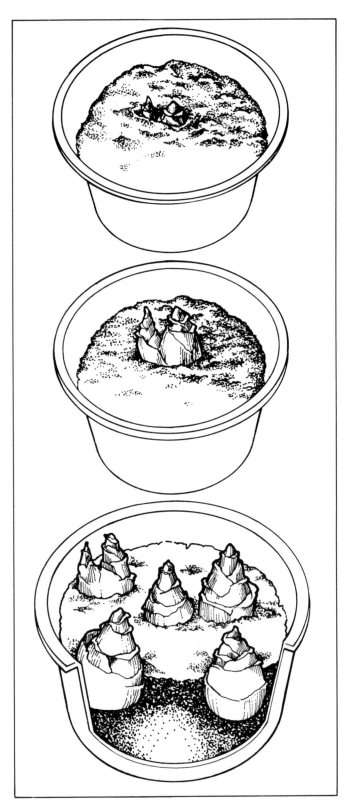

spaced out; it is important that the seedlings do not become drawn at any time, otherwise the adult plants will be leggy and will flower badly. The containers can be put in a frame outdoors, as schizanthus do not need great warmth for germination, but they should be covered until the seedlings do appear (see note on pricking-out, in Early Autumn).

Cyclamen should also be well spaced out, lightly covered with sieved compost and given a further covering of black plastic or glass and paper until they germinate. Keep the containers in the greenhouse; when sprouting starts, take off the coverings and put the seedlings in a shaded place, with a warm, even temperature. They will take several weeks to germinate and some seeds may take much longer.

## Potting

Although it seems unnaturally early to be thinking about it, flowering plants at Christmas will only be obtained if you start potting them now. Towards the end of late summer it should be possible to buy bulbs, such as hyacinths, daffodils and narcissus, specially prepared for early flowering. You will get good results with these and be able to keep them for future flowering if you pot them in a good, standard compost rather than bulb fibre, which contains practically no nourishment.

Hyacinth bulbs are large, so one will be plenty for a 12.5cm (5in) pot; two narcissus or daffodil bulbs, with offsets, will be enough for the same size pot. You can put more into this size pot but it gets so crowded with roots that they come out of the drainage hole and up onto the compost surface. All these bulbs should be planted with the 'nose' (tip) of the bulb above the surface of the compost; don't make the compost too firm beneath the bulb and don't press the bulb down hard, otherwise the roots grow upwards rather than downwards.

After potting, put them in a cool place with a temperature no higher than 7°C (45°F), in complete darkness, and leave for about ten weeks, checking occasionally to see if they need water.

You can also pot the miniature iris, *I. reticulata*, for flowering early in mid-winter; use a compost slightly on the sandy side and cover the bulbs to their own depth, putting five in a 12.5cm (5in) pot. Lachenalias for mid-winter flowering can be planted in the same way now and both these and the iris can go into a cold frame until late autumn; water them occasionally if need be.

*Bulbs for Christmas flowering need to be potted in late summer. Hyacinth bulbs should have just their tips showing, but daffodil bulbs should only be half-buried.*

If cyclamen were slow to start in mid-summer, they can be potted now; the timing of various jobs with plants is never exact because it is dependent on the weather and can vary each way in every season. Nor is it too late to pot freesia corms; they will merely flower a few weeks later than if potted in mid-summer.

Calceolarias, cinerarias and primulas (*malacoides, obconica, sinensis* and *stellata*) sown in early summer, will now need moving into 7.5-10cm (3-4in) pots; those sown in late spring (cinerarias and *Primula malacoides*) will need moving into 10-12.5cm (4-5in) pots. Fuchsia cuttings from the spring will need 12.5-15cm (5-6in) pots, if they have not already been moved and regal pelargonium cuttings, taken in mid-summer, will have rooted and need individual pots sometime during the next few weeks. The size of the first pot will be about 7.5cm (3in) but if they grew sufficiently fast to need potting at the end of mid-summer, they may be ready for a second move into 11cm (4½in) pots by the end of late summer.

The carnation layers which were prepared in mid-summer should have rooted well by now and can be cut from the parent plant, carefully dug out of the soil and put into pots in a cold frame for the winter.

Campanula isophylla *is not reliably hardy, but its prolific flowering ensures its place in the greenhouse or home.*

Above: *In spite of its fragile beauty, the lily-of-the-valley is a tough ground-cover plant which can become invasive in a border.* Opposite: *Lilies rival roses in popularity; this is a hybrid called Imperial Crimson.*

## Transplanting
Pansies can be removed to a nursery bed in the shade as soon as they are large enough to handle; lift them with great care and set them so that the leaves are only just above the surface of the soil. Doing this ensures short bushy plants, instead of straggly ones which can easily be beaten down by the rain.

## Disbudding
The remainder of the early-flowering chrysanthemums can be disbudded (see Mid-Summer) and the late flowering varieties can be treated towards the end of late summer for flowering late in mid-autumn and onwards.

## Deadheading
Continue to cut off dead flowers from annuals, bedding plants and pelargoniums to keep the displays of these plants as immaculate and brilliant as possible. Deadheading herbaceous perennials is not quite so important but you may be doing this in advance, in any case, by cutting the flowers for the house.

## Feeding
Continue to liquid-feed all chrysanthemums in pots, sweet-peas if they are being so treated and greenhouse plants, as in mid-summer. The lawn that is growing on light soil can have one, half-strength feed early in late summer, but no later, otherwise it may grow too lush too late in the year and be 'soft' when winter comes.

## Staking
Newly planted freesia corms should be staked now to support their long floppy leaves and stems later. Freesias growing from seed will nearly have finished their leaf growth, so will not need further training of foliage through the network of strings. Provided they have not been short of water during the summer, have been in a lightly shaded place and have not been subjected to too much warmth, they will begin to produce flowering stems in early autumn.

## Resting
Most hippeastrums will come to the end of their growing season now and can be left completely without water; put the pots on their sides underneath the greenhouse staging. However, because modern hippeastrums are hybrids and have an evergreen ancestor in their family tree, those few in whom this influence is strong will not die down but will keep their leaves but, they should not be fed and should be kept just moist, so their metabolism slows down.

## Increasing
You can take pelargonium cuttings at any time in late summer, the regals early and the zonals late. The regals have a much floppier habit of growth and fewer, but larger, trumpet-like flowers. The zonals have a dark band or zone on the leaves and heads of tightly clustered, small flowers; they are popularly known as 'geraniums'.

A shoot which will provide a good cutting will not have flowered or even have a flower-bud on it; the joints will be short, that is, the length of stem between the points where the leaves are attached will be 5 or 7.5cm (2 or 3in) long, rather than 10 or 12.5cm (4 or 5in). Lastly, the stem will not have started to harden but neither will it be soft

# Bulbs, Corms and Tubers for the Garden

| Name | Time of flowering; flower colour | Height cm/in | Position | Time to plant |
|---|---|---|---|---|
| Allium in variety | summer; purple, yellow, pink, lilac, rose | 15–90cm (6–36in) | sun | autumn, spring |
| Anemone, florist's | mid-spring–mid-summer; red, purple, white, pink, blue-mauve | 12.5–22.5cm (5–9in) | light shade | autumn, spring |
| Bluebell | mid–late spring; blue, white, lilac | 30cm (12in) | light shade | early–mid-spring |
| Chionodoxa (glory of the snow) | early–mid-spring; blue | 10–12.5cm (4–5in) | sun or shade | early–mid-spring |
| *Colchicum autumnale* (autumn crocus) | early–mid-spring; rosy lilac | 20cm (8in) | sun or dappled sun | mid–late summer |
| *Crinum* x *powellii* | late summer–early autumn; pink | 90cm (36in) | sun | mid-spring |
| Crocus | autumn, mid-winter–mid-spring; yellow, white, purple, lilac, blue-purple | 7.5–12.5cm (3–5in) | sun | late summer, early–mid-autumn |
| Crown Imperial (*Fritillaria imperialis*) | late spring; orange, yellow | 150cm (60in) | sun or shade | early–mid-autumn |
| Daffodil | early–late spring; yellow, white, orange, pink | 15–60cm (6–24in) | sun or shade | early autumn |
| Dahlia | mid-summer–mid-autumn; yellow, orange, red, white, purple, pink, magenta | 22.5–120cm (9-48in) | sun | late spring–early summer |
| Gladiolus | early summer–early autumn; red, pink, salmon, yellow, magenta, orange | 45–120cm (18–48in) | sun | early–late spring |
| Grape hyacinth | mid–late spring; blue, white, violet | 15–20cm (6–8in) | sun or shade | early–mid-autumn |
| Hyacinth | early–late spring; blue, pink, yellow, white, salmon, red; fragrant | 20–25cm (8–10in) | sun or shade | early–mid-autumn |
| Hyacinth, treated | early–late winter; as above | 20–25cm (8–14 in) | sun or shade | late summer – early autumn |
| *Iris reticulata* | mid-winter–early spring; blue-purple, blue, violet; fragrant | 15cm (6in) | sun | late summer – mid-autumn |
| Lily in variety | early–late summer; white, yellow, orange, purple, red, crimson, pink; some fragrant | 30–210cm (12–84in) | shade or dappled sun | late summer–mid-autumn |
| Montbretia | late summer–early autumn; orange | 30–45cm (12–18in) | sun | early–mid- spring |
| Narcissus | early–late spring; yellow, white, orange | 15–45cm (6–18in) | sun or shade | early–mid-autumn |
| Narcissus, treated | early–mid-winter | 15–45cm (6–18in) | sun or shade | late summer |
| *Nerine bowdenii* | early–mid-autumn; pink, salmon, white, scarlet | 30–45cm (12–18in) | sun | mid-summer |
| Scilla | late winter–mid-spring; blue, white, lilac-blue | 7.5cm–15cm (3–6in) | sun or shade | early–mid-autumn |
| Snowdrop | mid-winter–early spring; white | 15cm (6in) | sun or shade | mid-spring |
| Tulip | early–late spring; red, yellow, orange, purple, white, pink, bronze, magenta | 15–60cm (6–24in) | sun | mid–late autumn |
| Winter aconite | mid–late winter; yellow | 7.5–10cm (3–4in) | shade | mid–late autumn |

and sappy. You can also make cuttings of ivy-leaved and scented-leaved kinds now, though in fact they root so easily that any time in summer is suitable.

Make the cuttings about 11cm (4½in) long, cutting cleanly just below a leaf-joint and removing the lowest leaves. Put three or four round the edge of a 9cm (3½in) pot of sandy compost, cover with a clear plastic bag and put them in a cold frame outdoors, or in a shaded propagator, without the plastic bag, in the greenhouse. Watch their water needs.

## Routine work
Mowing, watering, weeding and compost-heap-making continue to be necessary, but on a smaller scale than in mid-summer. Watering outdoors may not be necessary at all, in which case, weeding and mowing will be correspondingly much more demanding.

## Treating pests and diseases
Capsids, leafminer, greenfly and caterpillars should be much less troublesome, though a last, precautionary spray against capsid and leafminer on chrysanthemum and dahlia and against leafminer on cinerarias is advisable. Continue to be on guard against whitefly, red spider mite and mealy bug under glass.

Earwigs will be the main problem, especially on dahlias, and there is still nothing much better than flowerpots filled with straw or paper and put upside down on top of the supporting stakes. Earwigs feed at night and hide during the day and such pots will be very convenient for them; check the traps daily and destroy any earwigs found.

*Taking a pelargonium cutting.* Left: *Use the top few centimetres (inches) of a new shoot. Lower leaves are removed and the cutting half-buried, at the side of the pot.*

Chemical sprays can be used but as the flowers have to be treated because they are the main targets, the sprays can do more damage than the insects.

A fungus disease that can spread rapidly during late summer is mildew; it infects many plants including Michaelmas daisies and chrysanthemums. There are varieties of both which are somewhat resistant to the disease. Mildew produces powdery white patches on leaves, stems and flower-buds sufficiently severely to kill leaves, malform flowers and stop the extension growth of stems. It appears during dry, warm weather and plants whose roots are short of water suffer heavy infections. Stuffy, badly ventilated conditions encourage its spread. Picking off affected leaves as soon as seen and spraying the remainder with a fungicide will help; alternatively, use a preventive systemic in advance.

*Golden Dragon is an Olympic Hybrid lily, a stem-rooting kind which is not difficult to grow, given shade and moisture.*

## Plants in flower

Antirrhinum, Annuals (hardy, etc), Japanese anemone, Campanula poscharskyana, Catmint (nepeta), Chamomile, Chrysanthemum (including Korean types), Colchicum, Crinum, Crocus, Dahlia, Daisy, Day lily (hemerocallis), Gaillardia, Geranium, Gentiana sino-ornata, Geum, Gypsophila, Lobelia, Michaelmas daisy, Montbretia, Nerine, Pansy, Pelargonium, Phlox, Red hot poker (kniphofia), Rudbeckia, Scabious, Sedum spectabile, Violet, Hardy annuals and half-hardy annuals and bedding plants

## Greenhouse

Achimenes, Begonia, Campanula isophylla (Italian bellflower), Cobaea, Fuchsia, Gloxinia, Ipomoea, Jasmine, Nerine sarniensis, Passion flower

# Early Autumn

With the beginning of autumn there comes a quite definite change in the tempo of plant growth. As plants reached their peak in early and mid-summer, they ceased to develop and remained static but the often fresher, cooler weather of autumn seems to induce a kind of second spring. It is for this reason that most bulbs are planted now, annual and other kinds of seed are sown and herbaceous perennials planted or transplanted.

It is almost as though the sap starts to rise again and plants which flowered in late spring and summer often flower again now. Biennials which have been ticking over suddenly start to bush out and become leafy. Chrysanthemums and dahlias come into their full glory, and on established lawns the grass grows with renewed vigour. Even the birds revive and begin a minor dawn chorus again, to say nothing of their daytime chattering.

The more and earlier that you can take advantage of this regeneration, the stronger and better established your plants will be by the time winter arrives, so early autumn will be a busy season. In fact, there will be a good deal of work until the end of early winter, but it can be a particularly good time for garden work, with the soil in good condition and the weather mild. Lastly, there will be none of the great rush that occurs in spring when the sudden changes in the weather alone are enough to disturb the average gardener's blood pressure.

The grass will need a good deal of attention now, whether it is established lawn or a new one started from seed. The greenhouse can be cleared up after the spring and summer displays and made ready for the winter flowering plants, and weeds will also need more attention as they join the general regrowth pattern.

# At~a~glance diary

**Prepare the soil for:** sowing seed and planting outdoors

**Prepare compost for:** sowing and potting under glass

**Sow seeds outdoors of:** some hardy annuals (see Table in Early Summer); lawn grasses

**Plant outdoors:** anemone, chionodoxa, crocus, Crown Imperial (Fritillaria imperialis), daffodil, grape hyacinth, Iris reticulata, Liliums auratum, bulbiferum croceum, davidii, formosanum, longiflorum, martagon, pardalinum, regale, speciosum, tigrinum, narcissus, scilla

**Transplant:** border carnation layers, pansy, polyanthus, primrose, primula

**Prick out:** cyclamen, schizanthus

**Pot:** calceolaria, cineraria, daffodil, hyacinth, Iris reticulata, lachenalia, narcissus, primula, rooted pelargonium cuttings

**Lawn care:** brush, feed, mow, rake, repair, topdress, spike,

**Greenhouse:** clean and disinfect, remove shading, move in all potted calceolaria, chrysanthemum, cineraria, freesia, pelargonium, primula

**Increase:** antirrhinum, pansy, pelargonium (zonal), viola from tip cuttings

**Routine work:** build compost heap, treat pests and fungal diseases, water, weed

# Jobs to do

## Preparing the soil for sowing seed outdoors

The soil can be prepared for sowing seed in beds and borders, in a nursery bed and on a site designated for a lawn. The preliminary digging and levelling where necessary should have been done in late summer, and now only the finishing touches need be applied early in autumn (see Early Spring for seed-bed preparation).

## Preparing the soil for planting outdoors

Most of the plants to be put in now will be small ones; it is also the planting time for bulbs. The small plants will take more happily if the soil is reasonably crumb-like, moist but not soggy and contains a dressing of a phosphatic fertilizer, such as bonemeal, worked in two weeks in advance of planting. Use it at a rate of 90g per sq m (3oz per sq yd).

Bulbs do better with good drainage, though any reasonable soil will maintain a satisfactory display of flowers, given the same phosphatic dressing. However, lilies are more demanding and should have grit or coarse silver sand mixed into the soil to lighten it, for average-to-heavy soils. Single digging will be sufficient for all these (see digging, Late Autumn).

You can also begin to prepare beds and borders where herbaceous perennials are to be grown for the first time; this is a much bigger job, since the plants will be in for some years and cultivation needs to be thorough. Many perennials are deep rooting and double digging is advisable, mixing in rotted organic matter as you go. However, if the topsoil depth is shallow, one spit deep will be all that can be managed; be particularly careful to mix compost or manure with the soil in the bottom of the trench, as well as with the topsoil (see Late Autumn for details of double digging).

## Preparing compost for sowing and potting under glass

Fortunately, there is correspondingly less work here, to compensate for the increase in outdoor work; there will be some sowing, a litting potting and some pricking out; you may have sufficient compost made up or bought.

*The hardy herbaceous geraniums thrive in sun and rather poor soils. The one shown here*, G. atlanticum, *is no exception and will be covered in flowers in summer.*

## Sowing seed outdoors

Early autumn is a good time to sow sweetpeas, for flowering in early summer; if you plant them in the soil of the greenhouse in mid-winter, they should begin to flower in late spring, given enough artificial heat to keep the frost out.

They will be in their pots through the winter, but not growing very much, so J.I. potting compost No. 1 or its equivalent will provide the right quantity of food. Sweetpeas grow a long tap root and there is a type of disposable plastic cup which is just right for them, as it is long in proportion to its diameter. A drainage hole in the base, made by applying heat, is necessary.

Sow the seeds, one to a 5cm (2in) diameter container, covered with their own depth of compost. Some varieties are slow to germinate but can be encouraged to do so by making a little nick in the seed-coat with a knife. Put the pots in a closed cold frame and expect germination to start in about ten days' time; make sure mice cannot get at them.

The best time to sow is the middle of early autumn for the colder gardens but for the sheltered and warmer ones the end of early autumn or even the beginning of mid-autumn is preferable. After germination, take off the light but protect the seedlings from sparrows, as they nip off the young tips and leaves at a very early stage.

Quite a good choice of hardy annuals can be sown now, in their flowering positions, for flowering late next spring onwards; these include annual chrysanthemum, clarkia, cornflower, eschscholzia, godetia, larkspur, limnanthes, marigold (calendula), nigella (love-in-a-mist) and viscaria. These are all particularly hardy and, provided they are sown sometime during the first two weeks of this season, will be of a suitable size to withstand cold by the time winter comes.

Grass seed for new lawns can be sown (see Mid-Spring for details of sowing).

## Planting outdoors

Autumn is the great season for planting spring-flowering bulbs and you can put in, the earlier the better, those listed for early-autumn planting in the table of bulbs given in Late Summer. Though none relishes organic matter, bonemeal or hoof and horn give them a good start, each mixed with the soil 10 days or so before planting at 90g per sq m (3oz per sq yd).

Lilies (except *Lilium candidum*) can also be planted in early or mid-autumn, giving them the same kind of soil treatment. An exception is *L. davidii*, which needs leaf-mould mixed into the soil before planting to flower at its best. The stem-rooting kinds, such as *Ll. auratum, bulbi-*

*Right: Dahlias are at their best in early autumn. This is Devil du Roi Albert, one of the most colourful decoratives. Below: For planting bulbs, a bulb planter can be used to remove a core of soil from turf, the bulb put into the resultant hole and the core replaced.*

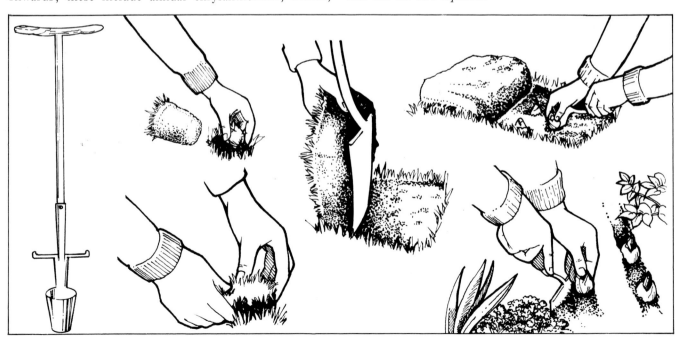

*Narcissus February Gold, one of the cyclamineus group of daffodils and one of the earliest to flower.*

*ferum croceum, davidii, formosanum, longiflorum, regale, speciosum* and *tigrinum*, should be planted 15cm (6in) deep; those that require acid soils are *Ll. auratum, formosanum, longiflorum, speciosum* and *tigrinum*, but *L. candidum* definitely needs a little lime. *L. martagon*, the purple turkscap, and *L. pardalinum*, the leopard lily, should be planted 10cm (4in) deep. Put them all in with a little silver sand beneath the bulb for perfect drainage.

## Transplanting

Pansy seedlings put out in a nursery-bed in late summer can be transplanted in early autumn to their permanent flowering positions, whether a bed outdoors or a windowbox or trough on a balcony or patio. Use a trowel and lift them with plenty of soil to keep the roots as complete as possible; replant slightly deeper than their previous level, firm in well and water. Distance to plant apart outdoors is 22.5-30cm (9-12in), the latter in heavy soils, but in containers they can be spaced 15cm (6in) apart.

The primulas and polyanthus which were sown in early summer, can be planted where they are to flower, spacing them 15-23cm (6-9in) apart each way and planting in the way described for pansies.

If border carnations were not planted directly into the soil, they can be transplanted from their pots now into a sunny position where they are to flower.

## Pricking out

The schizanthus sown in late summer will need pricking out. To keep them from growing thin and leggy, they should be moved as soon as large enough to handle. Put them 5cm (2in) apart in seed boxes. If the cyclamen have started to germinate, move them also when they have two leaves and a tiny tuber, and put them about 4cm (1½in) apart. Keep the temperature warm, especially at night towards the end of early autumn when the weather begins to cool off.

## Potting

There is still time, early on this season, to pot bulbs for winter flowering, by the methods described in late summer. Also pot *colvillei* gladioli. For early-spring flowering, put five into a 15cm (6in) pot, and put them in the dark with the other bulbs. Cuttings of zonal pelargoniums rooted in late summer can be given individual 9cm (3½in) pots. Calceolarias, cinerarias and primulas sown in early summer will need pots 10-15cm (4-5in) in diameter at some time during this season.

## Lawn care

Early autumn is a good time to repair, feed and topdress the established lawn, to get it into good condition for the winter. Bare patches can be forked up and re-seeded or cut out and replaced with turf; small bumps and hollows can be levelled out by cutting an H shape in the turf, rolling back the flaps and filling in or removing soil as needed.

Broken edges can be mended by cutting out a square of turf which includes the damaged edge, moving the turf forward and cutting off the broken part in line with the edge of the lawn. Fill in the gap behind it with soil and seed or more turf. (See details of turfing in Mid-Autumn.)

To maintain lawns in good health it is advisable to topdress them every autumn, but before doing this the lawn should be raked, brushed, mown and spiked. The topdressing can follow this treatment; put the mixture on in a dryish condition at 1-2kg per sq m (2-4lb per sq yd). Spread it evenly and work it in at once with the back of a rake or a stiff brush, otherwise it will have a smothering effect on the grass.

*Autumn lawn treatment: Repair bare patches by cutting a square of turf and replacing it with good soil and grass seed. Topdress with a mixture of loam, peat and sand.*

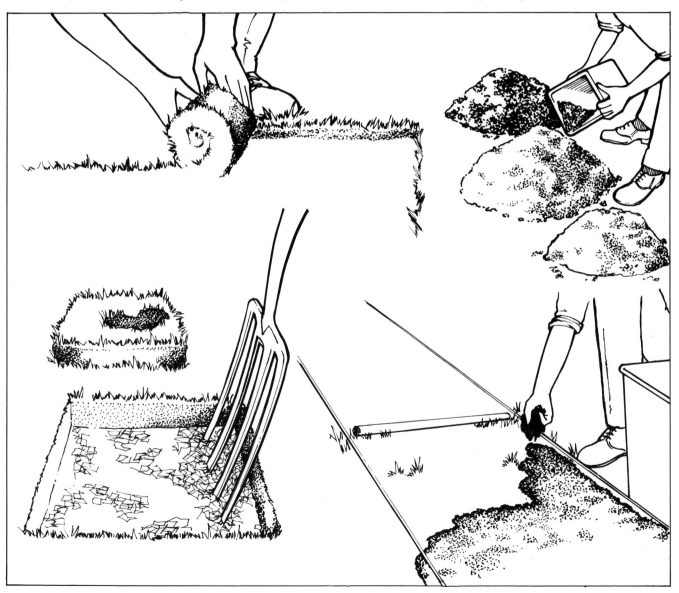

*Gaillardia Goblin is one of the dwarf varieties, growing to 23cm (9in). It is a useful variety to grow as its short, sturdy stems need no staking.*

The topdressing can contain loam, coarse sand and peat and for an average soil the proportions are about 6:3:1 but for heavy soils much more sand and much less loam are required and for sandy soils, much more peat, less sand and about the same quantity of loam are needed. Sometime during early autumn or at the beginning of mid-winter a fertilizer dressing can be given, either a proprietary autumn lawn feed, or a compound fertilizer, either of which contains much less nitrogen than the other two major plant foods. Too much in the way of nitrogen now will produce rapid, lush growth, which can be damaged by winter cold or badly infected by fungus diseases.

## Greenhouse hygiene

As early autumn is the time to move plants which have been outdoors all summer into the protection of the green-house and as much of the summer display under glass will be nearly finished, empty the greenhouse now and give it a thorough clean. Do this while the weather is mild enough to stand any pot plants outdoors.

Move all plants, such as gloxinias, streptocarpus, foliage plants and potential winter-flowerers out and remove from the inside of the greenhouse all debris such as fallen leaves and flowers and compost spilled on staging and floors. Then scrub or wash down the whole of the inside with soapy water, or water with a mild disinfectant in it.

If there was trouble with pests or fungus diseases, use a diluted solution of formalin but wear rubber gloves and a mask if possible, as the vapour is irritating to eyes, nose and throat. Wait until all the smell has dispersed before returning the plants; this may mean leaving the greenhouse empty overnight, so choose mild weather for this, so that the plants can stand out at night without harm.

Clean any shading off the glazing and renew whitewash on the back wall if the greenhouse is a lean-to, so that the plants get as much reflected light as possible during winter.

## Moving indoors
In the last week of this season, the late-flowering chrysanthemums can be housed; go over them for pests and diseases first, give them a good watering, make sure the ties are secure and put on a topdressing if the compost has got a bit low. Put them in the coolest part of the greenhouse and give them as much ventilation to start with as is consistent with the health of the other plants. Once the weather becomes changeable, ventilators need regulating from day to day.

All the freesias can go in; put them in a light place. Those grown from seed should be producing the first flowering stems by now. Cinerarias, calceolarias and primulas in a cold frame can be moved in as well but do make sure the cinerarias are free of greenfly and that leaf-miner is under control. Put them all in the least warm part, away from direct sunlight. If the weather is unseasonably warm, all can wait until mid-autumn before moving, as they are cool-temperature plants, and wilt quickly in warmth, especially cinerarias.

If fuchsias and pelargoniums in pots have been outdoors they can also be moved, depending on the weather. As soon as the night temperature drops appreciably, they are best given protection but this drop may not occur until mid-autumn.

*Red-hot pokers more than justify their name : this bi-coloured hybrid is an interesting modern variation.*

## Planting Depths for Bulbs

| Name | Depths cm/in |
|---|---|
| Allium | twice depth of bulb diameter |
| Anemone | 7.5cm (3in) |
| Bluebell | 10cm (4in) |
| Chionodoxa | 7.5cm (3in) |
| Colchicum | 7.5cm (3in) |
| Crinum | 15cm (6in) |
| Crown Imperial | 15cm (6in) |
| Crocus | 5-7cm (2-3in) |
| Daffodil | 10-15cm (4-6in) |
| Daffodil, miniatures | 5-7.5cm (2-3in) |
| Dahlia | 7.5cm (3in) |
| Gladiolus, large flowered | 10cm (4in) |
| *Gladiolus colvilei* in pots | 5cm (2in) |
| Grape hyacinth | 5cm (2in) |
| Hyacinth | 10cm (4in) |
| *Iris reticulata* | 7.5cm (3in) |
| Montbretia | 7.5cm (3in) |
| Narcissus | 10cm (4in) |
| Nerine | surface with necks protruding |
| Scilla | 5cm (2in) |
| Snowdrop | |
| Tulip | 10cm (4in) |
| Winter aconite (eranthis) | 5cm (2in) |

*Aquilegias grow wild in southern Europe. In gardens they are easily raised in sun or shade, in most soils.*

### Increasing
Zonal pelargonium cuttings can still be taken, early in the season; pansies and violas can be increased from soft tip cuttings, put to root in a cold frame and left there for the winter. Antirrhinums can also be increased in this way, if you wish to retain certain varieties.

### Routine work
Continue to mow the lawn, build the compost heap, water plants in the greenhouse and weed; the need for water by greenhouse plants will decrease from now on. Weeding may increase, particularly in a wet autumn. Pest and disease treatment is similar to late summer but should also become less demanding, though whitefly and greenfly in the greenhouse can go on being a nuisance until well into winter if not dealt with very firmly.

## Plants in flower
Anemone (Japanese), Antirrhinum, Annuals (hardy and half-hardy and bedding plants), Campanula poscharskyana, Catmint (nepeta), Centaurea, Chamomile, Chrysanthemum (including Korean types), Colchicum, Crinum, Crocus, Dahlia, Daisy, Day lily (hemerocallis), Gaillardia, Geranium, Gentiana sino-ornata, Geum, Golden rod (solidago) Gypsophila, Hosta (plantain lily) Lobelia, Michaelmas daisy

## Plants in flower
Montbretia, Nerine, Pansy, Pelargonium, Phlox, Red hot poker (kniphofia), Rudbeckia, Scabious, Sedum spectabile, Spiderwort (tradescantia), Veronica, Violet

## Greenhouse
Achimenes, Begonia, Campanula isophylla (Italian bell flower). Cobaea, Fuchsia, Gloxina, Ipomoea, Jasmine, Nerine sarniensis, Passion flower, Pelargonium (zonal), Streptocarpus, Thunbergia

# Mid-Autumn

By the time mid-autumn comes, in temperate climates, most of the plant growth for the spring and summer is finished and it is time to clear the garden up and make it ready for the winter. Summer bedding displays will be over, the last of the early-flowering chrysanthemums will have been picked and the first frosts blacken the dahlias and remind us that winter is only a few weeks away.

Protection needs to be given as soon as possible to the slightly tender plants that have been outdoors in pots all summer. Heat will be needed at night in the greenhouse and occasionally during the day towards the end of mid-autumn, earlier in the colder and more northern gardens. Plants in the greenhouse have been watered a good deal during the summer but now will gradually cease to extend their growth, so the job of providing them with moisture will be much less demanding.

Before last month's false-spring growth comes to an end, some mulching and feeding of permanent plants and those intended for spring displays can be done; if encouraged to build up larger crowns in a last spurt before winter, they will come through the cold weather much better, flower earlier and more profusely.

Another clearing-up job that will start towards the end of mid-winter is leaf removal from lawns, paths and drives but in borders and beds, where there are herbaceous perennials and bulbs planted, the leaves can be a very good protective mulch. For annuals and biennials, however, they should be removed, otherwise such small plants will be smothered.

The lawn is another major area which will not require much work, as grass growth slows down markedly; there is still just time to make a new lawn from seed and if you are planning to make one from turf, the soil for this can be prepared now, ready for turfing in late autumn.

# At~a~glance diary

**Prepare the soil for:** sowing seed and planting outdoors

**Prepare compost for:** sowing and potting under glass

**Sow seeds outdoors of:** some hardy annuals (see Table in Early Summer); lawn grasses

**Plant outdoors:** bulbs (as Early Autumn), also winter aconite and tulip; herbaceous perennials in well-drained soils; biennials Canterbury bell, double daisy, forget-me-not, foxglove, hollyhock, sweet william, verbascum, wallflower

**Thin:** hardy annuals sown in early autumn

**Pot:** calceolaria, cineraria, cyclamen, pelargonium, primulas, schizanthus

**Move indoors:** all potted calceolaria, late-flowering chrysanthemums, cineraria, freesia, fuchsia, pelargonium, primulas

**Clear up, cut back:** hardy annuals, half-hardy annuals and bedding plants, herbaceous perennials, rock plants

**Lift and shelter:** begonia, early-flowering chrysanthemum, dahlia, gladiolus, pelargonium

**Stop:** sweetpea

**Rest and store:** greenhouse-grown achimenes, begonia, dahlia, gladiolus, gloxinia, streptocarpus

**Feed:** herbaceous perennials, permanently planted spring-flowering bulbs

**Increase:** herbaceous perennials by division

**Greenhouse:** decrease watering and ventilation, stop feeding and damping down, watch for grey mould

**Routine work:** finish mowing and weeding by the end of mid-autumn, sweep up leaves, treat leather-jackets on lawns and under newly planted small plants

# Jobs to do

*The primrose-like flowers of the polyanthus, grown from un-named seed, show a marvellous range of jewel-like colours.*

### Preparing the soil for sowing seed outdoors
It will still be possible to sow seed in mid-autumn, though it should be done within the first week. Seed-beds will therefore need to be prepared; remember that any pre-seeding compound fertilizer or bonemeal to be used should be put on about a week in advance of sowing (see Early Spring for seed-bed preparation).

### Preparing the soil for planting outdoors
By the time late autumn comes, it is really too late to expect herbaceous perennials to establish successfully before winter and the only planting that can be done will be a few bulbs. However, turf can be laid at that time, so the site should be dug over in mid-autumn and prepared as for grass seed, but not to the fine tilth required for seed.

### Preparing compost
In the greenhouse some potting of various-sized plants will need to be done, so a supply of potting composts will be necessary. Seed composts will not be required until late winter.

### Sowing seed outdoors
There is still just time to sow the hardiest of the annuals and sweetpeas, if done right at the beginning of mid-autumn; they include those suggested for early autumn. It is particularly important that the soil is in good condition

*There are dahlias to suit all tastes, both in colour and form of flower. For exhibition they are classified into sections according to flower shape: this one—Lucky Fellow—is one of the cactus section.*

when sowing seed now, so that the seed germinates quickly and the seedlings can get themselves well dug in against gales, rain and snow.

Grass seed can still be sown, but the successful establishment of a good lawn from seed sown now depends a great deal on the weather of the next few weeks. If the temperature drops suddenly after sowing, the seed will take most of mid-autumn to germinate, and the seedlings are then very late and grow slowly. If bad weather sets in during late autumn, the result may be large bare patches, interspersed with sparse, weakly-growing seedlings and a good deal of time, money and energy will have been wasted. It is probably best to sow at this time only if you live in a district that continues to be warm until well into late autumn.

## Planting outdoors
Although planting the spring-flowering bulbs in early autumn produces earlier flowering and better plants than

planting now, such a planting will still give you a good display. In fact, mid-autumn is often regarded by many gardeners as the best time to plant bulbs but, if you dig up a bulb at the beginning of early autumn which has been left in the ground since the spring, you will find that it has already started to push out roots. New growth in the spring-flowering bulbs does start very early after the summer rest and they then go on growing underground all through the winter, except in extreme cold.

Put in the same bulbs as recommended for early autumn, with the addition of tulips and, towards the end of mid-autumn, winter aconites, which produce bright yellow flowers with frills of green in late winter. *Iris reticulata* planted now will not flower until early spring.

Herbaceous perennials can be planted in those gardens with a light, well-drained soil; newly planted perennials will not do well through the winter in a soil which tends to become waterlogged and may not establish at all. The same advice applies to rock plants and to perennials grown from seed sown in early and mid-summer; such small plants are more safely left in pots or nursery beds until spring and can be removed to shelter or otherwise protected if need be. However, lily-of-the-valley planted now should be successful, provided some grit is added to a heavy soil. It is relatively shallow-rooting, so should not suffer badly from heavy rain; plant it so that the roots are about 5–7.5cm (2–3in) deep, and the points of the crown just above the soil surface. A slightly shaded position is preferred.

The biennials which have been coming on in a nursery bed through the summer can now be planted in their flowering positions. If you are planting a whole bed of one kind, the following spacings will ensure good growth and a good display:

## Thinning
Hardy annuals sown outdoors in early autumn will probably need careful thinning by now. You can take the opportunity to weed at the same time, if this has not already been done and clear off any leaves so that the plants are not smothered. As well as being suffocated, they may be eaten by slugs, snails, and other pests sheltering beneath the blanket provided by the leaves and weeds.

## Potting
Plants to pot in the greenhouse include the schizanthus pricked out in early autumn, which can now be put into 5–9cm (2–3½in) pots, and the calceolarias, cinerarias and primulas sown in early summer, which will either need their final 15–17.5cm (6–7in) or a 12.5–15cm (5–6in) size. The late spring-sown cinerarias and *Primula malacoides* will probably be able to have their final move into 15–17.5cm (6–7in) pots, in which they will flower. Pelargoniums from cuttings may have grown well enough to need a larger, 10cm (4in) pot. Pricked-out cyclamen may have come on sufficiently to need their own pots but they are slower growing and should never be over-potted.

## Moving indoors
If the weather has been mild, tender plants in containers are probably in a cold frame but they should definitely be taken under greenhouse cover sometime during the next few weeks. Included in this are all the plants mentioned in Early Autumn for housing.

## Clearing up and cutting back
Hardy annuals, bedding plants and half-hardy annuals will have come to the end of their flowering and should be cleared off and put on the compost heap, leaving the ground ready for digging in late autumn. The aquatic plants will be dying back fast and their remains should be cleared out of the pool, together with leaves as they fall.

Herbaceous perennials and rock plants can be cleaned up by cutting off the flowering stems and leaves to crown level but it may be more sensible to leave them. Although it makes beds and borders look gaunt and untidy, the dead

## Planting Distances

| Name | Distance to plant |
|---|---|
| Canterbury bell | 22.5cm (9in) each way |
| Double daisy | 12.5cm (5in) each way |
| Forget-me-not | 15cm (6in) each way |
| Foxglove | 22.5cm (9in) each way |
| Hollyhock | 37.5cm (15in) each way |
| Sweet William | 22.5–30cm (9–12in) each way |
| Verbascum | 45cm (18in) each way |
| Wallflower | 15 × 22.5 cm (6 × 9in) each way |

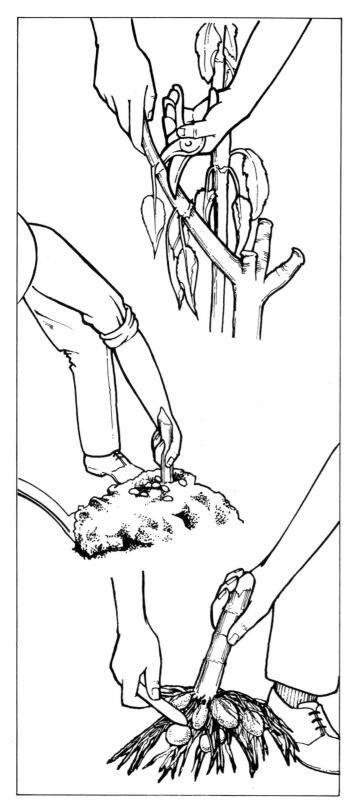

growth does provide protection from cold; this protection can just make the difference between life and death for some plants in a bad winter.

## Lifting and putting into shelter

Dahlias can be left until the first frost, in mid or late autumn, but once their leaves and stems are black, the remains should be cut off, the tubers dug up and the soil shaken off. Tubers which are firm and uninjured can be stored in a frostproof place through the winter; they should be put into 7.5cm (3in) deep boxes, in the bottom of which is a layer of peat, dry leaves or straw. Peat or soil is then worked in between the plants after they are placed in the box, to cover the tubers. Dusting them with sulphur beforehand will prevent the spread of storage rots.

Keeping the storage material slightly moist prevents the tubers from wrinkling and if placed under the staging and kept at about 7°C (45°F), they will tick over until spring. In its native habitat, the dahlia is a perennial and sometimes, in temperate climates, tubers left in the ground all winter survive and flower the following season, though not as well as new plants grown from cuttings.

Pelargoniums which have been planted outdoors all summer should be cut down to leave about 10cm (4in) of their main stem, dug up and put into pots or boxes containing compost; it will do no harm if they are slightly cramped for root-room. The containers are then transferred to the greenhouse staging.

Early-flowering chrysanthemums, the last flowers of which should have been cut by the end of mid-autumn, are another plant to move into shelter. Cut the top growth down to leave about 10cm (4in) of stem and put the crowns, packed closely, into boxes of compost or fine loam. Then put the containers into a cold frame for the winter, closing it when frost is forecast.

Large-flowered begonia tubers should be dug up and boxed, in peat, to go under the staging. Gladioli will have to be taken up, cleaned of any top growth and any small cormlets which have formed round the base, and put in single layers in seed trays in a dark frostproof place.

## Stopping

Sweetpeas sown in early autumn will need stopping: break off the tip of the main shoot just above the third pair of leaves. If this leading tip is allowed to grow, the resultant

*Preparing a dahlia for winter storage: Cut the stems right down after the first frost, dig up carefully and label before storing the tubers in a frostproof place.*

plant will be poor, if it ever reaches any length; its removal encourages two sideshoots to appear just below and these should be kept and used for training. They will need temporary support through the winter and any other sideshoots should be removed as soon as seen.

## Sweeping up leaves

Towards the end of mid-autumn one of the biggest autumn clearing-up jobs will start, that of sweeping up and removing leaves. In some years the autumn gales will largely do the job for you but leaf removal from lawns is important because leaf cover, if left to lie, discolours the grass and weakens it.

Leaves stacked separately from the general compost heap, with a wire-netting surround, rot down into good organic matter within a year; sieved leafmould used to be an ingredient of potting composts, before peat became so easily available. Leathery leaves, such as those of evergreens, which are shed at times, take so long to decay they are not worth including; oak and chestnut make excellent leafmould.

## Resting and storing

Summer-flowering tubers and corms in the greenhouse will be finishing their displays and as they do so, the dead and dying growth should be cut off and the containers put on their sides under the staging. There is no need to remove the tubers and corms from the compost; they can remain in it through the winter. *Nerine sarniensis* is the exception, as its leaves last through the winter; it should be watered occasionally, given a light place, kept free from frost and reasonably warm if possible. In spring it dies down and then rests through the summer.

*Increasing plants by division: Divide herbaceous perennials with the help of two forks, cut dahlia tubers with 'eyes' attached, and separate offsets from the parent bulb.*

## Feeding

Established herbaceous borders can be supplied with bonemeal now to good effect, also permanent plantings of spring-flowering bulbs; apply 120g per sq m (4oz per sq yd), preferably when rain is due. There is no need to continue feeding late-flowering chrysanthemums; in fact, it can damage them if continued later than mid-autumn.

## Increasing

This is a good time of the year to dig up herbaceous perennials and divide them. This job needs to be done about every four years, otherwise the plants flower less and less well. They should be taken up with as much root as possible intact; cut back very long ones to the main body of the root-ball. The plants are then divided, either by gently pulling them apart, by using a knife for solid crowns, or by using two forks, back to back. Replant the outside pieces and put the central parts on the compost heap or destroy.

## Greenhouse work

Damping down should cease, feeding will not be necessary any longer and watering can be considerably decreased. Ventilators will need to be closed very much more at night if the temperature drops and for the daytime they will need regulating from day to day, as the weather will be changeable. Gentle artificial heat will be needed some nights and towards the end of mid-autumn is a good time to line the inside of the greenhouse glazing with clear plastic sheet to

*A first-class herbaceous border, backed by immaculate hedges, takes a lot of beating as a garden feature.*

retain warmth. It is now possible to obtain sheet on which moisture does not condense. Grey mould (botrytis) tends to spread rapidly in autumn, so be careful to remove fallen leaves and stems. Watch for the disease on the plants; flowers can be infected just as much as leaves can.

### Routine work
Mowing will almost be unnecessary by the end of mid-autumn. The compost heap will be finished and can have a roof put above it to keep the worst of the winter wet off, weeding will be more or less at an end and pest and disease treatment will no longer be required, except for leatherjackets on lawns.

These grey-brown caterpillars are the larvae of the cranefly (daddy-long-legs); they hatch from eggs laid earlier in autumn in the soil and then feed on the roots of grass and also small plants. When adult they are about 2.5cm (1in) but the small caterpillars can do a lot of damage, feeding in groups in autumn and through the winter in mild weather; infested grass turns pale brown and dies, in roundish patches. Starlings digging into the turf are often a sign of their presence; watering it heavily, then covering overnight, brings some of them to the surface, where they can be collected and destroyed the following day (see Flower Garden Controls and Treatments for chemical insecticides).

## Plants in flower

Japanese anemone, Catmint (nepeta)
Korean chrysanthemums
Colchicum (Autumn crocus)
Dahlia, Daisy, Gaillardia,
Gentiana sino-ornata
Golden rod, Michaelmas daisy,
Nerine bowdenii, Sedum spectabile,
Violet Begonia, Campanula
isophylla (Italian bellflower)
Chrysanthemum, Cobaea,
Freesia, Passion flower,
Pelargonium (zonal),
Streptocarpus, Thunbergia.

# Late Autumn

As far as the ornamental garden is concerned, late autumn is one of the quietest times of the year. Most herbaceous plants become completely dormant during the next few weeks, in readiness for the freezing temperatures which start in earnest in early winter, and for lack of light which will become most marked at the same time. Late autumn is traditionally a dull period, when what light there is during the day is often obscured by cloud and sometimes fog.

Since light is needed for plants to manufacture the green colouring matter (chlorophyll) in their leaves and stems, any such growth now will be stunted, pale and extremely vulnerable to cold.

Most of the work is related to finishing off the mid-autumn jobs and doing one of the major jobs that is best done in winter, that of digging, whether single, half-trenching or double digging. Very deep digging is not generally as important as it is in vegetable cultivation and will perhaps only need to be done once every few years, possibly not even then, if the soil is in good condition.

Late autumn and winter are traditionally the times for producing a new lawn from turf, and late autumn is especially suitable, because the soil is still relatively warm and moist without being waterlogged. Laying turf in spring runs the risk of poor knitting of the individual turves as a result of spring drought and drying, cold, east winds and subsequent death of the grass. Summer is generally quite unsuitable unless you are prepared to water frequently and constantly.

A little planting can be done but plant propagation will not be possible, so there will be no seed sowing, and little potting. Plants in the greenhouse and cold frame will need attention, increasingly so, to make sure that they do not become frosted and they get as much light as possible, and as much air as can be managed; a little fresh air at all times is very important.

# At~a~glance diary

**Dig:** all sites where perennials, plants from seed, bulbs and sweetpeas are to be grown

**Prepare the soil for:** planting outdoors

**Plant outdoors:** winter aconites, tulips, spring-flowering bulbs for late flowering

**Turf:** new lawn

**Mow:** established lawns, new lawns lightly

**Stop:** sweetpea seedlings

**Protect:** woolly- and grey-leaved rock plants, Christmas rose (Helleborus niger), agapanthus, red hot poker (kniphofia)

**Light:** Christmas-flowering bulbs

**Cut down:** greenhouse chrysanthemums as they finish flowering

**Greenhouse:** heat, clean glazing, ventilate, water and watch for pests and diseases

# Jobs to do

*The autumn-flowering colchicum, sometimes called autumn crocus, only produces leaves when the flowers have died down.*

## Digging

Beds and borders in which the small, temporary plants are to be grown do not require tremendous excavations; provided the humus and nutrients are renewed in them every year, they need only be dug to the depth of a spade (spit), rotted organic matter being mixed into them at the same time. You can spread this on the surface first, or mix it in with a fork after the main digging has been done.

Loamy soils, which already have a good structure, drain well and contain nutrients easily available to the plant's roots, need only have a moderate dressing applied, about 2.5kg per sq m (5lb per sq yd). Those which are on the heavy side and contain clay, making them sticky when wet and concrete-like when dry, may need about 3.5kg (7lb) for the same area, but if you find plants become very leafy and large as a result, reduce the application in the following years to 2.5kg per sq m (5lb per sq yd), or less (a light dressing). Soils which contain sand, shale, pebbles, shingle or chalk in appreciable quantities will need at least 5kg per sq m (10lb per sq yd), in other words a heavy application. Even so, they should have mulches of organic matter given to the plants all through the growing season.

Organic matter consists of the remains of vegetable or animal organisms, rotted down into a dark-brown, moist, crumbly material without smell. Though farm manure is excellent, it is difficult to obtain, but a good substitute is compost made in the garden. Other materials to use are leafmould, rotted straw, spent mushroom compost, seaweed, poultry deep litter, treated sewage sludge, spent hops, or peat. Treated sewage sludge can be obtained from local councils, who should provide an analysis of the nutrient content; you should also find out what the heavy metal content is, otherwise you may unwittingly be building up toxic amounts of copper, zinc and other metals contained in, sewage sludge, in the soil.

Single digging should also be sufficient if you are planning to plant bulbs. Remember that they generally do best in light soil, so work coarse sand or grit into heavy soils at the same time, at up to 3.5kg per sq m (7lb per sq yd).

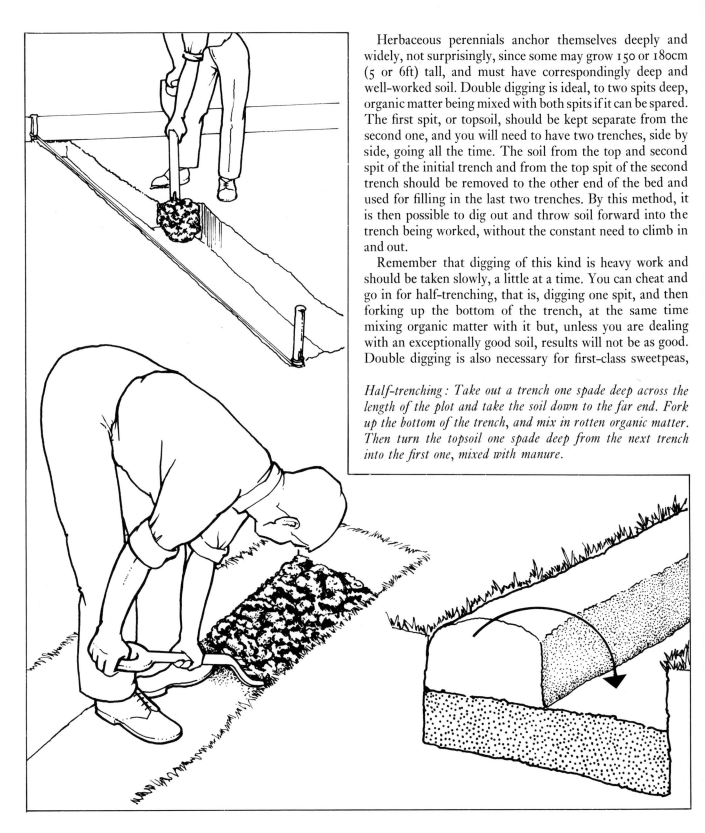

Herbaceous perennials anchor themselves deeply and widely, not surprisingly, since some may grow 150 or 180cm (5 or 6ft) tall, and must have correspondingly deep and well-worked soil. Double digging is ideal, to two spits deep, organic matter being mixed with both spits if it can be spared. The first spit, or topsoil, should be kept separate from the second one, and you will need to have two trenches, side by side, going all the time. The soil from the top and second spit of the initial trench and from the top spit of the second trench should be removed to the other end of the bed and used for filling in the last two trenches. By this method, it is then possible to dig out and throw soil forward into the trench being worked, without the constant need to climb in and out.

Remember that digging of this kind is heavy work and should be taken slowly, a little at a time. You can cheat and go in for half-trenching, that is, digging one spit, and then forking up the bottom of the trench, at the same time mixing organic matter with it but, unless you are dealing with an exceptionally good soil, results will not be as good. Double digging is also necessary for first-class sweetpeas,

*Half-trenching: Take out a trench one spade deep across the length of the plot and take the soil down to the far end. Fork up the bottom of the trench, and mix in rotten organic matter. Then turn the topsoil one spade deep from the next trench into the first one, mixed with manure.*

*The Siberian wallflower,* Cheiranthus allioni, *is a perennial species that does well in a sunny place.*

as they are strong, fast-growing plants with a large root system; even with the modern bushy sweetpeas you will get more flowers and brighter colours with thorough cultivation of this kind.

If you are fortunate enough to own a rotavator, this can be used, but unless it is one of the bigger, market-garden-type models, the tines will only penetrate about 22.5cm (9in) deep. Repeated use each year will result in the formation of a 'pan', a compacted internal surface just below the limit of the tine penetration, which will have to be dug or forked at some time.

Once the digging or cultivation has been finished, the soil can be left through the winter, even if it is still lumpy, because the action of rain, frost and snow will ensure that these lumps are easily knocked down into much smaller pieces by the use of a fork when spring comes.

### Preparing the soil for planting
Some bulbs planted now will still flower at the right time next spring, so soil should be prepared accordingly, if not already done in mid-autumn (see Early Autumn for method).

### Planting
Some experts advise that tulips should not be planted until the beginning of late autumn so, if you did not get them in earlier, little has been lost, even with the early spring-flowering species tulips. Winter aconites and other such bulbs as crocus, daffodils, narcissus and hyacinth will have a lot of catching up to do, so expect them to flower late from a planting of this date.

## Turfing

Although growing a lawn from turf is said to be seven times more expensive than from seed, it does mean instant lawn, with none of the anxiety associated with nursing grass seedlings through attacks by birds, competition with weeds, drought, cold, waterlogging and leather-jacket damage. Provided you lay the turves correctly, in suitable weather conditions, the lawn will be established, to all intents and purposes, from the first two or three weeks.

*Laying turf: Stand on a board, to prevent soil compaction, add or remove soil to adjust the level, and lay the turves staggered. Brush sand into the joins.*

Turves are either 90 × 30cm (3ft × 1ft), or 30 × 30cm (1ft × 1ft); they should be about 4cm (1½in) thick, consisting of a uniform mixture of grasses, without weeds.

You will have prepared the soil in mid-autumn and now you need only apply and rake in superphosphate at about 30g per sq m (1oz per sq yd) a week or so before laying the turves. Choose a day when the soil is moist and the weather mild, with the possibility of rain to come, and lay the first line up and down the length of the site, starting at the edge. Put each turf down slightly looped, and gently tap it flat when the line next to it has been laid. This ensures a tight fit, as does knocking the edge of the second line against the first, and so on, as the work progresses. In order to get a

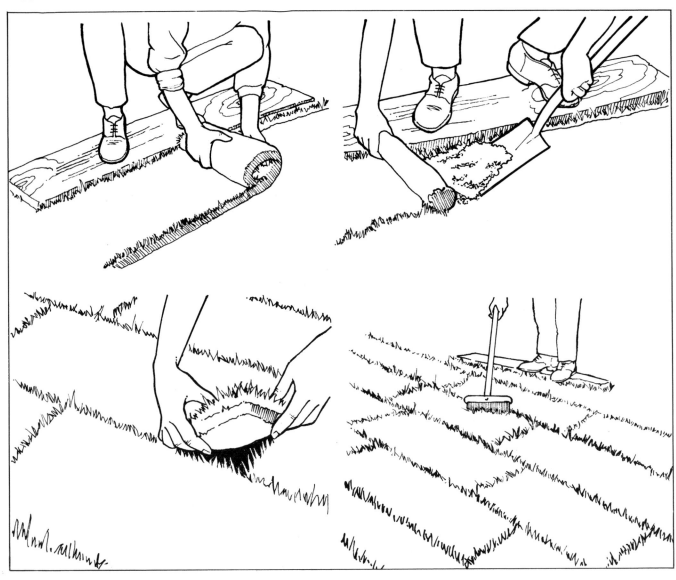

## Biennials

| Name | Time of flowering; flower colour | Height and spread cm/in | Sow | Transplant | Thin *in situ* |
|---|---|---|---|---|---|
| Canterbury bell (*Campanula medium*) | mid-summer; blue, white, pink, purple | 90 × 30cm (36 × 12in) | late spring | mid-summer | |
| Double daisy (*Bellis perennis flore-pleno*) | late spring–mid-autumn; white, pink, red, crimson | 7.5 × 10cm (3 × 4in) | late spring | mid–late summer | |
| Forget-me-not (*Myosotis scorpioides*) | mid–late spring; blue, red | 12.5 × 20cm (5 × 8in) | early–mid-summer | | 15cm (6in) apart |
| Foxglove (digitalis) | late spring–early summer, white, pink, purple, apricot, cream, yellow | 90–150 × 30–37.5cm (36–60 × 12–15in) | late spring | mid–late summer | |
| Hollyhock (*Althaea rosa*) | mid–late summer; red, pink, yellow, salmon | 150–180 × 60–75cm (60–72 × 24–30in) | late spring–early summer | mid–late summer | |
| Sweet William | early–late summer; red, white, purple, salmon, crimson | 15–45 × 30cm (6–18 × 12in) | late spring–early summer | mid–late summer | |
| *Verbascum bombyciferum* (mullein) | early–mid-summer; yellow; large, grey, very furry leaves, furry stems | 150 × 90cm (60 × 36in) | late spring–early summer | | |
| Wallflower | mid-spring–early summer; yellow, red, brown, orange, wine, crimson, cream, rose, purple | 37.5–60 × 20–30cm (15–24 × 8–12in) | late spring–early summer | either transplant mid–late summer, or thin *in situ* | |

**Greenhouse:** *Campanula isophylla* Christmas cactus Chrysanthemum Cyclamen Freesia Fuschia Pelargonium (zonal)

bonding effect, start alternate lines with half a turf. All this will ensure quick and successful knitting of the turves.

As you work, use a standing board to avoid compaction of the soil or turves; when the job is finished, do not use a roller, but fill in the cracks with topdressing mixture or coarse sand, brushing it in as you go. Make sure that all the edges finish with full size turves, not narrow strips, otherwise the edge will be ragged and messy. Push soil up against the outside turves when laid; this prevents the exposed face of the turf drying out and becoming uneven.

### Mowing
Established lawns may need one last light cut; turfed lawns can be topped, if required, two or three weeks after laying and a lawn from seed sown in early autumn may just need its first cut, as advised in mid-spring.

### Stopping
Sweetpea seedlings which have not been so treated should have the growing tip removed just above the third pair of leaves (see Mid-Autumn).

### Protecting
Rock plants with woolly or grey leaves will need a cover against winter wet; it is not so much cold which kills them as sodden roots and repeatedly soaked leaves. A gravel mulch round the plants to keep the leaves off the soil and cloches above them will keep them in good condition through the winter. Cloches put over the Christmas roses, too, will encourage them to unfold their petals and keep them free of mud. Agapanthus will be the better for a 15cm (6in) deep mulch of leaves, straw, peat or bracken and kniphofia can be treated similarly, to ensure their certain survival.

### Tidying/sweeping

The leaves start to come down with a vengeance in late autumn, and it is even more vital to clear them off lawns, especially newly sown ones, and off small plants, whether seedlings, rock plants or herbaceous plants. Get them out of the pool, too, and collect them off drives and paths before they begin to rot and become dangerously slippery. In general, there will be an over-all clearing up of rubbish blown about by autumn gales.

### Lighting

Christmas-flowering bulbs should be brought into light during late autumn when about 2.5cm (1in) of leaf and flower bud is showing and treated as specified by the nurseryman who supplied them. In general, they should be kept cool, at about 7°C (45°F) for the first few days while the leaves become green, and then given warmth gradually, with as much light as possible.

### Cutting down

As the earliest of the late-flowering chrysanthemums finish blooming, the stems should be cut back to leave about 7.5cm (3in) of stump and the crowns in their pots put under the staging, for the time being, keeping the compost just moist.

### Greenhouse work

As the light becomes less, in quantity and quality, with the approach of the end of the year, the glazing should be kept clean and clear of condensation at all times. Artificial heat will be needed most of the time, but not much ventilation, just enough to prevent a 'stuffy' atmosphere. Water in the mornings only, if needed, remove fallen and decaying vegetation and watch for missed pockets of greenfly or whitefly, especially on fuchsias, cinerarias and cyclamen. The greenhouse in winter is a haven for pests and diseases and is the one place where you will still have to be really vigilant.

*A new strain of smaller flowered, fragrant cyclamen is now available for growing in pots, to flower at Christmas.*

## Plants in flower

Chrysanthemum (Korean), Violet

## In unusual conditions

Bergenia, Michaelmas Daisy, Polyanthus, Primula, Christmas rose (Helleborus niger)

## Greenhouse

Campanula isophylla (Italian bell flower)
Christmas cactus, Chrysanthemum, Cyclamen, Freesia, Fuchsia, Pelargonium (zonal)

# Early Winter

It is a debatable point whether early winter or mid-winter is the quietest season in the flower garden: probably mid-winter, since that is when snow or hard frost tends to make it impossible to do any cultivation. In such weather plants certainly will not be growing and the majority of the herbaceous types will be underground, well out of the way of trouble.

Early winter, however, is still likely to have relatively reasonable weather; there may be some very wet days, and occasional frosty nights, but it should still be possible to get out and do some cultivation and some final tidying up. The grass can be lightly mown on established lawns and turf can be laid for new ones. Lawns seeded in the autumn may also need some attention.

It is a good season to undertake major construction jobs, such as building a rock garden, starting an excavation for a pool or re-designing the layout of beds and borders. Woodwork for the garden, such as pergolas, fences, arches and supports for climbers can be made and put into position and repairs done to any which already exist. However, any work which involves the making and laying of concrete should wait; because of the risk of frost, it is not a winter job and should be fitted in, if possible, with the summer or early autumn work.

The warmth in the greenhouse will ensure that there is still growing life in there and besides plants currently in flower, there will be others coming on for the weeks after Christmas and the beginning of spring. These will all need attention on most days and the greenhouse environment itself needs careful management, juggling with the necessities of warmth, light, ventilation and water and at the same time warding off pest attack. Plants in frames should not be forgotten; although hardier, they also need light, fresh air and protection from the coldest frosts.

# At~a~glance diary

**Dig:** sites intended for herbaceous perennial beds and borders, spring-sown hardy annuals and bedding plants to be planted late spring, spring-sown lawn from seed, nursery bed and cold frame, sweetpea trenches

**Construct:** rock garden

**Turf:** lawn

**Mow:** established lawns, new lawns lightly

**Light:** winter-flowering bulbs, Christmas cactus

**Cut back:** late-flowering chrysanthemums

**Greenhouse and cold frame:** ventilate, water, protect from cold

**Increase:** mid-autumn and late-autumn-flowering chrysanthemums from cuttings

**Routine work:** break any ice on pools; clear and tidy lawns, beds, paths, over-wintering annuals and biennials; overhaul tools and machinery

**Pests and diseases:** slugs, greenfly, red spider mite, whitefly

# Jobs to do

### Digging

The general digging that was described in late autumn can be continued or started while the weather permits, in early winter; this includes the preparation of beds for herbaceous perennials and borders, sweetpea trenches, sites for spring-sown hardy annuals and bedding and half-hardy annuals to be planted late in spring next year. You can also do the basic digging for a lawn to be sown in spring, leaving the surface rough over winter. It is probable that the weed seeds will not germinate as well in the interim as they would with a summer fallowing, but with a hard enough frost some seeds, especially those near the surface, may be killed.

If you have not already done so, early winter is a suitable time to choose a site for a nursery bed and prepare it. On it you can put a cold frame, a piece of equipment which has all sorts of uses. In order to avoid a lot of fetching and carrying, the nursery-bed should be next to or near the greenhouse. It should also be sheltered from wind, and from the north and east; it should receive both sun and shade. The soil needs to be especially good, well-drained and fertile, as it is to be used for seeds and growing on young plants before they are put into their permanent places. It is a good place to grow flowers for cutting too, so that the border is not vandalized by the flower arranger.

Frames can be used for hardening off plants, for sheltering real exotics during the summer, for containers of cuttings or seedlings or for direct planting. If for direct use, the base of the frame must be well drained. You may need to dig one or two spits deep, put in a layer of drainage material 5 or 7.5cm (2 or 3in) thick, then put on a covering of fibrous peat. Replace with only the topsoil if the subsoil is very heavy, and in that case bring up the level as required with additional compost mixture.

### Construction

The shortage of space in many gardens ensures that tiny is beautiful; it is not essential to have lots of ground in order to enjoy gardening. You can get as much, if not more, pleasure, out of a small rock garden and its plants and what

*Phacelias are hardy annuals which originate in South and Central America. They are good bee flowers.*

a big choice of plants there is, to provide you with flowers all through the growing season. The spring is generally known to be a rock garden's glory, but you can have a very good display of colour in summer and autumn; there are many small plants normally grown at the front of perennial borders which will fit equally well into a miniature alpine landscape.

The one thing above all else that rock garden plants must have is good drainage: whether you are dealing with a natural slope or producing an artificial mound, make sure that the subsoil is well-drained, mixing coarse grit with it if heavy. If it is really sticky subsoil, such as clay, it will have to be dug out, a spit deep, drainage material put in, and replaced with good topsoil mixed with grit. Ideally, rock-garden soil should be at least 60cm (2ft) deep and a good mixture would contain 3 parts loam, 2 parts peat or leaf-mould and 1 part grit (parts by bulk).

In a well-planned rock garden, the building is done from the bottom up, putting base layers of rock or stone first, adding soil, then planting and finally starting another layer. The rocks should be arranged to look as though they were there naturally and not artificially put into position; this natural look can be partly obtained by making sure the strata of any type of rock all run the same way. Each piece should be set into the soil so that it slopes back slightly, to ensure its permanence in that position and the drainage of rain off it, back into the soil.

When you are placing the rocks, remember that some plants like sun and some like shade, and construct crevices and gullies, as well as plateaux and peaks. The finished article should look as though you built the rest of the garden round it like a natural hump or bank, through which the underlying bed rocks are protruding due to centuries of soil erosion.

Two types of rock, sandstone and limestone, are most suitable and choice of either or both depends on the nature of your soil and therefore the kinds of plants you wish to grow. Sandstone is more likely to be acid in reaction; limestone is definitely alkaline and some rock plants (like other types of plants) are lime-haters. Hence a test of your soil (see liming, Mid-Winter) and an hour or so with a catalogue of alpine plants can save you a good deal of money and future frustration.

Left: *Build a rock garden from the bottom up, starting with a base layer of rock or grit and adding soil. Each piece of rock should slope backward slightly, so that rain drains off it, back into the soil, and so that it stays in position. The rocks should look as natural as possible.*

Limnanthes douglasii, *too, is attractive to bees, and will self-seed, to flower in autumn as well as late spring.*

### Turfing
Lawns can be made from turf laid in early winter, as well as in late autumn, if weather and soil conditions permit (see Late Autumn for method).

### Mowing
Although not generally realized, it is possible to cut the lawn during winter, under certain conditions. It does grow at this time, albeit very slowly, and becomes somewhat shaggy; you can take the top off it to leave it 4-5cm (1½-2in) long. The best time is the middle of a sunny day, not frosty, and preferably when the ground is as firm as it is likely to be in winter. Wet grass cannot be cut, as it becomes torn, and wet soil is soft, with the result that the mower gouges tracks in it. Top the grass of a lawn seeded in early autumn, if it has not yet been cut.

### Bringing plants into light and warmth
Bulbs for flowering at Christmas and in mid-winter should be brought out into light as soon as possible (see Late Autumn), and the Christmas cactus can now come into warmth, whether the greenhouse or the home. This will bring on its flower-buds very quickly; to time flowering to coincide with Christmas Day in the Northern Hemisphere, bring the plants in the second week of early winter.

### Breaking ice
If you have a pool with fish in it and it becomes completely frozen over in cold weather, break the ice gently to make a small hole and let in fresh air, and therefore oxygen. Non-tropical fish will be safe in cold weather, provided oxygen is available in the water.

### Clearing and tidying
Rake off any remaining leaves from grass, beds, paths and overwintering annuals and biennials, fork up established herbaceous perennial borders and work in a little bonemeal at 90g per sq m (3oz per sq yd) if not done in late autumn. Brush seedling lawns gently.

### Cutting back
Continue to cut down the late-flowering chrysanthemums as the blooms finish and put under the greenhouse staging temporarily until they begin to produce new shoots. Keep the compost moist.

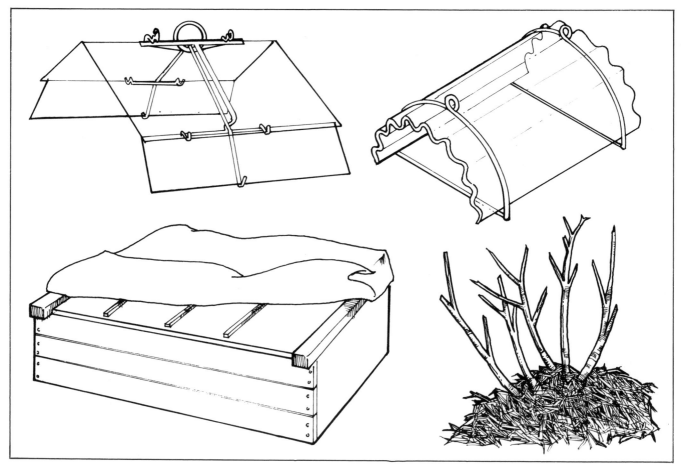

## Greenhouse and frame management

Be prepared for sudden, considerable drops in temperature at night and boost the heating in the greenhouse as necessary. Cover the frame light on particularly cold nights with sacking or other protective material. Also be prepared to decrease the heating on sunny, calm days and then open the ventilators as well and let in some much-needed fresh air. Wipe off condensation and water plants moderately. Keep house and frame free of dead plants, rotting leaves, and dying flowers and supply final support strings for the corm-grown freesias, which will be coming into flower soon. *Primula malacoides* and possibly *P. obconica* will be flowering in mid-winter, so their buds will be starting to show and they may need a little more water than previously.

## Increasing

Cuttings of chrysanthemums which flowered in late autumn may be ready for taking at the end of early winter, though mid-winter is more likely. Shoots will have been produced from below the soil round the old stems, since

*Above: Protection for grey- or woolly-leaved rock plants can be provided by cloches of glass or plastic; a frame with sacking on top is an alternative for slightly tender pot plants; a 15cm (6in) mulch will protect crowns of tender perennials. Opposite: The blazing sunshine yellow of chrysanthemum Cloth of Gold lights up the garden in autumn.*

they were cut back, and these should be used, not the shoots actually growing on the stems, or any produced while the plants were still flowering.

## Overhauling machinery and tools

A cold job, but a necessary one, conveniently done in winter, is cleaning and repairing garden tools and equipment. Inevitably, if you leave the sharpening of the mower blades and the servicing of the cultivator, hedge cutter, etc., until early spring, everyone else in the district will do the same and the delay until you get them back from the repair or maintenance centre can mean the ruin of the lawn and failure with crops and flowers for the season.

*Annual climbing plants like the Morning Glory are 'instant' sources of colourful cover for vertical space.*

## Plants in flower

Christmas rose (*Helleborus niger*), Violet

## In unusual conditions

Bergenia, Iris reticulata, Polyanthus, Primrose, Snowdrop

## Greenhouse

Christmas cactus, Chrysanthemum, Cyclamen, Freesia, Fuchsia, Pelargonium (zonal)

Hand tools should automatically be cleaned after use during the growing season, but in winter, oiling them is advisable while they are not needed for some time. You can take the opportunity now to sharpen spades, billhooks, shears – all tools with cutting edges in fact – to straighten teeth, strengthen handles and tighten screws, nuts and bolts. Wheelbarrows in particular take a lot of punishment; oiling the wheels, patching holes in the body and padding the handles are usually the most important attentions needed.

### Treating pests and diseases

Slugs are possible round the Christmas rose, so discourage them with 15cm (6in) bands of coarse grit round the plants or with slug-bait. Greenfly, whitefly and red spider mite may be persisting in the snug atmosphere of the greenhouse; either use finger and thumb or an insecticide (see Flower Garden Controls and Treatments for chemicals).

# Mid-Winter

The best that can be said about mid-winter, as far as the weather is concerned, is that the days are beginning to lengthen, so that there is at least more light, even if the temperature is low. Light is more important to green plants than warmth; without light they cannot live at all, but they will survive or grow slowly in relatively cold conditions, provided light is available. Hence the flowering of snowdrops, *Iris reticulata*, bergenias and some other tough herbaceous plants which have adapted to cold.

Hard frost, heavy rain and snow are all likely through mid-winter and you should not expect to be able to do much gardening, beyond small routine jobs in the greenhouse. Occasionally lawns can have a little work done on them; lime can be spread if needed, digging can be finished and occasional tidying is possible, on sunny, frosty days, of the results of winter gales.

Otherwise you can spend your time in the greenhouse or in an armchair planning your next growing season, with the seductive help of the new seed catalogues. It is a good time to take stock of your flowering display all round, including perennials, bulbs, annuals, bedding plants and rock plants. With experience you can arrange a continual show of flowers from early spring until winter; even in winter there are a few plants which will flower. Really, there is no end to the flowering season, merely a diminution at certain times.

Your efforts last summer in starting various plants from seed in containers will begin to show from now until early spring and you should have quite a lot of colour as well as fragrance in the greenhouse from flowering pot plants. A gently heated greenhouse in mid-winter is a great morale booster, as it can be the source of so much colour and the promise of spring for remarkably little expense, if you use paraffin heaters.

# At~a~glance diary

**Dig:**  finish all digging

**Lime:**  soil which is very acid, or soil which is very heavy, where plants need slightly alkaline rather than slightly acid soils

**Feed:**  spring-flowering bulbs

**Mow:**  established lawns, lawns grown from autumn-laid turf, lightly

**Pot:**  rooted chrysanthemum cuttings

**Start:**  early-flowering chrysanthemums to provide cuttings

**Sterilize:**  loam needed for use in composts in late winter and onwards

**Greenhouse:**  ventilate, water, heat, treat pests and diseases

**Increase:**  late-flowering chrysanthemums from stem cuttings; gaillardia, phlox and oriental poppy from root cuttings

**Routine work:**  break any ice on pools; plan and choose plants for the new season, and re-design the garden layout where necessary

# Jobs to do

*The petunia is one of the best plants for window-boxes and troughs, provided that it has plenty of sun.*

### Digging
Finish this as soon as possible as there is only just enough time left for the cultivated ground to be weathered sufficiently before the spring planting starts. Take advantage of hard frozen ground to wheel and place barrow-loads of organic matter, ready for mixing in when a thaw comes.

### Liming
The addition of chalk to the soil of the ornamental garden is not as important as with the kitchen garden, but no plant likes extreme acid conditions; most of them will grow best in soils which have a pH of 6.0-6.5, i.e. slightly acid. Some do better with a little alkalinity, of about 7.3-7.5. A test to discover the value of your soil is easily done and you can buy the materials for it in a kit, complete with instructions, from any good garden sundriesman.

A word about pH – it may sound mysterious and complicated, but as far as gardeners are concerned, all that it is, is a measure of how acid or alkaline the soil is. The reason for needing to know this is that, in very alkaline soils, some mineral nutrients – iron and magnesium are two – are present in a chemical form which makes it impossible for the roots of certain plants to absorb them. These plants are what is known as calcifuges and have to be grown in acid-reacting soils, if they are grown at all. The pH scale of acidity/alkalinity runs from 0-14; the lower figures show acidity, decreasing until they get to 7.0, which is the neutral point. After that increasing alkalinity is indicated up to the maximum of 14.0. In practice, most garden soils show a reaction somewhere between 5.0 and 7.5-8.0.

Besides altering the pH of the soil, lime has an effect on the soil structure, especially of heavy soils, and makes them easier to deal with and much less likely to be permanently saturated. Gypsum (calcium sulphate) is a particular form of lime which will break down such soils without altering the pH value, as it is neutral, and is particularly useful where the soil is heavy but already alkaline. Use a soil tester to find out whether this is the case in your garden.

There are various sorts of lime to use, the most common

*Most scillas are deep blue, but* S. tubergeniana *is a very pale blue. It grows to about 15cm (6in) in height.*

being chalk or ground limestone; both are calcium carbonate, ground limestone being slower in its action. Hydrated lime (calcium hydroxide) can also be applied; it acts more quickly. Rates of application will be given with the lime containers or with the soil-testing kit. Lime must always be put on with an interval of several weeks between its application and that of organic matter, to avoid a chemical reaction between them which results in the loss of plant foods.

## Feeding
Although it seems an unlikely time to supply food to plants, the spring-flowering bulbs – such as daffodils, scillas and crocus – will have poked through the soil by an inch or two. They at least are active and, provided snow is not lying

several inches deep, the ground is not hard with frost or sodden with moisture, they will appreciate a boost in the form of a general compound fertilizer at 90-120g per sq m (3-4oz per sq yd).

Plants are like other living organisms: they need food, not in solid form as with animals, but in the liquid state. The food they absorb from the soil consists of various mineral elements: phosphorus, potassium, sulphur and so on, each of which has a different function in the plant's metabolism. In order that the plants can 'eat' them, these minerals must be broken up into minute particles which become part of the soil moisture and form a solution with it.

This solution passes into the plant roots, and from there to the other parts, the stem, the leaves and the flowers in particular, and the minerals then interact with the results of the process, known as photosynthesis, which goes on in the green tissue of plants.

Each mineral nutrient has a chemical symbol, for instance phosphorus is P, potassium K and nitrogen N. A packet of fertilizer will have the 'analysis' of the contents on it, that is, the mineral nutrients present and their percentage in the fertilizer will be shown: for example, Nitrogen, N, 7%, Phosphorus, $P_2O_5$, 4% and Potassium, $K_2O$, 9%. The phosphorus and potassium have to be present as compounds for technical reasons; in this analysis the potassium present is slightly more than the nitrogen, which would be good for flowering. More nitrogen would favour leaves and a higher proportion of phosphorus would encourage root growth. These three nutrients are the ones usually given as a supplement to organic matter, as they are the most important ones to plants, but others can be obtained and used if need be.

If plants do not have the mineral foods they need they show various symptoms of ill-health and will die if the deficiencies are acute or continue for long enough. However, the average garden soil, provided it is kept in good condition by the regular addition of rotted organic matter and an occasional application of proprietary fertilizers, should not lack the various minerals needed and discolorations of leaves are more likely to be the result of infections.

## Mowing
It is unlikely that the next few weeks will be suitable for mowing, or even topping the grass, but occasionally a mild mid-winter occurs, when the birds sing, the sun shines and all sorts of plants show signs of growth, lulled into believing that spring has arrived. In such conditions, topping can be done, of established lawns, or those grown from autumn-laid turf, if it has put on some growth (see Early Winter for details).

## Breaking
Watch the pool for a solid sheet of ice and remember that taking a hammer to it will sound like an explosion to the fish beneath; melt a hole in it if it is really thick.

## Potting
Any late-flowering chrysanthemum cuttings taken in early winter should have rooted by mid-winter and will be ready for potting some time during this season. They can be transferred to individual 5 or 7.5cm (2 or 3in) diameter pots

of J.I. No. 1 potting compost and, as a precaution, you can keep them in the propagating frame (but without extra warmth), or put plastic bags over each pot for two or three days, while they settle.

## Starting
Early-flowering chrysanthemum crowns (stools) which have been overwintering in a cold frame may just be starting to produce new growth, so they can be encouraged by moderate watering near the end of mid-winter.

*Nemesias are half-hardy annuals in all colours, including blue. They flower continuously throughout the summer.*

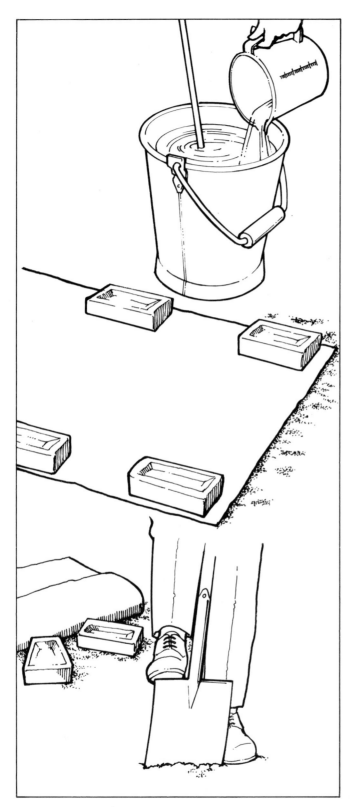

## Sterilizing

Unless you are buying seed and potting composts made up ready for use, you will need to sterilize the loam for them early in mid-winter. It is then certain to be entirely free from the sterilizing agent when needed in late winter. A formalin solution is the most effective, the dilution rate with water being 1 part formalin in 49 parts water; 9L (2 gal) will treat 36L (1 bushel) of loam. The best method is to spread the loam out in a thin layer on a hard surface, water it well with the solution, mound it up into a heap and then cover to trap the fumes for 48 hours. After this it can be spread out thinly again and left to dry; allow three to four weeks at least for the fumes to evaporate entirely. Once the loam no longer smells of formalin, it is safe to use. Do not do the sterilizing in the greenhouse; formalin and its fumes are lethal to plant life. Peat and sand are already inert, and do not need sterilizing.

## Greenhouse work

Continue to remove condensation from the inside of the greenhouse and leaves from the outside, to let in as much light as possible. You may have bonus light in the form of reflected light from snow. Keep the temperature as even as possible, not lower then 7°C (45°F) at night and 10-16°C (50-60°F) during the day, give a little ventilation during the day and shut down early in the afternoon, to retain as much of any sun warmth as possible. Water plants very carefully; give them just enough to wet the compost evenly all the way through and then leave them alone until the surface looks dry. At this time of the year, plants are touchy about their water needs: the amount should be exactly right.

## Increasing

You can continue to take cuttings from the cut-down late-autumn and early winter-flowering chrysanthemums until the end of mid-winter, and start with those produced by the early to mid-autumn-flowering kinds.

You can also use the roots of certain plants for cuttings; phlox, Oriental poppies and gaillardia are some. Phlox tend to suffer from a pest called stem and leaf eelworm, but if you increase the plants from root cuttings you avoid this trouble. Perfectly healthy plants can be produced from infested plants by this method of increase.

Left: *Sterilizing soil. Mix formalin with water, taking care not to inhale the vapour, saturate soil and cover for 4-8 hours, then turn and use when all smell has been dissipated.* Opposite: *Many border flowers can look rather ragged by late summer but perennial phlox are at their best then.*

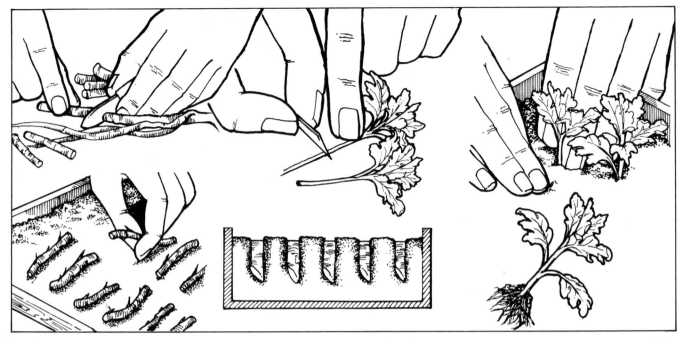

*Taking cuttings: Roots are cut into 5cm (2in) lengths and put vertically in, or on top of, the compost. Chrysanthemum cuttings are taken from crown shoots, not stem shoots. Below: Busy lizzies (impatiens)—the outdoor kinds—are superb plants for providing colour on shady patios.*

The roots are cut up into pieces about 2.5–5cm (1–2in) long; those from the poppies are put vertically into compost, the others laid horizontally on the surface and covered about 0.6cm ($\frac{1}{4}$in) deep. Kept in the gently heated greenhouse, they will root slowly, shoots will begin to appear and you can plant them out late in spring in their permanent positions after hardening off.

## Planning and choosing

All the best seasonal gardening books insist that the well-organized gardener does his or her garden designing and selection of plants in the depth of winter, partly because it helps to supply text at a time of year when there is little work to discuss. Nevertheless, it has to be admitted that mid-winter is a convenient time to take stock; for one thing, this is when the new seed catalogues are published, well in advance of the growing season. Since there actually is not very much to do outdoors and since spring, summer and autumn are times when you need running boots, the only peace you will have to consider and re-plan is the time when plant dormancy and hibernation have set in.

You could also make a resolution to keep a garden notebook. Details about times of sowing and planting, crop and flower yields, cultivations done, plant troubles, when pests and disease appeared and how you dealt with them, weed control and, above all, detailed daily notes about the weather, will all provide an extremely useful and entertaining garden work reference in future. Moreover, it will help to

# Half-hardy Annuals and Bedding Plants

All should be sown in a temperature of 13–16°C (55–60°F) in early spring, pricked out in mid-spring and planted out in late spring–early summer

| Name | Time of flowering; flower colour | Height and spread cm/in | Type of flower |
|---|---|---|---|
| Ageratum | mid–late summer; blue, white | 10–22.5 × 10–17.5cm (4–9 × 4–7in) | brush |
| Antirrhinum | early summer–early autumn; yellow, red, orange, pink, white, wine, salmon, bronze | 10–90 × 7 – 37.5cm (4–36 × 3 – 15in) | two-lipped, carried in spikes |
| Aster | late summer–early autumn; pink, mauve, lavender, rose, white, yellow, cream | 15–75 × 10–30cm (6–30 × 4–12in) | daisy |
| Begonia | mid-summer–early autumn; pink, red | 22.5 × 20cm (9 × 8in) | flat panicles |
| Cosmos | early–late summer; pink, red, white, orange, yellow, crimson; fern-like leaves | 45–90 × 20–30cm (18–36 × 8–12in) | daisy |
| Dahlia | mid-summer–mid-autumn; all colours but blue | 30–45 × 20–25cm (12–18 × 8–10in) | daisy or double forms |
| Helichrysum (everlasting) | mid–late summer; red, yellow, pink, crimson, orange, rose | 30–75 × 17.5–22.5cm (12–30 × 7–9in) | daisy |
| Impatiens | mid-summer–early autumn; pink, orange, red white, salmon | 15–22.5 × 10–15cm (6–9 × 4–6in) | flat saucer |
| Limonium (statice, sea-lavender, everlasting) | mid–late summer; lavender, pink, dark blue, yellow | 45–60 × 20cm (18–24 × 8in) | spike |
| Lobelia | mid-summer–mid-autumn; blue, red, purple, white, wine | 10–22.5 × 10–15cm (4–9 × 4–6in) | tubular or flat |
| Marigold, French and African | mid-summer–early autumn; bronze, deep red, orange, yellow | 15–90 × 10–37.5cm (6–36 × 8–15in) | daisy, ball |
| Mesembryanthemum (Livingstone daisy) | mid–late summer; salmon, cream, magenta, rose, white, carmine | 7–10 × 20cm (3–4 × 8in) | daisy |
| Nemesia | early summer–early autumn; red, yellow, orange, white, crimson, bronze, cerise, pink, blue | 15–30 × 10–15cm (6–12 × 4–6in) | trumpet |
| Petunia | mid-summer–early autumn; rose, white, pink, blue, purple, red | 15–30 × 10–20cm (6–12 × 4in) | flat |
| Portulaca | mid–late summer; yellow, red, white, magenta, orange, rose | 15 × 10cm (6 × 4in) | saucer-shaped |
| Salvia | mid-summer–early autumn; red, purple, violet-blue | 30–37.5 × 30cm (12–15 × 12in) | spike |
| Senecio (cineraria) | grown for silver-grey leaves | 22.5–30 × 30cm (9–12 × 7–8in) | insignificant |
| Stock, double and East Lothian | early summer–mid-autumn; pink, white, lavender, rose, mauve, crimson; fragrant | 37.5–60 × 12–20cm (15–24 × 5–8in) | spike |
| Tobacco plant (Nicotiana) | early summer–early autumn; white, yellow, red, rose, mauve, crimson, lime-green | 25–90 × 15–25cm (10–36 × 6–10in) | tubular |
| Zinnia | late summer–early autumn; all colours but blue | 15–90 × 15–30cm (6–36 × 6–12in) | ball or daisy |

*A well-grown bed of tobacco plants (nicotiana). These subtly-coloured flowers perfume the air heavily in the evening.*

explain a good many otherwise inexplicable failures or successes, and to prevent the repetition of mistakes.

The length of time it takes for various seeds to germinate is an extremely useful piece of information which is hard to come by and a note about whether they germinate better in darkness or light is another.

Setting up a table to show the times of flowering of perennials, bulbs and so on, will show you where the gaps are in continuity of blooming. It is, incidentally, an eye-opener as to how useful various plants are. Some may be literally continuously in flower for eight weeks or more; others, very showy and popular, may last only two or three weeks and take up room for the remaining fifty weeks of the year without paying their way by having attractive foliage or growth habit.

An experimental gardener cannot do without a notebook if he or she has set up comparisons between various methods of cultivation or control of troubles, or hybridizing programmes, and the notebook can be made visually interesting with sketches, paintings or photographic prints.

All in all, the winter, if not physically active, can be mentally busy and suddenly, without any help from you, you will find the snowdrops are in flower, the aconites are shining in a corner and the time for sitting is past.

## Plants in flower

Bergenia,
Christmas rose (Helleborus niger),
Eranthis (winter aconite),
Iris reticulata,
Iris unguicularis,
Snowdrop, Violet

## Greenhouse

Christmas cactus, Cyclamen,
Freesia, Hyacinth (treated),
Narcissus,
Primula obconica,
Primula malacoides

# Late Winter

Although the ground outdoors may be frozen hard or covered in snow at this time of the year, you can start the gardening season in the greenhouse, especially if you have a cool greenhouse, i.e. one which has a little artificial heat supplied, to keep the temperature at about 4–7°C (40–45°F) minimum.

Seeds of half-hardy annuals can be sown in a heated propagator and tuberous greenhouse plants can be put to sprout, with warmth. Tender annuals sown last summer or autumn will be coming up to flowering and will need more water. Cuttings of some plants can be taken now for the first time; chrysanthemums will continue to provide shoots for cuttings. Compost can be mixed up ready for use later this season or during early spring.

Watering of plants in the greenhouse will gradually need to be increased from about the middle of the season and some plants can be given their annual pruning. Late winter is the usual time of the year to prune or cut back many potted plants, though some are better done in autumn as soon as flowering has finished.

If the weather is not cold, then it is likely to be wet, but on non-rainy days, turf can still be laid to produce a lawn. Established lawns can be topped occasionally as they have been through the early part of the winter, but from next month, prepare for the frequency of cutting to increase. A little outdoor planting is possible, if the soil is in suitable condition.

# At~a~glance diary

**Prepare compost for:** sowing seed and potting under glass

**Sow seeds under glass (in heat) of:** ageratum, antirrhinum, fibrous-rooted and tuberous begonia, cosmos, dahlia, gloxinia (sinningia), impatiens, lobelia, mesembryanthemum, nemesia, petunia, dwarf phlox, portulaca, salvia, senecio, streptocarpus, ursinia

**Pot:** rooted cuttings of chrysanthemum, gaillardia and oriental poppy, schizanthus, hippeastrum

**Prune, cut back:** fuchsia, hoya, passion flower, pelargonium, tradescantia family and other climbing, trailing or shrubby plants

**Increase:** early-and late-flowering chrysanthemums from cuttings

**Start:** achimenes, large-flowered tuberous begonia, gloxinia (sinningia), streptocarpus

**Greenhouse:** water, ventilate and tidy

**Routine work:** brush and top established lawns, lay turf for new lawns, plant florists' anemones, weed and clear up generally

# Jobs to do

## Preparing compost for sowing seed under glass

If you have not very much time, you can buy these composts ready made up, but the advantages of making them up yourself are that you do know exactly what ingredients have been used in them, and they cost less. You should never use garden soil for container-grown plants; the alterations in aeration and drainage of the growing medium produced by the physical restrictions of containers result in poor root growth. Composts contain a mixture of ingredients balanced in their proportions and chemical contents so that the plant roots can develop to their maximum.

*This rock garden dianthus, La Bourbille, grows only 7.5-15cm (3-6in) tall: one of the best flowering rock plants.*

You will need both seed and potting composts and you can use those that contain soil or the more modern soil-less ones. One of the most commonly used composts is the one called John Innes; this can be bought ready-mixed for use. However, for home mixing you will need the following: 2 parts sterilized loam, 1 part granulated peat and 1 part coarse silver sand (all parts by bulk). To each 36L (1 bushel) of mixture, add 45g (1½oz) superphosphate and 21g (¾oz)

*The Christmas cactus will start to flower in early winter, provided that it is given short days from autumn onwards.*

chalk and mix all the ingredients thoroughly together. They should be capable of passing through a 0.6cm (¼in) sieve. This mixture is the John Innes Seed Compost.

The soil-less seed compost contains sphagnum peat and fine sand, usually in a 75:25 mixture, with lime and fertilizers added. There are many different formulae for these soil-less composts, depending on the plants and their needs and it is probably quicker and more satisfactory to buy them made up rather than make them up oneself and run the risk of damage to plants through wrong or excessive use of the ingredients. It is a matter of personal preference which you use, and you will probably find in time that you get better results with one or the other.

## Preparing compost for potting

As with the seed composts, you can make up those needed for potting in advance; give them at least a week to mature before using and leave them in the greenhouse to warm up to the surrounding temperature.

The John Innes potting compost contains the following: 7 parts sterilized loam, 3 parts peat and 2 parts coarse sand (by bulk); to 36L (1 bushel) add 120g (4oz) of fertilizer made up as follows: 2 parts superphosphate, 2 parts hoof and horn meal and 1 part sulphate of potash (parts by weight). The compost should also have 21g (¾oz) chalk added to every 36L (1 bushel).

This mixture is the J. I. Potting Compost No. 1; there are two more – No. 2 contains 240g (8oz) of fertilizer and 42g (1½oz) chalk per 36L (1 bushel), and No. 3 has 360g (12oz) of fertilizer and 63g (2¼oz) of chalk per 36L (1 bushel). Some gardeners occasionally need a No. 4 mix, for certain very vigorous plants.

The No. 1 potting compost is used for small plants growing in pots from 5-10cm (2-4in) in diameter; No. 2 is suitable for those in pots from 12.5-17.5cm (5-7in), and No. 3 for the larger plants, in pots from 20cm (8in) in diameter and larger. However, this is not a rigid rule; fast-growing plants may need the No. 2 in a 10cm (4in) pot and No. 3 in a 17.5cm (7in) pot. Others flower better if slightly starved, so will be all right in No. 1 for longer, and you will be able to vary the composts as you gain experience.

There are soil-less potting composts, too, consisting of a peat and sand mixture, to which fertilizer and lime are added. Such composts for potting are not as useful, as they have much less in the way of food reserves. Because they are light in weight, the large and medium-sized plants are top-heavy and tend to fall over, but for small plants they can be ideal, as they are exceptionally well-aerated and drained; some plants grow better in them than in the John Innes type.

When you become experienced at container cultivation, you can vary the contents according to the plants you are growing, so that the composts are tailored exactly to the plants' needs. For instance, cacti, not surprisingly, thrive in gritty mixtures, so you can mix an extra part of very coarse sand or grit into the basic potting compost; pelargoniums naturally grow in poor but well-drained soils, so their composts can also be given more drainage material. For cactus seed, the J.I. seed compost with about ¼ part sand added to it will be good; they also germinate and grow surprisingly well in a soil-less seed compost – surprisingly, since their native habitat is gritty, to say the least.

## Sowing seed in containers

Seed to sow in containers in late winter, during the last week, consists mainly of the half-hardy annuals and bedding plants: those which grow comparatively slowly and which are on the small side. Otherwise, by sowing at this time, you will be faced at the beginning of late spring with plants more than ready to be planted outdoors, when the weather may still be rather chilly, even for hardened-off plants. You can also sow seed of some tuberous plants: large-flowered begonias, dahlia, gloxinia (sinningia) and streptocarpus.

Wooden or plastic seed-trays are probably the most convenient containers to use, divided into sections, but pans are also very handy and, if any seeds are large, individual plastic, clay or peat pots can be used. Peat pots avoid the need for pricking out, as the whole pot can be planted or potted.

Fill the containers, press the compost down with the fingers at the sides and the corners first and then in the centre, and level the surface. Add more compost if necessary so that the final level is about 1cm ($\frac{1}{2}$in) below the top of the container and firm with a presser. Put partially in a tray of water so that the moisture is gradually drawn up through the compost; when the surface is obviously damp, remove the container and put to drain off the surplus water.

Sprinkle the seed evenly over the surface of the compost; if you sow it in clumps, the seedlings are more likely to be infected with damping-off, a damaging fungus disease. Sterilized loam avoids this, or watering them with a fungicide (see Flower Garden Controls and Treatments). Cover the seed with twice its own depth of compost, sieving it through a very fine sieve. If the seeds are minute, as begonia and cactus seeds are, don't cover them at all, simply press them into the surface. Cover the container with white plastic sheet, or brown paper and a sheet of glass, and put in a temperature of 16-18°C (60-65°F), away from the sun.

*Sowing seed: Fill the seed-tray with seed compost and firm the corners and sides first; divide into sections to save on seed, label each section and sieve compost over seed. Cover with glass and newspaper until seed germinates.*

You can vary these practices with experience; some seed germinates better in the light than in the dark and others need a higher temperature for germination or germinate more quickly with more warmth.

## Potting

Plants needing potting now may be schizanthus, rooted chrysanthemum cuttings and root cuttings which have taken. The schizanthus sown in late summer should be put into their final 15cm (6in) size pots, if this has not already been done, potting them firmly and re-staking if necessary. Chrysanthemum cuttings taken in mid-winter will need potting, into 5 or 9cm (2 or 3½in) pots, depending on the root development, and root cuttings taken at the same time will need similarly-sized pots.

Hippeastrums can be retrieved from under the staging and started off again sometime during late winter. They quite often start themselves off, like cyclamen, but whatever state they are in, the compost can be watered moderately and the pots put on to the staging and into the propagator, if possible with a temperature of about 16°C (60°F). When the tip is obviously sprouting well, take them out of the propagator; the top 2.5cm (1in) of compost can then be removed and replaced with a topdressing of fresh. This can be done annually for three or four years before there is a need for complete repotting, as hippeastrums grow better if undisturbed. However, they do need regular feeding during the growing seasons when they are not repotted. Give them as much light as possible.

## Pruning/cutting back greenhouse plants

Late winter is, in general, the best time to prune 'undercover' plants as early spring is when they start to grow again. In the cool greenhouse, the plants that will need pruning are climbers and fuchsias; pelargoniums can also be cut back now if they were not done last autumn.

Fuchsias should be pruned so that last summer's flowering shoots are cut back to leave one or two pairs of dormant buds, so that there is a kind of stub left. Older plants can have the main stem itself cut back by about half its length, to just above a good strong sideshoot, unless it is being grown as a standard. Short, thin shoots should be cut right off and the remainder thinned if crowded.

Left: *Hippeastrums, also sometimes called amaryllis, are tender bulbous plants for the greenhouse or home.*
Right: *Potting a hippeastrum. Use a 12cm (5in) pot, half fill with compost, centre the bulb on this and add further compost so that the bulb is half buried.*

Passion flowers can be pruned by removing all the weak shoots completely and cutting the strong shoots down to leave two-thirds of each stem. Hoya needs a little pruning to cut back straggling shoots to shape, and one or two of the oldest stems should be cut back by about a third. Trailing plants like tradescantias will probably need hard cutting as they are often very straggly at the end of the winter, so you can reduce the stems to about 7.5cm (3in) long. Pelargoniums can also be cut down hard, to leave stems about 10 or 12.5cm (4 or 5in) long. Remember that pruning cuts on all plants should always be made cleanly, just above a dormant bud or sideshoot, with no stub left.

## Increasing

You can continue to take cuttings of late-flowering chrysanthemums and, throughout late winter, early-flowering kinds will be producing suitable new growth, especially if the weather is getting markedly warmer (see Mid-Winter for method).

## Starting corms and tubers

Achimenes, large-flowering begonias, gloxinias (sinningias) and streptocarpus can all be encouraged to start growing by putting them into seed boxes containing moist peat. They should have the top of the corm or tuber just above the peat surface, except for the achimenes, which should be slightly below it. Space them out so that they do not touch one another. If you have room to put them in the propagator, they will come on more quickly.

## General greenhouse work

Start watering plants which have been dormant; some may have already begun to grow, but only give moderate amounts at first, just enough to moisten the compost right through. Do not saturate it. Give a little more ventilation, especially on sunny days, when you can turn the heat off altogether in the middle of the day provided the temperature outside is above freezing. Tidy out the winter accumulation of debris, fallen or rotting leaves and stems, scrub any green mould off the outside of containers, brush down staging and floors and generally give the greenhouse a mild springclean.

## Outdoor work

If the weather allows, top the lawn, brushing the grass first; also start a new lawn from turf (see Late Autumn for method). The tubers of the florists' anemones (St Brigid and de Caen strains) can be planted outdoors. Medium to light, sandy soil suits them and a sunny or lightly shaded position. Rotted organic matter should have been dug in some months earlier. Put the tubers 6.5-7.5cm (2½-3in) deep and about 15cm (6in) apart.

A general clearing up of leaves, twigs and other rubbish now will give you more time in spring; weeding can sometimes be done on fine days. Break the ice on pools if there are any fish in them and remove any leaves burying overwintering annuals.

*Crocuses naturalized in light woodland follow the snowdrop as the first of the spring flowers.*

## Plants in flower

Bergenia, Crocus, Eranthis (winter aconite), Iris reticulata, Iris unguicularis (syn. I. stylosa) Snowdrop

## In sheltered places

Anemone blanda, Chionodoxa, Lenten rose (Helleborus orientalis), Narcissi (miniature), Polyanthus, Primrose, Pulmonaria (lungwort), Scilla, Tulip (species)

## Greenhouse

Cineraria, Freesia, Lachenalia, Primula (from late-spring sowing) Daffodils and Narcissi, Hyacinth, Tulips (species)

# Controls & Treatments

The gardener who is interested in herbaceous flowering plants is the one with the fewest problems of pest and disease control and treatment of various other plant ailments. There will certainly be some troubles but in a general way; greenfly, blackfly and caterpillars will always be found where there is plant life but, unlike vegetables and fruit, there are not a great many specific to certain plants. Leafminer on chrysanthemum and cineraria, rust on hollyhocks and antirrhinums, wilt on asters and pansies, earwigs on dahlias and some others are the exceptions that prove the rule.

You may find all through the season apparently mysterious brown spots and brown edges on leaves, holes and tattering on leaves and petals, stems broken and small plants laid completely flat. Most of this can be put down to the weather; wind, hail, sunscorch, frost, heavy rain and salt spray are all sources of damage, about which little can be done, and they are just the luck of the game. Well-grown, healthy plants, staked, fed and watered, will take such trials in their stride, reviving or producing new growth in no time.

A lack of one or more mineral nutrients in a plant will declare itself in the form of various discolorations on the leaves, stunting of plants and poor flowering. Such deficiency symptoms are not easily diagnosed accurately without professional help; they can be confused with symptoms of virus diseases, or with natural variegations in colour, yellow or cream in most cases, but consistently bad growth and flowering of plants on a particular piece of ground is a good guide. If manuring and feeding do not improve matters after a year or two, then ask for specialist advice. However, real deficiency troubles are rare in gardens; you are much more likely to be contending with pests and blight.

Virus diseases are a real but simple problem, once diagnosed; there is no cure, and infected plants should be destroyed as soon as possible before other plants are contaminated. Viruses consist of particles so small that they can only be seen with an electron microscope; these particles are present in the plant's sap and are absorbed by sucking insect pests (greenfly, capsids, etc.) as they feed. By then feeding on healthy plants, the insects spread the virus and another

*One of the most convenient ways of applying a pesticide is as a powder from a puffer pack, aimed exactly where wanted.*

plant is doomed. Irregular yellow patches, circles and lines on leaves, twisted growth, streaking or alteration of flower colour, and slowly lengthening, stunted shoots are indicators of viral infection but, like deficiency symptoms, are best confirmed by those trained to do so.

Insect and other pests attack in one of two ways: either by biting or by sucking. Caterpillars, maggots, slugs and snails all come into the former category, being armed with, if not actual teeth, mouthparts which can tear or rasp off relatively large pieces of leaf, flower or stem. They are sufficiently sizable to be hand-picked when seen; in really bad epidemics caterpillars and maggots can be sprayed with derris or fenitrothion. Slugs and snails should have slug-bait containing methiocarb put down; they feed at night and need to be hunted with a torch for hand-picking.

The sucking insect pests such as aphids (greenfly, blackfly, root aphids, mealy aphid), capsids, thrips, leaf suckers and hoppers, whitefly, mealy bug, scale and red spider mite all pierce the plant tissue with needle-like mouthparts and draw up the sap through them. It therefore follows that insecticide sprayed on to the plant will be very effective and if absorbed into the plant's sap, even more so; such an insecticide is called systemic. This type of pest breeds extremely quickly and a plague will build up in a few weeks; although squashing with finger and thumb will help, other controls will generally be needed. Root aphids feed in the same way but below ground. Infested plants grow slowly, have a dull colour and wilt for no apparent reason. Derris and malathion are good general insecticides; bioresmethrin is good for aphids, whitefly (for which it was originally specified); dimethoate is best for dealing with capsid, mealy bug, leafminers and scale.

*On lawns, one way of dealing with earthworms is to sprinkle derris powder well into the turf.*

Woodlice frequently cause trouble by feeding on the roots of seedlings and young plants in pots and boxes, attacking them through the drainage holes. Move the containers frequently, raise them off the standing surface with pieces of wood or pot and dust the base with HCH (BHC).

But do remember that use of most of these insecticides harms the beneficial insects as well, including the pollinators such as bees and hover-flies. If you keep an observant eye on your plants, you can halt most of these pests before they get out of hand by killing the first one or two. Where one greenfly is obvious, there will be ten hidden, or there will be shortly, if you don't act immediately.

Grey mould (*Botytis cinerea*) infects through a previous injury and produces grey furry patches on leaves, stems and flowers, especially in cool, wet or humid conditions on practically any plant and can be treated with the systemic fungicide benomyl. Mildew produces white powder on leaves and flowers as well as buds and stems and causes most trouble from late summer onwards. Warmth, dewy nights and dry soil encourage its spread on plants; again use benomyl, or sulphur or dinocap.

Seedlings with stems reddish or black at soil level sometimes collapse; this is damping-off disease and is worst where seedlings are crowded. Use sterilized compost and water with Cheshunt compound to save remaining plants.

Weeds can cause a great deal of trouble in gardens but there are various modern chemical aids which kill them without harming cultivated plants growing nearby. Sodium chlorate is one which is watered in solution onto the soil so that it is absorbed by the plant roots; it remains effective for six months or more and is suitable for paths, drives, patios and all ground free of cultivated plants. Simazine is another of the same type, lasting twelve months, watered onto ground cleared of weeds, with the object of then keeping it clear. At certain dilution rates, recommended by the makers, it can be used round cultivated plants.

Dichlobenil is a third soil-acting weedkiller, applied dry in granular form to the soil to kill annual and perennial weeds. Like simazine, at certain application rates recommended by the makers, it can be used round some cultivated plants. It is effective for three to twelve months.

A second group of weedkillers consists of those sprayed on to the leaves and stems of weeds; they include those commonly known as 24D, 245T and MCPA. They are the so-called hormone weedkillers and will damage or kill any plant, not just weeds, as they are absorbed into the plant's sap, circulated round it and dislocate the normal working of its metabolism. Morfamquat is another of these, specific to weed seedlings growing in grass, so is used on newly germinated lawns; it is also effective on small-leaved weeds such as suckling clover or speedwell. Dalapon is also a translocated type, specific to couch grass and other grasses.

The latest weedkiller is glyphosphate, translocated, but not a hormone type. Sprayed on to the top growth, it deals with annuals and perennials but does not have its effect through plant roots.

A third type of weedkiller is that which is sprayed onto leaves and stems, but which only affects those containing chlorophyll – the green colouring matter of plants. It becomes inactivated on reaching the soil. For annual and small weeds it is very useful; paraquat and diquat are the chemical names. Directions for use of all these weedkillers must be read and followed for safe, satisfactory results.

# Pests & Diseases

*A bad attack of powdery mildew on chrysanthemums, which can be treated with benomyl or dinocap. This disease spreads rapidly in airless conditions and on plants short of water.*

## Pests and fungus diseases of particular plants

*Antirrhinum*

Rust: fungus disease. Symptoms are raised, bright rust-brown spots on undersurface of leaves and on stems; leaves wither. Some varieties are resistant; consult catalogues. Spray thiram at two-week intervals from end of early summer to end of late summer. Remove badly infected plants and burn.

*Aster, annual*

Aster wilt: soil-borne fungus disease which infects roots. Symptoms are wilting, then blackening of stems from base and browning of internal tissue of living stems. Wilt-resistant varieties are available; destroy infected plants, sterilize or replace soil.

Foot rot: soil-borne fungus disease which invades roots. Symptoms are blackening of base of stem, followed by sudden and total collapse of plant. Destroy infected plants, water soil round remaining plants with thiram or a copper-containing fungicide.

*Begonia*, see *Cyclamen*

*Chrysanthemum*

Leafminer: insect pest. Symptoms are wavy white lines on upper surface of leaves, in bad infestations leaves brown and wither. Hand-pick and spray with dimethoate; do not spray flowers.

*Cineraria*

Leafminer, see *Chrysanthemum*

*Cyclamen*

Vine weevil: insect pest. Symptoms are leaves wilting for no apparent reason, fat cream-coloured grubs in corms and compost. Adults are black, 0.6cm ($\frac{1}{4}$in) long, with a long, two-pronged snout; they eat holes in margins of leaves. Hand-pick grubs, water compost with HCH (BHC), trap adults in small pieces of rolled up sacking or paper placed on the soil.

*Dahlia*

Earwig: insect pest. Symptoms are holes and ragged edges to petals and leaves, flowers may then be infected with grey mould. Nocturnal feeder; trap in flower-pots stuffed with straw or paper, placed upside down on tops of stakes and spray plants and ground with trichlorphon or carbaryl.

*Gladiolus*

Thrips: insect pest. Symptoms are small silvery streaks on leaves and buds, later turning brown. Thrips are tiny, yellow-to-black pests, known as 'thunder bugs', most frequent during hot, dry weather. Remove affected buds, and spray with malathion.

*Hollyhock*

Hollyhock Rust: fungus disease. Spray thiram at two-week intervals from the end of early summer to the end of late winter. Remove badly infected plants and burn.

*Hyacinth*, see *Narcissus*

*Lawn*

Leather-jacket: insect pest. Symptoms are roundish patches of beige-coloured grass, slowly enlarging during late autumn, winter and spring. Grass is killed. Leather-jackets are grey-brown, slowly-moving caterpillars found in top 2.5cm (1in) or so of soil. Mature size is 2.5-3cm (1–1½in) long, adults are cranefly (daddy-long-legs). Water lawn with HCH (BHC) solution.

Fusarium patch: fungus disease (sometimes known as snow mould). Symptoms are pale yellow-brown patches of dead grass, edges sometimes fringed with white, fluffy growths. Disease most common autumn and winter. Remove infected areas, replace with fresh soil and turf or seed; water neighbouring turf with copper-containing fungicide.

Fairy ring: soil-borne fungus disease; symptoms are rings of toadstools in grass, 90cm (36in) and more in diameter. If grass within and around ring is dark green and does not die, spike 10cm (4in) deep and water with sulphate of magnesium at 60g in 4.5L per sq m (2oz in 1 gal per sq yd), two or three times at four- or five-week intervals.

If the grass has died completely within ring, leaving a bare patch, remove soil and turf to a distance of 60cm (24in) beyond ring and a depth of 30-45cm (12-18in); replace with fresh, or sterilize the same area, forked up, with formalin, using a dilution rate of 1 part formalin to 39 parts water, and applying 18L per sq m (4gal per sq yd). Cover for ten days, then fork soil and replant when smell of formalin has gone (about six weeks).

*Narcissus*

Bulb fly: insect pest. Bulbs grow and flower poorly, do not flower at all, or die and do not appear in the season following infection. Bulbs become soft and contain white maggots internally. Destroy such bulbs and dust soil round remaining bulbs with HCH (BHC) from end of late spring at two-weekly intervals until end of early summer.

*Pansy*

Black-root rot: soil-borne fungus disease. Symptoms are yellowing leaves followed by withering, death of plant and blackening of roots. Destroy affected plants; rest soil for three years, or sterilize, or replace.

Stem rot: soil-borne fungus disease. Symptoms are yellowing of leaves which then die, main stem rots at base. Destroy affected plants; dust soil with fungicide containing mercury (calomel) and improve drainage, or plant in different site.

*Pelargonium*

Black-root rot, see *Pansy*; rust, see *Antirrhinum* (N.B., no resistant varieties of pelargonium).

*Peony*

Blight: fungus disease. Symptoms are wilting of plant and death of young shoots at base of main stem, following browning. Remove affected parts where possible. Treat plants and soil round them with benomyl fungicide; dig up and destroy plants if they do not recover and plant new specimens in a different site.

Bud disease: physiological. Symptoms are stem just below flower bud shrivelling and turning brown; bud hangs down and does not open. Supply potash in spring; make sure plant does not run short of water or become waterlogged. Protect from hot sun after cold nights.

*Phlox*

Eelworm: pest. Symptoms are twisted, narrow leaves, turning brown from base of plant and falling, stems swollen and splitting from base upwards, flowering poor or non-existent. Dig up plants in winter, use roots for cuttings, and destroy remainder of plant. Plant in different site.

*Salpiglossis*

Foot rot, see *Aster*

*Stock*

Wire-stem, see *Wallflower*

*Sweetpea*

Thrips, see *Gladiolus*; black-root rot, see *Pansy*

*Tulip*

Fire: fungus disease. Symptoms are blackened patches on leaf tips and later rest of leaf, and on buds and flowers; bulbs have blisters on the outside. Destroy badly infected plants; spray remainder and soil with captan or thiram, avoiding flowers. Following year start spraying when growth 2.5cm (1in) tall, until flowers unfold.

*Violet*

Leaf-midge: insect pest. Symptoms are thickened leaves, rolling inwards from margins. Plants small and poorly flowering. Pick off infested leaves and spray plant with dimethoate early in late spring, the middle of late summer and in mid-autumn.

*Wallflower*

Flea-beetle: insect pest. Symptoms are small round holes in leaves of seedlings and very young plants; tiny, hopping irridescent beetles present. Dust derris or HCH (BHC) on to leaves when dry.

Wire-stem: fungus disease. Symptoms are brown, constricted stem near base, plant stunted if not killed. Destroy infected plants; use sterilized soil for seed compost or seed-bed. Dust seed with captan or thiram.

# THE SHRUB & TREE GARDEN
## Early Spring

For some weeks now, the days will have been getting noticeably lighter for longer, the dawn chorus will be under way and the temperature will have a slow but steady tendency upwards—even if it does seem to be a case of two degrees up and one down. Another sign that spring is definitely on the way is the fattening and bursting open of buds on roses, shrubs, trees, hedges and some of the fruits. In fact, apricots, nectarines and peaches may optimistically be trying to flower outdoors.

Since plant growth is very much on the move, some pruning will have to be finished fairly quickly before it is too late; summer-flowering clematis and buddleia are examples. Annual pruning of large-flowered and cluster-flowered roses can be done. Similarly, winter-flowering shrubs can be tidied up; they rarely need annual or rule-of-thumb pruning. It may also be mild enough to prune some late-summer- and autumn-flowering shrubs.

It is a good time to renovate older and worn-out or straggly hedges, and some shrubs, including the old varieties and hybrids of rhododendrons (not the modern kinds, which do not take kindly to such attacks) by cutting them hard back. Such severe pruning, provided it is done at the right time and combined with feeding, can produce very good results.

A job which can only be done in early spring is grafting various kinds of fruit, either to change the variety or to produce one's own young trees by grafting stocks. Grafting is not a technique often used by the gardener, but it can be useful, if you find that a particular variety of fruit does not have a good flavour or if you need more or different pollinators.

However, as with vegetables and soft fruit, the real rush of plant growth and work does not start until mid-spring; the remainder of the jobs will mostly consist of finishing the winter ones, tidying up, protecting and making preparations for the next season.

# At~a~glance diary

**Prepare the soil for:** planting outdoors

**Plant:** finish planting deciduous trees, shrubs, climbers and roses; plant evergreens and the hardier grey-leaved shrubs

**Prune:** large-flowered, cluster-flowered and climbing roses; winter-flowering cherry (Prunus subhirtella autumnalis), Garrya elliptica, heather (Erica carnea in variety), laurustinus (Viburnum tinus), Mahonia Charity, sarcococca, Viburnum Dawn and V. farreri, winter sweet (Chimonanthus praecox), witchhazel (Hamamelis mollis); late-summer-flowering shrubs: abelia (deciduous), Buddleia davidii, campsis, caryopteris, Ceratostigma willmottianum, fuchsia, heather (Calluna vulgaris in variety), hippophae, hydrangea, hypericum, indigofera, leycesteria, lupin (tree), potentilla, Sambucus nigra Aurea, solanum, sorbaria, southernwood (Artemisia abrotanum), spiraea, symphoricarpos, tamarisk; finish pruning fruit and summer-flowering clematis

**Cut back hard:** overgrown hedges; informal flowering hedges; old or overgrown shrubs grown as specimens; dogwood (cornus) and willow (salix)

**Feed:** all roses, summer-flowering shrubs and summer-flowering clematis; sites prepared for planting

**Pollinate:** apricots, peaches and nectarines

**Protect:** fruit trees and spring-flowering shrubs against pecking by birds; wall-grown apricots, peaches and nectarines against cold; newly planted shrubs and trees against rabbits, voles and hares

**Pests and diseases:** scab on apples and pears; greenfly in general; mildew on roses, gall on azaleas, wilt on young clematis

**Routine work:** inspect all for winter weather damage; firm in new plantings where lifted by frost; tie in grape vines

**Increase:** fruit by grafting. Clematis by layering

# Jobs to do

## Preparing the soil for planting

It is still not too late to plant the various kinds of shrubs and trees which would have been better put in during late autumn or early winter. If you are expecting an order to arrive from a nursery, have bought container-grown plants from a garden centre or have some plants heeled-in waiting for better weather, the soil can be prepared for these any time up to within a day or two of planting (see Mid-Autumn for details of method). Heavy soils may still be too wet for digging comfortably and any soil may be frozen, so always wait until it is possible to get a fork or a spade into it. If you find the soil difficult to penetrate, the plant roots will not find it easy either.

## Planting

Once the dormant buds on woody plants begin to pop open and sprout stems and leaves, it is really too late for totally successful planting. As this will start happening shortly, you should plant roses, the hardy deciduous shrubs, including hedges and climbers, trees, vines and other fruit, as soon as possible. Towards the end of early spring is the time to plant many evergreens and a few of the hardiest grey-leaved shrubs, such as santolina and *Senecio greyi*. However, if there is some risk of a dry spring with strong cold winds, it would be better to wait until mid-spring or even early autumn, before planting these evergreens and evergreys (for details of planting all these see Late Autumn).

## Pruning

The groups of plants which need pruning at this season are the large-flowered and cluster-flowered (hybrid tea and floribunda) and climbing roses, the late-summer-flowering shrubs and winter-flowering shrubs and trees. If the fruit and summer-flowering clematis have not been finished (or even started), their pruning should be completed as soon in early spring as possible, particularly as clematis may already have new shoots up to 30cm (12in) long (see Early and Late Winter for pruning details).

*Senecio greyi is an extremely attractive shrub with evergreen leaves and bright yellow daisies in summer.*

*Roses* Early spring is generally accepted as the time to prune the most popular group of roses: the large-flowered and cluster-flowered modern bush types. Some gardeners start doing it in mid- or late winter because they maintain that flowering starts earlier as a result. However, as the tips of the shoots, pruned or unpruned, are likely to be damaged or killed by cold, later pruning, when one can see any damage, may mean less damage and only one lot of pruning.

Rose buds generally start to sprout towards the end of early spring, so pruning should be started at the beginning of the season. Large-flowered kinds need moderately hard cutting back to stimulate as many and as strong new shoots as possible. Weak, spindly shoots should be cut back flush with their parent stem; shoots growing into the centre or across the bush should also be removed, together with dead shoots.

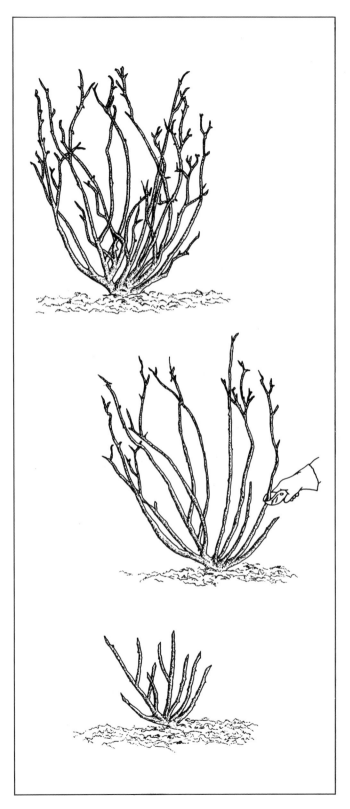

The remaining healthy and vigorous shoots should then be pruned to remove about half to two-thirds their length; try to place each cut so that the bud immediately below it points outwards and the one below that, too, if possible. It is often the case that the dormant bud you assumed would sprout and grow outwards to form a perfect, goblet-shaped bush either dies, gets attacked, knocked off or otherwise assaulted and the one below it grows beautifully, straight into the centre.

The majority of large-flowered roses produce a good display and plenty of blooms for the house if pruned like this, but the tall-growing, vigorous kinds such as Queen Elizabeth and Peace need lighter cutting, otherwise they get taller at the expense of flowers. For best results only one-third of the main stem is cut off and lesser stems are merely tipped. Occasionally, one of the old main stems can be cut down to ground level to encourage new wood.

Cluster-flowered rose pruning is not so simple; with some varieties the recommendation to remove last year's flowered stems can mean that virtually no growth is left above ground level. In order to produce the best show possible, pruning should ensure that the main stems are cut back to markedly differing lengths. For instance, those stems which are 'middle-aged' can be cut back moderately, to half to two-thirds their length, as the large-flowered kinds are. Any of last year's shoots produced at or close to ground level should have only about one-third of their length removed and the oldest stems, perhaps one, two or three of them, should be pruned hard to leave 7.5 or 10cm (3 or 4in) only. Besides this, there is the routine pruning to remove weak, diseased, crowded or crossing shoots, if any remain.

By treating each main stem individually like this, and pruning to different lengths, it is possible to maintain a renewal of growth each year throughout the bush so that strong new shoots are constantly being encouraged, while older ones which are still capable of flowering are retained to ensure as good a display as possible. For the details of pruning climbing roses, see Late Winter.

The winter-flowering shrubs and trees include autumn-flowering cherry (*Prunus subhirtella autumnalis*), *Garrya elliptica*, heather (*Erica carnea* in variety), laurustinus (*Viburnum tinus*), *Mahonia* Charity, sarcococca, *Viburnum* Dawn and *V. farreri*, winter sweet (*Chimonanthus praecox*) and witch hazel (*Hamamelis mollis*). All of these except the ericas need only a little pruning. Quite often you need not

*Pruning roses: Large-flowered (hybrid tea) roses need to be pruned hard in early spring. Cuts should be made close to outward-pointing buds.*

*The winter-flowering heathers are some of the best small shrubs for providing colour at a dull time of the year.* Erica carnea alba *will grow in chalky soil.*

do any pruning at all if they are growing naturally into an attractive shape, and they will still flower perfectly well.

However, most shrubs have some dead shoots, broken branches, thin, spindly shoots shorter than the rest, or crowded together and crossing over. Cutting away this sort of growth, even if you do nothing else, will always ensure that the shrub grows more healthily and has better flowers and leaves. At the same time you can deal with the odd long stem which protrudes far beyond the main body of the bush; if it is as strong as that it will not flower well in any case, so it is better removed altogether, back to its point of origin. You can also cut back some of the oldest shoots, once the shrubs have been planted a few years, to just above a new or strong younger shoot.

A general rule when pruning flowering shrubs is to cut off the shoots which have had flowers on them, with the object of inducing the shrub to produce new shoots to take their place and flower the coming season. However, winter-flowering shrubs on the whole are rather slow-growing and such cutting-back is more likely to mutilate their appearance and discourage growth, rather than encourage it. So, on the whole, the rule is not to cut off old flowering growth unless it comes into any of the categories that have just been mentioned above.

*Viburnum farreri* and *V*. Dawn tend to be awkwardly shaped and often do need to have their figures improved; laurustinus turns itself into a nicely rounded bush without help. The autumn-flowering cherry may stick a stem straight up out of the otherwise weeping head; don't hesitate to cut it right away, or the tree's head will become more and more grossly unbalanced.

The mahonia will probably produce new shoots at or near ground level as the central stem extends; if the latter becomes too tall, it can be cut right down and the younger shoots allowed to grow into its place.

*Erica carnea* and its varieties are pruned quite differently; as soon as flowering is really finished, but before new growth starts, they may be not so much pruned as sheared. Trim them straight across with shears to cut off the dead flowers and shoots; this need only be done in alternate years.

*Garrya elliptica* can be pruned in this season (see Pruning, Late Winter, for details); the remaining winter-flowering plants need not be pruned, except in occasional years in a general way.

The late-summer-flowering shrubs are generally considered to include those which flower in mid-summer, late summer and through early autumn into mid-autumn and pruning can be done towards the end of early spring or the beginning of mid-spring.

These shrubs generally flower on shoots produced earlier in the same season, i.e., a new shoot which starts to grow in early or mid-spring will bear flowers some time during the later part of summer or in autumn of the same year. As it is a principle of growth that the removal of shoots from a plant results in the plant replacing them with new shoots, so pruning in spring will—or should—automatically ensure that it will have a new crop of blossom later on. Therefore, if you do not have time to prune this type of shrub in the early part of spring and decide to make up for lost time by doing it in early summer, you will remove most of the new growth and flowering display. Not only that: the plant will try to make good the loss by developing a new batch of shoots, but too late for them to ripen by the time winter comes, so that tips will be killed, the shoots die back and disease infect the dead growth. The result is a weakly growing, poorly flowering shrub which may never recover.

The late-summer-flowering shrubs to prune towards the end of early spring include the following:

*Abelia* deciduous  Prune only to tidy, cut out weak and straggling growth and one or two of the oldest shoots; regular annual pruning not necessary.

*Berberis* deciduous  Prune only those with coloured leaves, e.g., Rose Glow, Aurea, and purple-leaved kinds except the dwarf form, since the young leaves and stems have the best colouring. Cut the main stems to strong new side-shoots and occasionally cut out one or two of the oldest shoots completely.

*Buddleia davidii* and varieties (butterfly bush)  Cut last year's long shoots back hard to leave a length of stem with only three or four dormant buds on it. In cold districts wait until mid-spring.

*Campsis*  This is mostly spur-pruned: the new shoots are cut back to stumps with two buds on them, once the main shoots have filled the space available, but a few new shoots are left at their full length in suitable positions to clothe the support and the plant.

*Caryopteris*  Cut flowered shoots moderately hard to leave about 23cm (9in) of stem, and cut weak shoots back hard, to

Buddleia davidii, *the butterfly bush, blooms late in summer; other colours are deep purple, plum and white.*

leave a stub with one or two buds. In cold districts wait until mid-spring before you do this pruning.

*Ceratostigma willmottianum* (plumbago) Cut back hard almost to ground level; in cold seasons or districts leave until mid-spring.

*Fuchsia*  In mild districts cut off dead shoots and parts of shoots now and cut live side-shoots back to one or two pairs of buds. In other districts and cold seasons leave this until mid-spring.

*Heather* (*Calluna vulgaris* in variety)  Trim with shears to cut off the flowered shoots.

*Hydrangea* (round headed) in variety Cut off old flower-heads to just above a pair of good buds; cut back some of the oldest shoots to ground level and those shoots killed by cold. Thin new shoots coming from ground level, otherwise they will be crowded.

*Hippophae* Hardly any pruning; remove weak shoots.

*Hypericum* Cut back the tall kinds hard so that last season's new shoots are reduced to a quarter of the length. Be careful with *H. x moseranum*; remove dead shoots only when new ones start to sprout.

*Indigofera* Annual pruning is not essential but better flowering will be obtained by cutting last season's new side-shoots back to leave stubs to produce new stems. Dead tips should be cut off and weak shoots removed to avoid overcrowding.

*Leycesteria* Remove some of the oldest stems at ground level and cut back last season's flowered growth by about half. In cold districts and seasons wait until mid-spring.

*Lupin*, tree  Cut out the oldest stems and weak shoots completely and cut the strongest growth from last season by a half to two-thirds.

*Potentilla*, tall kinds to 1.5m (5ft)  Cut to ground level to produce small, bushy and very floriferous plants or prune in mid-autumn.

*Sambucus nigra* Aurea (yellow-leaved elder)    Cut last season's new shoots back to leave stubs 5 or 7.5cm (2 or 3in) long, so that plenty of new foliage is produced.

*Solanum* Every year, before new growth begins to appear, the weakest shoots should be cut back hard to leave one or two buds, and some of last year's strongest shoots pruned to leave three or four buds. Choice of shoot for cutting should ensure that the space allowed for growth is covered adequately and evenly.

*Sorbaria* Prune very hard, almost to ground level, leaving stubs with strong buds on them

*Southernwood* (*Artemisia abrotanum*)  Prune last year's new growth to leave only 1.2cm ($\frac{1}{2}$in) stubs of it. Do not cut into growth older than this.

*Spiraea*, late-sumer-flowering kinds    Cut last season's shoots back very hard to within a few centimetres (inches) of ground level; in some years cut out completely one or two of the oldest shoots also.

*Symphoricarpos* (snowberry)  Cut out the weakest, oldest and straggling shoots completely and thin the remainder, making all cuts to ground level.

*Tamarisk*, autumn-flowering  Cut last season's new growth back to leave stubs with dormant buds on them.

This list does not include all the summer-flowering shrubs shown in the table below, because some are more safely pruned in mid-spring.

## Cutting back hard
Old deciduous hedges which have got rather gaunt and bare at the base can still be cut back hard in early spring, down to half or even less, of their height. Sometimes better results are obtained doing it just before new growth starts, rather than at the beginning of the dormancy period. Furthermore, you can remove growth killed by the winter's cold at the same time. Dormant buds, low down, will sprout as a result of the hard cutting.

If evergreen hedges are to be treated, early or, preferably, mid-spring is the time to cut them, but very hard cutting back is generally not advisable. The cypresses and brooms in particular object to this treatment and may die as a result. It is quite enough to remove about half the height of a hardy evergreen hedge and only about one-third of the sensitive ones. If the hedge has got too broad, as well as too high, wait until the second spring before cutting the sides, so that the vertical growth has a chance to grow and keep the hedge going while the sides recover from drastic trimming.

Informal flowering hedges which bloom from mid-summer onwards should be cut back now before growth really gets going. Cut last year's flowered shoots off to leave stubs a few centimetres (inches) long, on which there are dormant buds. Slow-growing hedges of this kind need not be trimmed except to cut back long straggling shoots now.

Individual shrub specimens which have grown tall or rather old can be rejuvenated by hard cutting at this time; *Buddleia davidii* and varieties and the tall hypericums can be pruned to leave stubs at ground level late in early spring. Doing this every few years is an alternative to moderate pruning every year. Hippophae, too, can be cut down to about 90cm (36in). The older and hardier rhododendron hybrids and varieties will tolerate cutting back to about 60-90cm (24-36in).

There is another reason for hard cutting back in spring, if the shrubs concerned have attractively coloured bark. There are varieties of dogwood (cornus) and willow (salix) which have brilliantly red, orange or yellow bark on the young shoots. If such plants are cut down hard to leave about 15cm (6in) of stem, they will produce a great number of these young shoots; all or about half of last year's shoots can be pruned, depending on how ruthless you feel.

## Feeding
Roses can be given their first feed of the growing season as soon as pruning is finished. You can use one of the proprietary compound fertilizers, or a general one which is high in potash, to help with flowering. Summer-flowering shrubs and the later summer-flowering clematis can also be

fed with similar fertilizers. If you still have shrubs or trees to put in, dress the site with bonemeal about a week before planting, forking it in evenly at about 120g per sq m (4oz per sq yd). Give hedges and shrubs which have been hard-pruned a dressing of a general compound fertilizer, forking or hoeing it in if practicable, or watering it in.

## Pollinating
The only blossom likely to be out at this time of the year is that of peaches, nectarines and apricots. Such fruits are natives of much warmer climates than the temperate zone and so flower earlier, with the certainty of being pollinated

*Peaches are self-fertile, but they flower so early in the year that hand-pollination is advisable in many cases.*

by insects which also come out of their winter hibernation much earlier. Pollinators from temperate climates do not appear in large quantities until mid-spring, so you must help the process of fertilization with a child's paint-brush, doing it preferably in the middle of a sunny day.

## Protecting
The fruit and the shrubs which have had cover on them all winter to guard against bullfinches, sparrows and other birds nipping out the flower or fruit buds should be gone over carefully, as the birds can do a lot of damage now, at the end of winter. The forsythia and flowering cherry displays can be non-existent as a result of bud pecking, and sprays and protective webbing may need renewing.

Apricots, peaches and nectarines growing with wall protection may already be in flower, or just coming up to it, and if you want to be certain of a crop, you should insulate against frost and cold winds. A polythene net dropped in front of them from battens on the wall will do the job, or you can have a more elaborate arrangement with clear plastic sheeting. Remove it as soon as the temperature goes up, otherwise any pollinating insects about cannot do their work.

## Treating pests and diseases
In early spring there is little more to do to woody plants than examine them to discover how they are. New growth will only just be starting to appear, so pests and diseases will not yet be visible in large quantities. Greenfly, of course, may start to hatch from their over-wintering eggs, in town gardens and others where the district is mild or the season an early one. The opening buds of roses, apples and pears are likely to be their main targets.

The fungus disease, scab, on apples and pears (a different strain on the latter) may start to infect leaves as they unfold, if temperature and humidity are high enough, but mid-spring is usually the season when it becomes really dangerous. Mildew may attack the new growth of roses, especially if it were present the previous year. Fruit can be infected by mildew and there are different mildews according to which fruit is being infected. However, they can all be treated with the same chemicals. If mildew does appear, it is worth removing the ailing growth now, cutting off the shoot well below the infection, even if it does mean removing apparently healthy growth.

The fungus disease on azaleas which makes the leaves become thick and curled up, with grey bloom on the surface, is called azalea gall; cutting off the affected parts is usually all that need be done. Gall does not appear on outdoor azaleas very much; the indoor potted types are more likely to get gall as it thrives in close, humid conditions (see Controls and Treatments section for details of chemical sprays, and the spray chart in Mid-Winter).

## General work
If it has not been done before, taking a good look round the plants is advisable, to discover broken branches, stakes which have been blown askew, loosened ties, trees which have been wind-rocked (so that a hollow full of water has formed round the base of the trunk), and freshly planted trees and shrubs which have been lifted out of the soil as a result of the action of frost. Any of these troubles left unrepaired will at best result in a damaged and weakened

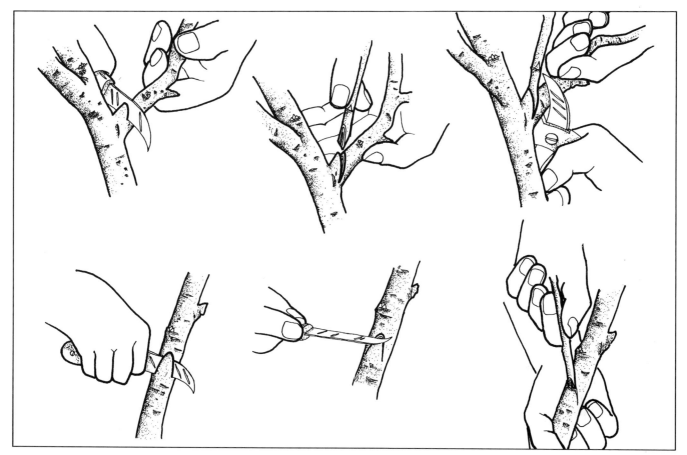

plant and at worst a dead one. Wind-rocking causes some of the most serious trouble, because the collected water starts a rot of the bark of the trunk. Once the bark has been killed all the way round, it is only a matter of time before the tree dies.

Check that protective coverings and barriers against cold are still intact and in place; although this is the beginning of the spring some of the coldest weather of the winter can occur during the next four or five weeks.

The main stems of grape vines, which were loosened and allowed partially to hang down in mid winter can now be tied back in position again.

## Increasing

Early spring is the recommended season for grafting fruit trees. The grafting the gardener will most likely want to do will be the kind that changes the variety of a mature tree and this is most frequently done with apples and pears. By now the sap has begun to run again and the chance of the grafts 'taking' is much more certain than at any other season.

*Framework grafting: If a fruit tree is to be changed to another variety, its branches are cut back and grafted by two methods. Above: Stub-grafting. The scion is cut into a wedge shape and the branch forced open, then cut off just above the graft. Below: Side-cleft. A tongue is lifted and the scion's end is tapered.*

For grafting you will need a really sharp, straight-bladed, grafting knife (not an ordinary penknife and not one with a curved blade), grafting wax (proprietary hot and cold waxes can be bought from garden shops) and a brush; a rag always seems to be useful, too.

On a mature tree with a cup-shaped arrangement of main branches, the latter should be left to almost their complete length, so that the growth at the end of each is not less than two years old. The side-shoots and side branches should be cut back to about 20cm (8in) long.

The pattern of grafting should be herring-bone, so that the new branches come out alternately on each side of a main branch; any original side branches which do not fit into this pattern should be removed completely. So, too, should any main branches growing into the centre of the tree or straight upwards; if any are too close, now is the time to remove one here and there.

The secret of successful grafting is to get what are known as the cambium layers matching. The cambium is a layer of tissue composed of cells which divide and create new woody cells, just below the bark; in most plants the cambium is bright green, The sloping cuts made in both scion and stock expose as much of this layer as possible and so increase the chances of the graft being successful.

The scion is the new variety to be grafted on to the parent tree, or stock, and for the average bush apple or pear on dwarfing stock, about a hundred scions will be required. You should have already obtained them (see Early Winter) and they can now be cut so that they are about 10 buds long. For a stub graft, the end of the scion should be cut to form a short wedge. The side branch or side-shoot to be

*Mahonis japonica is strongly fragrant, like lily-of-the-valley. It flowers on and off all through winter and early spring, and sometimes in late autumn, too.*

grafted has a sloping cut made partially through its upper side; this cut is pulled open and the scion pushed into it, matching the cut surfaces. Once the scion is in, the stub can be cut back to just above the graft and grafting wax painted completely over the whole stub and cut so that there are no gaps at all.

If there is no stub in a suitable position, a side-cleft grafting may be used instead. Cut the branch to be grafted to lift a tongue of bark and wood, cut the tip of the tongue off and push the scion in with the cut surfaces facing and matching. The end of the scion for this type of graft should have a single flat, tapered surface; finish by waxing, as before. The ends of the main branches should be stub grafted.

After grafting, as the tree begins to grow, sucker shoots will appear from trunk and main branches; these suckers should be removed while still only a few centimetres (inches) long.

Clematis can still be layered, but mid-spring will be too late (see Late Autumn for method), so do it early in the season.

## Plants in flower

Apricot, Camellia, Flowering cherry, Clematis armandii, Corylopsis, Flowering currant, Forsythia, Gorse, Japonica, Jasmine (winter-flowering, Jasminum nudiflorum), Laurustinus, Magnolia stellata, Mahonia japonica, Pieris, Peach, Rhododendrons in variety, Skimmia, Spiraea thunbergii

## Fruits in store

Apple, Pear, Quince

# Mid~Spring

Spring might have been a little hesitant in appearing during the last few weeks, but there will be no doubt about its presence by now. Cherries, pears and plums will be in flower, wall-grown peaches and nectarines will be setting their fruit, many shrubs and trees will be blossoming. New leaves and shoots will be sprouting everywhere, and so will the weeds. The places most likely to need urgent weeding will be rose-beds, hedge bottoms, trained fruit grown against walls or as dividers and specimen trees grown in beds.

Pruning will continue to be a major activity. There will be some planting and this is also the time to start layering various shrubs. Seeds which have been stratified through the winter, and others, can be sown; there may be cuttings to take in sheltered gardens.

Although woody plants are apparently not much affected by bad weather, it is only short spells of bad weather to which they are immune. Prolonged cold, drought, waterlogging and wind take an equally prolonged and severe toll, but it does not show on this type of plant until months, perhaps even a year, have passed. Unfortunately, by that time, some other type of unfavourable weather may have ensued and the compound damage results in a small, unhappy plant, if it lives at all.

It is extremely important to foresee these problems and take steps to ameliorate them before they have lasted more than a week or two. For instance, in early spring, strong, cold wind, bright sun and drought can set in and continue for six weeks or more. The effect of this on newly-planted evergreens can be death, unless you put up a barrier in the path of the prevailing wind, keep the soil moist and spray the top growth every day.

Friends and foes in the insect world will be on the move, like everything else; disease spores will be floating about in their millions, and there may still be trouble from birds and animals. A variety of jobs will be started now, to be carried on through the season; these include blueing hydrangeas, making compost, mowing orchard swards and deadheading flowering shrubs.

# At~a~glance diary

**Prepare the soil for:** planting outdoors

**Plant:** the hardier grey-leaved shrubs and evergreens; finish any planting left from early spring; young shrubs, roses and trees grown from seed

**Prune:** large/cluster-flowered and climbing roses if in cold districts or if the season is late; finish planting winter-flowering shrubs and late-summer-flowering kinds. Also prune: Buddleia globosa, evergreen berberis, brooms, camellia ceanothus, flowering currant, daisy bush (olearia haastii), dogwood, forsythia, fuchsia heather (calluna and Erica carnea), hebe (shrubby veronica), hibiscus, hydrangea, ivy, lavender, lavender cotton (santolina), tree mallow (lavatera), mahonia, pyracantha (firethorn), romneya (Californian poppy), rue, Senecio greyi, yucca

**Disbud:** peach, nectarine, vine

**Cut back hard:** evergreen hedges

**Deadhead:** rhododendrons and pieris

**Pot:** rooted vine-eyes

**Feed:** planting sites; roses, summer-flowering shrubs and summer-flowering clematis if not done in early spring; hedges and shrubs cut back hard for rejuvenation

**Blue:** hydrangea

**Water:** newly planted specimens, plants growing close to walls or fences

**Support:** climbers

**Protect:** new shoots against frost, remove protective mulches from tender plants

**Thin:** apricot, peach, nectarine grown against walls

**Increase:** tree fruit by grafting; shrubs, climbers and roses by layering; a variety of plants by seed

**Weed:** where necessary

**Mow:** orchard swards

**Compost heap:** start to build

**Ring:** pear trees

**Pests and diseases:** aphids (greenfly, blackfly, mealy-aphid, etc) caterpillars, vine weevil, mildew, scab, rose black spot, peach leaf curl, clematis wilt; remove grease-bands from fruit trees

# Jobs to do

### Preparing the soil for planting

Mid-spring is a better time to plant some of the shrubs mentioned in early spring, and there are others which should not be planted until now, so soil will need to be prepared for these in the usual way by forking it, clearing it of winter weeds and mixing in fertilizer (see Feeding).

### Planting

Finish any planting left from early spring. You should be able to plant the hardier grey-leaved shrubs towards the end of mid-spring and most of the evergreens at any time (see tables for tender species). However, if you are in the middle of a cold, sunny period, and you have somewhere to heel in open-ground plants, it is better to wait until the weather improves. Warm, showery springs are ideal for planting, but drought combined with cold wind can be as damaging as when it is combined with heat, in summer.

Shrubs, roses and trees grown from seed sown last spring can now be planted in their permanent positions (see Planting, Late Spring).

If planting in bad conditions is unavoidable, do all that you can to insulate the plants from them. Mix coarse sand and granulated peat into wet soil to mop up and drain at the same time. Remember that evergreens lose water through their leaves constantly and while their roots are settling down, they will not be absorbing water to replace that being lost by the top growth. The result is brown leaves or brown needles, particularly on the windward side. A daily spray overhead with water is essential in cold or windy dry weather, together with a wind barrier and some soil watering.

### Pruning

If you were unable to finish pruning the roses in early spring, you should do so in the first week of this season. In all but cold districts, shoots and leaves will be developing fast; pruning once the plant is growing again weakens it. Those with chilly gardens will not normally expect to prune roses until now in any case, but wherever your garden

*The brooms are handsome shrubs which cover themselves in flower in late spring and summer.* Cytisus scoparius *Andreanus grows to about 2.4m (7ft).*

is, be guided by the stage of growth the bushes have reached. Pruning just as the buds begin to swell is a good time, although, if you have a lot of roses, you may have to start earlier, in order to get round them all before it is too late.

Any of the winter-flowering shrubs which were not pruned in early spring should be dealt with early this season, also the late-summer-flowering kinds as listed (see **Pruning, Early Spring**). In addition the following can now be pruned; they include some of the more tender species and some evergreens, as well as the early-spring-flowering shrubs and less hardy, late-summer-flowering subjects.

If in doubt about pruning any shrub, mid-spring is usually safe; although many do not need annual pruning, they do occasionally, every five years or so, need cutting to a better shape, restricting to the space provided instead of overflowing it and dead, ailing, crowded or stunted shoots cleared out.

*Buddleia globosa* This tends to become rather leggy and awkwardly shaped, so it should be cut back by about half towards the end of mid-spring, every few years, instead of pruning later, after flowering. However, in cold districts this may kill it, and it would be better to start again from rooted cuttings.

*Berberis*, evergreen Cut some of the oldest shoots down to the ground so that the remainder have more air and light; also cut some other shoots down to the origin of strong one-year-old growth, but wait until flowering has finished before pruning. Do all this occasionally.

*Broom* (*Cytisus battandieri*) Regular pruning is not necessary, but occasional cutting back of straggling shoots and branches in mid-spring will improve its appearance.

*Camellia* (*japonica* types) If space has been outgrown by rather elderly specimens, cut back by about half or a little more; any other pruning is not necessary. These shrubs are amongst the best for arranging themselves in a shapely way and producing a mass of flowers. They are hardy enough to withstand several degrees of frost at least and can be covered in icicles without harm to the leaves or shoots.

*Ceanothus*, autumn-flowering Prune those with a wall backing them in mid-spring—if the weather is not cold—by cutting back strong-flowered shoots to leave about 30cm (12in) of stem. They also tend to grow a lot of short, weak, crossing shoots which do not flower and clutter up the bush, so these should be removed as well.

*Currant, flowering* (ribes) No regular pruning; prune to shape every few years and cut out old shoots to just above strong young shoots.

*Daisy bush* (*Olearia haastii*) Can be trimmed with the shears in mid-spring or cut back hard if you want the bush to put out a lot of new growth.

*Dogwood* (Cornus), see Pruning, Early Spring.

*Forsythia* Specimen bushes should have some of the flowered shoots cut back after flowering, to newly growing stems. If the bush is rather thick and overgrown in spite of this, the oldest shoots can be cut right down to the ground and others cut hard to let in light and air. Wall-grown forsythias, such as *F. suspensa*, need regular pruning every spring; the flowered shoots are cut back to a stub 5 or 7.5cm (2 or 3in) long.

*Fuchsia* By now most fuchsias will be showing some signs of life and dead shoots and dead shoot tips will be obvious; these should be removed and remaining side-shoots cut back to one or two pairs of dormant buds. Weak shoots should be cut right off.

*Heather* (calluna and *Erica carnea* in variety) If not already done in early spring, trim off the flowered shoots with shears, annually for calluna, alternate years for the ericas.

*Hebe* (shrubby veronica) Being evergreen, hebes must be **treated with care**. Prune every three years or so, late in mid-spring or in late spring, if they are outgrowing their space or getting leggy.

*Hibiscus* Pruning is usually not needed, but if they are getting too large, they can be pruned hard, by half their growth, early in mid-spring.

*Hydrangea* (round-headed) If pruning were not done at the end of early spring, it can be done early in this season by cutting off the old-flower-heads to just above a pair of good buds, removing some of the oldest shoots completely, and thinning out the new shoots, again to ground level. Alternatively, pruning can be done every few years, cutting the whole bush back to stubs with one or two buds on them.

*Ivy* Rarely needs any treatment, but if it is colonizing too much, trimming can be done now.

*Lavender* Cut back last season's shoots to within a couple of centimetres (about an inch) of their origin. Lavender tends to become leggy within a few years and should be replaced, but as it roots easily from cuttings this is no problem.

*Lavender cotton* (santolina) This can be cut back hard once a year, in spring, to just above the new growth which will be appearing by now. Alternatively, it can be trimmed two or three times in the growing season to keep it tidy.

*Mahonia* *Mahonia japonica* need not be pruned at all unless one of the main stems is getting rather leggy, in which case it can be cut low down and new shoots will come from the

*The ceanothus are shrubs which deserve to be grown much more as they are one of the few with blue flowers.*

base to fill the gap. Normally, however, it grows into a leafy, rounded shrub. *M. aquifolium* does not need pruning; *Mahonia* Charity can have one of its main stems cut down to near ground level if getting too tall as it produces shoots from the base without any fuss.

*Tree mallow (Lavatera arborea)* A fast-growing shrub, so cut back low down on each main shoot to where new growth is beginning to appear.

*Pyracantha (firethorn)* If it is wall-trained and has got rather large and untidy, it can be cut back hard into shape, though there will not be any flowers for the coming season.

*Romneya (Californian poppy)* Being on the tender side, this may well have had all its stems killed during winter, but if not, they should be cut down practically to ground level. It will grow well again and can be regarded somewhat in the same way as herbaceous peonies.

*Rue (Ruta graveolens)* Last year's growth can be cut back hard, close to its base, so that it produces as much of its grey-blue ferny foliage as possible.

*Senecio greyi* Cut back towards the end of mid-spring, removing last year's growth to leave stubs. It is not essential to do all this every year; you can get away with simply cutting off straggling stems, those that are outgrowing the space and those lying on the ground. The latter will provide new plants as they will probably have rooted.

*Willow (salix)* see Pruning, Early Spring.

*Yucca* Remove all dead leaves every year at this time.

## Disbudding

It could be said that disbudding is a form of pruning, as it involves the removal of shoots, but they are taken away when only 2.5 or 5cm (1 or 2in) long. Fan-trained peaches and vines grown against walls are treated like this during spring and later as needed. For peaches and nectarines, each side-shoot should have left on it, one new shoot at its base, one about half way along it to act as a 'feeder' (or replacement if need be), and the new growth at its tip, the leader. All the rest should be rubbed off, except the shoot growing immediately next to a fruit, which is pinched back to one leaf. Do this disbudding gradually in about three stages, to avoid shock to the tree. This treatment ensures the growth of new shoots for next year's crop and the prevention of bare leggy shoots which do not fruit.

Vines are disbudded in spring so that there is only one shoot left at each spur and one shoot at the end of the main branch, or rod. Wherever there is a pair of shoots, the weaker of the two is rubbed off. The remaining shoots on both peaches and vines are tied in as they grow, spacing them evenly.

## Cutting back hard

Evergreen hedges that have become too tall and bare at the base can be rejuvenated now by removing about half their height (see Early Spring). Laurel hedges can be more drastically treated, if your district has warm, wet weather now, by cutting down to stumps about 30 or 45cm (12 or 18in) tall. You will have to do without the hedge for a season or so, but it is a strong shrub and will quickly produce new growth, which you can keep bushy at the base from the start.

## Deadheading

You may have already cut some flowers in the natural course of events for the home, but any that have finished on the rhododendrons and pieris should be cut off, otherwise the plants' energy is concentrated on forming seed instead of new flowering shoots.

*Opposite: Peaches are thinned from the time when they are marble-sized, to one every 23cm (9in) square. Below: The firethorns (pyracantha spp.) set berries which often last through the winter.*

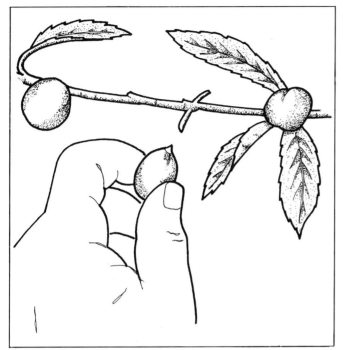

## Potting
Vine-eyes, put to root in late winter, should now be ready for potting into a 13.5cm (5in) pot of good potting compost. They should be kept protected.

## Feeding
Sites prepared for planting should have bonemeal mixed into them at 120g per sq m (4oz per sq yd), if possible a week or so in advance, otherwise the day before. Try to avoid mixing the fertilizer with the soil as you plant, because some roots will inevitably come into contact with the fertilizer; this results in 'burning' and the root dies back.

If it has not been done in early spring, feed roses, summer-flowering shrubs and summer-flowering clematis now; also give a general compound fertilizer to hedges and shrubs cut back hard for rejuvenation.

## Blueing
At the beginning of mid-spring, if you want blue hydrangeas rather than pink or red, you can begin to water the soil round the plants with a solution of aluminium sulphate and iron sulphate. Mix 7g ($\frac{1}{4}$oz) of each in 4.5 litres (1 gal) soft water, leave the solution to stand for a few hours and then give each plant 9 litres (2 gal), watered all over the area which the roots are likely to have reached. Apply every week until flowering time and then give one more dose at some point in early autumn.

## Watering
You should keep an eye on anything which is newly planted, particularly in dry cold springs, and especially evergreens, wisteria, hydrangea, and any plant planted close to a wall or fence. They are all very vulnerable to a few days without water, unless planted in rather wet soil, and a gentle shower from the hose for a couple of hours every few days until there is rain will help them survive without any harm through a dry period.

## Supporting
If you have not already got supports in place for some of the climbers, you should get them fixed early this season. Clematis will be growing very fast and may be halfway up a wall; in warm gardens eccremocarpus shoots may be long enough to start flowering. Panels of plastic-covered trellis, or horizontal wires spaced 30cm (12in) apart, attached to wall nails, are amongst the strongest and most convenient supports for wall climbers.

If you have climbing roses, wisteria, Russian vine (*Polygonum baldschuanicum*) or honeysuckle scrambling over pergolas, archways or fences, make sure that they are stout enough to support what will eventually be a considerable weight of vegetation when dry, and half as much again when wet. Summer gales can be almost as fierce as winter gales and, once these climbing plants are blown down, their effect will never be the same again for the rest of the season. Repairing the damage is such a thankless and complicated job that it is tempting to cut everything off at ground level and be without any display until next year. So, if you make everything much stronger than you think it need be, you will be greatly relieved later on.

## Protecting
New growth on any plant is vulnerable to cold but, unfortunately, frost at night, and even during the day, is still possible. Young shoots caught by frost will die back from the tip and can then be infected by fungus diseases, such as grey mould; this compounds the damage, and flowering will be delayed. Although it is probably not practicable to protect all the new growth, you will have favourite shrubs, fruit or roses, and plastic netting, newspapers or thin material (cotton or nylon) can be draped over them until the risk has passed.

Protective mulches which have been put over the crowns of tender plants, such as fuchsias, eccremocarpus, romneya, solanum and ceratostigma, in late autumn, should be removed carefully, as the plants will have started to sprout at the beginning of this season.

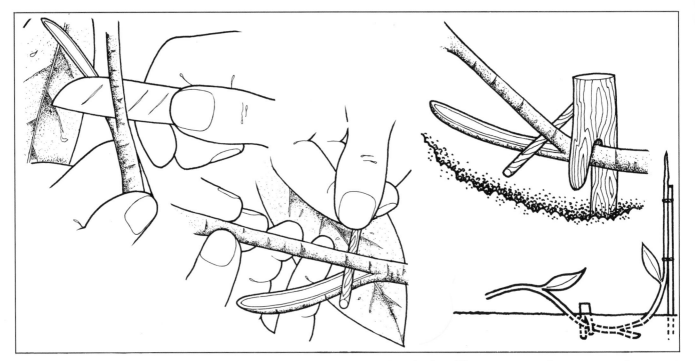

## Thinning

Apricots, peaches and nectarines, which are wall-grown, will have set their blossom by now in all but the coldest gardens; when the fruits are about the size of a marble, you can start thinning. Do it gradually over about two weeks until they begin to 'stone', the sign of which is that the fruit stops swelling. After this, they will have a small natural drop and you can then do a final thinning, if necessary.

Start by taking off fruit growing towards the wall, then take one away from every pair and eventually remove some of the remainder so that there are about 12 peaches to every sq m (sq yd) and 20 nectarines for the same area.

Apricots have a heavy natural drop and should not be thinned until after this, when they can be spaced in the same way as nectarines.

## Increasing

There is still time to graft, as the bark will lift easily all the time the sap is rising, from early to late spring; if, however, the buds on the scion start to sprout, the scions will no longer take and the grafting cannot be done for another year.

Another method of increase, used on ornamentals, is layering, and there are many shrubs, climbers and roses which can be easily propagated in this way. Choose a good shoot which grew last year and which is growing close to the ground; make a cut upwards on the underside, opposite a joint, through part of the stem. Pull the stem down to the

*Layering shrubs: Choose a young shoot near to the ground, make a cut partially through it on the underside, wedge open, and pin down into good soil or compost.*

soil so that the cut is in contact with it and peg the shoot down or hold it in place with a stone. The cut should be made several centimetres (inches) from the tip. When the layer is pegged down, the end of the shoot should be bent gently upward and tied to a cane.

If you layer the plants now, they should have rooted and be ready for lifting and planting in the autumn. Many will root if layered any time between spring and autumn, but doing it now does mean that they can be planted at one of the most suitable times. Plants to layer include rambling and climbing roses, rhododendrons, viburnums, magnolia, laurel, spotted laurel and various other evergreens. It is worth trying this method on any shrub with conveniently low-growing shoots; even if you do not want the rooted layers as new plants, they increase the visual effect of the parent plant so that it provides an even better show.

Many woody plants can be grown from seed sown in spring, and mid-spring is probably the best period. It can be sown outdoors in a seed bed, where the soil has been dug in winter, and then raked to crumb-like consistency on the day of sowing. As seedlings have a particular need for the mineral nutrient phosphorus, superphosphate should be mixed in a week or so before, at 30g per sq m (1oz per sq yd). Seeds of the more tender species can be sown in cold frames using seed compost and seed pans or direct into the frame soil suitably prepared. Germination may take any time from a few days to a year.

Seeds of some plants need stratifying (see Mid Autumn). Top-fruit stones and pips will germinate well but the resultant plant will not be the same variety as its parent. Moreover, seedlings tend to be very vigorous and either do not come into bearing at all or do so after ten years or more. Seedlings of ornamentals will also be different from their parents, and if you want exactly similar varieties or hybrids, you will have to use vegetative methods of increase: layering, cuttings, budding or division.

## Weeding
From now until the end of autumn, weeding will be necessary at intervals, but it is not nearly such a problem as in the kitchen garden or where the herbaceous plants are grown. If you like clean rose-beds, there is a weedkiller which will keep the weeds at bay for the season, or you can use mulches. Ground-cover plants are another possible way of keeping down weeds, but it does mean trampling on them when pruning and feeding the roses can be awkward.

The same weedkiller can be used round certain shrubs, climbers, hedges and fruit, as the makers direct, but a better method is to mulch heavily. It does the plants a power of good as well. Of course, if you have specimen shrubs, trees and fruit growing in a lawn, or if you have an orchard down to grass, the weed problem can be ignored, if you like. Lawn weeds can be left alone, provided they do not overwhelm the grass, and an orchard mixture of grasses and clovers will effectively keep out other plants (see Controls and Treatments section for chemical weedkillers).

## Grass cutting
Orchards down to grass should be cut now and kept at about 10cm (4in) until the end of mid-summer, when they can be left, though for convenience at fruit-picking time; the grass is probably better kept short.

## Making a compost heap
Do not put prunings on the compost heap unless summer ones, of soft green shoots; those with bark or hard, tough tissue should be burnt. The resulting ash will be rich in potassium.

You can make the heap out of the orchard mowings, weeds, dead flowers, leaves (not evergreens, they are too tough to rot down well) and soft prunings. Build it with 23cm (9in) layers of vegetative material alternating with

5cm (2in) soil layers, up to 120-150cm (48-60in) high, enclose it with wood or polythene and cover when finished. It should be ready for use in autumn.

## Ringing
Pear trees can be ringed at blossom time; see Late Spring for details.

## Treating pests and diseases
This is the season when greenfly and caterpillars will eat blossom as well. Vine weevils start eating holes in the edges

*The barberries (berberis spp.) are splendid shrubs, with flowers, berries and good leaves, some evergreen.*

of rhododendron leaves nearest the ground; slugs will attack the new shoots of fuchsias, hydrangeas, romneya and tree peonies. Rabbits may also attack these succulent shoots. Mildew may appear or continue to spread on roses, apples and pears, and infected shoots should be cut out. Scab on apples and pears may infect leaves and bad infections are likely to occur in warm, rainy springs. Rose black spot may appear or continue to spread. If peach-leaf curl on peaches, nectarines, almonds and apricots appears, pick off infected leaves and cut out infected growth as necessary; destroy all diseased prunings.

Young clematis may go off suddenly with clematis wilt; cut the shoots concerned down to ground level as soon as seen and cover the cut surfaces with a fungicidal wound-sealing compound. Spray new growth with a fungicide.

If you had grease-bands on the trunks of fruit trees, they can be removed now, as they will not be needed until late summer, when the adult winter moths begin to appear.

Chemical fungicides and insecticides for all these troubles are given in the Controls and Treatments section.

*Skilfully placed and selected shrubs, mingled with trees, give a garden depth, as well as colour and line.*

## Plants in flower

Apple (early varieties and crab apples), Apricot, Berberis in variety, Cherry (ornamental and fruiting), Clematis alpina and C. armandii, Corylopsis, Flowering currant, Cytisus × kewensis and C. praecox, Damson, Eccremocarpus (shelter), Forsythia, Fothergilla, Gorse, Greengage, Heathers (tree), Japonica, Mahonia aquifolium, Magnolia in variety, Medlar, Osmanthus, Peach (bush), Pear, Pieris, Plum, Quince, Rhododendron in variety, Skimmia, Spiraea × arguta and S. thunbergii, Viburnum burkwoodii and V. carlesii

## Fruits in store

Apple, Pear

# Late Spring

Late spring is one of the best seasons for display as far as shrubs are concerned. Many of them burst into full flower now and rhododendrons and azaleas will be at their most beautiful. If your garden contains alkaline soil, you can still have a marvellous display and a greater variety of flower and leaf shape than gardeners who rely solely on rhododendrons. Much of the fruit will be in full bloom, too, and it would be hard to beat an apple orchard on a sunny day for beauty. Some of the smaller trees, such as laburnum, the Judas tree and hawthorn, come into flower to join the show. Wisteria, clematis and the early climbing or rambling roses are in bloom now as well.

However, there is another side to every story; tree fruit is the target for a great number of insects and fungus diseases. Roses are another main source of food for these pests, and the rest of the shrubs, trees and climbers have their own special predators. The main hatch or appearance of all these occurs in late spring, so that much finger-and-thumb work and spraying may have to be done for the next few weeks. If controlled early in the growing season, there should be no serious trouble for the rest of it.

There is still a good deal of surgery required, mainly on shrubs, but also on peaches, vines, some of the tree fruit and the fast-growing hedges. Pruning, pinching back, trimming, disbudding, deadheading and cutting away remaining winter-killed shoots should be done. None of this is absolutely obligatory; most of the plants will produce some flowers or fruit if left to themselves but the quantity and quality will gradually tail off over the years. The life of a plant will also be short if its growth is not judiciously controlled with the knife or secateurs.

# At~a~glance diary

| | |
|---|---|
| **Prepare the soil for:** | planting |
| **Plant:** | tender and some grey-leaved shrubs; container-grown shrubs; seedlings |
| **Prune:** | (if necessary) berberis, Clematis alpina, C. armandii, C. montana, corylopsis, forsythia, fothergilla, tree heather, japonica, osmanthus, Senecio greyi, skimmia, Spiraea x arguta, tamarisk (Tamarix tetrandra), |
| **Pinch back:** | cistus (rock rose), fuchsia, phlomis (Jerusalem sage), apricot, grape vine |
| **Disbud:** | Morello cherry, nectarine, peach, vine |
| **Deadhead:** | azalea, camellia, lilac, pieris, rhododendron |
| **Trim:** | hedges of gorse, hawthorn, Lonicera nitida, myrobalan (Prunus cerasifera), privet |
| **Mulch:** | shrubs, climbers, roses, trees, wall-grown peaches and vines; tree fruit in dry soil |
| **Water:** | wall-grown plants; newly planted specimens |
| **Thin:** | apricot, nectarine, peach fruits; vine flower clusters |
| **Support:** | wall-grown plants |
| **Ring:** | apple |
| **Pests and diseases:** | bacterial canker (cherry and plum), blackfly, black spot (rose), capsid, caterpillars, sawfly caterpillars (apple and pear), clematis wilt, fireblight, greenfly, grey mould, holly-leaf miner, leaf hopper, leaf sucker, mealy plum aphis, pear leaf-blister mite, pear midge, peony wilt, red spider mite, scab, slug |
| **Routine work:** | weed, build compost heap, blue hydrangea, mow orchard sward |

# Jobs to do

### Preparing the soil for planting

Late spring is the only safe time to plant some of the grey-leaved or tender shrubs, if ordered from a nursery; you may be buying container-grown plants in any case, so a little soil preparation will probably be necessary. Problems with frost and waterlogging should no longer occur and the difficulty in late spring, when forking the soil, may be hardness due to drought. However, this is easily remedied. Most weeds will be seedlings, also easily dealt with. Remember to add phosphatic fertilizer some days before planting (see Mid-Autumn for details of soil preparation).

*Clematis are justifiably popular climbing plants, and* jackmanii *is one of the best of its colour.*

### Planting

Shrubs which should not be planted before late spring include cistus (rock rose), fuchsia, romneya (Californian poppy), ceratostigma (plumbago) and phlomis (Jerusalem sage). In cold districts, hebe and hibiscus are better left to the beginning of late spring before planting.

Seed which was sown in mid-spring may have produced seedlings large enough to handle by now. If so, they can be transplanted to a nursery bed where they should be left for about a year before moving to their permanent places.

From now until the end of summer, there is always the possibility of heat, combined with drought, and to endure survival of newly planted shrubs under these conditions you should have a look at them every few days and supply water if need be. Container-grown plants, whether fruits, shrubs, trees or climbers can, in theory, be planted at any time during late spring or summer, but they do seem to have a struggle to establish and need a good deal of cosseting.

### Pruning

Mid-spring pruning should be finished as soon as possible; the main group of shrubs to be pruned during this season are those flowering from early spring to the middle of late spring, as named in the following list. You can do some pruning when cutting flowering sprays for the house; make sure that the cut is made just above a strong, new shoot.

*Berberis*, deciduous or evergreen Cut some of the oldest shoots down to ground level, cut flowered shoots back to strong new growth and thin out the remainder. This need only be done every three years or so.

*Clematis* The *montana* types can be cut back hard immediately after flowering to leave a few centimetres (inches) of the flowered growth every year or they can be pruned every four years or so in the same way, but further back, to the oldest growth. If *C. alpina* and its varieties needs treatment, do it after flowering, to thin out the oldest shoots and cut back others to strong new growth, also every few years. *C. armandii* can grow extremely large against a sunny wall but is a little tender, and does not take well to any more pruning than occasional thinning out and cutting back to the space available.

*Corylopsis* Virtually no pruning needed, as its habit of growth is naturally tidy and well-spaced but occasional removal of weak shoots and those which are old and hardly flowering improves its appearance even more.

*Forsythia* If late in flowering or not yet pruned, forsythia should be pruned now; remove flowering sprays and thin out remainder (see Mid-Spring for details).

*Fothergilla* A charming shrub, with its white chimney-sweep's brushes of flowers, it hardly needs any cutting beyond the removal of dead shoots, weak ones and any which cross or are too close to each other.

*Tree heathers*, spring-flowering (*Erica arborea*, *E. australis*, etc.) These can be left alone and will still flower well but are bushier and more floriferous if cut back after flowering by about 30-60cm (12-24in).

*Japonica* (chaenomeles) The oldest shoots or spurs can be removed altogether after flowering, some of the flowered

shoots cut back by about half and a little thinning done. Those grown as wall shrubs should be pruned to produce spurs; cut back the flowering shoots after flowering to leave one or two buds.

*Osmanthus* Virtually no pruning is necessary, except to cut the oldest shoots down to about half their length occasionally.

*Senecio greyi* If plants have become gaunt and leggy and if you live in a mild district, you can cut them down hard at the end of this season. This treatment may prove fatal, if the weather turns cold unexpectedly, but as they root so easily from layers or cuttings, pruning is probably not worth the risk involved.

*Skimmia* Leave well alone and do not prune except occasionally to remove dead and diseased shoots, broken ones and weak or crowded ones.

*Spiraea* x *arguta* Cut off some of the flowered shoots after flowering, back to strong new or potential new growth. Remove some of the oldest growth to ground level.

*Tamarisk* (*Tamarix tetrandra*) Little pruning needed but cut back some of the flowered shoots to new ones, to keep the size under control.

## Pinching

Although there are some shrubs which flower quite well if left more or less alone, pruning which takes the form of nipping out the tips of the new shoots makes them produce more side-shoots and so become even more flowery. Shrubs which can be treated like this in late spring are fuchsia, cistus and phlomis (Jerusalem sage). When the new shoots are a few centimetres (inches) long, or have about three lots of buds, the tip can be pinched off as far as the next bud or pair of buds down the stem. It delays flowering, of course, but is well worth it. At the same time, if you see any dead growth left over from winter, you can clear it out and leave more room for living stems.

On grape vines, the shoot carrying the flower cluster should be stopped at just above the second leaf beyond the cluster. Any shoots without flowers should have the tip removed at the fourth leaf and minor shoots coming from either of these should be stopped hard, just above the first leaf. This kind of stopping is preferably done when it

Left: *A good heather garden can be a patchwork of colour, especially if the coloured-leaved kinds are grown.* Opposite: *Disbudding peaches. The peach is a prolific bearer of shoots, so unwanted ones are rubbed off to leave the leader, the feeder and the replacement, which are tied in to form an evenly-spaced fan.*

just means taking off the tip. If the shoot has been allowed to grow six or seven leaves long, removal is a much greater shock to the plant and it may retaliate by becoming even more vigorous (see also Pinching, Early Summer).

## Disbudding

It may be necessary to do more peach and nectarine disbudding in late spring; the shoots which were left to grow in mid-spring should be tied to the wires as they grow, spaced evenly from one another. If they prove to be crowded, or if other shoots have grown meanwhile, they should be removed. Vines need the same treatment and it is important to tie the retained shoots carefully to the wires. They are brittle and should be tied loosely to start with, gradually tightening the string or raffia until they are close against their supports. Fan-trained, wall-grown Morello cherries are pruned and trained like fan-trained peaches and tying-in of new shoots, as well as removal of unwanted ones, can start now.

Fan-trained, wall-grown apricots seem to fruit much more satisfactorily in temperate climates if only pruned a little, but this leads to bare branches in the centre and fruiting towards the tips. It can be avoided by pinching out most of the new, strong, unwanted shoots from spurs or branches early in late spring, keeping one or two in the centre, to replace the bare oldest shoots which have been removed in winter.

## Deadheading

The shrubs which benefit from this and look better as a result, are rhododendron, azalea, pieris, camellia if the dead flowers tend to hang and lilac as it finishes flowering.

## Trimming

Some formal hedges are exceedingly quick growing and need a clip over several times a year. If you only trim them once or twice a year they will gradually become taller, bare at the base and will eventually need a ruthless, hard cut. Hedges to trim towards the end of late spring include *Lonicera nitida* (it has tiny round evergreen leaves), gorse, hawthorn, privet and myrobalan (*Prunus cerasifera*). If you are short of time, this trimming can wait until the beginning of early summer without much harm.

*The main flowering season for rhododendrons is late spring but it can extend to winter and late summer.*

## Mulching

Late spring is the time when the soil should be moist, as well as warm; putting on a mulch now, once the ground has been freed from weeds, helps make sure that roots will have a supply of moisture deep down when the hot weather comes. Organic mulches stop the soil from cracking in a drought, encourage worms in the soil and supply nutrients. They can be rotted garden compost, spent hops, leaf-mould, seaweed, rotted, chopped-up young green bracken, which contains a lot of potash, farm manure, spent mushroom compost or peat. Don't be put off by the word 'spent' to describe mushroom compost; it still contains a good deal of food and humus-providing material, which makes it extremely good for ordinary plants. However, if it is being sold in sacks door-to-door, be careful that it does not contain lumps of chalk, otherwise it can wreak havoc on your rhododendrons. Peat is quite safe for plants that like acid soil; the drawback is that it contains very little plant food besides nitrogen and even that is released to plant roots only very slowly.

Mulches should be at least 5cm (2in) thick, spread all over the area which the roots reach; they can spread sideways underground as far as the branches or top growth do above ground. Trees, climbers, and roses can all be mulched, as well as the general run of shrubs; it does no harm to mulch hedges, too, if you have enough material to spare. Plants growing close to walls benefit particularly from mulching; the soil there may already be getting dry, so water first if need be.

Tree fruit is generally given a top dressing in autumn, but if the soil is a 'hot', quick-draining one, a mulch now would be preferable. Straw is better than nothing and will have rotted down by autumn. Water-in an application of hoof and horn meal or sulphate of ammonia before putting it on, otherwise a temporary shortage of nitrogen will occur, while the bacteria get to work on decomposing the straw. Wall-grown vines will give the best crops if mulched heavily, with a 10cm (4in) layer.

## Watering

Any plant which grows next to a wall or a fence is not only sheltered from cold, but from rain as well. As it is often facing south or west, the temperature gets hotter than other parts of the garden, so water is at a premium. Wisteria is practically always grown up a house or garden wall and is a very thirsty plant. Lack of water is probably one of the main reasons for lack of flowers on wisterias; the buds simply drop off, as they do from runner beans or sweetpeas, when they are growing in drought conditions. Fan-trained

Wisteria sinensis *is one of the many Chinese plants which grow well in Europe, in most soils and sites.*

peaches grown with a wall backing them must have enough water all the way through the growing season. If they have a feast-or-famine water supply, the fruit drops or splits, or the stones crack.

A good watering with a sprinkler for two or three hours may be necessary every fortnight, or even every week, depending on the weather and soil type, for all plants in this position.

## Thinning

The peach, nectarine and apricot thinning started in mid-spring may run on into late spring, depending on the season and district, but it should be possible to finish it early in late spring.

If vines start to flower during the next few weeks, they should be thinned to leave one bunch of embryo fruit to every 30cm (12in) of main stem.

## Supporting

Continue to tie in climbing plants, trained tree fruit and wall-grown shrubs as they grow. Rambling roses and clematis in particular will need regular tying if they are to provide their best displays.

*Right:* *Bark-ringing. Remove a 6-12mm ($\frac{1}{4}$-$\frac{1}{2}$in) wide strip of bark in two half-rings from the trunk of a fruit tree, and cover with grafting wax or insulating tape.*

## Ringing

If you have any apple trees which are producing many strong new shoots but only a little fruit, you can encourage them to carry blossom and set fruit instead, by removing two half-rings of bark from the trunk. The rings should be 0.6-12cm ($\frac{1}{4}$-$\frac{1}{2}$in) wide, one 2.5cm (1in) above the other. Using a sharp knife, take the bark away down to the wood and then cover the exposed surface with insulating tape while it heals.

## Treating pests and diseases

The tree fruits are the main targets for attack in this and the remaining seasons of summer and autumn. Besides such plagues as peach-leaf curl, greenfly, scab, mildew and caterpillars already mentioned, there may also be capsid bug, sawfly caterpillars (which eat the fruitlets), red spider mite, leaf sucker and leaf hopper, pear midge and pear-leaf blister mite, and bacterial canker of cherry and plum liable to infect the shoots, flowers and fruit.

On the ornamentals, peony wilt, clematis wilt, holly-leaf miner, rhododendron bud blast, black spot, mildew and leaf-rolling sawfly on the roses, slugs and fire-blight are possible plagues. The latter can infest tree fruit as well, and grey mould (*Botrytis cinerea*) is a universal fungus disease.

This seems a formidable list of troubles, but it only consists of the most common ones, perhaps a tenth of all those which might infect your plants. However, it is unlikely that what you grow will be affected by even the common kinds all at once, all the way through the growing season. This is the time when they hatch or come to life but it is probable that you will have to deal only with a few of them and—if your plants are well grown and strong—they will be much less severely damaged.

For descriptions of all these and their chemical controls, see the Controls and Treatments section. Remember that cutting out as soon as seen or hand-picking often does all that needs to be done; the birds, too, will help you for a change, as they will have nests full of newly hatched young, demanding food.

## General Work

Regular jobs include weeding, compost-heap building, hydrangea blueing and orchard-sward mowing (see Mid-Spring for details of last two).

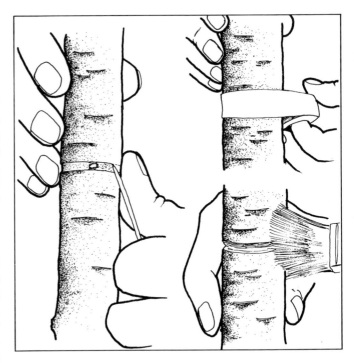

## Plants in flower

Apple (including crab apple), Azalea, Berberis in variety, Buddleia globosa, Ceanothus in variety, Flowering cherry Cotoneaster franchettii, Clematis alpina, C.montana, and some large-flowered hybrids, Cytisus (in variety), Daphne, Deutzia, Eccremocarpus scaber, Fremontodendron, Gorse, Genista, Hawthorn, Heathers (tree), Hebe hulkeana, Horse chestnut, Jew's mallow (kerria), Judas tree (cercis), Kalmia, Kolkwitzia, laburnum, Lilac, Magnolia, Medlar, Mexican orange blossom (Choisya ternata), Mountain ash, Peony (tree), Pieris, Piptanthus, Pyracantha (firethorn), Rhododendron in variety, Rosa banksiae, Spiraea × van houttei, Tamarix tetrandra, Viburnum in variety, Weigela, Wisteria

# Early Summer

Early summer is a glorious time in any garden and particularly so where roses and other flowering shrubs are garden features. Large-flowered and cluster-flowered roses, polyanthas, climbers, ramblers, miniatures and the old garden roses provide a tremendous variety of flower colour, fragrance and shape. By making a careful choice it is possible to have roses in flower from late spring until the end of autumn and even then the modern bush roses will often go on producing blooms beyond late autumn. It is not unknown in some gardens to pick the last rose of summer in early winter.

The early-summer-flowering shrubs such as philadelphus (mock orange), rock roses, honeysuckle, clematis, escallonia and weigela overlap the late-spring-flowering sorts and, with sunshine and warmth, the display should draw praise even from the vegetable fanatic, who usually only sees beauty in a well-grown row of spinach or football-sized lettuces.

It is a good season to take time off working in the garden; let the plants get on with growing themselves and wander round the garden to enjoy it and plan some replanting or redesigning. With the roses particularly, you can see if there are any mistakes or gaps during the next few weeks.

Watering begins to be an important job; some feeding will be needed and control of growth by various discreet forms of pruning will still be necessary for shrubs, hedges, fruit and climbers. Some propagation from cuttings will begin to be possible, as new growth becomes established on most plants by now. Pest and disease control becomes less alarming; the onslaughts from the first spring hatches will lose their intensity as insects come to the end of their first—or perhaps only—life-cycle.

# At~a~glance diary

**Prune:** broom (cytisus and genista), ceanothus (spring-flowering), clematis (C. alpina, C. montana) if not done last month, deutzia, lavender cotton (santolina), peony (tree), Spiraea x vanhouttei (S. x arguta if not already done), Tamarix tetrandra

**Trim:** quick-growing formal hedges; informal hedges

**Pinch back:** shoot tips of rock roses (cistus), fuchsia, Jerusalem sage (Phlomis fruticosa), young tree lupins

**Disbud:** apricots, nectarines, peaches, vine; roses for exhibition

**Tie~in:** tie-in new shoots of fan-trained Morello cherries

**Deadhead:** azalea, kalmia, lupin (tree), peony (tree), rhododendron

**Remove:** suckers from roses; plain green shoots from variegated-leaved plants; suckers from framework-grafted trees, suckers from stone fruits

**Thin:** apple, apricot, peach, pear and nectarine fruits; vine flower clusters if still necessary; vine fruits in early seasons and if early varieties

**Water:** all wall-grown plants especially wall-grown fruit; wisteria, clematis; newly-planted specimens

**Plan:** rose gardens, beds and borders

**Increase:** by soft cuttings, deutzia, fuchsia, hydrangea, Jerusalem sage (Phlomis fruticosa), lavender, lavender cotton (santolina), rock rose (cistus), southernwood (Artemisia abrotanum), spiraea; by seed, any plants which have flowered and set seed

**Pests and diseases:** as for late spring; also codling moth caterpillars on apples; woolly aphis (American blight) and canker on fruit; canker on roses mow orchard swards, weed, blue hydrangea, build compost heap, support climbers

# Jobs to do

## Pruning

The major part of pruning in early summer is taken up with the late-spring-flowering shrubs and some of those flowering early in this season. It may also be necessary to finish off the pruning of the mid-spring bloomers, if they were late flowering because of the weather or an exposed site. Shrubs to prune now are given in the following list.

*Broom* (Cytisus and Genista) *Cytisus scoparius* and its varieties are shrubs which really need annual pruning, otherwise they get very leggy and sparsely flowered. The flowered sprays should be cut to leave about 2.5cm (1in) of their previous summer's growth; always leave this and do not cut into older growth. Other cytisus species and varieties can also be pruned if flowering has finished, being careful not to prune old wood or unbalance their natural shape.

Most genistas do not need pruning except for the Mount Etna broom (*G. aetnensis*) and one or two others in late summer, and the Spanish gorse (*G. hispanica*) which benefits from a light trim all over with shears after flowering. On the whole, genistas have a tendency to flower themselves to death and there is no need to encourage flowering—rather discourage it.

*Ceanothus*, spring-flowering. As soon as flowering has finished, the sideshoots on a specimen grown against a wall should be cut back hard, to leave only a few centimetres (1 or 2 inches) of stem. Weak shoots should be removed altogether. Plants growing in the open need not be cut back so hard but if you cut some of the sideshoots by about half the bushes will be denser and the deciduous kinds, in particular, will be less vulnerable to cold.

*Clematis* Some of the *alpina* and *montana* types may have continued to flower until the end of late spring, so will need dealing with at the beginning of this season. However, it does no great harm if you leave them alone, and *C. alpina* will then produce attractive, fluffy seed-heads, like a cultivated form of old man's beard (see Late Spring for details of pruning).

Kolkwitzia amabilis, *a shrub with charming flowers in late spring, is commonly called the beauty bush.*

Above: *Rose suckers develop from the roots of the stock; they are usually very prickly and have more leaflets. Pull them off: do not use a knife unless it is unavoidable.*

Opposite: *The peach's home country is hot all summer, but with wall protection and a sunny place, the fruit will ripen well in temperate climates.*

*Deutzia* An easy shrub to prune, as the new growth will be very obvious by now. The flowered shoots at the base should be cleared out and weak shoots removed unless they fill a gap, when they can be left until next spring.

*Lavender cotton* (santolina) If you did not prune it hard in mid-spring and intend trimming it through the growing season, you can give it the first trim with shears now; the object is to make it bushier and better covered in its silver-grey filigree foliage.

*Peony, tree* Pruning is not necessary except occasionally, and then only to cut one or two of the oldest stems out completely; tips of shoots infected with grey mould should be removed as soon as seen.

*Spiraea* The species *S. van houttei* will need its flowered shoots removing at the end of the season, down to where strong new shoots are already growing. The same technique can be applied to *S. x arguta* if not pruned in late spring.

*Tamarisk* (*Tamarix tetrandra*) Prune early this season as described in Late Spring.

## Trimming

The quick-growing, formal hedges should be clipped in early summer, if not done in late spring; they provide good, thick hedges, especially the evergreen ones, but they do need quite a lot of attention to maintain their precise shape (see Late Spring for details of hedge cutting).

The informal hedges which have finished flowering can now be trimmed also. However, trimming these is much more like pruning, in that flowered shoots are removed and the new growth thinned a little, if very crowded. If any of these hedges are formed of slow-growing plants, there is no need even to do this, simply cut off dead flower-heads.

## Pinching

The removal of the tips of new shoots to just above the first leaf or pair of leaves is called 'pinching'. It is done when the shoots are still young and soft and the tips can literally be pinched between the thumb and first finger nipping them off finally with the nails. It restricts the size of the plant and results in the growth of more side-shoots on the treated stem, so producing more flowers and leaves. Small, quick-growing shrubs, such as rock roses (cistus species), fuchsia, Jerusalem sage (*Phlomis fruticosa*) and young tree lupins benefit from this treatment.

Pinching will also be required for wall-grown vines, removing the tip of a flowerless shoot just above the fourth leaf, and that of a sub-side-shoot above the first leaf. If a shoot has a flower cluster on it, stop it above the second leaf beyond the flowers.

## Disbudding

Continue to disbud peaches, nectarines and vines as advised in mid-spring and apricots as advised in late spring.

If you are growing large-flowered or cluster-flowered roses for exhibition, the buds should be thinned during the next two or three weeks to leave only the central one at the end of each main stem.

## Tying-in

Continue to tie-in the new shoots of fan-trained Morello cherries as they grow.

## Deadheading

As in late spring, rhododendrons and azaleas can be dead-headed and tree lupins will exhaust themselves more quickly if allowed to form seed-pods. Kalmia and tree peony can be similarly treated.

### Removal of unwanted shoots

This is not standard pruning, as it refers to the elimination of very specific growth. In the case of grafted or budded roses, it is the sucker growth from the rootstock which, if left on the plants, will rapidly and easily overcome the named variety. Suckers nearly always come up from soil level, near to a plant, and if the soil is dug away, it will be found growing from a root, usually close to the soil surface.

It should, ideally, be pulled off, to make sure that its point of origin is removed. You can cut it, but because its 'roots' remain, other suckers will sprout from the same point. Some rose stocks sucker particularly badly; those that are least troublesome are the Laxa stocks, said to be hybrid between *Rosa alba* and *R. canina*.

Don't forget that standard roses are budded at the top of the main stem, so that the main stem is in fact stock and any buds on that which sprout, as well as any coming from

the roots, are suckers and should be taken off. The leaflets on suckers are generally different in colour and size to those of the true variety.

Suckers on frame-work grafted fruit trees should also be removed; they will be any shoots not growing from the grafts and similarly may result in the tree returning to the original and now unwanted variety. Suckers from the roots of cherries, plums, peaches and all fruits associated with them, should also be dealt with.

Another kind of unwanted shoot is that which has plain green leaves, growing on a shrub or tree with variegated leaves. Sometimes shoots or branches will revert in this way, to the original species; they grow very strongly because they contain much more chlorophyll than the cream- or yellow-variegated form, and eventually take over the plant. Variegated forms are thought to be mutations in some cases, and are not always completely stable, but taking out these rogue shoots as soon as seen is usually sufficient.

### Thinning

The wall fruits such as peaches, nectarines and apricots, and vine flower clusters may still need a little thinning if they are late varieties or if the season is cold. Vine fruits may already need thinning, if early (see Mid-Summer for method). Apples and pears can be thinned, if they have set heavily, near the middle of early summer, before the 'June drop' takes place. Thin to leave about three or four fruits to a cluster, removing the centre or 'king' fruit first and then any which are small, damaged or misshapen. After the natural fall, remove any fruits in excess of one or two per cluster.

### Watering

Continue to supply all wall-grown plants with water, especially fruit and remember, too, that wisteria and clematis are thirsty plants. If the weather is droughty, newly planted specimens of all kinds will be vulnerable and may even need their top growth sprayed every day as well, if they are evergreen.

### Planning

Early summer is a good time to take stock of your rose display and decide whether, and if so where, it needs re-designing and improving. As the large-flowered and cluster-flowered climbers and old shrub roses come into flower, you will be able to see the best 'doers', the colour clashes and the weak or badly flowering varieties. By now, you will also be able to pick out the disease-prone kinds; unless you are very partial to them, they are not worth keeping, as they serve as centres of infection.

It is the best time, too, to visit rose nurseries and see how well their stocks are doing in the open, rather than on the bench at a show, where only the best will appear. A visit to your national rose society gardens during the next few weeks could be of great help in obtaining detailed cultural advice, ideas on design of rose gardens and use of roses in a garden, as well as information on new and particularly good varieties.

## Increasing

From now until the end of summer it will be possible to take 'soft' tip cuttings of shrubs and climbers. Subjects which can be rooted from such cuttings include: deutzia, fuchsia, hydrangea, Jerusalem sage (phlomis), lavender, lavender cotton (santolina), rock rose (cistus), southernwood (artemisia) and spiraea. Rooting will be quicker if you can give them a little bottom heat, keeping the compost warm in some way. All can be rooted later in the summer

*In this cottage garden, old-fashioned shrub roses and tree peonies mix in delightful profusion, while climbing roses soften the walls of the house and link it with the garden.*

from half-ripe cuttings (see Increasing, Late Summer for details of this.)

All tip cuttings should be of the end 7.5cm (3in) or so of new shoots, without flower buds (otherwise they will not root), cut just above a leaf or pair of leaves. Two or three cuttings, stripped of their lowest leaves, are put into 9cm (3½in) pots, to half their length. Firm in and lightly water, then cover with blown-up polythene bags or put into a closed frame and keep warm and shaded until they root.

Many shrubs, trees and climbers which have flowered and set seed can be grown from seed sown now, in an outdoor nursery bed; some will need stratifying first (see Mid-Autumn). Once the seed has got to the stage when it can easily be detached from the plant, it is ready for sowing.

Grafts which were made in early spring may now have grown and taken so well that the wax is acting as a constriction. If it has not cracked, it would be best to remove it.

*Softwood cuttings of roses, taken as shown in early summer, are quite as likely to root as hardwood cuttings.*

## Treating pests and diseases

In addition to the troubles listed in Late Spring, there may be an infestation of codling moth caterpillars, which feed on the pips and the flesh at the centre of apples. Damage can be considerable and the only real answer is to spray; the birds do not seem to be able to get at the small caterpillars before they go into the fruit and other predatory insects appear to be non-existent.

Roses can still be infected by such plagues as black spot, mildew, greenfly, leaf-rolling sawfly grubs, leaf-cutting bees and chafer beetles. Scab, mildew, aphis, particularly woolly aphis (American blight) and canker, as well as codling moth, can infest fruit. For chemical controls, see the section on Controls and Treatments of plant troubles at the end of the book.

## General work

The tasks are much what they were in the latter parts of spring. Continue to mow orchard swards, weed, blue hydrangeas, build the compost heap and support climbers as required (see Mid- and Late Spring for details).

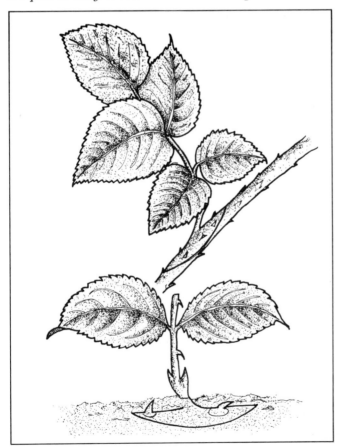

## Plants in flower

Broom (Cytisus scoparius and varieties, genista and Spanish broom), Buddleia globosa, Ceanothus, Clematis, Cotoneaster, Deutzia, Eccremocarpus, Escallonia, Fremontodendron, Fuchsia, Hawthorn, Hebe, Honeysuckle, Jasmine (summer-flowering), Jerusalem sage, Kalmia, Kolkwitzia, Laburnum, Lilac species, Lupin (tree), Magnolia, Mexican orange blossom (Choisya ternata), Mountain ash, Peony, Philadelphus (mock orange, syringa), Potentilla, Pyracantha (firethorn), Rhododendron (late), rock rose (cistus), Roses, Solanum, Tulip tree (liriodendron), Viburnum, Weigela, Wisteria

# Mid-Summer

Early summer and mid-summer are the main seasons for large-flowered, cluster-flowered and shrub roses, old and new. The latter flower in mid-summer and some kinds will continue to flower for the rest of the summer, following their first heavy flush of blooms. Some of the climbers are repeat-flowering, too.

Mid-summer is also the time when there is a new wave of shrub-blooming; after the spring flowers, the fuchsias, hydrangeas, hypericums, hebes, hibiscus and many other plants which prefer summer warmth come into their own and decorate the garden all over again. Fruit, such as cherries, mulberries and the very earliest pears and apples will begin to ripen. Towards the end of mid-summer in sheltered places, picking of the early varieties of peaches, apricots and nectarines can start.

Much of the month's work consists of routine jobs but pruning takes on a new pattern, as the restricted fruit trees begin to need their summer cutting, cherries require their annual pruning and the hybrid tea and floribunda roses need treatment after flowering. There will still be a little pruning of flowering shrubs, left over from early summer, and some hedges may need trimming.

If you have plants which you would like to increase, mid-summer is the time to start taking what are known as semi-ripe cuttings from shrubs, and to start budding roses. It is also a good time to order new stock from the nurseries, to make sure that it arrives when you want it to, in the autumn.

# At~a~glance diary

**Prune:** Buddleia globosa, deutzia, escallonia, kolkwitzia, lavender cotton (santolina), philadelphus (mock orange), Senecio greyi, weigela; summer-prune restricted pears, fan-trained and bush cherry

**Trim:** fast-growing formal hedges; informal flowering hedges

**Deadhead:** rock rose (cistus), roses, rue, Senecio greyi

**Thin:** fig, grape, fruits

**Feed:** camellia, peony (tree), roses; plants growing in light soil

**Water:** newly planted specimens, wall-grown plants; all in drought

**Order:** all plants to be delivered from specialist nurseries

**Increase:** roses by budding; various shrubs and climbers from semi-ripe cuttings, tip cuttings, layering

**Pests and diseases:** as for early summer; in addition red plum maggot, silver leaf of plums and other plants, tortrix caterpillar on apple and pear, rose rust, earwig on clematis and other plants

**Routine work:** weed, mow orchard sward, build compost heap, blue hydrangea, remove suckers and plain green shoots, tie-in climbers

# Jobs to do

## Pruning

For the flowering shrubs, there is not a great deal of pruning during mid-summer, possibly a few left over from late spring and the few that have flowered last season. However, even if a shrub does not need formal pruning every year, it nearly always accumulates dead shoots; just clearing these out completely seems to give many a new lease of life. Anything which flowers or grows poorly, including weak shoots, diseased ones and broken or crowded growth, should be cut off completely to its point of origin.

*Buddleia globosa* When the flowers have finished, a little of the oldest growth can be removed, cutting these stems back by about a quarter of their length.

*Deutzia* If not dealt with already, this should be pruned

*Rosa Mundi, or Rosa gallica Versicolor, one of the oldest shrub roses, can be traced back to the Middle Ages.*

early in mid-summer, as detailed in Early Summer.

*Escallonia* These shrubs can have their flowered shoots pruned off as soon as flowering has finished, back to a strong new shoot. Those kinds with long arching shoots can become rather untidy and need this pruning every year; others can be missed occasionally. If grown as wall shrubs, they will need hard cutting to leave only a few centimetres (inches) of the flowered shoot, so that they remain compact.

*Kolkwitzia* (beauty bush) Prune off the flowered stems and cut out one or two of the oldest main stems to ground level occasionally, to encourage new growth from the base.

*Lavender cotton* Trim all over with shears towards the end of mid-summer.

*Philadelphus* (mock orange blossom) Cut the flowered sprays back to strong new growth and thin out some of the new growth if getting too tall or crowded.

*Senecio greyi* If it has been allowed to flower, clip immediately after flowering with shears, to give it plenty of time to renew itself before winter.

*Weigela* Like deutzia and philadelphus, easily pruned by removal of flowered growth as soon as flowering has

*For those who like their apples crisp and juicy, Granny Smith is ideal for dessert, and stores late into winter.*

finished, to allow space for the new shoots already growing.

Summer-pruning of espalier or cordon-trained apples can sometimes be started at the end of mid-summer, if the season is dry, but is normally begun in the first week of late summer. Pear growth matures a little earlier than apples, and does have to be treated late in mid-summer (for details see Pruning, Late Summer).

The pruning of fan-trained sweet cherries grown against walls consists of cutting the new side-shoots back to just above the fifth or sixth leaf in late mid-summer, with further pruning following in early autumn. Leading shoots which were bent over last autumn, should be cut back to a weak side-shoot.

Bush sweet-cherry trees grown in the open need little pruning, beyond removing dead, diseased, broken, crowded or weak shoots and occasional cutting back of the main branches or leaders to keep within bounds. This should be done as soon as the crop is picked.

## Trimming

The fast-growing formal hedges will probably need a second clip early in mid-summer, depending on when they had their first one; informal flowering hedges will need cutting if they have finished blooming (see Early Summer for details).

## Deadheading

Remove the dead blooms of rock roses (cistus) as they form seed easily and then flower less. If you prefer the foliage of rue to its mustard-yellow flowers, these will need cutting off and *Senecio greyi*, if allowed to flower, should at least have the dead flower clusters clipped off. Large-flowered, cluster-flowered, climbing and rambling roses should all be deadheaded, unless their hips are wanted for decoration or seed. Large-flowered should be cut back by about half their length; cluster-flowered, climbers and ramblers should have the complete flower cluster cut off. All cuts should be made just above a leaf with an outward-pointing bud in its axil.

## Thinning

Figs should be thinned round about mid-summer; they are fertile trees and in warm countries ripen heavy crops, in successive stages. However, in temperate climates the small, hard figs which are present in autumn will never ripen and only hinder the production of more fruit. As soon as these can be seen to be developing in mid-summer, they should be removed. The result is that more embryo fruit forms but remains dormant until the following growing season, when it starts to swell in late spring and is large enough to ripen by late summer.

Grapes will need thinning early in this season, if not already done, starting when the fruit is about the size of a sweetpea seed. Remove the smallest berries and the innermost ones first; then, starting at the bottom of the bunch, remove at least half the remainder, until the shoulders are reached, where very few should be removed. Thinning should be done in two stages, before and after stoning, as with peaches, and sufficient space should be left to accommodate the berries comfortably when they are fully grown—about 2.5cm (1in) diameter, depending on variety. Use sharp, pointed scissors to cut out the unwanted berries.

## Feeding

This is a good season to feed one or two spring-flowering shrubs which begin to form their flower-buds for next spring now, on this year's new shoots. They include camellia and tree peony, which is a notoriously greedy plant.

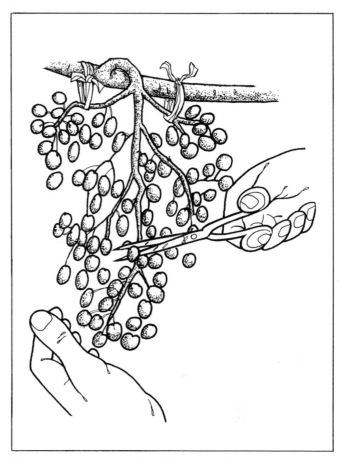

*Grapes set a great number of berries and in order to be well-sized they must be thinned to remove more than half.*

A general compound fertilizer with a high proportion of potash can be used, potash alone as sulphate of potash at the rate of 15-30g per sq m (½-1oz per sq yd) or ash formed as a result of burning wood—about 150g per sq m (5oz per sq yd). Roses can have a second feed after their first flowering, and if your soil is light, all will be grateful for a feed with a balanced compound. Watering-in of any fertilizer application at this time is advisable.

## Watering

Be very careful to make sure plants do not go short of moisture now. Drought in summer followed by winter waterlogging is death to many woody plants but if kept in good health in summer, they can withstand winter weather better. Container-grown specimens, newly planted, are very much at risk, as are all wall-grown plants, especially the fruits. Shortage of water now results in their dropping the whole crop on the ground.

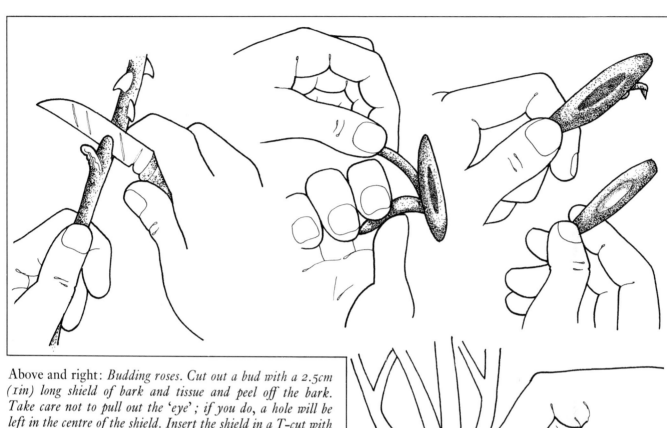

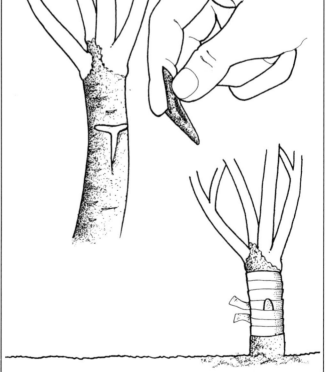

Above and right: *Budding roses. Cut out a bud with a 2.5cm (1in) long shield of bark and tissue and peel off the bark. Take care not to pull out the 'eye'; if you do, a hole will be left in the centre of the shield. Insert the shield in a T-cut with the bud facing outwards. Bind with raffia. Insert in the main stem close to soil level on bushes, and just below the head on a standard.* Opposite: *A perfect large-flowered (hybrid tea) rose.*

## Ordering
Mid-summer is a good time to get ahead in the queue for plant delivery; ordering what you need now from the nurseries will ensure that your plants arrive when you want them to, weather permitting. You will not be so far down the list that you have to wait till mid-winter.

## Increasing
If you want to increase the number of your rose varieties, do it by budding in mid-summer. Basically the method consists of making a T-shaped cut in the bark of the rose stem to be budded, and then slipping into this a bud, backed by a sliver of woody tissue, of the new variety. You can take the buds from new shoots of the selected variety, about half-way up the stem, and use as stock either a variety you no longer want or one of the special rootstocks used for roses: *Rosa canina* (the wild dog-rose), or *R. x laxa*, which you have to buy. These are themselves grown from hardwood cuttings taken in mid-autumn.

In mid-summer, some shoots of shrubs and climbers will be sufficiently mature to supply semi-ripe cuttings (see Late Summer for details). You can also take tip cuttings of the plants listed in Early Summer and the layering method of increase is still possible for many plants.

## Treating pests and diseases

Another spray for codling moth caterpillars will be necessary, as well as one for red plum maggot, which can decimate plums in mid and late summer. Silver leaf on plums and other fruit can be cut out now. Woolly aphis (American blight) may be a considerable problem and tortrix caterpillars on apples and pears can do a lot of damage without being noticed until picking time. Red spider mite and mildew are still other potential menaces on fruit. Black spot, rose rust and mildew on roses will need treatment, and earwigs on clematis and other plants will be in evidence. The remaining pests mentioned in early summer should be much less troublesome.

*Honeysuckles will flower in succession from early summer until autumn, depending on variety; they need little care.*

## Plants in flower

Abelia grandflora, Broom (cytisus and genista in variety), Spanish broom (Spartium junceum), Buddleia davidii in variety, Ceanothus, Clematis, Cotoneaster, Daisy bush (Olearia haastii), Deutzia, Eccremocarpus scaber, Escallonia, Fremontodendron Fuchsia, Heather (ericas), Hebe, Honeysuckle, Hydrangea, Hypericum, Indigofera gerardiana, Jasmine (summer flowering), Jerusalem sage (Phlomis fruticosa), Kalmia, Koelreutaria, Lavender, Lavender cotton (santolina), Leycesteria formosa, Lupin (tree), Magnolia, Philadelphus (mock orange, syringa), Rhododendron, Rock rose (cistus), Roses, Russian vine (Polygonum baldschuanicum), Senecio greyi, Solanum, Spiraea, Tamarisk (Tamarix pentandra) Tulip tree (liriodendron), Yucca

## Harvest

Apple (early varieties), Cherry, Mulberry, Pear (early varieties)

# Late Summer

Most activity in late summer is related to fruit crops, rather than ornamentals; you will find that much of your time is taken up with picking and harvesting various kinds of tree fruits. A good deal of the pruning needed is associated with the fruits, too, if you are growing the restricted forms, such as fans, espaliers and cordons.

There will still be a little shrub pruning; late summer is the season for trimming formal hedges, both deciduous and evergreen. The fast-growing kinds may be needing their third clip and some deadheading and sucker removal will still also be necessary.

Semi-ripe cuttings of many shrubs, including climbers, can be taken now. At this time of the year, they have the best chance of rooting and surviving, while conditions are still warm and there is plenty of time for them to build up a good root system and top growth. Other methods of increase include budding early in the season and layering.

The pest and disease war will begin to peter out and though you may still be fighting off mildew, earwigs and woolly aphis, the remaining plant troubles will definitely be diminishing. Many pests will have come to the end of their life-cycle and will be looking for suitable places in which to winter. Birds and wasps will be problems on the fruit, particularly the wall-grown crops.

# At~a~glance diary

**Prepare the soil for:** planting outdoors in early autumn — e.g. evergreens, and/or winter-flowering shrubs and trees

**Prune:** wisteria; restricted forms of apple, pear; bush plum, greengage; bush cherry, fan-trained Morello cherry

**Trim:** formal, deciduous and evergreen hedges: examples are beech, cypress, holly, hornbeam, privet, yew; informal flowering hedges, provided the flowering has finished

**Deadhead:** Buddleia davidii, lavender, lavender cotton, roses, rock rose (cistus), rue, Senecio greyi, yucca

**Feed:** camellia, peony (tree), roses

**Pot:** rooted cuttings from mid-summer

**Increase:** roses by budding; various shrubs by layering or by semi-ripe cuttings

**Pests and diseases:** codling moth caterpillars (third spray), tortrix caterpillars and woolly aphis on apples; red plum maggot (second spray); black spot, mildew and rust on roses; red spider mite, mildew, earwigs, birds and wasps generally; put corrugated cardboard or sacking bands round trunks of apple trees

# Jobs to do

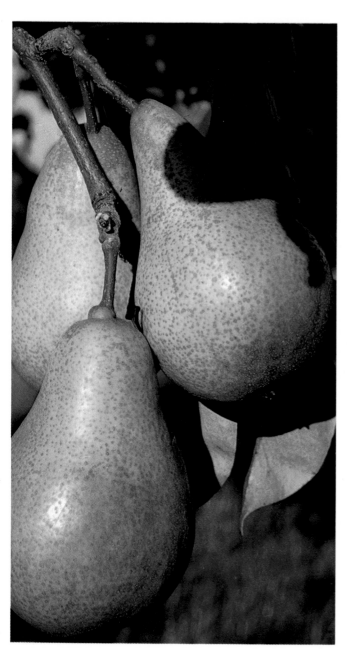

### Preparing the soil for planting

Early autumn is one of the best seasons for planting evergreens, conifers in particular, and so, some time in late summer, the soil of the chosen site should be dug and rotted organic matter mixed in as in the preparations for planting detailed in Mid-Autumn. If the soil is dry, a thorough watering a day or two beforehand will be necessary. Evergreen planting does, of course, include evergreen hedges, so preparation could mean digging out trenches, not merely individual planting sites.

### Pruning

Virtually no shrub and climber pruning will be needed in late summer, except to wisteria. This is done to encourage more flowering, but you can leave it alone and simply prune it to fit the space available in winter. For summer pruning wisteria, all this year's new side-shoots are cut back to leave a length of about 30cm (12in), or about six leaves. The leading shoots should be cut back similarly.

Summer pruning of both apples and pears grown as cordons or espaliers is as follows. When the new side-shoots have matured to the stage at which the bark is light brown for about half the length of the stem, the rest gradually changing colour until it is a fresh green at the tip, the shoot should be cut to leave a length of about 15 or 17.5cm (6 or 7in). This applies to sub-side-shoots as well. Shoots which are not sufficiently mature should be left until they are, and then pruned. After the middle of early autumn it is too late to summer-prune, however, and they should be left alone.

It is important that the shoots are pruned at the right stage of maturity; too soon, and the buds which should have turned into fruit buds instead produce new shoots which do not mature by winter and are then killed. Too late, and the shoot does not bud up to form fruit buds. The first week of early summer is often the best time for the majority of trees and gardens but warm conditions can mean pruning

*Pear Beurré Clairgeau is an early-flowering culinary variety which is ready for picking in mid-autumn.*

Left: *Summer-prune cordon and espalier apples and pears by cutting the new growth just above a leaf, to leave 15-17cm (6-7in) of stem.* Below: *Cobaea scandens,* the cup-and-saucer plant, *is a half-hardy climber for the greenhouse or warm garden.*

much earlier, during the latter half of mid-summer and cold ones will put pruning back to the second or third week of late summer.

Bush-grown plums may also have what little pruning is necessary done after the fruit has been picked. Infection by silver-leaf fungus is much less likely at this time; it infects through wounds and is most troublesome in winter, so that pruning then can be disastrous. Plums fruit on two-year-old shoots and on naturally formed spurs, so all that has to be done is to encourage some new side-shoots to form every year. Too much pruning results in a great deal of strong vegetative growth, so perhaps only a quarter of the season's new side-shoots should be cut back to four or five leaves or cut out completely. If there are any strong, new shoots growing straight upwards from the lower branches, these should have the tips removed; in time they can be used to replace the drooping branches which become unfruitful. Keep the tree clear of crowded, diseased or weak growth.

Bush forms of sweet cherries can be pruned after the fruit has been picked (see Pruning, Mid-Summer, for details). Fan-trained Morello cherries should be pruned after picking by cutting the fruited shoots off, back to a stub, on which is the replacement shoot.

## Trimming

Some time in late summer the formal deciduous and evergreen hedges can be given the annual clip; you could leave the deciduous kinds until winter but it is much less pleasant then and you may be prevented by the weather from doing it until too late.

You can make the job easier, if doing it by hand, by using really good quality, sharp, shears. If you have great lengths of hedges, a powered hedge-trimmer is a very worthwhile investment; it is now possible to obtain battery-driven models. When choosing one, make sure the weight is not going to be overpowering after half-an-hour or so of use; also, make sure the grip is completely comfortable and the right size for your hands. This applies to shears as well. Handles which are too thick are very tiring and rapidly produce blisters.

As soon as you start having to stretch up to cut, stand on a tripod ladder, steps or stool. Start from the bottom

# Plants for Hedges

**Plants for formal hedges**
Beech
Berberis
Box
*Cotoneaster simonsii*
Cypress
Escallonia
*Euonymus japonicus*
Hawthorn
Hebe
Holly
Hornbeam
Laurustinus
Laurel
Spotted Laurel (aucuba)
*Lonicera nitida*
Privet
Pyracantha (firethorn)
Tamarix
Yew

**Plants for informal hedges**
Berberis
Cotoneaster
Currant, flowering
Daisy bush (olearia)
Deutzia
Escallonia
Forsythia
Fuchsia
Gorse
Hawthorn
Heather
Hebe
Hydrangea
Japonica
Lavender
Lavender cotton (santolina)
Philadelphus
Pyracantha (firethorn)
Rhododendron

Roses
Spiraea
Tamarix
Viburnum
Weigela

**Roses for hedges**
*Rosa moyesii*
*Rosa rugosa*

Blanc Double de Coubert
Frau Dagmar Hastrup
F. J. Grootendoorst
Roseraie de l'Hay
Sarah van Fleet
Schneezwerg
Frühlingsgold
Frühlingsmorgen
Pemberton Musk roses
Penzance Briars
Zephirine Drouhin

when cutting the sides of the hedge and use a line stretched along the top to prevent the appearance of scallops on the horizontal edge. If, however, you want scallops or castellations, use two lines to mark both the dips and the tops. Hedges of laurel and bay are better cut with secateurs, otherwise the leaves are badly damaged.

Although most hedges can be dealt with once a year, in late summer, there are exceptions, as given in the accompanying table. This also details the method of cutting hedges after the second winter from planting, to ensure that they have leaves down to ground level.

## Deadheading
Plants to deadhead through late summer include rue, lavender cotton (santolina), *Senecio greyi* if not already done, rock rose (cistus) and roses in general. New subjects to treat will include lavender, yucca and *Buddleia davidii* varieties.

Magnolia denudata, *or the Yulan lily, whose home is China, bursts into fragrant flower in spring.*

## Feeding
It is still worthwhile giving a potash-high fertilizer to camellias, tree peonies and roses as mentioned in Mid-Summer, as early as possible this season.

## Potting
Some, if not all, of the shrub cuttings taken in mid-summer will have rooted by now and will need larger pots and a good potting compost. The size of pot depends on the amount of root produced and should be large enough for the roots not to be cramped. The young plants can be kept outdoors quite safely and will need regular watering.

## Increasing
Rose budding may be possible early this season, provided the bark still lifts easily (see Increasing, Mid-Summer, for details). Any increase by the layering method also needs to be done early, so that the layers are well rooted by autumn.

Late summer is a good time to make semi-ripe cuttings

Opposite: *Those exotic flowers of the South Seas, the hibiscus, have some hardy relatives in the shape of the shrubby H. syriacus. Blue Bird is one variety, flowering in late summer.*
Right: *Before planting a semi-ripe cutting, trim the heel. Plant the cuttings round the rim of the pot to about half their length. Cover the pot with plastic to keep the atmosphere at the level of warmth and moisture the cuttings need.*

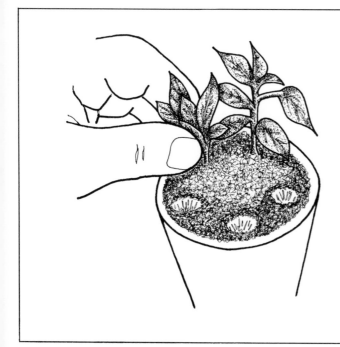

of shrubs and climbers. These cuttings should be about 5-17.5cm (2-7in) long, made from this year's shoots. The shoot will have begun to mature so that the bark is starting to brown and harden from the base of the shoot but the tip will still be green and soft. The cutting is made in the usual way (see Increasing, Early Summer).

## Treating pests and diseases
Troubles to contend with now will probably be earwigs eating the petals and leaves of clematis, mildew, which causes most trouble in early autumn, especially after dry summers, woolly aphis on apples and pears and birds and wasps on fruit of all kinds. Wall-grown fruit can be protected with netting against birds and jam jars full of sweet liquid will sidetrack the wasps from the fruit.

*The St John's Worts all have yellow saucer flowers with long stamens in summer; Hypericum x inodorum Elstead mixes red berries with the flowers in late summer.*

Late summer is the time to put corrugated cardboard or sacking collars, about 10-15cm (3-6in) wide, round the trunks of apple trees, just below the main branches. These collars provide places for codling caterpillars to pupate and their removal in autumn ensures a good deal of control and reduction of damage to next year's crop.

Other pests and diseases will be as for mid-summer but by now the need for spraying should virtually have finished.

## General work
Continue to water, build the compost heap and remove suckers and plain green shoots. Hydrangeas will be flowering and should not need any more blueing treatment for the time being; weeding will be much less, unless the summer is wet. Climbing plants will have grown to their limit and may now only need to have their ties reinforced after summer gales. Orchard swards need not be mown if time is short.

## Plants in flower

Abelia grandiflora, Buddleia, Campsis Mme Galen, Ceanothus, Ceratostigma willmottianum, Clematis, Daisy bush (Olearia haastii), Eccremocarpus, Escallonia, Eucryphia, Fremontodendron, Fuchsia, Gorse, Heather (Calluna vulgaris and ericas, including E. cinerea), Hebe, Hibiscus, Honeysuckle, Hydrangea, Hypericum, Indigofera gerardiana, Jasmine (summer-flowering), Koelreuteria paniculata, Lavender, Leycesteria formosa (himalayan honeysuckle), Magnolia, Mallow (tree), Potentilla, Rock rose (cistus), Roses, Russian vine (Polygonum baldschuanicum), Solanum, Spanish gorse (Spartium junceum), Spiraea, Tamarix pentandra, Wisteria, Yucca

## Harvest

Apple, cherry, Greengage, Mulberry, Nectarine, Peach, Pear, Plum

# Early Autumn

Quite often at this time of the year some of the spring-flowering shrubs bloom again. Repeat-flowering of large-flowered and cluster-flowered roses is almost taken for granted now, but Mexican orange blossom (choisya), ceanothus, weigela and berberis may produce more bloom and even wisteria has the occasional flower cluster on it late in the season. This revival of growth is not confined to flowering; new leaves and shoots sprout, orchard swards often start to grow again and some hedges may even need another clip.

Plants seem to be taking in one last helping of food and consolidating the season's growth in preparation for the winter. It is a good idea to take advantage of this and mulch all top fruit and any plants which were not so treated in late spring. Although not standard practice, a dressing of potash-high fertilizer now could just tip the balance between the formation of flower or fruit buds, instead of vegetative buds, next spring and summer.

The main pruning consists of treating the rambler roses, though there is still some general summer pruning of fruit to finish. Hedges will need clipping, if this has not already been done in late summer.

The main planting season is not far away and soil can be prepared now for a good many shrubs and climbers and also for rooted layers and plants formed from cuttings. Routine jobs will continue to tail off; most of them will come to an end this season.

# At~a~glance diary

**Prepare the soil for:** *planting*

**Plant:** *evergreen and evergrey plants, except the least hardy kinds; winter-flowering plants; rooted layers and plants grown from cuttings*

**Prune:** *rambler roses; fan-trained sweet cherries and peaches; plums; finish summer-pruning restricted apples and pears*

**Trim:** *formal deciduous and evergreen hedges if not done already*

**Deadhead:** *Buddleia davidii, hebe, lavender, roses, rue; hydrangea in warm districts*

**Feed:** *with potash-high fertilizer*

**Mulch:** *shrubs, climbers, top fruit that has cropped, rambler and climbing roses, hedges*

**Water:** *if weather dry*

**Increase:** *evergreens and deciduous plants from semi-ripe cuttings*

**Pests and diseases:** *birds, wasps, mildew, especially on vine and roses, black spot on roses, earwigs; apply greasebands to fruit trees*

**Routine work:** *weed, finish compost-heap making, remove suckers and plain green shoots, blue hydrangeas*

# Jobs to do

## Preparing the soil for planting

Ideally, soil should be dug, manured, fed and cleared of weeds about four or five weeks before planting but it is often difficult to get the timing right, taking into account delivery from the nursery and the fickleness of the weather. The object of this early preparation is to ensure that the additions to the soil become broken up and absorbed to some extent by the time the plants are put in, so that they can make use of the added goodness at once. Then their establishment is much quicker and your chances of success are much greater (see Mid–Autumn for details).

## Planting

Early autumn has been found to be the best time to plant most winter-flowering and evergreen or evergrey shrubs and

*A garden with a superbly-kept lawn, planted with conifers, will be a pleasure to look at in summer and winter.*

trees. The least hardy kinds can be left until mid- or late spring if time is short now or if your district is a cold one. Sometimes the autumn is dry and warm and, if so, the planting sites should be thoroughly watered a day or two before planting, as well as immediately after preparation. Make sure that all the plants are well firmed in and securely attached to supporting stakes before the big autumn gales start (see Late Autumn for details of planting).

## Pruning

Roses, particularly the ramblers, are one of the main groups of plants to need treatment in early autumn; they flower profusely on the previous season's new growth and can be encouraged to produce good long stems if the flowered shoots are cut right away to ground level. The job can be simplified by untying both flowered and new shoots and placing them full length on the ground; weak and stunted growth should be pruned off as well. The new canes are then retied to their supports, well spaced out.

Fan-trained sweet cherries grown against walls should have the side-shoots, which were cut to five or six leaves in

Left: Potentilla fruticosa *is a shrub whose flowers vary in colour from primrose to deep gold.*

Below: *Planting a conifer. Plants supplied by mail-order should have the sacking removed from the root-ball and the ball planted intact, with soil filled in over it.*

mid-summer, further cut to three or four now. If the leading shoots have grown too tall, they should not be pruned, but bent over and tied down, when they should produce side-shoots.

If the peach harvest has finished, the trees can be pruned in the way described in detail later, under Pruning, Early Winter.

Plums which have finished cropping can be pruned by the methods recommended in Late Summer and will be all the better for being cleared, not only of their fruit, but of unnecessary shoots and twigs.

The summer pruning of restricted apples and pears should be finished early in autumn; at the same time, if any secondary shoots have grown after the earlier summer pruning, these should be completely removed. They will never mature satisfactorily and the tips will be damaged by cold, which can lead to fungus infection setting in.

As far as the shrubs and climbers are concerned, both flowering and foliage kinds, no pruning is required in early autumn unless it was missed in late summer and some catching up has to be done.

Right: Solanum crispum *Glasnevin is a slightly tender climber, which flowers intermittently all through summer.*

Below: *A temporary screen should protect the conifer from wind, and the foliage should be sprayed daily from planting time until the plant is well established.*

## Trimming

There is still time, early this season, to trim formal deciduous and evergreen hedges, if they were not done in late summer. In fact, some are best left until now; these include bay, elaeagnus, laurel and spotted laurel (aucuba).

## Deadheading

Plants to deadhead include *Buddleia davidii* varieties, late-flowering lavenders, all types of roses where necessary, rue if still flowering, and hebe. In warm districts the flower-heads can be taken off hydrangeas, but otherwise they provide a little protection from cold for the buds just below them which will flower next year.

## Feeding

Although feeding plants is not generally recommended at this time of the year, it is the leaf-and-shoot-producing nutrient, nitrogen, that could result in trouble. Its application would encourage rapid, 'soft' growth, easily burnt by frost and cold wind. Phosphorus and potassium, however, will make the roots stronger and mature the shoot growth without increasing it, thus making it harder and more resistant to low temperatures. A compound fertilizer with a small nitrogen content could therefore be applied now and would be particularly beneficial to plants growing in sandy or shingly soil.

## Mulching

By now the compost heap started in spring should have rotted down to the brown, crumbly substance which does so much good to the soil structure. It can be used as a mulch for shrubs, climbers, top fruit that has been picked and pruned if necessary, rambling and climbing roses and hedges. Privet has a bad reputation for taking all the goodness out of the soil and herbaceous plants growing close to privet hedges grow poorly because of this, so it pays to mulch such hedges well now, besides feeding them in spring.

## Watering

There are some autumns when the idea of artificial watering is that season's joke but, equally, there can be others which make the Gobi Desert look wet! Whatever the weather, keep an eye on the wall plants, the evergreens and the new plants so that they never become parched.

## Increasing

Semi-ripe cuttings of deciduous shrubs and climbers can still be rooted this season, preferably early rather than late.

It is a good time to increase conifers, such as cypresses, juniper, cedar and larch from heel cuttings and other evergreens, for which semi-ripe cuttings are used (see Late Summer). Heel cuttings are much used for the conifers, and may only be 5 or 7.5cm (2 or 3in) long. The shoot is pulled off, not cut, so that a sliver of bark and older wood is attached to the shoot; this 'heel' is trimmed of its ragged edges and the cutting then put into a moist sandy compost, or moist silver sand alone. If the latter is used, the cuttings must be potted as soon as rooted, as there is no food in the sand.

Opposite: *Dessert plums take a lot of beating as to flavour if eaten when freshly picked and still warm from the sun.* Below: *The shrubby veronicas, now called hebes, carry their flowers in spikes, long or short. Autumn Glory will flower until early winter in mild seasons.*

*In their native Mediterranean regions figs will set at least two crops of fruit a year. In colder climates only one is possible in sheltered places outdoors. In order to obtain this, the small hard fruits present in mid-summer should be rubbed off the shoots.*

Some conifers, such as spruce (picea) and fir (abies), have a good deal of resin in them. Dipping the ends of the cuttings in hot water for a few minutes prevents this resin from forming a callus over the end of the cutting, which would prevent rooting.

After potting, the cuttings can go into a shaded cold frame.

## Treating pests and diseases
Birds and slugs will still be damaging fruits a good deal and mildew on vines and roses can be very troublesome in early autumn. Black spot on roses, and earwigs generally, are other current plagues. Female winter moths and March moths will be preparing to lay eggs on branches of apples, pears and plums and can be prevented by putting grease-bands round the trunks of the trees (and supporting stakes) about 60-90cm (2-3ft) above the ground. Grease-bands can be bought ready for use from garden shops.

## General work
It is a good idea to get on top of weeds in rose beds, in beds round specimen plants and those growing beneath wall or fence-trained plants and hedges, in early autumn. Otherwise, by next spring, they can easily have got completely out of hand. Orchard swards may need mowing, depending on the weather. The second compost heap or heaps will be nearly finished. There will be few, if any suckers and plain green shoots to remove and climbing plants will have finished their upward growth. Hydrangeas should be given one more blueing treatment.

## Harvesting
The apple and pear harvest will be in full swing during early and mid-autumn. If you are in doubt about the maturity of a fruit, test it by holding it in the palm of your hand and pushing it gently upwards. The stalk should come away easily, but if it needs a good tug, leave the crop for a few more days. A colour change from green to yellow is another indication and a third, if you can bear to cut a fruit open, is the colour of the pips. They should be dark brown when the fruit is ripe. Other fruits to harvest include: apricot, damson, fig, greengage, nectarine, peach, plum and vine.

## Plants in flower
Berberis, Buddleia davidii, Campsis Mme Galen, Caryopteris, Ceanothus, Ceratostigma Clematis, Fremontodendron, Fuchsia, Gorse, Heather (Calluna vulgaris and ericas including E. cinerea), Hebe, Hibiscus, Honeysuckle, Hydrangea, Hypericum, Indigofera, Jasmine (summer-flowering), Leycesteria formosa, Magnolia grandiflora, Mexican orange blossom (choisya), Potentilla, Roses, Russian vine (Polygonum baldschuanicum), Solanum, Sorbaria, Spanish gorse (Spartium junceum), Spirea, Tamarix pentandra, Weigela, Wisteria

## Harvest
Apple, Apricot, Damson, Fig, Greengage, Nectarine, Peach, Pear, Plum, Vine

# Mid-Autumn

In general, mid-autumn is a quiet time as far as shrubs and trees are concerned. Their growth has largely finished; the main planting and pruning season does not start until late autumn and much of mid-autumn's work consists of finishing off, clearing up, harvesting and making preparations to make later work easier.

The emphasis at this time is on increasing your stock; you may be planting bought-in plants ordered from nurseries or container-grown plants picked up from garden centres. You may be planting cuttings and layers rooted earlier, in spring or summer, or you may be taking hardwood cuttings, using completely mature, new season's shoots. Some roses can be propagated like this, as well as shrubs and climbers and if you want to put in a new hedge, hardwood cuttings are a much less expensive way of obtaining it. For all these, soil preparation will be required, whether you plant later this season or during late autumn.

Harvesting fruit will continue and most apples and pears picked now will be storable. Mulching the trees after picking, or mowing for the last time before winter, and tying-in the wall-trained fruit will be the remaining jobs on the fruit front. A little spraying to control peach leaf-curl, if present, is done now; other troubles will be few.

# At~a~glance diary

**Prepare the soil for:** planting at the beginning of early spring —e.g., deciduous shrubs, climbers, ornamental and fruit trees

**Plant:** deciduous shrubs and trees; evergreens if not done; rooted layers and cuttings taken in spring and early mid-summer, rooted vine eyes

**Prune:** rambler roses, potentilla, summer jasmine

**Mulch:** all shrubs, climbers, fruit trees (even if the crop is not yet picked), ornamental trees

**Deadhead:** hebe, hydrangea, roses

**Sweep up:** leaves to form a heap to rot down into leafmould (do not use diseased or leathery leaves)

**Increase:** by hardwood cuttings rambling and climbing roses, shrub roses, some species and some cluster-flowered roses, deciduous and evergreen shrubs in variety; by seed, trees

**Pests and diseases:** peach leaf-curl, black spot, mildew, birds

**Routine work:** weed, complete compost heap, water new plants, mow orchard sward for the last time

**Store:** apple, pear, quince, in a dry, cool, frost-proof place, safe from vermin

# Jobs to do

### Preparing the soil for planting

The woody plants are the most permanent part of the garden, and the most costly, so it pays to take steps to avoid death of the plants shortly after planting. It is essential to supply the roots with as favourable conditions for re-growth as possible. Late autumn is the best time, as far as weather is concerned, for planting roses, deciduous shrubs, climbers and trees; advance soil preparation in mid-autumn (except for light soils) will result in food, aeration and drainage being at their best by the time the plants are put in.

Unless your soil is a well-drained, deep, fertile loam, it will be the better for the addition of rotted organic matter. Use any of the materials suggested in Late Spring for mulches: farm manure, garden compost, leafmould, spent hops or spent mushroom compost. It must be rotted, because unrotted material may remain in the state in which it was added to the soil for many months. Heavy soils can have about 3kg per sq m (7lb per sq yd) mixed in, medium soils about 4½kg (10lb per sq yd) and sandy, shingly or chalky soils need about 6½-8½kg per sq m (15-18lb per sq yd).

In the case of these light soils, preparation should be left until a few days before planting, otherwise the organic matter added will be absorbed too quickly by the soil flora and fauna and be less useful.

Soil should be dug two spits deep, keeping the topsoil separate from the lower spit. The bottom of the second spit should be forked up, mixing organic matter with it at the same time. Planting holes should be at least 60×60cm (2×2ft) square; as the soil is replaced, organic matter is mixed with it, and the whole left to settle until planting.

If you are planting at the beginning of late autumn, bonemeal should be added about a week before the end of mid-autumn, at the rate of about two large handfuls per sq m (sq yd); mix it into the top spit with a fork. Bonemeal contains phosphorus, the mineral plant food so much needed by developing roots.

When preparing the site, large stones and weeds should

*The colour of the leaves of many shrubs and trees in autumn can be spectacular and is a point to remember when choosing varieties. Acer nikoense is a slow-growing tree to 12m (40ft), with particularly brilliant leaf colour.*

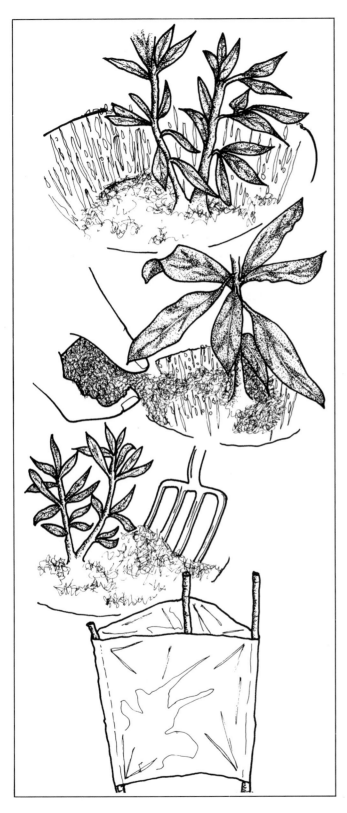

be cleared away; roots of perennial weeds should be dug out completely. Bindweed, ground-elder, couch grass and horsetail will be a particular nuisance later if not thoroughly dealt with now.

You may want to grow rhododendrons, azaleas and other plants that love acid soil in a neutral-to-alkaline soil, but although you can create pockets of acid soil for them, in time these will become alkaline, due to soil drainage and rain. It is a constant fight to grow plants under these conditions and, in any case, they never look quite right in their surroundings. On the whole, it is better not to go against the grain: try, instead, some of the many attractive lime-tolerant trees and shrubs available: clematis, coton-easter, buddleia, box, ceanothus, cistus, forsythia, fuchsia, laburnum, syringa and viburnum, for example.

## Planting

It is not too late to plant evergreens, except in cold districts, though even in the warmer ones they should go in as soon as possible. Deciduous shrubs and trees can also be planted now, as well, though it is better to wait until leaf fall, and rooted layers and cuttings, including vine eyes, will be ready (see Late Autumn for details of planting).

## Pruning

Rambler roses can be pruned in mid-autumn if not so treated in early autumn.

If potentilla was not pruned in spring, and it has some rather old, non-flowering growth, this growth, which may be several stems, can be removed to ground level. Such pruning need only be done every few years. Potentilla is one of the few shrubs which naturally has a brown cambium layer, rather than a green one, below the bark, so do not assume that it is dead because of this.

Summer jasmine produces a lot of annual growth which gets much tangled; flowering falls off unless one or two of the oldest shoots are cut off to soil level in mid-autumn and the remainder thinned by cutting shoots back here and there. In cold districts this can be left until spring.

Left: *Planting rhododendrons. Plant so that the root-ball is undisturbed, with the soil mark on the stem at the same level as the soil surface; crumble soil on to and around the root-ball to fill the hole; rake or lightly fork the surface of the firmed-down soil and give temporary protection from the wind or cold.*
Right: *A corner of a rock garden with an attractively mixed planting of rhododendrons and dwarf shrubs. These include a Japanese maple and an upright juniper.*

## Mulching
All fruit trees can be mulched now, even if a crop is not yet picked, as later mulching will not be made use of to the same extent. Keep the mulch clear of trunks, otherwise mice and voles nest in it and feed on the bark of the trees during the winter months.

## Deadheading
Roses will still need removal of finished blooms; hebe flower spikes are better removed and so are hydrangea flowerheads if the garden is warm and the buds below the flower heads do not need their protection from cold.

## Sweeping up
In the last week or so of this season, the leaves will start to fall; rather than let them smother the ground-cover shrubs and provide a place for pests and disease to winter, they should be collected up into a heap to rot down into leaf-mould. Leaves which should not be added are the leathery kinds, usually evergreens, and those infected with diseases such as scab, black spot and mildew; these are better burnt.

## Increasing
Mid-autumn is the best season for increasing woody plants from hardwood cuttings. These consist of the end 22.5-

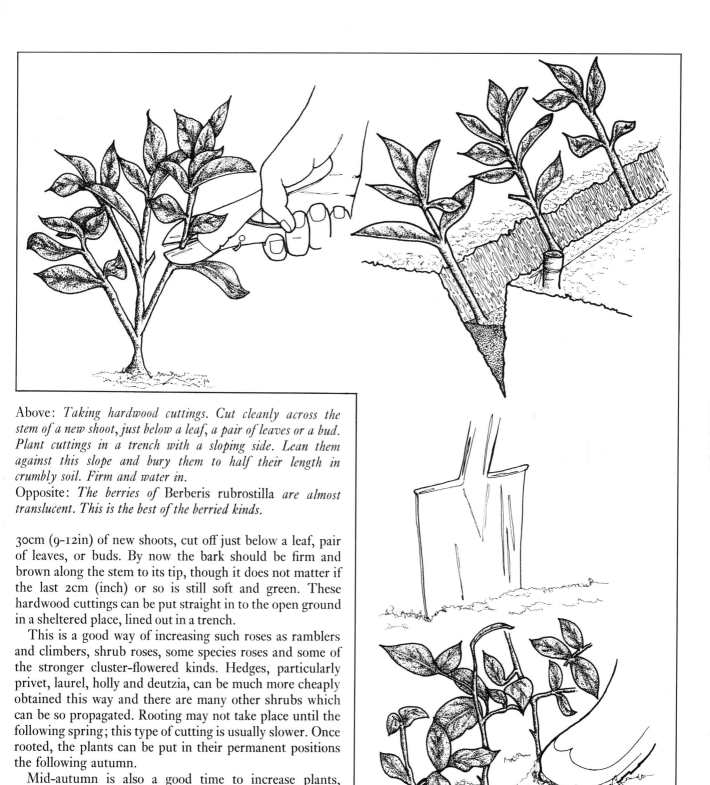

Above: *Taking hardwood cuttings. Cut cleanly across the stem of a new shoot, just below a leaf, a pair of leaves or a bud. Plant cuttings in a trench with a sloping side. Lean them against this slope and bury them to half their length in crumbly soil. Firm and water in.*

Opposite: *The berries of* Berberis rubrostilla *are almost translucent. This is the best of the berried kinds.*

30cm (9-12in) of new shoots, cut off just below a leaf, pair of leaves, or buds. By now the bark should be firm and brown along the stem to its tip, though it does not matter if the last 2cm (inch) or so is still soft and green. These hardwood cuttings can be put straight in to the open ground in a sheltered place, lined out in a trench.

This is a good way of increasing such roses as ramblers and climbers, shrub roses, some species roses and some of the stronger cluster-flowered kinds. Hedges, particularly privet, laurel, holly and deutzia, can be much more cheaply obtained this way and there are many other shrubs which can be so propagated. Rooting may not take place until the following spring; this type of cutting is usually slower. Once rooted, the plants can be put in their permanent positions the following autumn.

Mid-autumn is also a good time to increase plants, particularly trees, from seeds which are to be stratified through the winter. Stratifying simply means putting the seeds, in layers, into containers filled with a mixture of peat, coarse sand or a mixture of the two. The containers are then plunged (sunk up to the rim) in a bed or border close to a north-facing wall or fence. They should be covered with close-mesh netting to prevent mice getting at the seeds. Seeds treated like this are those with hard coats; roses (the whole hip is buried), hawthorn, peach and plum stones and holly are examples. They may need to stay there until spring only, or a year and a half, and the more they are frozen the better.

## Treating pests and diseases

Be sure to spray for peach-leaf curl, just as the leaves are about to fall (see Controls and Treatments section for fungicide required). Black spot and mildew may still be present on roses; birds may be menacing fruit.

## General work

There may be a little weeding left to do. The compost heap will be completed now and can be covered for the winter;

*In Mexico,* Choisya ternata *is a common shrub; its fragrant flowers justify its English name of Mexican Orange Blossom.*

in a dry autumn newly planted specimens should be kept well watered. Give the orchard sward a last mow.

## Storing

Certain varities of apples, pears and quinces can be stored through the winter until late spring, but they must be in a frostproof place and they must be safe from mice and rats. Sheds and garages are not necessarily frostproof in bad winters and storing the fruit in wooden boxes or on slatted racks invites trouble. Thick, wooden chests, with slatted shelving inside, lagged against the cold with fibreglass wool or several layers of sacking should be safe, but a cellar, unheated attic or spare room is better.

Apples, pears and quinces should be stored separately from one another; they can be placed four or five in a clear plastic bag, stored singly, or wrapped in oiled paper. If stored in a pile in a box or chest, all must be quite free from injury or disease, otherwise trouble spreads rapidly, and you do not want to turn out several hundredweights of apples every few weeks to see whether the bottom ones are rotting.

## Plants in flower

Caryopteris, Ceanothus, Ceratostigma, Cherry (autumn-flowering, Prunus subhirtella autumnalis), Clematis, Fatsia, Fuchsia (shelter), Gorse, Heather, (Calluna vulgaris and ericas, including E. carnea in variety), Hebe, Honeysuckle, Hypericum, Hydrangea, Mexican orange blossom (choisya), Roses, Russian vine (Polygonum baldschuanicum), Strawberry tree (Arbutus unedo), Witch hazel (Hamamelis virginiana)

## Harvest

Apple (late varieties), Fig, Grape, Pear (late varieties), Quince, Sloe

# Late Autumn

Your main job in late autumn will be planting. Although it can, in theory, be done at any time during winter, late autumn or early winter are best. Roses, deciduous shrubs, trees, climbers, tree fruits, vines and hedges can all go in now; the hardier evergreens can also be planted but are less likely to survive in very cold winters. Staking and pruning will be part of the process.

Pruning the tree fruits can be started towards the end of late autumn, once the leaves are completely off. Wall-grown fruits can be re-tied after spacing and possibly cutting if necessary and some shrubs and climbers may need surgical treatment. Another form of late-autumn pruning is root pruning, done to fruit which is obstinate about cropping.

The end of late autumn is also a good time to cover vulnerable plants with netting to protect them against birds, cold or wind, and to make sure that all those needing supports are securely attached before gales, snow and heavy rain start. Apart from these, there are various odd jobs to do, which are mostly a matter of finishing off; these include picking the remaining fruit, sweeping up leaves and taking hardwood cuttings.

# At~a~glance diary

**Prepare the soil for:** planting at the beginning of winter all subjects except evergreen and tender plants

**Plant:** deciduous shrubs and trees, climbers, roses, hedges, tree fruits, the hardier evergreens

**Transplant:** deciduous shrubs and ornamental trees, climbers, roses, hedging plants, fruit trees, and the least tender evergreens

**Prune:** tree fruits, rambler roses; root prune unfruitful tree fruits

**Mulch:** finish mulching; give tender plants extra deep mulch at least 15 cm (6in) deep above crowns and the side root area

**Sweep up:** leaves

**Protect:** tree fruits and some ornamentals against bud pecking by birds; newly planted and young plants against cold and wind

**Increase:** by hardwood cuttings taken early this season, rambling and climbing roses, shrub roses, some species and some cluster-flowered roses, deciduous and evergreen shrubs in variety; by stratified seed trees, shrubs and roses; clematis by layering

**Routine work:** finish weeding, store fruit; examine supports and ties and repair where necessary

# Jobs to do

## Preparing the soil for planting

You may not be able to plant until the end of this season, or even sometime during early winter, but soil will need digging and manuring a few weeks in advance, as detailed in Mid-Autumn. If it is very wet, due to early autumn rains, leave the soil alone, especially clay soil, which can become severely compacted if trampled on while wet. It will also be very heavy work.

## Planting

The reason for planting at this time of the year is that the soil is still relatively warm from the summer, the air temperature has not fallen really low and the plants are not completely dormant, but still capable of growing new roots.

At this time of the year, it should be possible to put in plants directly they arrive when bought by mail-order from a nursery. If, however, conditions are cold and the soil frozen or waterlogged, they can be left in their wrappings for a few days, provided the roots have moist peat, compost, or sacking round them. If the weather looks like being difficult for some time, as it may do in winter, they should be heeled in to a shallow trench in a sheltered place for the time being.

If you are using container-grown plants from a garden centre or bare-rooted plants from the gardening department of a general store, you can, of course, choose your time for buying, so that it coincides with good weather.

Spacing of plants is very important. You need to know the spread, almost more than the height, of a mature tree

Left: *The winter jasmine,* Jasminum nudiflorum, *is a weakly climbing shrub in flower from late autumn to spring.*
Below: *Stratifying seeds. Tree and shrub seeds are sown in a peat/sand mixture, protected from mice with netting.*

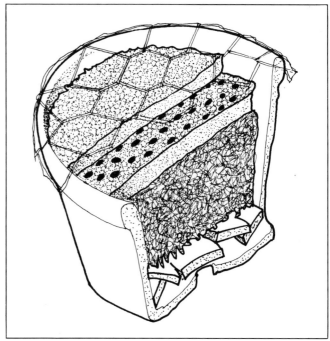

Above: Viburnum x burkwoodii *is a heavily fragrant spring-flowering shrub ; height is about 2.4m (8ft).*
Opposite: *Williams' Bon Chrétien, or the Bartlett pear, is good to eat raw, and also bottles and cooks well.*

## Fruit Tree Spacing

| | |
|---|---|
| Apple, bush | 2.4-4.5m (8-15ft) |
| cordon | 60cm (2ft) |
| espalier | 3.6m (12ft) |
| Apricot, fan | 3-7.2m (10-24ft) |
| Cherry, sweet bush | 4.5m (15ft) |
| fan | 4.5m (15ft) |
| Morello | 4.2-6m (14-20ft) |
| Damson, bush | 4.5-5.4m (15-18ft) |
| Fig, fan | 2.4m (8ft) |
| Grape vine, single rod | 1.2-1.5m (4-5ft) |
| Greengage, bush | 3-4.5m (10-15ft) |
| Medlar, bush | 4.2-4.8m (14-16ft) |
| Mulberry, bush | 9m (30ft) |
| Peach (nectarine) fan | 4.2m (14ft) |
| bush | 4.5-6m (15-20ft) |
| Pear, bush | 3.6-5.4m (12-18ft) |
| cordon | 90cm (3ft) |
| espalier | 3.6m (12ft) |
| Plum, bush | 4.5-5.4m (15-18ft) |
| Quince, bush | 3.6m (12ft) |

or shrub (see table of ornamental shrubs and trees for these dimensions). In nearly every case, not enough space is allowed, and the plant has cramped growth, flowers and leafs less well than it might and becomes much more prone to infection and pest epidemics. If proper spacing means rather large gaps for some years, you can fill them up with annuals, herbaceous plants or quick-growing shrubs like the tree lupin, rock rose (cistus) or broom. For spacing of fruit, see the list.

There is one major rule about planting, which really amounts to the difference between success and failure: always make sure that the roots are spread out to their fullest extent in the planting hole. Never plant so that the roots are in a doubled-up handful; it is tantamount to strangling them, and even if the unfortunate plant survives, it never grows well.

Dig out a hole which is more than wide enough and deep enough. Make a shallow mound in the centre and set the plant in the hole so that the roots spread naturally over and down the mound. Crumble good topsoil or a compost mixture in over the roots, shaking the plant gently every now and then so that all the crevices are filled and firming as the hole fills. Firm by treading, starting at the perimeter of the hole; firming from the centre outwards will result in the tips of the roots pointing upwards rather than downwards. Do not tread on the roots unless they have soil on them.

If any roots are torn or broken off with a jagged edge or are much longer than the others, cut them cleanly below the damage. Plants produce two sorts of roots; anchoring kinds which are long and stout and fibrous ones which are fine and short and which are the feeding roots. It is these that the plant will need most urgently; anchoring can come later. This is why you should plant firmly and provide a stake and/ or shelter from wind while the plants are young and establishing.

Planting should generally be at the same level as in the nursery or container, shown by a soil mark on the stem, but fuchsias can be about 5cm (2in) lower if planted now and will then survive the winter with a heaped-up protective mulch over them. Roses must always be planted so that the grafting bump is above the soil.

Some plants will arrive from the nursery with the root-ball wrapped in sacking or other material, having been lifted with the soil because they have formed a tightly packed mass of fine roots. Rhododendrons, azaleas and many conifers are examples. When planting, the roots should be left undisturbed and the soil-ball planted intact, with a little topsoil crumbled over the top.

If a stake is needed, put it in position in the hole before planting, to avoid later injury to the roots and, if you are dealing with standards, use a stake which reaches to just below the main head of branches. Bush tree fruits can have shorter stakes.

After planting, water the plant in and rake the topsoil gently to produce a rough rather than a smooth surface, for better drainage and aeration. It is advisable to keep the soil round the plants clear of grass or weeds, in a circle about 60cm (24in) in diameter for two or three years, to avoid competition for water and food while the plants establish.

Unless there are any very strong or ungainly shoots on the plants, there is no need to do any initial pruning at this time except to the roses. The large-flowered and cluster-

Opposite: *Planting trees. Spread the roots out, and position the tree on a shallow mound in the centre of the hole. Line up the soil mark with the soil level, using a board, and stake. Fill in soil; support tree with a suitable tie.*

Below: *The berries of* Symphoricarpos albus, *the snowberry, last a long time as they are not at all popular with birds.*

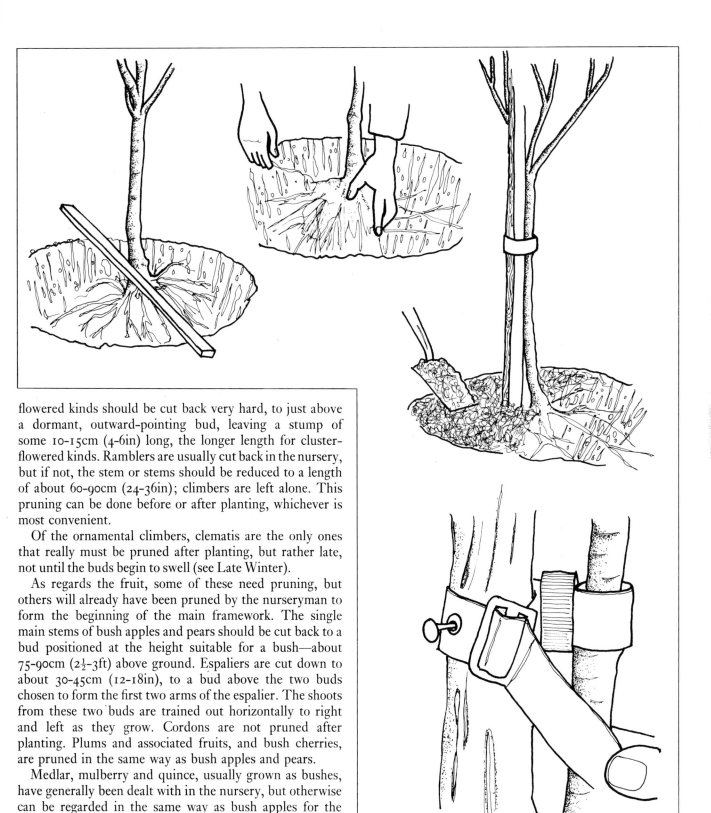

flowered kinds should be cut back very hard, to just above a dormant, outward-pointing bud, leaving a stump of some 10-15cm (4-6in) long, the longer length for cluster-flowered kinds. Ramblers are usually cut back in the nursery, but if not, the stem or stems should be reduced to a length of about 60-90cm (24-36in); climbers are left alone. This pruning can be done before or after planting, whichever is most convenient.

Of the ornamental climbers, clematis are the only ones that really must be pruned after planting, but rather late, not until the buds begin to swell (see Late Winter).

As regards the fruit, some of these need pruning, but others will already have been pruned by the nurseryman to form the beginning of the main framework. The single main stems of bush apples and pears should be cut back to a bud positioned at the height suitable for a bush—about 75-90cm (2½-3ft) above ground. Espaliers are cut down to about 30-45cm (12-18in), to a bud above the two buds chosen to form the first two arms of the espalier. The shoots from these two buds are trained out horizontally to right and left as they grow. Cordons are not pruned after planting. Plums and associated fruits, and bush cherries, are pruned in the same way as bush apples and pears.

Medlar, mulberry and quince, usually grown as bushes, have generally been dealt with in the nursery, but otherwise can be regarded in the same way as bush apples for the purposes of after-planting pruning.

## Hedge-trimming Table

| Group A | Group B | Group C |
|---|---|---|
| Clip several times a year; cut leading shoots lightly until height required is reached, then cut at that height always. Cut sides hard always. | Cut once a year in late summer; cut leaders lightly until height required is reached, then cut hard. Cut sides hard always. | Clip once a year, in early autumn. Cut sides fairly hard, and leaders as advised for Groups A and B |
| Cherry plum (*Prunus cerasifera*), hawthorn, gorse, *Lonicera nitida*, privet | *Berberis buxifolia nana*, beech, cotoneaster, all cypresses, escallonia *Euonymus japonicus*, hebe, holly, hornbeam, juniper, laurustinus, *Osmanthus delavayi*, pyracantha, snowberry, tamarix, *Thuja plicata*, yew | Bay, elaeagnus, laurel, spotted laurel (aucuba) |

*Berberis darwinii* and *B. stenophylla* : treat as Group B, but in late spring

Left: *Types of tree support vary according to the shape of the tree for which they are required. Illustrated here are the wire support for a fan-trained tree, types of wooden stake to support a standard, and the support for cordons.*

Fan-trained wall-grown fruit, such as peach and Morello cherry, are cut down to about 30cm (12in) above the grafting union, and the growth from the two topmost buds about 20cm (8in) above the union used to form the first ribs of the fan. These are tied down gradually as they grow to a final angle of 45°. Figs usually have the basic fan formed in the nursery and need not be pruned immediately.

Grape vines should be cut down to leave two or three dormant buds, which may mean reducing the stem to about 15-45cm (6-18in). However, if they are planted later than the end of mid-winter, do not prune, otherwise they will 'bleed' and this will weaken them. The leading shoot which then grows strongly from the top bud in summer is used to form the fruiting 'rod' and will also need to be cut hard in late autumn by as much as two-thirds of its length.

Newly planted hedges will need some degree of cutting back directly after planting, but if planted in late winter or early spring, should not be so treated. They should be left to grow during the summer and then cut back in late autumn as directed for those planted in autumn and the early part of winter.

The informal hedges, with the exception of the brooms and the evergreens, should be cut down hard to leave about 30cm (12in) of stem. This will ensure good bushy growth right from the base.

In the second winter after planting, Groups B and C are treated as in the first, but Group A should be cut back hard so as to remove half the growth produced in the summer.

## Transplanting
As with planting, this is a good season to transplant woody plants. The method is much the same; when lifting the plants, try to keep the roots as intact as possible and re-plant as quickly as possible. This means having the holes dug ready beforehand. Keep a good ball of soil round the roots. If the plants have to be out of the ground for a while, cover the roots with moist peat or wet sacking as soon as dug up. If they become dry and then wither, especially the rootlets, their chances of establishing and developing successfully are much decreased.

## Pruning
Towards the end of late autumn, after finishing any mulching left over from mid-autumn, you can start to prune the bush-tree fruit and finish the pruning of the restricted forms, such as cordons, fans and espaliers, started in summer (see Early Winter for details). Rambler roses can still be pruned, if there has not been time to do it so far (see Early Autumn).

Late autumn is a suitable time to root-prune fruit trees to encourage them to fruit. Some trees, in a very fertile, deep soil, become too strong and put all their energy into producing shoots instead of fruit. One way to overcome this is to dig a trench round the tree about 30cm (12in) deep and 45-60cm (18-24in) wide, so that the roots can be seen and loosened. The smaller and finer ones are tied back out of the way and the thickest sawn off; then the fine roots are replaced in position and the trench filled in with fine soil. With established trees, this should be done in two stages, half one autumn or winter and half the next year.

## Mulching
Any mulching not done or finished in mid-autumn should be completed early this season; on romneyas, eccremocarpus and fuchsias it will serve as a frost protection if 15cm (6in) or more deep.

## Sweeping up
This is the season for collecting leaves. All will make good leafmould, except the leathery and/or evergreen kinds.

Those infected with fungus disease, such as black spot and scab, should be burnt and it is particularly important to sweep these up so that fungus spores do not overwinter on them.

## Protection
Although it is difficult to believe, bullfinches and other birds are quite likely to start pecking out the fruit buds of gooseberries, greengages, damsons, plums, pears, cherries

*The spindle-tree is a plant of North European hedgerows, but its bright berries make it gardenworthy.*

and apples at any time from late autumn through winter to spring, so protective netting, webbing, or bird-repellent sprays should be put on now before they start.

### Increasing

Hardwood cuttings can still be taken early in late autumn and seeds stratified. If you have clematis you would like to propagate, you can do so by layering, at any time from now until spring. Use a shoot which was produced the spring before last, i.e., about 18 months old, close to the ground. Plunge a 15cm (6in) pot full of cutting compost into the soil to its rim, bend the shoot to form a 'U' into the pot so that it is buried in compost and keep it in place with a wire hook or wooden peg. By the following autumn it will have rooted and can be detached and planted.

### General work

There may be a little weeding to do; the summer spraying of pests and diseases is over and winter spraying, if it is necessary, need not be started until pruning is finished. Securing of ties, stakes and supporting trellises should be done before gales start in earnest. The last late varieties of apples and pears can be put into store.

## Plants in flower

Cherry (autumn-flowering, Prunus subhirtella autumnalis), Fatsia, Heather (Erica carnea varieties), Hebe, Jasmine (winter-flowering, Jasminum nudiflorum), Laurustinus, Mahonia Charity, Roses, Strawberry tree (Arbutus unedo), Viburnum farreri, Witch hazel (Hamamelis virginiana)

## Harvest

Apple, Grape (last), Medlar, Pear

Below: *Apples can be stored in single layers, in shallow trays stacked so that air can circulate between them.*

# Early Winter

The weather at this season generally continues to be reasonable for working in. Although the temperature will have gone down, the really cold weather, wet and snow should not start until early mid-winter. Then there will be very little that can be done outdoors, so that such jobs as planting, pruning and spraying should be finished during the next few weeks.

Planting can continue through early winter; tree fruit pruning can be started and, it is to be hoped, completed. Vine pruning should certainly be finished, as the sap in this fruit starts to rise much earlier than in the others. Wisteria can be winter-pruned, also some other ornamental climbers and one or two shrubs.

Once the pruning is finished, tree fruits can be given a winter wash against pests and diseases, if the spray programme you follow includes it. Protection will be required to prevent damage from cold, wind, birds and rodents, and weather damage should be looked for and remedied.

There will also still be a mixture of small jobs to do, such as leaf clearing, mulching and trimming hedges if not finished in summer. A rather bigger one is that of basic digging, to get the soil into good condition for planting next spring. Thorough preparation of this kind really does result in better and stronger plants and is particularly useful if they are to be grown in sticky, heavy soils containing a lot of clay.

# At~a~glance diary

**Prepare the soil for:** planting for double digging (digging to two spades' depth)

**Plant:** hardy deciduous shrubs and ornamental trees, climbers, roses, hedging plants, fruit trees (not evergreens or grey-leaved shrubs)

**Prune ornamentals:** large-flowered and cluster-flowered roses, if rather leggy, shrub roses if necessary, campsis, overgrown or crowded honeysuckle, summer jasmine, wisteria

**Prune fruit:** apple, apricot, Morello cherry, fig, medlar, mulberry, nectarine, peach, pear, quince, vine

**Save:** prunings from apples and pears for framework grafting

**Protect:** against birds; protect the following against wind, cold, winter weather. Abelia x grandiflora, campsis, ceanothus, Clematis armandii, eccremocarpus, escallonia, fremontodendron, fuchsia, hebe, hibiscus, summer jasmine, Mexican orange blossom (choisya), phlomis, piptanthus, privet, rock rose (cistus), romneya, Senecio greyi, solanum, yucca

**Sweep up:** leaves

**Increase:** by hardwood cuttings, vine

**Pests and diseases:** black spot and rust on roses; spray apples, pears, cherries, plums, greengages and other tree fruits with tar-oil winter wash to control over-wintering eggs of aphids and apple sucker, and adult scale insects; spray vines with sulphur to control scale insects, and with soft soap for mealy bug

# Jobs to do

## Preparing the soil for planting

Early winter is usually a good time to do some basic digging of previously uncultivated soil or to improve badly structured soils. These include those which are markedly quick-draining, such as chalky, sandy and shingly soils or heavy and water-retentive ones, such as sticky clay, peat and silt. To grow plants successfully in these soils, it is advisable to dig them a few months in advance of planting, mixing in soil improvers, such as rotted organic matter, coarse sand or grit, peat, and lime if very acid. The soil should be dug to a depth of two spades, the bottom of the hole or trench forked up and mixed with rotted manure, garden compost or similar material and the soil, together with the soil improvers, returned. The top spit should be kept separate from the second, so that they can be returned in order, and unmixed.

If lime is thought to be necessary, to break up a heavy soil or to decrease extreme acidity, it should be mixed in some weeks after adding organic matter, otherwise a chemical reaction occurs which results in loss of nutrients from the soil.

Once the soil has been roughly dug, it can be left until early spring before doing the final preparation for planting.

## Planting

General planting can still be done in early winter, if not finished in late autumn but never when the ground is frozen or waterlogged.

## Pruning ornamentals

If the large-flowered and cluster-flowered roses have grown rather leggy, it does no harm to shorten them back a few centimetres (inches) to prevent wind-rocking.

Shrub roses can also have done what little pruning may be needed, to tidy their outlines. Remove old growth and

*Callicarpa bodinieri giraldii has spectacular berries, but, sadly, they are seldom seen except in hot summers. The foliage has warm autumn tints.*

Above: *Make pruning cuts cleanly, as close as possible to a bud. Begin them on the side opposite to the bud.*
Below: *An amber-yellow-berried form of the guelder rose,* Viburnum opulus *Fructu luteo fruits in autumn.*

any shoots which are badly diseased or cluttering up the bush, preventing the good new growth from getting the light and air available.

Wisteria which was partially pruned in summer can be finished now by cutting back the shortened shoots to leave 5 or 7.5cm (2 or 3in) of stem. This method of pruning gradually builds up a spur system, and in time a few of the oldest spurs should be cut right away, once they begin to flower badly.

Climbing honeysuckle can be thinned now by cutting one or two of the oldest stems right out, and removing dead, diseased and weak shoots.

Campsis is mostly spur-pruned, with the new shoots cut back to stumps like wisteria, once the main shoots have filled the space allowed, but about four or five strong new shoots are left full length to clothe the support, and plant.

Summer-flowering jasmine can be treated now, if missed earlier (see Mid-Autumn), but in cold districts it is better to leave it until spring.

### Pruning fruit

Once the leaves have fallen and the trees have become dormant, pruning can safely be done, even in frosty weather, provided it is not severely cold.

Trees which were framework-grafted in the spring should be pruned by cutting the new growth from the grafted shoots at the ends of the main branches by a quarter to one third its length; one third of the remaining new shoots, spaced evenly over the tree, should be cut to about half their length, and any further sucker growth or badly placed grafts should be completely removed. In future winters, renewal prune in the usual way, as for bush apples and pears.

### Apples and pears

*Apples and pears*, cordon- and espalier-trained. The new shoots partially cut back in summer can now be shortened to about 7.5-10cm (3-4in) if they are primary side-shoots, but if secondary, should be reduced to about 2cm (1in). The leading shoots should be kept cut back, if need be, to the space available.

*Apples and pears*, bush trees. The most productive method for the amount of labour involved is the system of pruning called renewal, based on the fact that a shoot will fruit in its third year. The object of this pruning is to get a good supply of new side-shoots growing all the time to replace, or renew, the fruiting wood.

At the end of the summer a new shoot will have leaves all along it. During the following summer—the second one— buds will grow in the axils of these leaves; they will be round and fat, and are blossom buds. At the same time the tip bud will grow out to produce a new length of stem. In the third summer, the blossom buds will flower and fruit, growing out as they do so on a short length of stem, the beginning of a spur. The second summer's new growth, at the tip of the shoot, will form blossom buds, and at the same time, its own extension of the stem at the tip.

By cutting back the two-year-old growth and three-year-old growth, the amount of fruit produced can be manipulated and the production of vegetative growth regulated, so that there is a balance in the tree each season between fruit and shoot production. Heavy cutting encourages shoots to form and takes away potential fruit; very light pruning can result in overcropping and no renewal of shoots.

Depending on the vigour of the tree, about one-third to a half of the two- and three-year-old shoots can be cut, to leave about four or five fruit buds on the two-year-old growth, and one fruit bud or spur on the older. The growth at the ends of the main branches, the leaders, is pruned by one-third, a half, or two-thirds, depending on whether it is strong, moderate or weak, until its full length is reached. Then it is treated like a side-shoot.

The weather, the soil, the feeding programme, the root-stock and the variety will all affect the fruiting potential of the tree; if you find that the amount of pruning you are doing each winter is producing too much fruit or too much leaf, it must be adjusted, remembering that the more pruning, on the whole, the less fruit and the more shoots.

*Apricots*, fan-trained. Most of the pruning for these is done in spring and summer, but after fruiting or in early winter, one or two of the oldest main branches can be taken away completely, not necessarily every year.

*Morello cherry*, fan-trained. Cut very long bare shoots, which have been fruiting badly, back hard to a conveniently placed dormant bud, untie the remaining shoots, and re-tie, evenly spaced. Cut out any of these which are crowded.

*Figs*, fan-trained. Little needs to be done to figs in winter. New growth is constantly required for fruiting, so two or three of the oldest branches forming some of the ribs of the fan can be cut right down to leave stubs with dormant buds on them. Any shoots with long bare sections which are unlikely to be covered by other new growth are cut to below the bare section, and new shoots should appear from the remaining stem.

*Grape vines*, wall grown. Once the leaves have fallen, vines can be pruned by cutting the side-shoots back to a stump with one or two buds on it, and the topmost leading shoot back by about two thirds.

Liriodendron tulipifera (*tulip tree*) *is a hardy deciduous tree from North America, up to 60m (200ft) tall.*

# Small Trees

| Name | Height metres/ft | Time of flowering; flower colour | Fruit/foliage | Soil/aspect |
|---|---|---|---|---|
| Bay, sweet (*Laurus nobilis*) | 5-9m (15-30ft) | Late spring; creamy | Evergreen; culinary | Any soil; sun and shelter |
| Cornelian cherry (*Cornus mas*) | 5-6m (15-19ft) | Late winter—early spring; yellow | Variegated and yellow-leaved forms available | Any soil; and site |
| Cotoneaster (*Hybridus pendulus*) | 3m (10ft) | Early—mid-summer; cream | Semi-evergreen; red berries | Any soil; shelter |
| Crabapple (*Malus* spp.) | 5-7.5m (15-25ft) | Mid—late spring; white, pink, red | Green or purple; good fruit, edible | Any soil and site |
| Eucryphia | 3.5-9m (12-30ft) | Late summer; white | Evergreen | Acid soil; sun or some shade; shelter from wind |
| Hawthorn (May) *Crataegus* spp.) | 3.5-7.5m (12-25ft) | Late spring—early summer; white, pink, red, some double | Red berries | Any soil and site |
| Holly (*Ilex* spp.) | 3-7.5m (15-25ft) (slow-growing) | Flowers inconspicuous | Evergreen; some variegated, red berries | Any soil; sun or some shade |
| Judas tree (*Cercis siliquastrum*) | 6m (19ft) | Late spring; purple-pink | Flat, dark-red seed pods in autumn | Any soil; sun |
| Laburnum in variety | 5-7.5m (15-25ft) | Late spring—early summer; yellow, some fragrant | Seeds poisonous | Well-drained soil; sun |
| Magnolia in variety | 3-6.5m (10-20ft) | Early spring—early autumn; white, purple, pink; some fragrant | Some evergreen | Preferably acid soil; sun; shelter from wind |
| Maple, Japanese (*Acer palmatum* in variety) | 1.5-2m (4-7ft) (slow-growing) | Flowers inconspicuous | Ornamental leaves | Preferably acid soil; shelter from wind; any aspect |
| Mountain ash (*Sorbus aucuparia* in variety) | 5-9m (15-30ft) | Late spring—early summer; cream | Red, yellow, pink berries | Any aspect and soil |
| *Parrotia persica* | 5m (15ft) spreading | Late winter—early spring; red but insignificant | Good autumn leaf colour | Any soil and site |
| Pear, ornamental (*Pyrus salicifolia pendula*) | 7.5-9m (25-30ft) weeping, slow | | Silver-grey leaves | Well-drained soil; any site |
| Prunus in variety (almond, cherry, plum) | 3-7.5m (10-25ft) | Early—late spring; white, pink, yellow, red | Leaves green, red, purple | Any soil and site |
| Strawberry tree (*Arbutus unedo*) | 5m (15ft) | Mid-autumn—early winter; white, fruit at the same time as the flowers | Evergreen; red fruit | Any soil and site |
| Whitebeam (*Sorbus aria*) | 5-6m (15-19ft) | White; spring | Silver-grey leaves | Any soil and site |
| Willow (*Salix purpurea pendula*) | 5-6m (15-19ft) | Flowers inconspicuous | Blue-green | Any moist soil |

*Medlar, mulberry and quince.* Virtually no pruning is needed for these fruits, beyond the standard treatment of clearing out weak, crowded, dead, diseased or crossing growth. All will fruit satisfactorily without further cutting.

*Peaches and nectarines,* fan-trained. These can be pruned immediately after picking the fruit, or after leaf-fall. The shoots which have fruited are cut back to the replacement shoot and each of these spaced out regularly and tied to the wires. If crowding is unavoidable, some thinning of these shoots can be done.

## Saving scions

If you are proposing to framework-graft apples or pears in the spring to change the variety, the one-year-old shoots cut off in the course of renewal pruning can be used as scions. They should be strong and mature. Heel them in, tied in small bundles, about 15cm (6in) deep in a trench on the north side of a fence or wall; label them securely.

## Protecting

From now until spring, it will be necessary to keep an eye on supports and protection of tender plants, climbers and those which are favoured by birds. Plants vulnerable to

*Protecting plants: a sheet of glass for small alpine plants, sacking right round larger plants, or two rolls of wire netting, padded with straw or bracken and staked.*

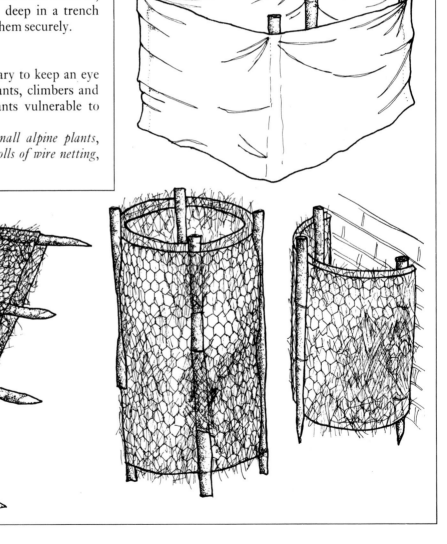

cold, especially north and east winds, are: *Abelia grandiflora*, campsis, ceanothus, *Clematis armandii*, eccremocarpus, escallonia, fremontodendron, fuchsia, hebe (some), hibiscus, summer jasmine, Mexican orange blossom (choisya), phlomis, piptanthus, privet, rock rose (cistus), romneya, *Senecio greyi*, solanum and yucca. All these need some sort of protection.

Weather damage can be in the form of rocking, when hollows form round the trunk or stem bases, which fill up with water and rot the bark, or plants being lifted by frost after planting. Snow and wind can break shoots and branches; bark can split due to cold (cover wound with sealing compound or glasshouse sealing tape), and young shoots are burned by strong cold wind.

Protection against birds may be destroyed by the weather, so renew sprays after heavy rain or snow and make sure that netting is still tightly secured and without unwanted holes after wind.

*A double-flowered form of the almond,* Prunus triloba, *needs to be pruned hard after flowering to encourage the production of new flowering shoots.* P. triloba *is one of a genus of about 430 species of trees and shrubs, including almonds, apricots, cherries, peaches, plums and nectarines, and ornamental plants such as cherry-laurel.*

## Sweeping up
Leaves may still be in need of sweeping up, after a late fall, or burning, if diseased.

## Increasing
When pruning vines, cuttings can be made and used now or stored for increase later. Mature one-year-old shoots are used, to provide cuttings about 30cm (12in) long; these are put in to half their length in a sheltered place outdoors or in a cold frame. In good conditions, these will root without any further ado, but if not, they can be used to provide vine 'eyes' in late winter.

## Treating pests and diseases
Once the pruning is finished, tree and climbing fruits can be winter washed if necessary (see spray chart in Mid-Winter).

To prevent rose black spot and rust overwintering, as far as possible, leaves, fallen shoots and flowers should be raked up from round the plants and burnt. If the large-flowered and cluster-flowered roses are fully dormant, they can be sprayed with a solution of Bordeaux mixture, but it should not be applied if there are still leaves on the plants.

Vines should be brushed down thoroughly with a stiff brush before spraying or painting to get rid of loose bark in which pests and diseases can lurk.

## Plants in flower
Cherry (autumn-flowering, Prunus subhirtella autumnalis), Fatsia, Heather (Calluna vulgaris, Erica carnea varieties), Jasmine (winter-flowering, Jasminum nudiflorum), Laurustinus, Mahonia Charity, Roses, Viburnum farreri and V. Dawn, Winter sweet (Chimonanthus praecox), Witch hazel (Hamamelis mollis)

## Fruits in store
Apple, Medlar, Pear, Quince

# Mid~Winter

Mid-winter is not a good time for outdoor gardening; if the ground is not covered in snow, it is likely to be frozen hard or so wet that it is waterlogged. There are often strong and penetratingly cold winds blowing or thick mist or fog, making it thoroughly unpleasant to be out-of-doors. However, the occasional, sunny, less cold day does occur and mid-winter can be unnaturally mild, resulting in cold and snow in early and mid-spring.

When the weather does improve, you can take the opportunity to finish pruning, do some basic digging and even plant, if the soil is workable; otherwise heel the plants in.

Weather damage should be checked and plant protection, supports and ties reinforced or repaired. Fruit in store should not be forgotten, neither should stratified seeds.

Once pruning is finished, tree fruit can have a winter wash applied to it, if thought necessary. However, unless moss and lichen on the bark of the trees has become very thick, it is preferable to rely on a lightning attack with a spray during the growing season, and let the beneficial insects do most of the work for you.

# At~a~glance diary

**Prepare the soil for:** planting by double digging, manuring at the same time and liming if necessary (but do not lime at the same time as adding manure)

**Plant:** hardy deciduous plants if the weather permits, such as deciduous shrubs and ornamental trees, climbers, roses, hedging plants and fruit trees

**Prune ornamentals:** cut back climbing ornamentals, such as overgrown or crowded honeysuckle, finish pruning of wisteria begun in summer, and prune campsis and summer jasmine before really cold weather;

**Prune fruit:** apple, Morello cherry, medlar, mulberry, pear and quince; finish pruning as early in this season as possible apricot, fig, nectarine, peach and vine

**Protect:** plants against birds, cold, wind, bark gnawing by small/large mammals

**Pests and diseases:** black spot and rust on roses; spray apples, pears, cherries, plums, greengages and other tree fruits with tar-oil winter wash to control over-wintering eggs of aphids and apple sucker and adult scale insects; spray vines with sulphur to control scale insects, and with soft soap for mealy bug

**Check:** stored fruit for damage; stratified seed for attack by mice

**Plan:** garden design and/or cropping programme

# Jobs to do

### Preparing the ground for planting
Basic digging can be started or continued (see Early Winter for method). If the addition of lime will be necessary, digging should be finished as soon as possible, to allow for several weeks between adding organic material and lime.

### Planting
If the weather allows, you can plant any of the woody plants except the evergreens; once planted they must have protection from wind and some protection from frost would be advisable, though snow will act as a protective blanket. If plants have arrived just as the weather becomes unsuitable, heel them in for the time being (see Planting, Late autumn).

### Pruning
By now the pruning of the tree fruits and climbing ornamentals should be finished or well on the way to it. Grape vines in particular should be finished as soon as possible.

### Training
Grape vines which were pruned in early winter should now be partially untied from their supports and allowed to hang downwards for about half their length. This is to make certain that when the buds begin to sprout, growth occurs evenly the whole length of the stem (rod), otherwise too many strong shoots are produced near its end and very few lower down. However, tie them in loosely to prevent wind damage.

### Protecting
It is even more important now than in early winter to make sure that plants are safeguarded against bud pecking

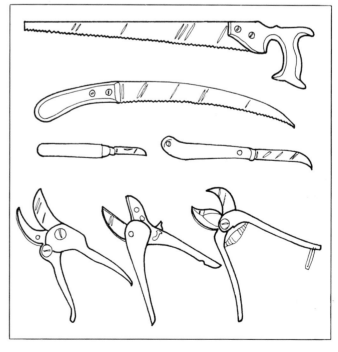

Above, right: *Ivy climbs until it reaches the light and then become tree-like, when it flowers in late summer.* Right: *Tools for pruning include rolcut or parrot-billed secateurs, knives, and various types of saw, including both the folding saw and the rigid straight saw.*

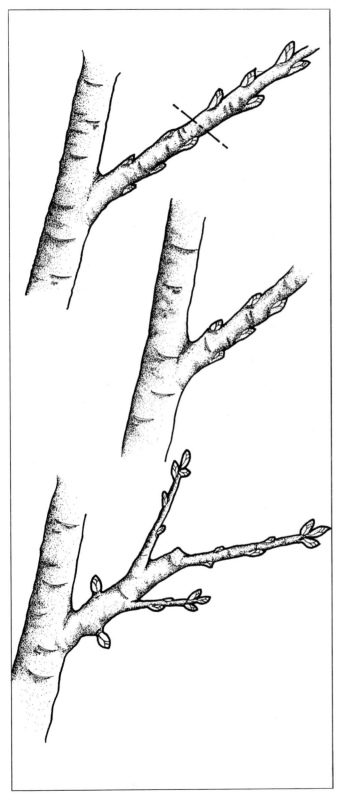

Above: *Berries of* Viburnum davidii *last through winter.*
Left: *Results of pruning. A shoot left unpruned fruits in the third year of its life all along the portion which grew in the first year. If cut, it produces some fruit buds (round and fat) and some new shoots from this length of stem.*
Opposite: *This lawn is shaded by the branches of an apple tree, with euphorbias and ferns clustered at its foot.*

by birds, that supports and ties are secure and strong and that the tender plants have sufficient coverings to enable them to shrug off frost and cold wind.

If real cold has set in, trouble with bark gnawing will start as the small mammals, such as rabbits, hares, mice, voles and rats, begin to run out of their normal food. Young plants recently put in are particularly vulnerable, with their narrow trunks or main stems, from which the bark is easily eaten or torn off in a complete circle. A mature plant will have some difficulty in recovering from this kind of onslaught, but a young one will more than likely be dead by the end of winter.

A cylinder of wire-netting of 1.2cm ($\frac{1}{2}$in) mesh put round the trunk and reaching up to the head, even of a standard, will stop most of the damage. Bush trees sometimes have their lowest branches attached by hares, which are quite capable of standing on their hind legs and leaning on the wire-netting while they gnaw, but this is less serious than attack on the main trunk.

# Control Guide to Fruit Troubles

| Time to spray | Troubles | Treatment |
|---|---|---|
| **APPLES AND PEARS** | | |
| early—late winter (dormant) | aphids, scale and apple sucker | 5% tar-oil winter wash |
| early spring—mid-spring | caterpillar (including winter and | derris |
| (bud burst to green cluster stage of apple | March moths) | |
| or early white bud stage of pear) | | |
| | aphids, apple sucker, capsid bugs, | derris or bioresmethrin |
| | scale insects and pear midge; | |
| | mildew | benomyl or dinocap |
| repeat every 2 weeks | scab disease | benomyl or captan |
| until mid-summer | | |
| mid-spring—start of late spring | mildew | benomyl or dinocap |
| (pink bud stage of apple, | | |
| petal fall stage of pear) | | |
| mid-spring—late spring | apple sawfly | derris |
| (80% petal fall stage of apple) | mildew | benomyl or dinocap |
| start of early summer | red spider mite | derris |
| | mildew | benomyl or dinocap |
| | codling moth | derris |
| 2-3 weeks later (mid-summer) | red spider mite — repeat | derris |
| | codling moth | sacking bands round tree trunks |
| early autumn | winter and March moths | greasebands |
| **PLUMS AND DAMSONS** | | |
| early—late winter (dormant) | aphids | 5% tar-oil winter wash |
| early spring (bud burst to white bud stage) | caterpillars | derris |
| | aphids | derris or bioresmethrin |
| late spring (cotyledon split) | sawfly | derris |
| late spring (post blossom) | red spider mite | derris |
| 10 days later | red spider mite — repeat | derris |
| early summer | red plum maggot | derris |
| 2 weeks later | red plum maggot — repeat | derris |
| **CHERRIES** | | |
| early—late winter | aphids | 5% tar-oil winter wash |
| mid-spring—late spring | caterpillars | derris |
| (bud burst to white bud stage) | aphids | derris or bioresmethrin |
| late summer and twice more | bacterial canker | Bordeaux mixture |
| at 3-week intervals | | |
| **PEACHES, NECTARINES AND APRICOTS** | | |
| early—late winter (dormant) | aphids | 5% tar-oil winter wash |
| mid-winter (bud swelling stage) | peach leaf-curl disease | Bordeaux mixture or lime sulphur |
| 2 weeks later | peach leaf-curl disease — repeat | Bordeaux mixture or lime sulphur |
| early—mid-spring | caterpillars, aphids | derris or bioresmethrin |
| mid-spring (petal fall stage) | red spider mite | derris |
| early summer | aphids | bioresmethrin or quassia |
| mid-summer | aphids | bioresmethrin or quassia |
| early autumn (just before leaf fall) | peach leaf-curl disease | Bordeaux mixture or lime sulphur |
| **GRAPE VINE** | | |
| early winter | scale | sulphur |
| | mealy bug | soft soap |
| early spring | mildew | dinocap, benomyl or sulphur |
| mid-spring | mildew — repeat | dinocap, benomyl or sulphur |
| late spring | mildew — repeat | dinocap, benomyl |
| early summer | red spider mite | derris |
| | mildew | dinocap, benomyl |
| 3 weeks later and at similar intervals as | red spider mite — repeat | derris |
| necessary until the end of summer | mildew | dinocap, benomyl |
| throughout growing season | vine weevil | carbaryl |
| whenever present | | |
| as above | mealy bug | methylated spirits |

Cylinders made of plastic, with ventilation holes in them, can be obtained and used instead of netting. They may be more effective in preventing damage by mice, but it is advisable to lift the cylinders occasionally and make sure the mice have not adopted them as a highly convenient nesting place, with food ready to hand.

There are harmless repellents for small mammals, applied in liquid or powder form, and if you live in an area where deer roam wild, these repellents can be used against them also. Deer can be a great problem to shrubs and trees and sometimes the only solution is a 1.8m (6ft) high barrier all round the orchard or entire garden.

Corylopsis spicata *prefers an acid or neutral soil, but will grow in a chalky one, provided it is deep.*

## Treating pests and diseases

Once fruit trees become fully dormant, they can be sprayed with a winter wash of tar-oil, if thought necessary. However, it has been found that such a wash kills the over-wintering forms of a good many beneficial insects which are predators of the pests and it also destroys the mosses and lichen on which red spider mite feeds in summer. Thus, with the removal of predators and its natural food, the mite attacks leaves and builds up very large populations in summer. This seriously weakens the trees but, unfortunately, chemical control is now very difficult as the mite is resistant to the sprays based on phosphorus, such as malathion and dimethoate.

Tar-oil washes now are mainly used for removing lichens and moss from mature and old trees and should only be used occasionally.

The control programme which follows gives details of various troubles which may occur on tree fruits and grape vines, the control method and the time to apply it. However, there is no need to use all the chemicals mentioned every year; in fact, it is preferable not to. Apply them only as a preventive, if trouble occurred the year before, in the case of scab, mildew, peach-leaf curl and bacterial canker. For insect pests, such as greenfly and caterpillars, it is generally sufficient to spray or treat when the first one or two are seen, but for sawfly, codling moth, red spider mite, red plum maggot and capsid, they should automatically be applied when suggested.

It is quite possible to obtain perfectly adequate fruit crops without doing any spraying at all, particularly if you ensure that the trees are properly pruned, fed and watered all through their lives. They may not be completely free of the odd spot or nibble but a natural balance will be set up between beneficial and damaging insects, so that no one species gets out of hand. The fungus diseases can cause more trouble, but even so, a constitutionally strong tree will be much less badly infected.

## Checking

Some varieties of apples and pears may have been in store now for three months and a thorough looking-over will decrease wastage from rots, frost and attack by mice and rats. Seeds which have been stratified will not be harmed by cold; the colder it is the better, as this 'vernalization', as it is called, is nature's way of breaking dormancy. Without it some seeds never germinate. However, hungry mice can quietly decimate your seed collection, and a check to make sure the frame gauze or netting is in place takes only a minute or two.

## Planning

You can take the opportunity resulting from this lull in active gardening to do some thinking and planning, to look back over your garden notebook for the year and consider changes or innovations in the garden layout or cropping plan. One of the fascinations of gardening is that you can always improve on your garden's appearance, as your experience and knowledge increases.

Specialist books, catalogues from specialist nurseries, the year books of specialist societies such as those for roses, camellias, fruit, and so on, will all supply more information and more help for good cultivation. New methods of growing some plant or other frequently appear, new ways and chemicals for controlling or preventing disease and pest trouble are regularly produced and new hybrids and varieties provide mouth-watering choices every year.

*Cercidiphyllum japonicum is an easily-grown tree, $4\frac{1}{2}$-12m (15-40ft) high, with good autumn leaf colouring.*

## Plants in flower

Cherry (autumn-flowering, Prunus subhirtella autumnalis), Garrya elliptica, Heather (Erica carnea in variety), Jasmine (winter-flowering, Jasminum nudiflorum), Laurustinus, Viburnum farreri and V. Dawn, Winter sweet (Chimonanthus praecox), witch hazel (Hamamelis mollis)

## Fruits in store

Apple, Pear, Quince

# Late Winter

After the peace of mid-winter, there begins to be a definite feeling of revival in the air in late winter. Even if there is still snow about, the days are appreciably longer and the earliest shrub and tree buds, willow, clematis and perhaps even roses, will begin to sprout towards the end of this season. You will need to finish the winter pruning as near the beginning of late winter as possible and some advance rose pruning may be necessary.

Similarly, planting of deciduous shrubs and trees should be finished, digging completed, and winter tar-oil spraying must be got out of the way before the buds begin to unfold, otherwise they will be damaged.

With the rising of the sap, there are two new jobs to do which would not have been of much benefit done earlier: feeding the tree fruit and mulching some of the shrubs and climbers. Vacant soil can also be treated, with lime.

# At~a~glance diary

**Prepare the soil for:** planting heeled-in plants now, or for planting in early spring such subjects as the hardier evergreens and deciduous shrubs and trees; also double dig if not already done for planting tender shrubs in mid-spring–late spring

**Plant:** deciduous shrubs, trees and climbers, provided that the ground is not water-logged, frozen or covered in snow

**Prune:** finish tree fruits; finish climbing ornamentals as for Early Winter; also prune Abelia x grandiflora, clematis, Garrya elliptica, japonica, winter jasmine, roses (early seasons)

**Feed:** tree fruit, vines, with a compound or straight fertilizer as necessary

**Lime:** acidic soils

**Check:** protection against birds, cold, wind, mammals; check ties and supports

**Increase:** vines from vine 'eyes'

**Pests and diseases:** spray tar-oil winter wash on fruit trees (not apricots, nectarines or peaches) as early as possible, as it will damage shoots and leaves which may soon appear; spray apricots, peaches and nectarines with fungicide for peach leaf curl; spray vines against scale or mealy bug if not already done

# Jobs to do

### Preparing the ground for planting

As you may still have heeled-in plants to put in or may be expecting new arrivals in early spring, such as evergreens, the ground will need forking and dressing with bonemeal (see Mid-Autumn). If it is still hard with frost, covered with snow or sodden, wait until soil conditions improve.

It is rather late to do basic digging, unless it is of ground in which you intend to plant tender shrubs in mid- or late spring; the two- to three-month gap in that case will be sufficient to allow the soil to digest the organic matter and other nutrients added and settle down again.

### Planting

Although late autumn and, to some extent, early winter, are the best times for planting, deciduous woody plants (unless tender) can be put in at any time when dormant. The only restrictions are the state of the soil and very bad weather. If you do plant now, make sure those that need it are firmly supported and protected against prevailing winds which, with the change of season in a few weeks' time, will begin to blow with gale force strength.

### Pruning

If tree fruit pruning is not finished in late winter, it will be too late to do it afterwards without damaging the trees and upsetting their management. Wisteria should be pruned, if not yet done, together with other climbing ornamentals mentioned in Early Winter. Other shrubs to prune now include the following:

*Abelia* x *grandiflora* At the end of late winter, these can be tidied up by cutting off weak new shoots completely, cutting back long shoots and removing one or two of the oldest stems to ground level in some years. In cold seasons and districts, wait until late in early spring before doing this.

*Clematis* The large-flowered kinds which flower from late in early summer right through almost until autumn will probably start to sprout this season, if they have not already done so; some shoots, in early seasons, can be

*The camellia's flowers may be pink, white, red, rose-pink or striped with any of these colours. It grows in acid or neutral soil, with a little shade and protection from the sun in the early morning in spring.*

30cm (12in) long by now. Even if they are, the main stems should still be cut hard back to within 90cm (36in) of the ground, to just above a pair of buds. As they are very low down on the stems, this pair of buds will probably be still dormant, but cutting will encourage sprouting.

The large-flowered clematis that flower in late spring and early summer do better with much less ruthless treatment. Since it will now be possible to see where the dead growth is, this can be cut off; the live new shoots are then cut back to remove not much more than the tips, to just above the first pair of dormant buds. To make the most of their flowering display, these shoots should then be spread out evenly and separately and tied in position.

Clematis planted in autumn and earlier in the winter should now be cut back hard to just above a pair of still dormant buds, about 15–30cm (6–12in) above ground.

*Garrya elliptica* Pruning of this is mainly to prevent the bush becoming too crowded, as it is enthusiastic about growing, so some catkin-bearing growth should be removed as soon as the catkins have finished, to let in light and air, and some of the oldest shoots can be completely removed. Pruning should always be done before new growth begins.

*Japonica* The tendency of this shrub to produce thin, straggly shoots without flowers needs checking, so such growth can be cut back now before flowering, to leave a stub with one or two buds on it. Watch for the flower buds, which will be round and fat.

Above: *The evergreen hedging plants, such as box or yew, are very suitable for topiary work of the kind shown here.*
Below: *Stretch a line taut along the top of a hedge as a guide for keeping the top level while you trim it.*

*Winter jasmine* As soon as this has finished flowering, which may not be until early spring, cut the strong flowered shoots back by about three-quarters of their length and the remainder to leave stubs with one or two pairs of buds on them. Alternatively, this rather hard pruning can be replaced by simply thinning some of the flowered shoots, to give the remainder room to breathe. In this case when pruning, remove about half the length of flowered shoot.

*Roses* In some seasons and some districts, pruning of large-flowered and cluster-flowered kinds can start during late winter. Climbers can have what little pruning they need done at the same time; dead growth is cut off, flowering growth which has become too old to flower well should be cut back to a strong new shoot, and small side-shoots can be cut to about 7.5cm (3in) or one bud.

## Feeding

Late winter is an appropriate time to feed tree fruits, if they need it. If the soil was carefully prepared before planting and is subsequently regularly topdressed with rotted organic matter fertilizers may not be necessary at all. However, sandy or shallow soils are likely to need annual additions of fertilizer, unless you are clever with the use of manure or garden compost.

*The leaves of the stag's-horn sumach*, Rhus typhina, *turn to glorious shades of orange and then crimson in autumn. The fruiting spikes also turn crimson.*

Main mineral nutrients needed are nitrogen, phosphorus and potassium and these can be obtained singly as, for example, sulphate of ammonia (nitrogen, N) or sulphate of potash (potassium, K), or as compounds containing all three in varying percentages. The percentage will be shown on the container in the form of an 'analysis'—thus: N 5 per cent, $P_2O_5$ (phosphorus, P) 7 per cent, $K_2O$ 9 per cent, so helping you to decide which is the most suitable for your plants.

Nitrogen helps with shoot and leaf growth, phosphorus is needed by the roots and potassium is the maturing nutrient, encouraging flower and fruit production. These divisions are very general and the subject of nutrients and their interaction is extremely complex, but remembering that the above are the main roles of these nutrients, you can apply them according to whether your plants are cropping too much, moderately, or running to leaf.

Rates of application of the compound fertilizers will be given on their containers; the 'straights' are applied as follows:

Sulphate of ammonia (N),
15–30g per sq m (½–1oz per sq yd)
Nitro-chalk (N and lime)     30g per sq m (1oz per sq yd)
Hoof-and-horn meal (N)     60g per sq m (2 oz per sq yd)
Superphosphate (P)     30–90g per sq m (1–3oz per sq yd)
Bonemeal (P)     up to 180g per sq m (6oz per sq yd)
Sulphate of potash (K) 15–30g per sq m (½–1oz per sq yd)
Wood ash (K)     up to 240g per sq m (8oz per sq yd)

Nitro-chalk is a convenient way of ensuring that the stone fruits get the calcium they need but if nitro-chalk is not used, lime should be applied every four or five years or so at about 240g per sq m (8oz per sq yd), depending on the degree of acidity of the soil.

There are many other mineral nutrients also required by plants; some are called the 'trace' elements as the plant requires them only in minute quantities, to the order of parts per million, and others such as sulphur, iron and calcium are the minor elements, coming between the two. All have different functions within the plants and are dependent on one another to some extent and all are present in the average garden soil, provided it is treated with rotted organic matter in sufficient quantity to ward off deficiencies.

If the state of the soil permits, grape vines can also be fed and topdressed. Weeds, leaves, last spring's mulch remains and other rubbish should be raked carefully off the area beneath which the roots are growing. Then a mixture of rotted organic matter and loam in equal parts, combined with a proprietary vine compound fertilizer, can be spread over the clean soil surface to a depth of about 7.5cm (3in).

## Liming

Soil that is proved by a soil test to be very acid in its reaction can be treated by liming so that it becomes only slightly acid. This degree of acidity is probably the most suitable one for growing the widest range of woody plants; tree fruits, the ericaceous plants such as rhododendrons and most of the heathers, in particular, do not do well on

Left: *Winter flowers are often fragrant, and the winter sweet,* Chimonanthus praecox, *is no exception.* Opposite: *The Kurume azaleas are a selection of some of the best and grow superbly in light woodland conditions.*

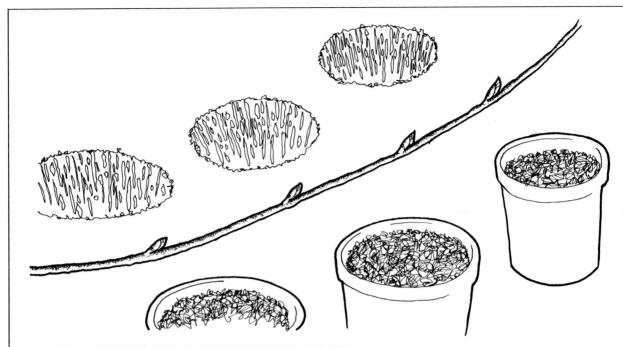

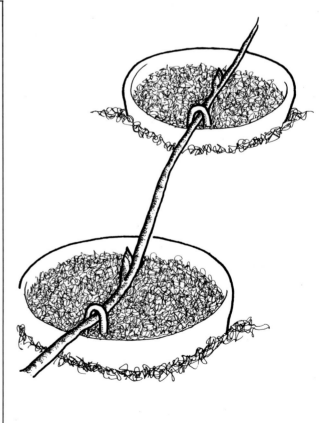

*Layering a clematis: Use a shoot at least 18 months old, bend it to form a U, peg it down into a potful of compost, and plunge the pot. Do not layer in cold weather.*

chalky soils or those with a markedly alkaline reaction. If you have a choice, choose a neutral to mildly acidic soil when planting.

Be very careful not to overlime, as reduction of alkalinity is a slow and difficult process; from the soil-testing kit you will know the quantity to apply, depending on the degree of acidity. Ground limestone or chalk are slow acting and can be used at up to 1 kg per square m (2 lb per sq yd), though this amount is a rather heavy dressing.

Do not apply lime until at least six weeks have elapsed since the application of organic matter and do not apply at the same time as sulphate of ammonia, basic slag or super-phosphate.

## Checking
Routine checks of protections of various kinds, supports and ties are advisable some time in late winter. Bark gnawing may still be a serious potential problem, as the animals get hungrier towards the end of winter.

## Increasing
The only plant which can be multiplied now is the grape vine and then only if you can supply warmth. The hard-

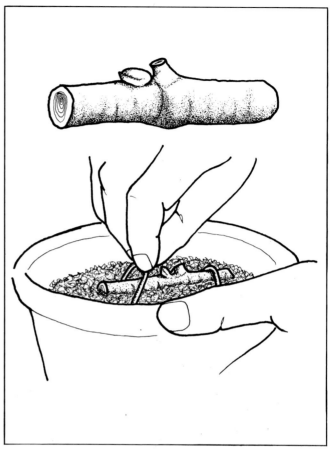

Above, left: *Cornelian cherry, Cornus mas, is a small tree which flowers in late winter, and has bright red, edible fruits in hot summers. In autumn, the leaves are a red-purple.*
Above, right: *Vines can be increased from vine 'eyes'. Cut a short length of stem with a dormant bud, pin it down in compost, and it will root with the help of heat.*

wood cuttings made in early winter can be used to supply 5cm (2in) lengths of shoot, each with a bud or 'eye' on it. The cutting is pegged down into cuttings compost in a 7.5cm (3in) pot. In a temperature of 10–15°C (50–60°F) and with bottom heat of 21°C (70°F) supplied to the compost rooting will take about three weeks.

### Treating pests and diseases
If you propose to use a tar-oil winter wash on fruit trees in winter, to cut out some of the summer spraying and to clean the trees of mosses and lichens, it should be applied early this season, as it damages leaves and young shoots which can soon start to appear. Peaches, nectarines and apricots may need a fungicidal spray against leaf-curl, put on just before the buds sprout and repeated two weeks later to cover the young developing leaves (see chart in Mid-Winter for control of fruit troubles and treatment section at end of book).

## Plants in flower
Camellia (shelter), Cornelian cherry (Cornus mas), Cherry (Autumn-flowering, Prunus subhirtella autumnalis), Clematis, Honeysuckle (Lonicera standishii), Japonica (Chaenomeles speciosa), Jasmine (winter-flowering, Jasminum nudiflorum), Laurustinus, Mahonia japonica (shelter), Rhododendron, Sarcococca, Skimmia (shelter), Viburnum farreri, V. Dawn, Winter sweet (Chimonanthus praecox), Witch hazel (Hamamelis mollis)

## Fruits in store
Apple, Pear, Quince

# A Small Selection of Flowering & Foliage Shrubs

| Name | Height spread cm/in | Time of flowering; flower colour | Foliage/bark/ berries | Soil/aspect | Remarks |
|---|---|---|---|---|---|
| Azalea in variety | 45-150 x 45-120cm (18-60 x 18-48in) | mid-spring—early summer; all colours except blue | some evergreen | acid soil; light shade | |
| Berberis | 30-300 x 30-300cm (12-120 x 12-120cm) | spring, summer; orange, yellow | some evergreen, leaves coloured; berries red or blue | any soil and aspect | |
| Broom (Cytisus and Genista spp.) | prostrate 270 x 60-300cm (108 x 24-120in) | spring—summer; yellow, pink, white | some have bright green stems | well-drained soil; sun | not very limy soil |
| Buddleia in variety | 180-240 x 150cm (72-96 x 60in) | early—late summer; purple, blue, red, white, orange | | any soil and aspect | *B. globosa* needs shelter |
| Camellia in variety | 300 x 180cm (120 x 72in) | early—mid-spring; pink, white, red | evergreen | acid/neutral soil; light shade | shelter from north and east |
| Ceanothus in variety | 120-360 x 150-210cm (58-144 x 60-84in) | mid-spring—autumn; blue | some evergreen | well-drained soil; sun | some slightly tender |
| Cistus in variety (rock rose) | 90-240 x 90-150cm (36-96 x 36-60in) | late spring—mid-summer; pink, white, purple | evergreen, aromatic | well-drained soil; sun | slightly tender |
| Clematis | From 300cm (120in) to 7.5m (8yd); some climbing | spring—summer; purple, blue, white, pink, red | | any except light | some are better colour with north aspect |
| Deutzia in variety | 90-180 x 90-150cm (36-72 x 36-60in) | late spring—early summer; white, pink, purple-pink | | any soil and site | |
| Fuchsia in variety | 30-300 x 30-240cm (12-120 x 12-96in) | mid-summer—early autumn; purple, red, white, pink magenta, blue-purple | | any soil and aspect | slightly tender |
| Heather | From 12.5 x 45cm (5 x 18in) to 300 x 240cm (120 x 96in) | winter—mid-autumn; pink, red, purple, white | foliage yellow, red, orange, bronze, grey, green | acid soil; sun | add peat to soil |
| Hebe in variety | 22.5-150 x 22.5-120cm (9-60 x 9-48in) | late spring, summer—autumn; purple, blue, white, pink, red, magenta | evergreen, green, grey yellow-variegated | any well-drained soil; sun | |
| Honeysuckle | 300-600cm (120-240in) climbing; 90-300 x 90-240cm (36-120 x 36-96in) shrubby | early summer—mid-autumn, winter; red-purple, cream, yellow, orange; some fragrant | some evergreen, or variegated | most soils; a little shade | |
| Hydrangea (round-headed) | 90-180 x 90-180cm (36-72 x 36-72in) | mid-summer—early autumn; red, pink, blue, white, mauve | | moist soil; a little shade | good by the sea; blue varieties in acid soil |

# A Small Selection of Flowering & Foliage Shrubs

| Name | Height spread cm/in | Time of flowering; flower colour | Foliage/bark/ berries | Soil/aspect | Remarks |
|---|---|---|---|---|---|
| Hypericum in variety | 30-150 x 120cm (12-60 x 48in) | mid-summer—early autumn; yellow | some evergreen | any soil; sun or little shade | *H. calycinum* invasive |
| Ivy (hedera) in variety | climbing | flowers inconspicuous | evergreen, some variegated cream or yellow | any soil; a little shade | small-leaved varieties slow-growing |
| Japonica (chaenomeles) | 90-240 x 120-300cm (36-96 x 48-120in) | early—late spring; pink, red, white | | any soil and site | |
| Jasmine, winter (*J. nudiflorum*) | 360 x 300cm (144 x 120in) | late autumn/late winter; yellow | | any soil and site | good facing north |
| Jew's mallow (kerria) | 240 x 180cm (96 x 72in) | mid—late spring; yellow | | any soil and site | double form the best |
| Lavender | 45-90 x 60-120cm (18-36 x 24-48in) | mid—late summer; lavender, white, blue; fragrant | evergrey | well-drained soil; sun | |
| Lilac in variety | 90-450 x 150-360cm (36-180 x 60-144in) | spring—summer; white, red, lilac; fragrant | | any soil; sun or some shade | |
| Magnolia in variety (shrubby) | 210-360 x 150-300cm (84-144 x 60-120in) | spring—early autumn; white, purple; some fragrant | some evergreen | acid soil; sun | need shelter |
| Mahonia in variety | 120-300 x 150-210cm (48-120 x 60-84in) | winter—spring; yellow; fragrant | evergreen | any soil and site | do better with shelter |
| Mexican orange blossom (*Choisya ternata*) | 180 x 120cm (72 x 84in) | late spring, early autumn; white; fragrant | evergreen | well-drained soil; sun | not quite hardy |
| Philadelphus (mock orange) | 90-450 x 90-300cm (36-180 x 36-120in) | early—mid-summer; white; fragrant | | any soil and site | |
| Pyracantha in variety | 180-360 x 210-300cm (72-144 x 84-120in) | early summer; white | evergreen; berries red, orange, yellow | any soil; sun or some shade | good as wall plants |
| Rhododendron in variety | 23-600 x 23-300cm (9-240 x 9-120in) as shrubs | late winter—late summer; all colours | evergreen | acid soil; a little shade | |
| *Senecio greyi* | 90-120 x 120cm (36-48 x 48in) | early—mid-summer; yellow | evergrey | any soil; sun | not hardy in severe winters |
| Spiraea in variety | 45-210 x 45-150cm (18-84 x 18-60in) | spring, mid—late summer; white, pink, red | | any soil; sun or some shade | |
| Virginia creeper (*Parthenocissus quinquefolia*) | 21m (70ft) climbing | inconspicuous flowers | brilliant autumn leaf colour | any soil and aspect | |
| Weigela (diervilla) | 90-150 x 50-150cm (36-60 x 36-60in) | late spring—early summer; pink, red, white, salmon | one variety, yellow-leaved | any soil and site | |
| Wisteria | 30m (100ft) climbing | spring—early summer, late summer; purple, white | | rich moist soil; sun | |
| Witch hazel (hamamelis) | 210-300 x 150-240cm (84-120 x 60-96in) | winter, autumn; yellow or bronze-red | | acid soil; sun or some|shade | slow-growing |

# Fruit Varieties

The following list of fruit varieties gives a description of the fruit, the season of flowering, the season of ripening, the period of storage (if any) and the names of suitable pollinators. A few varieties are self-fertile, others must have pollinators, and a few others will only set fruit with certain varieties, or need two different pollinating varieties. Fig, medlar, mulberry and quince are not included in the list, delicious though they are, because, in each case, there is only one variety available.

C=Culinary     D=Dessert

| Name | | Description | Season of flowering | Ripe | Storage | Pollinators |
|---|---|---|---|---|---|---|
| **APPLE** | | | | | | |
| Bramley's Seedling | C | green | late spring | mid-autumn | late-autumn—mid-spring | Cox's Orange, Grenadier, Tydeman's Early Worcester (T.E.W.) |
| Cox's Orange Pippin | D | yellow, flushed orange | late spring | early—mid-autumn | mid-autumn—mid-winter | Sunset, Fortune, Grenadier, T.E.W. |
| d'Arcy Spice | D | brown-green | late spring | late in mid-autumn | late autumn—mid-spring | Winston |
| Egremont Russet | D | yellow, with brown russet | early in late spring | mid-autumn | late autumn—early winter | Fortune, James Grieve, Sunset |
| Fortune | D | yellow-striped red | late spring | early—mid-autumn | | Cox's, James Grieve, Sunset, T.E.W. |
| Grenadier | C | yellow-green | late spring | late summer—early autumn | | Cox's, Fortune, James Grieve |
| James Grieve | D | heavily striped red | late spring | early autumn | | Egremont Russet, Fortune, Grenadier |
| Sturmer Pippin | D | pale green, some russet | late spring | late in mid-autumn | late autumn—mid-spring | T.E.W., Grenadier, Cox's, Fortune |
| Sunset | D | dull yellow, flushed red | late spring | mid-autumn | late autumn—early winter | James Grieve, Egremont Russet |
| Tydeman's Early Worcester (T.E.W.) | D | green, striped red | late spring | late summer | | Grenadier, Cox's, James Grieve, Fortune |
| Winston | D | flushed and striped red | late spring | late autumn | early winter—early spring | d'Arcy Spice, Cox's |
| **APRICOT** | | | | | | |
| Farmingdale | | yellow-orange, pink-flushed | early spring | early in late summer | | self-fertile |
| Moorpark | | brown-orange | early spring | late summer | | self-fertile |
| **CHERRY** | | | | | | |
| Bigarreau Napoleon | | yellow, flushed red | mid-spring | late summer | | Merton Glory |
| Early Rivers | | black | mid-spring | early summer | | Merton Favourite |
| Merton Bigarreau | | black | mid-spring | mid-summer | | Merton Glory, Merton Favourite, Morello |
| Morello (cooking) | | red | mid-spring | late summer | | self-fertile |
| **DAMSON** | | | | | | |
| Farleigh Damson | | blue-black | mid—late spring | middle or early autumn | | Shropshire Damson |

| Variety | | Colour | Flowering | Ready | Keeping | Pollination |
|---|---|---|---|---|---|---|
| Shropshire Prune | | blue-black | mid—late spring | middle of early autumn | | self-fertile |
| **GRAPE** | | | | | | |
| Black Hamburgh | | black | early summer | late summer—early autumn | | self-fertile |
| Buckland Sweetwater | | green to pale yellow | early summer | middle of late summer | | self-fertile |
| Royal Muscadine | | green to pale yellow | early summer | early autumn | | self-fertile |
| **GREENGAGE** | | | | | | |
| Cambridge Greengage | | green | mid-spring | late summer | | Victoria plum |
| Jefferson's Gage | | yellow-green | mid-spring | early autumn | | Reine Claude de Bavay |
| Reine Claude de Bavay | | yellow-green | mid-spring | mid-autumn | | self-fertile |
| **NECTARINE** | | | | | | |
| Humboldt | | orange with red flush | mid-spring | late summer | | self-fertile |
| Lord Napier | | green-yellow, crimson flush | early in mid-spring | late summer | | self-fertile |
| **PEACH** | | | | | | |
| Duke of York | | crimson | early-mid-spring | late in mid-summer | | self-fertile |
| Peregrine | | red with yellow flesh | early-mid-spring | early in late summer | | self-fertile |
| Rochester | | yellow, red flush | early-mid-spring | middle of late summer | | self-fertile |
| **PEAR** | | | | | | |
| Beurré Hardy | D | russet with red flush | mid-spring | early autumn | mid-autumn | Conference, Fertility |
| Catillac | C | green | late in mid-spring | late autumn | late autumn/mid-winter | Fertility, Williams', Beurré Hardy |
| Conference | D | pale green | mid-spring | early in mid-autumn | late autumn | self-fertile |
| Doyenné du Comice | D | yellow, pale red flush | mid-spring | pick late in early autumn | mid-late autumn | Conference, Fertility, Josephine de Malines, Beurré Hardy |
| Fertility | D | orange-brown | late in mid-spring | early in mid-autumn | | Conference, Vicar of Winkfield |
| Jargonelle | D | pale yellow | mid-spring | late summer | | Beurré Hardy, Conference |
| Josephine de Malines | D | yellow with grey russet | mid-spring | late in mid-autumn | late autumn—early winter | Conference, Comice, Fertility, Williams' |
| Vicar of Winkfield | C | green to yellow | early in mid-spring | late in mid-autumn | early—mid-winter | Easter Beurré, Conference |
| Williams' Bon Chrétien | D | pale yellow | mid-spring | early autumn | | Josephine de Malines, Fertility, Conference |
| Winter Nelis | D | green-yellow | late in mid-spring | late in mid-autumn | late autumn—mid-winter | Beurré Hardy, Josephine de Malines |
| **PLUM** | | | | | | |
| Czar | C | reddish purple | mid-spring | mid-summer | | self-fertile |
| Kirke's Blue | D | reddish blue | late in mid-spring | early autumn | | Farleigh Damson, Marjorie's Seedling |
| Marjorie's Seedling | C & D | black | late in mid-spring | early—mid-autumn | | self-fertile |
| River's Early | C | blue-purple | mid-spring | mid-summer | | self-fertile |
| Victoria | C & D | red | mid-spring | late summer | | self-fertile |

# Controls & Treatments

Prevention is better than cure—if you follow this principle when growing plants, you will save yourself time and expense. A good start with proper planting, followed by ensuring that food and water are supplied as needed, combined with careful pruning and safeguarding against extreme weather conditions, will result in strong plants able to withstand pest and disease infestation with little or no appreciable effect.

Occasionally you may have to resort to a specific method of control, in epidemic years especially; try to choose the most natural method first and use chemicals only as a last resort. If you have to use chemicals regularly, it is a sign that your plant management is poor or that you are trying to grow plants unsuited to the conditions of your garden.

Insect pests can be divided into two groups: the suckers and the biters. Aphids (greenfly, blackfly, mealy plum aphis, woolly aphis), leafhoppers, scale and mealy bug are some of the suckers, which live on the sap they withdraw from leaves, shoots and sometimes flowers. Derris, bioresmethrin and quassia are some of the safest chemicals to use against such pests.

The biters are mostly caterpillars, also slugs, maggots, wasps and such insects as the rose leaf-cutting bee, rose chafer beetles and vine weevils. Derris can be used for most of these also and is most efficient when at its freshest and

Above, left: *Aphids of various kinds cause a great deal of trouble by sucking the sap from leaves. These green fly are shown in their winged and unwinged forms.* Above, right: *The tawny mining bee, a solitary bee, makes holes in soil and helps to pollinate blossom.*

there is a good quantity of rotenone present. If slugs appear, methiocarb pellets will be an effective control, or use grit on the soil round soft, vulnerable shoots.

Some of the fungus diseases can be very serious: these include honey fungus, cherry bacterial canker and fireblight, and control is more difficult. Others are persistent, needing regular spraying for several months, although the new systemic fungicide, benomyl, has proved to be very useful for these. Many fungicides are protective rather than eradicant and so need to be applied repeatedly.

Bacterial diseases are hardly troublesome on woody plants; virus diseases occur mostly in the tree fruits in such forms as 'chat' fruits and rubbery wood. However, nurserymen take great care to use clean stocks and scions and much of the fruit available in Britain has been cleared under the EMLA testing programme, run jointly by East Malling and Long Ashton fruit research stations.

Nutrient deficiencies are mainly of iron or magnesium and appear on plants growing in strongly alkaline soils;

they can be put right with sequestered compounds of these nutrients and by reducing the alkalinity with peat, acidic fertilizers and sulphur. Such remedies are long-term ones and need skill in use; it is better to test the soil before planting, so that you can put in plants appropriate to the soil acidity.

Harmless repellents can be used to ward off such small mammals as mice, rabbits and voles and larger ones, too—deer in particular; quassia, extremely bitter, is a good one. Aluminium ammonium sulphate, anthraquinone and thiram are others.

Remember that there is a whole army of 'beneficial' insects, which are predatory on the pests, working for you; the less you spray, the more they will thrive and so maintain a balance between the various insect species. Once you begin to spray, especially the tree fruits, you run a great risk of ensuring that one pest breeds unchecked; in a monotype planting of—say—apples, it then spreads rapidly.

Remember also that bees and other pollinating insects are harmed by most chemical sprays, so never spray when the plants are in flower, except possibly when most of the blossom has set or fallen, and then do it late in the evening. When you have finished spraying, clean thoroughly all the sprayers and apparatus used and keep all chemicals out of the reach of pets and children at all times. Also, make sure the containers remain clearly labelled.

Another group of chemicals you may wish to use are those contained in weedkillers. Some are undoubtedly very useful and so far their application has not appeared to harm the soil. Simazine will keep the ground clear of weeds for twelve months; paraquat and diquat will kill seedling, annual and small weeds by disrupting the mechanism which produces chlorophyll, and dichlobenil will keep the ground round certain shrubs, roses, and trees free of all weeds, including perennials, for at least the growing season.

The latest weed killing chemical, glyphosate, combines some of the virtues of paraquat and dichlobenil, since it kills the plants through the top growth but is inactivated when it reaches the soil and will effectively control perennials as well as annuals and small weeds. Even the most persistent of weeds, such as bindweed, ground-elder, oxalis and horsetail, succumb to it. It has no effect on the soil flora and fauna.

The following is a list of pests and diseases specific to certain shrubs, trees, fruit and roses; details are given of appearance, damage, life-history and control. Do not assume that they will all automatically ravage your plants; one or more may do so, in some years, but some you may never have to contend with.

*The cockchafer beetle can do much damage by eating flowers; its grubs feed on the roots of plants.*

### Roses
Black spot: fungus disease; fringed black spots 0.6cm ($\frac{1}{4}$in) wide on leaves. May start from early spring and can defoliate bushes in bad attacks. Pick off, rake up and burn infected leaves; spray with benomyl or captan as makers direct.

Canker: fungus disease; bark on stems cracked and flaking off in patches, especially near to soil level. Worst in humid districts and badly drained soil. Pare off with knife to healthy wood or cut infected shoots off to healthy growth. Improve soil drainage and increase supplies of phosphorus, calcium and/or magnesium.

Chafer beetle: insect; large brown or black flying beetles, which eat holes in flowers, flower buds and leaves, present in late spring and early summer. Control difficult; HCH (BHC) sometimes helps.

*Mildew on roses infects the leaves and flower stems, as well as the shoot stems; it can badly stunt a plant.*

Leaf-cutting bee: insect; adults similar to honey bees, remove semi-circular pieces from edge of leaf for making nests. Effect on plant is negligible and control is unnecessary.

Leaf-rolling sawfly: insect; maggots feed in rolled-up leaf margins and leaves wither. In bad attacks much defoliation occurs. Adult lays eggs on leaves in late spring and mid-summer. Spray HCH (BHC) at two- to three-week intervals to prevent adults laying eggs, otherwise hand-pick infested leaves as soon as seen and destroy.

Mildew: fungus disease; white powdery patches on young leaves and tips of shoots from early spring; flower buds and flowers can also be infected. Disease spreads rapidly in badly ventilated sites, at beginning of growing season and in late summer and early autumn. Cut the infected parts off as soon as seen; make sure plants have sufficient soil moisture and improve spacing of plants, branches or shoots. Spray benomyl, dinocap or a sulphur-containing fungicide.

Rust: fungus disease; raised brown-red spots, later turning black, on undersides of lower and older leaves, from late spring to late summer, mostly late in the summer. Collect and destroy infected leaves, as spores can overwinter on them; spray plants with a protective spray such as thiram or zineb, at two- to three-week intervals.

*Shrubs, trees and fruit*

Apple and pear canker: fungus disease; bark cracks, swells and flakes off. If branch or shoot encircled, it dies above canker. Disease enters through injuries, is worst in humid conditions and wet soil. Pare off diseased area back to healthy wood and paint wound with sealing compound or grafting wax. If too large, cut off affected part to below infection and treat cut area as above.

Apple codling moth: insect; pinkish grub feeds on pips and centre of apple from middle of early summer to end of mid-summer. Attacked apples may turn reddish, fall prematurely; collect and destroy. Apply sacking or corrugated cardboard bands to tree trunks late in mid-summer. Spray derris in the middle of early summer and again three weeks later if a bad attack is suspected. Repeat in late summer for second generation.

Apple (and plum) sawfly: insect; caterpillar which is dirty white with brown head, feeds on the flesh of young apples in late spring and early summer. Long, ribbon-like, corky scars on apple skin are also sawfly damage. Destroy infested fruits; spray g-HCH (BHC) at 80 per cent petal fall stage in bad infestations.

Apple and pear scab: fungus disease; infects leaves from early spring to mid-summer and is particularly bad in warm, rainy seasons. Black spots on leaves, brown markings down central vein of leaf and black spots on fruits, which later crack and rot. Infected young shoots have blistered bark, in which spores over-winter, for one year on apples and up to five years on pears. Cut off all such shoots when pruning in winter and destroy; collect and burn all fallen infected leaves and fruits during season and in autumn and spray with captan, benomyl, or sulphur-containing fungicide as in spray guide (see Mid-Winter).

Armillaria mellea *see* Honey fungus.

Azalea gall: fungus disease: young leaves thickened and twisted, with grey-white bloom on upper surface, and plants can be killed. Evergreen azaleas only are attacked. Pick off leaves and destroy; spray remainder with zineb to maintain protection.

Cherry (plum, peach) bacterial canker: bacterial disease; leaves in late spring have small round brown spots, which drop out, leaving 'shotholes'. Bark cracks and flakes off, may girdle shoot, branch or main trunk, all of which subsequently die. Leaves on such branches are pale green or yellow. Canker infection occurs in autumn through injuries. Obtain trees with resistant rootstocks; spray Bordeaux mixture at leaf-fall in autumn, again just before blossom opens and at petal fall. Remove unhealthy parts, treat wounds and do any pruning in spring or in summer immediately after picking.

Capsid bug: insect pest; distorts apple fruitlets badly as well as feeding on leaves. Control difficult without resorting to phosphorus insecticide such as dimethoate, but this may lead to build-up in red spider mite. Rely on predators if possible.

Clematis wilt: fungus disease; shoots of young plants wilt and collapse rapidly and suddenly. Cut off, to healthy growth, back to soil level if necessary, paint all cuts with sealing compound and spray subsequent growth with copper fungicide.

Fire blight: bacterial disease infecting shrubs and trees belonging to the rose family; flowers and leaves at tips of shoots turn black in spring, oozing patches appear just below bark; later, leaves wither and shoots appear to be burnt. Disease spreads rapidly in wet seasons and trees can be killed. No effective chemical control; cut out unhealthy shoots as soon as seen and destroy.

Holly leaf miner: insect; leaves have pale tunnels and blisters on surface, eventually wither and fall in bad attacks. Maggots feed within leaf tissue. Pick off and destroy infested leaves, spray remainder with dimethoate.

*Apple blossom which has been caught by frost will have blackened centres and stamens. Such blossom will never set fruit and an entire crop may be destroyed.*

*The caterpillars of the lackey moth feed on the leaves of fruit trees and can cause severe defoliation.*

Honey fungus: fungus disease; infects roots of woody plants. Toadstools with honey-coloured surface appear at base of affected plant, bark peels off to show white covering on wood beneath; spreads by means of black threads or 'bootlaces' in soil. Affected plants stop developing, leaves wilt and shoots and branches die. Burn dead plants, including roots; do not replant in same site. Treat roots of still living specimens and soil with creosote-based fungicide specific to honey fungus.

Mildew *see* Roses.

Peach-leaf curl (apricot, nectarine): fungus disease; spores over-winter beneath scales on outside of buds, infect leaves as they unfold in late winter and cause thickened, yellowish, later pink-to-red, distorted patches on leaves. Grey bloom on surface of patches in summer is spore-bearing stage which further infects leaves. Defoliation occurs, shoot growth stops and trees can be killed. Spray as buds open with copper or sulphur fungicide, repeat two weeks later and again in autumn, just as leaves start to fall. Destroy affected leaves as soon as seen and cut shoots back to healthy wood.

Pear-leaf blister mite: mite; in spring leaves have small, yellowish blisters which turn reddish and then black, fall prematurely. Fruitlets affected similarly. Hand-removal of affected parts is usually sufficient, otherwise spray lime-sulphur at bud burst stage.

Pear midge: insect; fruitlets deformed and enlarged, with central black cavity, in which will be one or more white maggots. Such fruitlets crack and fall prematurely. Hand-

removal is usually sufficient, but in bad infestations, spraying with fenitrothion can be tried, remembering the possibility of red spider mite build up in consequence. Maggots may hibernate in soil two winters in succession.

Peony blight: fungus disease; new young shoots and young flower buds wilt suddenly; buds lower down on the stem turn brown and brown patches, later coated with grey mould, may appear on older leaves. Spray thiram or captan as leaves appear in spring and repeat at two-week intervals until flowering. Cut off all affected parts to healthy growth and paint cut surfaces with sealing compound.

Red plum maggot: insect; red caterpillar feeds in centre of fruits from early summer to early autumn and then hibernates in suitable hiding place until following spring. Treat as for apple codling moth.

Rhododendron bud blast: fungus disease; buds turn brown or grey-brown from autumn onward and by winter have growth of black bristles on them. Buds are killed; frost-damaged buds do not have black bristles. Remove infected buds and a little stem and destroy. Control leaf-hoppers, by spraying in mid-summer with derris or malathion, as they indirectly help to ensure the spread of the disease.

Silver leaf: fungus disease; infects plum, cherry; apple, pear, peach, nectarine and apricot to a lesser extent, also shrubs, especially laburnum and laurel. Leaves silvered on one complete shoot or branch, wood stained brown internally. When tree or shrub killed, purple and yellowish brown, plate-like growths appear from the branches. In advanced attacks, infected branches of tree should be removed and burnt and wounds covered with sealing compound. Improved feeding and manuring should enable remainder to recover. Prune when infection unlikely, from early to late summer.

Vine and clay-coloured weevil: insect; adult beetles, small and black or brown, eat holes in margins of rhododendron, rose and vine leaves. White grubs feed on roots of various shrubs and vines. Fork HCH (BHC) dust into soil occasionally from mid-summer to late winter, to deal with the grubs, and dust leaves lightly from early spring to early autumn, for adult control.

Woolly aphis (American blight): insect; patches of white cotton-wool appear on bark of apple trees, especially at junctions of shoots and branches. Does little direct harm, but looks unsightly, makes picking messy and provides entry for disease through injury made by feeding. Brush away with stiff brush, paint patches with methylated spirits or spray forcibly with derris, from early summer, as necessary.

# The Kitchen Garden

# Index

# The Flower Garden

# Index

# The Shrub & Tree Garden

# Index

**Picture Credits:**
A-Z Collection 90
Bernard Alfieri 87
Alpine Garden Society 215
*Amateur Gardening* 143, 154, 177, 237
D. Armison 125, 301
P. Ayers 102
Barnaby's Picture Library 264
Beckett 227
Ann Bonar 58
P. Booth 168, 210, 212, 318
Pat Brindley 50
Roger Charity 35
Chevron Chemical Company 7
Eric Crichton 23
R. J. Corbin 3, 88, 105, 112, 199, 210, 221, 222, 232, 323
J. Cowley 164, 202
Dobies 28
J. E. Downward 40, 207, 287
Mike Duff/Marshall Cavendish 15
V. Finnis 45, 98, 163, 174, 178, 259, 263
Brian Furner 19
P. Genereux 229
Iris Hardwick Library 67, 272
Grant Heilman 54, 315
Peter Hunt 64, 189, 191, 255, 280, 327
A. J. Huxley 194, 322
G. Hyde 48, 153, 197, 258, 290, 313, 332, 333, 334, 336
L. Johns & Associates 49, 240
D. Kesby 127
Mark Lawrence/Marshall Cavendish 89
J. Markham 147, 239
E. Megson 182
Murphy Chemical Company 109, 110, 223
Natural History Photographic Collection 332
Opera Mundi 130
Muriel Orans 97
R. Parrett 186
Clay Perry 9, 43, 47, 79
Photo Researchers 206
Picturepoint 66
R. Procter 104
J. Ruthven 315
courtesy of Shell 335
D. Smith 71, 73, 302
Harry Smith Horticultural Photographic Collection 30, 33, 39,
  64, 66, 84, 115, 135, 138, 148, 171, 176, 230, 243, 244, 248,
  251, 257, 268, 276, 282, 283, 295, 296, 305, 306, 310, 314,
  317, 324, 325
V. Stevenson 205
D. Wildridge 247